NEW DIRECTIONS IN WORLD ARCHITECTURE AND DESIGN

EARTH is an epic publishing feat never to be repeated, proudly created by Millennium House

Western Europe

Locator box indicates location of map within world

Locator box indicates location of map within region

Color-coded bars make identifying each continent easy

Each page is edged with silver gilding to help in the preservation of the book over time

Comprehensive labelling with current data

Specially created state-of-the-art full-color background relief

Colored relief bar indicating elevation

Feature boxes throughout the book focus on milestone events in a country's history or take an in-depth look at a unique feature about a country

Exquisite full-color images are used throughout, with more than 800 images in total

Scale bar and map scale information

A profile of each country provides a snapshot of vital information, including official name, population, area, capital city

A map of each country shows the major cities, highest point, and neighboring countries

Handy map reference information will take you straight to the corresponding map for each country

A locator map pinpoints the location of the country within the region

This limited edition atlas—the world's largest modern atlas—is bound by hand in beautiful custom-dyed leather with silver-gilded pages for preservation and silver-plated corners for protection. *Earth* establishes a new benchmark in the world of atlases, with highly detailed mapping and comprehensive country profiles. With 580 pages, including 355 maps of 194 countries, more than 800 images, 4 breathtaking gatefolds, and information on every country, territory and dependency in the world, *Earth* will appeal to book collectors, libraries and institutions, map lovers, and anyone wishing to enjoy now, and preserve for the future, a record of our world today.

Earth can be ordered from all good book stores or contact Millennium House for your nearest supplier

www.millenniumhouse.com.au

NEW DIRECTIONS IN WORLD ARCHITECTURE AND DESIGN

MILLENNIUM HOUSE

First published in 2006 as *Home* by
Millennium House Pty Ltd
52 Bolwarra Rd, Elanora Heights
NSW, 2101, Australia

ISBN 978-1-921209-68-0

SALES
For all sales, please contact:
Millennium House Pty Ltd
52 Bolwarra Rd, Elanora Heights
NSW, 2101, Australia
Phone: (612) 9970 6850   Fax: (612) 9970 8136
Email: rightsmanager@millenniumhouse.com.au

PHOTOGRAPHERS
Millennium House would like to hear from photographers
interested in supplying photographs

Printed in China
Color separation by Pica Digital Pte Ltd, Singapore

Publisher Gordon Cheers

Associate publisher Janet Parker

Project manager Tracy Tucker

Art director Stan Lamond

Chief text editor Loretta Barnard

Editors Monica Berton, Helen Cooney, Heather Jackson,
        Susan Page, Janet Parker

Coordinator, Parts 1 & 3 Monica Berton

Picture research Monica Berton, Helen Cooney, Tracy Tucker

Cover design Stan Lamond, Anthony Wyld

Designers Stan Lamond, Lena Lowe, Ingo Voss

Initial design concept Anthony Wyld

Digital image control Andrew Davies

Index Di Harriman

Production Simone Russell

Publishing assistant Bernard Roberts

Photographers are acknowledged on page 514

Photographs on preliminary pages:

Pages 2–3: Crescent House, Wallace E Cunningham
Pages 6–7: Chesa Futura, Foster and Partners; Küchel Architects
Pages 8–9: Quito House, Carlos Zapata Studio
Page 11: Mataja Residence, Belzberg/Wittman Collaborative
Page 13: Skybox, Melling:Morse Architects
Page 14: Casa Cusenza, Van Tilburg, Banvard & Soderbergh

Consultants

Michael Webb lives and works in Los Angeles, USA, and is the author of more than twenty books on architecture and design including *Art/ Invention/House*, *Adventurous Wine Architecture*, and *Brave New Houses*. He is also a regular contributor to *Architectural Digest*, *The Architectural Review*, and *Frame and Mark*.

Chris Abel is an architecture writer and lecturer of international renown, based in Sydney, Australia. He has taught at major universities in many parts of the world and is the author of more than 100 publications of theory and criticism.

Professor Alexander Cuthbert, University of New South Wales, Australia, has had more than 30 years academic and professional experience, living and working in Europe, North America, Asia, and Australasia, in the fields of architecture, urban design, and urban planning.

Professor Philip Goad, Melbourne University, Australia, is internationally known for his research in a variety of areas, including architectural theory and design. He is an authority on modern Australian architecture and has worked extensively as an architect, conservation consultant, and curator.

Douglas Lloyd Jenkins is one of New Zealand's best known and most respected design, art, and architecture writers. In 2005 he was awarded the Montana Medal for Non-Fiction, New Zealand's top literary prize, for his book *At Home: A Century of New Zealand Design*.

Professor 'Ora Joubert, University of Pretoria, South Africa, is an acclaimed architect, with work featuring in more than fifty national and international publications. As well as academic commitments, she is the editor of a forthcoming book on contemporary South African architecture.

CONTRIBUTING WRITERS

Part 1 Alexander Cuthbert, Ayu Suartika

Part 2 Nigel Bartlett, Philip Goad, Linda Hunt, Marlowe Richards, Barry Stone, Russell Walden, and the architects

C O

ntents

contents (continued)

Preface

Home is an enlightening tribute to architecture, containing rich illustrative photos, technical drawings, and descriptive text. The pages depict the cultural traditions of housing throughout history, featuring a broad range of innovative homes of the present day, and a guide to architects who are leaders in their field.

In the Introduction, architectural writer Michael Webb looks at the evolution of home in the Americas, from the dwellings of early settlers to the Modernist creations of Frank Lloyd Wright and Irving Gill, and the South American push inspired by Le Corbusier. Michael Webb puts the American homes featured in this book into context.

In Part 1, Professor Alexander Cuthbert considers the home as the universal physical medium of expression for humans. Drawing examples from across the globe and across time, he considers the cultural, symbolic, religious, and spiritual dimensions of home.

Part 2 of the book is devoted to exploring an international array of homes, designed by some of the most significant architects of the modern era. A wide selection of images provides a spatial context to plans, elevations, and section drawings. The home descriptions are written by the architects themselves, or a nominated writer, and these provide invaluable insights into the architects' design intents and their creative solutions to logistic, heritage, and environmental problems. The descriptions also provide an appreciation of the architects' design philosophy. The homes have been ordered alphabetically by name within broad categories, including In the City, Outer City, Future City, In the Country, By the Water, and In Your Dreams. Readers can seek out their favorite architects in the book's index.

Enjoy viewing some of today's most significant, architecturally designed homes from around the world created by the artists of modern-day architecture.

Introduction
Houses of the Americas

SETTLERS' HOMES

The Americas span the entire range of the world's geography, from polar ice caps to tropical rainforests by way of arid deserts, lofty mountains, vast plains, and the longest coastline of any continent. Culturally, the range is much narrower. The British took over from Dutch and French rulers in North America; the Spanish settled Central and South America, and the Portuguese seized control of Brazil. That established distinct legacies of building that initially overrode local conditions, just as the colonialists ignored or suppressed whatever native traditions they encountered.

The Spanish were even more determined than the British to impose their will on their new domains and the Laws of the Indies provided a blueprint for every new town and city from the sixteenth century on. And yet, the remoteness of these settlements and the scarcity of sophisticated materials encouraged local builders to create a simpler architecture of adobe blocks, clay tiles, and rough-hewn wooden beams, reserving dressed stone and rich ornament for cathedrals and centers of administration. The hacienda was a model that provided security and enclosure for families and livestock.

In North America, early settlers adapted the same models of wood-frame and brick construction they had practiced at home, and utilized the same pattern books for ornament and the treatment of facades. The cottages and mansions of New England played subtle variations on English styles until well after the original 13 states declared independence. As settlers moved westward through the nineteenth century, they developed new models, and absorbed the Spanish traditions of Texas and California. The false fronts of Main Street in every western town, the Victorian exuberance of the merchant class, and the Arts and Crafts bungalows are now cherished as historic relics.

THE AMERICAN HOME

As the United States became richer, more populous and diversified, architectural eclecticism flourished. The new rich sought an instant pedigree, as they still do, by building extravagant copies of European castles and palaces, and the middle classes sought status with decorative overlays on humbler structures. Regional styles spread across the country, starting with the wood-frame houses that were shipped as kits around Cape Horn to San Francisco following the Gold Rush of 1849. Today's tract builders offer a menu of styles, from Mediterranean to Cape Cod, in suburban developments that have a cookie-cutter sameness in every state. The house became the "home," a stand-alone symbol of personal status and the American way of life, with deep emotional and economic associations. Huge resources are poured into the construction, furnishing, and landscaping of homes. Although American-style suburbs now encircle the globe, no country has such a fixation on size and surface style as the USA.

In contrast, poverty and corruption has held back development in most Latin American countries. Tradition still rules, and the opulent estates and luxury apartments of the affluent are a shocking contrast to the teeming shanty towns that surround most cities. Houses that would excite no attention in the USA are protected by high walls, surveillance cameras, and armed guards. Bodyguards drive owners to work or to shop in armored cars. The open plans and clean lines of contemporary architecture are compromised by the pervasive feeling of insecurity.

Modernism was a late arrival and has shallow roots in the Americas, except for office towers where the USA led the world. In southern California, Irving Gill used thin planes of concrete to create a pared-down version of the Spanish Missions, and Frank Lloyd Wright employed textured concrete blocks to build houses that were inspired by Mexican temples. In the 1920s, R.M. Schindler and Richard Neutra moved to Los Angeles from their native Vienna, transplanting progressive European ideas to this far shore. Philip Johnson popularized the concept of the International Modern style in an exhibition that was inaugurated in 1932 at the fledgling Museum of Modern Art in New York. It provoked a lively debate, but few Americans wanted to live that way until postwar euphoria and an emphasis on the practical over the pure made it seem less threatening. Even then, the Case Study House program yielded only 24 realized designs in the years 1945–63, and few developers embraced those ideas.

LEFT
The House of Courts in Texas, features three internal courtyards. Architects Lake | Flato were inspired by the Spanish missions, warehouses, and early stone houses common in the Texan landscape.

ABOVE
The "Miesian box" visible at the front of Studio Pali Fekete's House on Blue Jay Way creates an arresting facade for the home. The glass-walled sitting room doubles as a protective eave for the home's entry.

In South America, Le Corbusier spread the Modernist gospel on lecture tours and through his writings, but local architects had to wait to realize their dreams – in Uruguay from 1930 on, and later in Mexico, Brazil, and Cuba, but rarely elsewhere. The forces of reaction were deeply entrenched, especially in Argentina and the Andean republics, and the visionary capital of Brasilia was completed just as a military coup over-threw the elected government and drove Oscar Niemeyer, the godfather of Brazilian Modernism, into exile. The Modernist honeymoon in Cuba ended soon after Castro seized power and took the geriatric Soviet Union as his model. Architects and their clients emigrated en masse.

Whatever a country's politics or wealth, innovative residences are always rare. With few exceptions, builders and their customers prefer the tried and true — the house that doesn't stand out from the crowd. A family may crave larger rooms and the badges of wealth (from lofty porticoes to fancy cars), but they also want to fit in with their neighbors. Home-owners typically reject every departure from the norm, as spontaneously as small children refuse to eat the unfamiliar. Community design codes mandate shapes and color palettes, seeking a respectable uniformity. The challenge for the few enlightened clients and talented architects is to maneuver around these whimsical constraints or find a site that's unregulated, while responding to the topography and climate, as well as to the scale and character of the surroundings.

ABOVE
At the entry to Kanner Architect's Malibu House, the varied roof lines preview the "ladder of space and volume" that awaits. This Californian home by the sea was inspired by the work of Mexican Pritzker-winning architect Luis Barrigan, who was famed for the way he worked with space and light. The Cubist work of Irving Gill was another important influence.

RIGHT
In House C, TEN Arquitectos have achieved a vivid sense of space on a relatively small building site by incorporating large voids into a three-level residence. The Modernist design of the home is representative of a range of cosmopolitan homes found in Mexico City today.

approval. The review board had heard of Meier and treated him with respect, but were deeply disturbed when they saw that the pitched roof they had mandated was apparently upside down. Meier calmly responded that nothing in their exhaustive code said it had to be done in the conventional way and, to their fury, he prevailed. The constraints inspired him to do one of his finest, most original designs.

Ever since Ayn Rand's lurid novel, *The Fountainhead,* and the real-life example of Wright tyrannizing his clients, architects have enjoyed an unjustified reputation for arrogance and imposing their own ideas on reluctant clients. A few have tried, but it's not good strategy; the choice is too wide and most people call on former clients to ask if they are well satisfied. In contrast to the off-the-shelf models builders offer, architects can tailor a house to your personal needs and desires. It will take much longer and cost more, but it's a life-long investment that will bring untold rewards. The houses included in this book may be rooted in place and the local vernacular, but they make daring leaps into the unknown, carrying their lucky owners to places they never dreamed of.

For sheer exuberance, it's hard to surpass the house that Carlos Zapata designed for a young art-loving couple high in the Andes, just outside Quito, the historic capital of Ecuador. The Venezuela-born architect lived in the area as a child, although he now practices in New York, and the clients are friends. They asked him for a house that would make them feel as though they were levitating, and Zapata sketched a plan that resembles a bird in flight, with an extended terrace and main bedroom oriented toward one lofty peak and a partially covered pool branching off toward another.

Things used to be a lot simpler. In 1946, Palm Springs was a scattered community of second homes, a two-hour drive across the desert from Los Angeles. Frank Sinatra had just made his first million and strolled through the open door of an architect's office on Palm Drive. E. Stewart Williams had taken over the practice from his father, but he was out, and the entertainer spoke to his brother. He wanted a house with a pool, to be finished in three months so that he could spend Christmas there with his family. And it should be Colonial style. Williams met the deadline, but built a modern, flat-roofed residence. "Sinatra had heard of Colonial but he'd probably never seen one, and he was entirely satisfied with what I gave him," Williams later recalled. The nearest neighbor was probably a mile

away, and many of the free spirits who wintered in Palm Springs in those early years were willing to try something new. Edgar Kaufmann Sr, a department store mogul, had commissioned Frank Lloyd Wright to build Fallingwater as his summer house in Pennsylvania, outraging his peers, but he encountered no opposition to his 1947 Neutra desert house.

Today, every move may be contested. A German art-collector bought a waterfront lot on the Gulf Coast of Florida, and commissioned a purist white house from Richard Meier. When the architect heard it was in a gated community he feared the worst and tried to back out, but the client insisted, and he built a model with a dramatic V-profile roof and submitted it for

The hillside house that John Patkau designed on the Vancouver waterfront is tightly confined by its neighbors, and its exuberance is contained within a narrow slot of space. The client, a Chinese businessman, wanted a house that would maximize views of the natural harbor and pull light into every room, and the architect has achieved this by raising the lap pool and allowing the light to filter though the water and splash down from skylights, turning the simple linear volume into a luminous, multi-leveled belvedere.

Builders prefer flat sites that speed construction, but architects are inspired by steep gradients, and some of the best houses are perched on precipices. Will Bruder is a man of the desert who has built several expressive houses around his home base of Phoenix. In contrast, Sky Arc, a recent residence for a software inventor who sold his company at an early age to enjoy his family and music, hugs a wooded hillside looking out to San Francisco Bay. Poured concrete anchors the house to the slope, curved canopies of aqueous fiberglass modulate the light, and the woodsy, colorful interior makes a connection with the pines and madrona trees to either side. It's a house that embraces and frames the landscape; and it is both free-flowing and snug within.

Sharon Johnston and Mark Lee, a husband–wife partnership in Los Angeles, were commissioned to build a spec house on the edge of Santa Monica Canyon. To maximize the volume while minimizing the number of caissons required for the foundations, they designed a flared concrete base and a steel frame that tapers in at the top, and is covered with a spray-on polymer skin that unifies roof and walls. The owner parks her car and enters at the middle level, where glass sliders open two sides of the lofty living room to a panoramic view over the canyon.

Some houses take their character from one or two materials that are employed in a boldly expressive way. A house by Brigitte Shim and Howard Sutcliffe in the suburbs of Toronto is named the Weathering Steel House for its rusted steel (Cor-Ten) cladding, which requires no maintenance and withstands the rigors of the Canadian climate. Within this hard carapace is a house that contrasts exposed poured concrete with the rich tones of fir, mahogany, and cherrywood.

David Chun was commissioned to build an expansive family house for his Korean-born parents in a leafy neighborhood of West Los Angeles. As a Modernist, he had no compunction in creating a base of poured concrete, but he overcame the reservations of his clients by treating the lofty living room as a giant cabinet with maple floors, cherry paneling, redwood soffits, and straight-grain Douglas fir doors and windows. He demonstrated that wood is the magic button, convincing skeptics that modern does not need to feel cold and alien.

ABOVE LEFT
Architect John Patkau describes Shaw House, on the Vancouver waterfront, as an "essay in light, water, and concrete." The entrance to the home is located directly under the lap pool, so the whole area is illuminated by the pattern of light that passes through the pool's glass bottom.

TOP
With Weathering Steel House, Brigitte Shim and Howard Sutcliffe set out to create a home that would make an emphatic statement in its suburban Toronto neighborhood. The "no maintenance" steel cladding was chosen because of the way it interacts with nature, darkening slowly as it weathers.

ABOVE
From the exterior, Hill House, by architects Johnston Marklee & Associates, looks like a white geometric sculpture built into the hillside. The interior, created by the dynamic form of the home, makes the most of the views across Rustic and Sullivan canyons to Santa Monica Bay.

Many of the best architect-designed houses are studies in minimalism, eliminating everything that's inessential to focus attention on the landscape and the life within.

The planned community of Sea Ranch on the northern California coastline began, 40 years ago, with woodsy houses and a condo block that drew inspiration from the past and from the rugged landscape. Buzz Yudell, who was a partner of the late Charles Moore, and his wife Tina Beebe, who was employed by Charles and Ray Eames, worked in the spirit of those original buildings in designing their own stripped-down summer house. They built a Cubist compound of redwood siding with shallow-pitched corrugated metal roofs that seem to disappear as you approach.

Another bucolic hideaway is located at the bottom of a canyon in Big Sur, an area of stunning natural beauty to the south of San Francisco. French-born architect Anne Fougeron employed cedar battens to screen the street facade, copper that will weather to a soft brown, and glass clerestories to pull in natural light when the sun dips below the walls of the canyon. Thanks to the earthy tones of the natural materials and the refinement of the detailing, this house sits lightly on the land.

Many of the best architect-designed houses are studies in minimalism, eliminating everything that's inessential to focus attention on the landscape and the life within.

A patron of contemporary art invited Jim Jennings to design a guest house for visiting artists on a ranch in the Alexander Valley of northern California. Jennings made a cut through a grassy knoll, and treated the poured concrete retaining walls as a container for two identical suites that open up to precisely framed views at either end and also share a central courtyard. The walls are slightly angled to each other to force the perspective, and are incised by New York artist David Rabinowitch.

The houses of the two Iranian-born sisters, Gisue and Mojgan Hariri, are celebrated for their elegant simplicity, and both qualities are evident in their Belmont House residence, near San Francisco, in which they deftly combined the dominant types of "architecture" in the region: Mexican pueblo style and the mobile-trailer home. A paradoxical mix that inspires.

ABOVE
Yudell-Beebe House at Sea Ranch was designed by and for its inhabitants, architect Buzz Yudell and design colorist Tina Beebe. The house was developed in response to the rhythms and elements of the rugged coast of northern California.

TOP RIGHT
Acknowledging the ecologically fragile nature of the site in Big Sur, northern California, Jackson Family Retreat, by Fougeron Architecture, is a Modernist structure that sits lightly on the land. Steel columns lift the structure 3 ft (1 m) off the ground, to reduce its impact and to protect it from flooding.

ABOVE RIGHT
The two dominant architectural styles of the San Francisco suburb of Belmont (the mobile-trailer home and the pueblo style of housing) have been captured by Hariri & Hariri – Architecture in the design of Belmont House. The Mexican-influenced heavy stuccoed walls are visible at the lower level of the house; the metal-clad volume sits atop its solid base.

RIGHT
The starkly minimalist walls of Jim Jennings' Visiting Artists House mark the entry to one of two self-contained suites in which visiting artists might stay. The long walls integrate with the curve of the land by literally cutting through the hill on which the home sits.

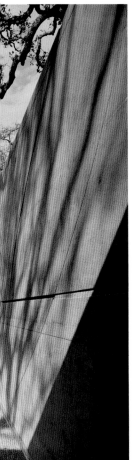

ABOVE
With Desert House, Marmol Radziner + Associates developed an exciting prototype for an eco-friendly prefabricated custom house. The home consists of four prefabricated house modules and six deck modules, all built off-site and transported to the client's chosen location.

ABOVE RIGHT
Pugh + Scarpa's Solar Umbrella is situated in an area populated mostly with single-story bunga- lows. The home, inspired by Paul Rudolph's Umbrella House of 1953, incorporates both passive and active solar design tech- niques and is a bold precedent for the Venice area of California.

From the birth of the modern movement 80 years ago, architects have dreamed of making good design available to a broad public, employing prefabrication to simplify construction and achieve cost savings through standardization. Few designs have progressed beyond the prototype stage. The design-build firm of Leo Marmol and Ron Radziner has established its own factory in an effort to control quality and offer a variety of customized models. Marmol created the first house for himself and his wife, shipping steel-framed modular units and assembling them on a desert site outside Los Angeles. The product of this initial venture has the solidity and refinement of the firm's site-built houses, but the cost was lower, and the time required for site preparation and final assembly was substantially less.

The late Franklin Israel was a master of subtle inflec- tions, imparting a dynamic sense of movement to every space he designed. Before his death, in 1996, he sketched a house for a cliff-side site in West Los Angeles, and this was fleshed out by his partners, Barbara Callas and Steven Shortridge, who now have their own firm. A steel-troweled gray stucco facade shuts out traffic noise, and its sharp angles herald the interlocking volumes of the interior, which step down the precipitous slope and open up to decks overlooking the ocean. There's a harmonious balance of solid and void, and axes that tie the varied spaces together.

Energy conservation has become an increasingly high priority as public awareness of global warming becomes more widespread and the cost of power escalates. Green architecture is the hallmark of build- ings designed by Gwynne Pugh and Lawrence Scarpa, a partnership in West Los Angeles, and Scarpa named his own house the Solar Umbrella. A steel-framed addition to a modest bungalow contains a new living area that opens to a walled yard and a master suite that is cantilevered over the old structure. The entire house is naturally ventilated, and an array of photo- voltaic panels generates more energy than the house consumes, doubling as a sun shade. Recycled materials are used throughout, thus reducing costs.

INNOVATION AND COLLABORATION

Most of the houses featured here are one-offs, but they display a wealth of ideas that other architects and clients can adapt to their own projects. Creativity and practicality, elegance and economy, adventure and a sense of rootedness are carefully balanced. They represent a collaboration between audacious clients and innovative designers who shed all preconceptions in the search for a fresh approach. These are houses that point the way forward, in contrast to most of their neighbors, which vainly attempt to recreate the past.

Michael Webb

*Los Angeles writer Michael Webb is the author of
more than twenty books on architecture and design.*

Part 1
Home
in the Past

Introduction

Home is the ultimate paradox: It can be a building, a destination, or a concept. Home at its most elementary is merely a house – a place where we perform functional tasks for ourselves such as washing, cooking and eating, personal hygiene, storing material possessions, investing money, and other activities. But home has purposes beyond the material; it has an historical and spiritual purpose. We say: "Home is where the heart is" – a thought which opens up a universe of emotion. Here we use the idea of home to signify the place where journeys end; a place we somehow arrive back to, though not necessarily from where we departed. Despite this, home also connotes the idea of a return – a homecoming of some kind to the same people, whether it is to where a partner resides, to one's children or friends, or to a familiar landscape. Here the connection in our minds moves beyond the functional into the realm of feelings.

In this section we integrate function and emotion with concept, as we set out to illustrate the complexity of home and its historic, symbolic, religious, and spiritual dimensions. In essence, home reflects an archeology of qualities that are integrated in highly complex ways. In exploring the idea of home over historical time, it is fair to say that while homes range from primitive grass huts to immense palaces, they all perform the same tasks in different ways and in different proportions. Neither can we draw any conclusions about the symbolic richness of people's lives from the physical quality of their houses. The Aboriginal people of Australia had the most elementary shelters, yet lived in a world without parallel in our modern societies. Their concept of home stretched out to encompass the entire symbolic universe of the Dreamtime. Conversely, the physical dimensions and apparent wealth of grand castles and palaces were no indication of a similar richness in the lives of kings and queens, or of dictators and other tyrants.

Homes in the past have also had a significant impact on the homes of today in form, design, and appearance to the extent that it is impossible to isolate ourselves from the effects of history. At whatever time, homes have had to adapt to similar climates, geographies, systems of beliefs, and the adoption of the family unit as a universal norm. However grand, most homes have used certain basic features such as pitched roofs for insulation and drainage, windows for daylight, and doors for access. In this manner our homes are a direct reflection of our physiology and in most cases mirror the human condition. In many areas, building materials are limited and homes, however large or important, have a similar appearance dictated by nature.

The effects of history are also revealed in the work of famous architects, each one being significantly affected by their own learning, and also by each other. Hence today we see stylistic and design influences continuing over thousands of years, from ancient Greece and Rome and the Italian Renaissance, to the Georgian architecture in Britain and into contemporary design today. Much of this has been directly copied as a vocabulary or "language" of architecture. Architects have also adopted the spirit of home as personal influences, and we find examples such as traditional Japanese architecture, the Greek villages in the Cyclades, Italian hill towns and Scottish castles personally affecting many of the great contemporary architects.

TOP
Trulli houses from Puglia, Italy. These houses display the timeless qualities of utility and beauty. They also combine together into one continuous facade, hence helping to form a town as well as a series of homes.

LEFT
Homes in the Cyclades, Greece. The islands of the Cyclades form part of the mythology of ancient Greece and are steeped in history and legend. The villages of Mykonos, Ios, and Santorini have inspired architects for generations. Absolute simplicity of color and a complex integration of individual architectural elements have created unique and beautiful homes for the islanders.

TOP RIGHT
Fishing boats in a canal, Venice, Italy. This view shows another side to the usual grandeur of Venice. An ordinary street in an ordinary neighborhood displays a rich tapestry of color alongside the canal, demonstrating how even the most elementary of buildings can contribute vibrancy to urban life.

FAR RIGHT
Courtyard of a building, Jaipur, India. This building, with its elegant and spacious courtyard, is well adapted to the heat of the Indian climate. The richly decorated facades with crafted balconies, doors, windows, and entry way, show how a simple courtyard and a single tree can provide a beautiful living environment.

But we must also remember that the concept of home cannot be isolated from that of community. As home is a reflection of the self and family, it is also a reflection of a larger social world, varying from a small tribe to today's mega-urban regions. Lifestyles, customs, and traditions practiced at home are seldom unique and are connected to society by systems of communication such as language, mail, boats, roads, air transport and today's mass media and electronic communication. Even the actual form of home is in many cases sacrificed to the greater social good. At the village level, homes are frequently organized in some collective configuration for defense, against some form of adversity in nature, or from other people. Homes may be designed to symbolize a god or gods, so that the ritual display of a particular deity will grant protection from evil forces. Similarly, in larger settlements and cities, high-rise apartments (that even existed 2000 years ago in the *insulae* of ancient Rome) represent a singular loss of identity in the interests of collective life.

In the following pages we illustrate the wonder that is home in many examples drawn from across the world – from the polar icecaps and the tropics, to outer space. These all attest to the sheer vastness of creativity and imagination that characterizes the human condition in its responses to nature and function, to family, spirituality, aesthetics, and social life. In all of this, home is the universal medium where these qualities become distilled and refined in physical space, a testament to the singularity of our collective universe.

Chapter 1
Home as Nature

The terms "refuge" or "sanctuary" are ways of expressing the meaning of home in relation to the natural world. Refuge implies a passive attitude and experience: Some place to which one can escape, or flee from enemies; a place of security or asylum; a sanctuary or a place where people go for safekeeping. There we can avoid the fear associated with natural forces such as earthquakes, tsunamis or other extreme climatic changes. In this context home reflects attitudes to nature, and as a refuge, is designed to mitigate its worst effects. There is also a significant overlap between humanity's relationship to other peoples and animals, and its attitude to the natural world. While both are extremely material considerations, relationships to nature are also philosophical, religious, and spiritual (as discussed in Home as Spirit).

AN ENEMY TO BE TAMED?

Western civilization has for centuries followed the dictum "multiply and subdue the Earth:" A philosophy which might just see the extinction of the human species. India's renowned political and social reformer, Mohandas Gandhi, when asked about his views on western life, replied that he thought it would be a good idea. Western attitudes accepted humanity as the predominant force in the world. Attitudes to nature as a world to be conquered, and imperialism as a political philosophy, were not wholly unrelated. In contrast, there have been countless examples of

the huge respect that early nomadic and hunter-gatherer people had for nature, as it provided refuge, food, and overall prosperity. From the Inuit people in the Arctic Circle and the Plains Indians of North America (the Sioux, Blackfoot, Cheyenne, Crow, Kiowa, and Comanche), to the Dayak people of Borneo and the Maori in New Zealand, nature was God and their survival was ensured by this belief. However, nature within western civilization has been viewed as an enemy to be tamed, its resources exploited, and all assistance denied in time of need. This is seen in humanity's struggle to preserve rainforests, agree on carbon dioxide emissions, reduce the use of fossil fuels, and the destruction of animal and marine species. Today, these same attitudes are slowly bringing us to the point where our beliefs may not survive because they will have destroyed the material basis upon which they were constructed. Nature will no longer be capable of providing the refuge that it has so generously allowed in the past, since it has been suffocated by its own inhabitants.

The first of our species survived by hunting animals and gathering food from their environment. Hence, they were known as "hunter-gatherers." Few such people remain, most having become extinct as civilization gradually evolved into the globalized world of today. The ones that do exist in minute numbers are found in such places as Papua New Guinea (the Dani and Tambanum), the Amazon Basin (the Yanoamo,

Tampiri, Bororo and Guarani), and up until relatively recently, in Australia (the Australian Aborigines). Their lives remain threatened by development that is not only destroying their culture, but also the plant and animal species that they depend on for their survival. For many of these peoples, and others like them, scattered across the planet, home has no material existence – the actual creation of permanent structures is unknown. Most use temporary dwellings for protection from the elements, from wild animals if such creatures exist, and even from the spirit and other worlds that structure their cosmology. Home is built, if it is built at all, from basic natural materials, in most cases from vegetation in the form of tree bark, branches, strong grasses such as papyrus, bamboo, leaves, and other substances. In other situations, cave and cliff dwellings abound, either underground or cut into rock.

In nomadic hunter-gatherer societies, people saw themselves as part of nature, somehow balancing off advantages against disadvantages, but without the idea that nature was somehow an enemy. Dependence on nature was respected and worshiped in a multitude of ways, where animistic beliefs allocated god-like powers to inanimate and animate objects and creatures. Forests, lakes and streams, plants and animals were alive with spirit, and integration with nature was absolute. Nonetheless, home still had to be located and designed in such a manner as to fend off wild animals, vermin, and insects, and to provide insulation from heat and cold. Torrential rain, typhoons, dust and snow storms also had to be resisted, as well as earthquakes, volcanic eruptions, and serious flooding. Therefore, the evolution of home gave rise to infinite and progressive forms of refuge, as well as a unique use of natural materials depending on which force of nature happened to predominate in any region. Examples include the use of steeply pitched roofs to resist torrential rain or mud-brick for insulation.

LEFT
A local village hut, Sepik River, Papua New Guinea. In contrast to the various types of natural disasters that mother Earth may bring us, it also provides an immense range of basic natural materials. This house is almost entirely built from grass and leaves collected from its surroundings. Being built on stilts, the structure protects its occupants from flooding as well as providing cooling ventilation.

TOP
An illuminated igloo, Hudson Bay, Manitoba, Canada. The word "igloo" is derived from the Inuktitut word *iglu* which means "house." Nowadays, the igloo is commonly associated with the snow house – a form of shelter protecting its occupants from the freezing harsh climate of the Arctic. Its construction requires blocks of hard field snow which are structurally sufficient to condense and interlock ice crystals that hold the dome.

OPPOSITE
Rock-hewn dwellings, Uchisar, Turkey. This is an example of home situated in the Cappadocia region. These homes represent an amazing adaptation of people to the hilly and rocky living environment. Earthquakes and volcanic eruptions are believed to be the major reasons for the formation of such strange terrain then, for hundreds of years, the people of this region dug into the soft but firm rock to create these unusual dwellings.

MUD-BRICK AND STRAW

The geographic distribution of similarly built forms and spaces are referred to as "typologies," and while the range of individual types of building are infinite, certain generic or commonly held features in mass construction of structure and form can usually be identified. The simple reason for this resides in the properties and qualities of materials, which are derived from nature. While the contemporary use of brick, for example, is widespread, buildings are restricted by the fact that brick cannot be used in tension, limiting brick to specific dimensions that utilize its compressive stress to best advantage. Combined with the type of kiln and the heat of the firing process, the use of different types of clay also decides strength, what color bricks or tiles eventually adopt, and therefore the height of walls that can be constructed. Similar considerations apply to all other materials, limiting and influencing how home materializes from nature, and deciding how efficiently home can be adapted to its environment.

Heat and cold have been tamed for millennia by the use of mud-brick structures, which are simultaneously extremely cheap, widely available, and incredibly effective. In many cases, the only difference between mud-brick and brick is that the former is only fired by the heat of the sun, and therefore has a much weaker crushing strength. Mud-brick remains the predominant building resource for the majority of the Earth's population, as is thatch as a roofing material. Mud-brick has a multitude of local names, one of the most common being the word "adobe," which is used in North and Central America. Adobe bricks are without doubt one of the most superior building materials ever invented, being readily available for free, and an efficient insulator against heat and cold. Frequently made from a mixture of mud and straw, adobe has been used to build whole cities; the largest pyramid ever built was constructed at Chan Chan in Peru from mud-bricks. Entire towns such as Gao and Timbuktu in Mali, or the desert cities in the Yemen are built from adobe. San'a, the Yemeni capital, is largely constructed from mud-brick, and buildings can reach ten stories in height. Taos Pueblo in New Mexico, built by the Tiwi Indians, is also a wonderful example of the combined use of mud-brick with a defensive structure. The building complex is up to five stories high in places, and houses cannot be distinguished from each other or from the settlement as a whole. Even the traditional ovens, which were used for baking, were built from adobe. The Tiwi created an extremely efficient defensive system by only allowing access to homes through the roof of the structure, and in historic photographs there are only a few doors visible. Photographs that are more recent show an increase in doorways. Given the transition to modern society, this suggests that the need for floor level access has been increased. While Taos Pueblo is relatively "modern" in the ancient world, Catal Huyuk in Anatolia in Turkey has a similar form. So in this context the confluence between nature, refuge, home, and settlement becomes absolute.

After mud-brick for building walls, strong grasses in the form of straw have traditionally been used as a walling and roofing material, either independently or in combination with mud, although adobe could also be adapted to roofing over small areas. Straw was frequently used as an additive to mud-bricks for increased strength, resilience or insulation, depending on the use to which it was put. The addition of straw increased the tensile quality of the brick, which only had strength in compression and cracked easily under differential loading. The essential property of any insulating material is that it does not allow the efficient passage of heat across its width. Adobe did this due to its high insulating properties, and straw had similar abilities since it contained a sealed air space between each joint in the material. When straw was used for roofing, and laid at a reasonable pitch, rotting was prevented through the efficient drainage of rainwater. It could then last many years without replacement, and has been used across the world, from the romantic thatched cottages of rural England to the Batak houses in Sumatra and the kainga and pataka houses built by the Maori in New Zealand.

Thatch has therefore been used in a plethora of forms as defense against nature and as a refuge for local people. Probably the best example of its use has been by the Marsh Arabs (Ma'dan) of Iraq. Reed boats were used for transport, and on top of reed islands, entire houses were built from the same material, which could last up to 20 years – even longer on dry land. The Marsh Arabs nearly became extinct under Saddam Hussein's rule, when the supply of water to the marshes was cut off. Fortunately, this situation has now been corrected and the Ma'dan is returning to their traditional way of life.

In many early societies, stored crops also required a refuge in the form of granaries, which had the same thatched roof as home. The granaries of early people became an art form in themselves, as in the Gurunsi of Upper Volta or the Tata in Chad. Even today, grain silos are one of the most dominant architectural features of the American mid-west, and have provided inspiration for many modern architects.

LIVING WITH THE ELEMENTS

Torrential rains and tropical storms usually have been resisted in several different ways. The best forms were those that had steeply pitching roofs, as we can see from many indigenous homes, such as those of the Batak in Sumatra, the Jolong people of South Vietnam and the various peoples from the islands of Micronesia. In addition, flooding was frequently dealt with either by having floating structures or through the use of stilts, which raised the building above the water level, such as those in Papua New Guinea or the Solomon Islands.

Even today, grain silos are one of the most dominant architectural features of the American mid-west, and have provided inspiration for many modern architects.

TOP LEFT
A traditional thatched cottage in Great Tew, Oxfordshire, England. In thatched houses the main structure is built from stone, brick or wood, and the roof from straw or other dried grasses. Organic materials such as straw, water reed, sedge, rushes, and heather have been long-crafted for roofing purposes. In most European countries, for example, wheat stems have been widely used.

TOP FAR LEFT
Taos Pueblo village, near Taos, New Mexico, USA. This is one of the ancient settlements of the Pueblo people, a native American community who have continuously maintained their original form of habitation up to the present time. Its uniqueness is inextricably linked to the existence of multi-storied residential dwellings whose strength relies in the use of adobe or mud-bricks.

RIGHT
A farmhouse with a grain silo in the American mid-west. While this type of dwelling fulfills its residential purpose, it is designed to accommodate farming activity. The grain silo is usually used for storing wheat. They are a feature of home in many American mid-west states, and their cylindrical forms signify their relationship to nature and food storage.

FOLLOWING PAGES
A traditional guesthouse of the Marsh people between the Euphrates and Tigris rivers in southern Iraq. This form of dwelling has its entire structure made out of bundles of reeds, and can be easily rebuilt when the structure becomes weak from flooding, age, or accident.

Earthquakes were quite another story, and there was little or no defense against volcanic eruptions, mud slides and tsunamis, except not building in areas prone to these natural disasters. Nonetheless, the design of home remained ingenious. Wooden structures were frequently designed with flexible joints, which allowed for settlement and lateral movement, since rigid structures were most at risk from earthquakes. In Bali, for example, the actual structure of the traditional Balinese house was also partially isolated from the dividing walls, offering an additional level of protection from the shifting of tectonic plates under the earth, by partially separating form from structure. In other areas, such as Japan, which is seriously earthquake prone, nature provided bamboo, allowing traditional buildings to be lightweight and sliding panels for walls (*shoji*) to be largely made out of paper. Without doubt, traditional Japanese architecture represents the pinnacle of technology when it comes to carpentry in wooden buildings. Joints between wooden members were arguably the most complex ever created, with hundreds of different types to suit all known circumstances. In many cases, joints were manufactured without even the use of wooden dowels, let alone the steel nails popularly used in the west. While buildings frequently burned down, they were relatively safe during earthquakes because of their flexibility and absence of mass. Lightweight homes using traditional materials were also less prone to damage during a storm, and in cases where houses collapsed, allowed

the salvaging of materials for reuse. While firestorms were also threatening, it was a singularly easier task to rebuild such homes than those made from heavier and more enduring materials.

In South America, the Inca people also invented polygonal walling to resist earthquakes. This method of construction used stone as a material, which settled and became stronger when it was vibrated, although this method of construction was probably not used to house the poor. Nonetheless, excellent examples of polygonal walling remain visible in Cuzco, Peru, where Spanish colonists used structures as the foundations for their own homes. The colonists, however, proved to be a worse disaster than that of any natural force, decimating the population through war and pestilence, particularly smallpox. Therefore, the Incas used the power of nature as a refuge when they fled the advance of the Spanish conquistadors, escaping to the inaccessible regions of the Andes, and to fortresses such as those at Machu Picchu, Pisac, and Ollantaytambo.

So the landscape itself can provide refuge in a variety of different ways. Fortresses were built on hilltops, the very vastness and heat of the desert offered protection, islands created isolation, and even marshes allowed for sanctuary. Indeed the city of Venice was first established by a group of refugees fleeing from Padua around about the sixth century. (The great historian Lewis Mumford notes that the marshes and

shallow waters of the Adriatic replaced the defensive properties of stone walls, while observing that other forms of refuge can be as effective without the construction of massive defensive systems.) The marshes were slowly turned into islands through dredging, and over one and a half millennia later, Venice developed into the city it is today. Italy is also home to another form of refuge – the hill town. These were not the same kind of hill town as the Incas had built, which relied on the secrecy of remoteness as well as mountainous terrain. Towns such as San Gimignano, Todi, Montepulciano, Montefalco, Montecastello and a host of others were permanent settlements where the hilltop and town had the same identity. The people of San Gimignano even enhanced this situation by building tower homes that can still be seen today. Combined with a maze of streets, the town became an even more impenetrable refuge.

While early habitation was undoubtedly crude and unsophisticated, this held no implication for the sensibilities of early peoples. The Aboriginal population of Australia possessed a highly advanced consciousness in relation to a unified cosmology of matter, energy and spirit. Arguably, their awareness went well beyond that of contemporary modern life by several levels. The world was not measured by possessions or defined by omnipotent and fearful gods. Not only was their relationship to their environment unsurpassed, it was inextricably linked with their concept of existence

in the Dreamtime: A world where spirituality, mythology, consciousness and home as refuge blended into a single integrated universe. The idea of possessions did not occur, and any instruments required for survival were held in common. Even clothes were unnecessary. There was no intermediate world between that of the self and that of the spirit, so nature and consciousness merged into one reality. As such, "home" provided no refuge for the Australian Aborigines since it was not required, and they built neither settlements nor any fixed abode. Their traditional way of life was largely nomadic, where "humpies" or small temporary shelters made from whatever resource was available, provided some immediate protection from the weather.

Nature as refuge has therefore had a massive effect on home, as well as settlement. Nature has provided an infinite variety of climates, geographies, and materials that have supported habitation for countless millennia. There is no doubt, however, that we have not chosen to learn from our ancestors. Nature can no longer provide unconditional refuge from its own power, nor can it survive without our active participation. Since we have now achieved the Biblical mandate of dominion over nature, it is now time to question whether another strategy based on worship and respect for nature might be a more effective way to guarantee our refuge and hence our survival for the foreseeable future.

TOP FAR LEFT
Interior of a traditional Japanese house. Traditional Japanese house design is a consummate example of relating interior and exterior elements to create a balanced living environment. Natural building materials are used. Wide sliding doors and mobile internal partitions create an unsurpassed sense of space.

FAR LEFT
Polygonal walling in Cuzco in the Peruvian Andes. The city is believed to have been the center of the Inca Empire from the fourteenth to the fifteenth century. Such walls had defensive purposes, as well as protection from earthquakes due to their extreme stability and size. As structures, they are also a high art form.

TOP CENTRE
An Italian hill town forming the background to the San Biagio Church, Montepulciano, Tuscany, Italy. The hilly contours of the region inspired the Italians to form tower homes at the summit. Hilltops have always been considered a safe living environment against attack from enemies.

ABOVE
Gamble House, Pasadena, California, USA. Commissioned by David and Mary Gamble, this outstanding house was designed by architects Charles Sumner Greene and Henry Mather Greene in 1908. The use of timber, wide terraces, cross ventilation, and an indoor-outdoor living environment are carefully designed and crafted to create a harmonious home.

TOP
Fallingwater, Bear Run, Pennsylvania, USA. Built by the legendary architect Frank Lloyd Wright for Edgar Kaufmann in 1935, Fallingwater is perhaps one of the most famous homes in America. In this design, Wright creates an organic relationship with nature, mimicking the natural rock ledges that are created by a rushing mountain stream.

Chapter 2
Home as Defense

The concept of home as defense looks at home as protection from living creatures, including other human beings. This concept is primal and remains with us today. Home as defense is also dictated by climate, geography, and nature. This view is discussed in Home as Nature.

ACTIVE DEFENSE

As society has evolved from its primitive origins, it has become clear that the idea of defense has intensified and is of greater concern. There is a well-known saying in Britain that "an Englishman's home is his castle:" An unambiguous reference to the defensive structures that castles represent. The phrase "an Englishman's home is his palace" would have an altogether different significance; palaces being a place for display and entertainment, where any external threat has already been accommodated. These days, people define their lives by the ownership of commodities – cars, jewelry, computers, plasma televisions – so there is much more to be protected than just our physical bodies, as was the only requirement in ancient times. While modern life has unquestioned benefits over prior standards of living, it is also permeated by criminal

activity from the state and corporate level, down to individuals. This generates the need not only for extensive security systems in homes, but also for complex surveillance systems throughout most cities in the developed world.

Active defense has from time immemorial been concerned with building walls, usually against warring neighbors, and the concept of "wall" is also used as a metaphor for a variety of defensive conditions – in technology, in psychology, and physically. Walls have adopted many forms and in the past have been physically built from every possible material available, including wood, stone and water (moats), often in combination. Israel is in the process of building a wall 800 miles long (650 km) along the West Bank, and the United States of America is considering a similar wall along its entire border with Mexico. At one level, the history of civilization is the history of progressive warfare between individuals, tribes, fiefdoms, states, and nations. The Great Wall of China is probably the greatest of these, built to keep out nomadic Mongolian and Manchurian tribes from the 3rd century BCE onwards. From Biblical times, the walls of Jericho remain an archetype for all defensive structures, and

even the Romans had to build Hadrian's Wall across the whole of Britain to keep the blue woad-painted savages from Scotland on their own territory. Even animals have been used as defensive elements during warfare – Hannibal is well remembered for using elephants to fight the Romans – and movies of the Wild West are replete with images of cowboys using their horses as a protective wall against the original inhabitants. At the other end of the scale, animals also represented a need for serious defense, and many early forms of settlement constructed defensive walls against predators. Africa and India were home to the most dangerous species of animals – lions, tigers, cheetahs, and rogue elephants – and protection from these marauding carnivores was ubiquitous. Mass settlements from the Cameroon exhibit a huge range of huts constructed in a circle that were simultaneously defensive fortifications from animals, storage places for grain, and rooms for various sizes of family where more than one wife was the norm. The same is true of the Zulu Kraal in South Africa. Therefore, from our beginning as a species, humanity has viewed home both as a place to be defended and as a refuge for protection and solace.

TOP
A medicine man in front of his beehive hut, Natal, South Africa. This kind of house is decorated with various types of animal heads which are believed to have the power to defend against unwanted forces such as evil spirits. Evil spirits are considered to harm human health, bring bad luck, and affect relationships with others.

LEFT
Buckingham Palace, London, England. This is the official residence of the British head of state. To a great extent the palace is a symbolic representation of British sovereignty and the strength of its defenses that were part of the historic success of the British Empire. Buckingham Palace is a venue for numerous official state occasions and celebrations.

OPPOSITE
The Great Wall of China. Built from the 3rd century BCE onwards, the wall was intended to form a defensive structure, and coincidentally isolated China from the rest of the world. Attacks by the Mongols, however, demonstrated that the wall was ineffective and could be easily breached. It has been recognized as a UNESCO World Heritage Site since 1987.

Home then became the second "wall," since most cities were forced to construct defensive systems in the form of immense battlements and moats, or to locate on unscaleable hilltops.

POWER AND PROTECTION

As society developed and nomadic peoples everywhere became organized into communities of fixed settlements based on agriculture, surplus energy became stored not only in agricultural products, but also in materials mined from the earth, such as precious stones, gold, silver, and copper. A materialized concept of history proposes that communities are only representative of human labor – the labor it took to make them. An extended division of labor was created when social production reached a point where manufacture exceeded consumption and a quantum of labor could be freed to perform work not related to survival. This is how priests, artists and other professions arose. Progression from one historical period to another depended on how much labor had been stored in specific material forms. In turn new forms of power came into being, which were built on sectarian knowledge (priests), collective energy (armies), or organized social life (governments). The first forms of social organization that superseded hunter-gatherers, tribes and nomadic peoples are traditionally referred to as slave states, slavery representing the next level of social development. Not only did home remain a

defensive environment, it now became located in towns and cities where slavery was a defining form of wealth, with slaves being variously used for physical labor, their intellectual abilities (not all slaves were uneducated and many were used as scribes, doctors or for whatever skill they owned), a form of currency, and even substitute foot soldiers. Slave states abounded over historical time. The worlds of the ancient Sumerians, Egyptians, Olmecs, Toltecs and Aztecs were all built on slavery. Slaves were one-third of the population of ancient Greece, the birthplace of democracy. More recently, the Incas of South America also based their culture on slavery, as indeed did the United States of America up until the civil war. Hence, another layer of defense was added to the idea of home, since it was not merely individual, house, or family that had to be protected, but states that had acquired enemies. Defense fell into the hands of professional armies conscripted by the state, whose job it was to protect its citizens from becoming slaves themselves. Home then became the second "wall," since most cities were forced to construct defensive systems in the form of immense battlements and moats, or to locate on unscaleable hilltops.

TOP LEFT
Thatched huts, Machu Picchu, Peru. An example of the 150 houses discovered in Machu Picchu, a sacred site to the Inca people located in the Peruvian Andes, 9060 ft (2800 m) above sea level. It was the main center to which the Incas fled in order to escape the invasion of the Spanish in 1532.

ABOVE
The hill town of San Gimignano, Tuscany, Italy. The selection of a hilltop as the site for this town provided a prime defensive opportunity as well as a unique urban form. The town built a series of towers to exaggerate the height of the village, which offered a more threatening image to any potential enemy.

Not only did "home" become secondary to "wall," and "citizen" to "soldier," the concept now acquired a whole new meaning since different classes of people had come into being. While hunter-gatherers existed in a state of shared wealth and power, slave states had allowed social stratification, and hence an unequal distribution of wealth to come about. On this basis, new forms of home evolved across the medieval period into the Renaissance that had never previously been contemplated. The beginning of conspicuous consumption was born, where excess wealth was not merely possessed; it was also

exhibited, albeit for the specific function of protection. Where defense was concerned, this meant citadels, castles and fortresses, usually at the center of a settlement or town. There are few places in the world where defensive homes for those in power were not constructed. The home of the king, prince, dictator, or demi-god needed protection both from other powers, and frequently from their own people. Even today, there are few governments that do not possess special silos for the powerful, such as bunkers for the defense of the privileged in the event of a nuclear war.

In medieval times, warring states or fiefdoms built fortresses all over Europe. Scotland is a first-class example of this, where the country is littered with castles of all kinds. Edinburgh Castle is a perfect model of home as defense, as are the castles at Craigievar, Fyvie and Huntly. Similarly the Bastide towns of France such as Carcassonne, Villereal, and Monpazier are outstanding showpieces of walled towns of the medieval period. Italian hill towns such as San Gimignano, Assisi and Todi, also made effective use of the landscape, where hilltops provided near perfect defense against attack.

From the late Renaissance onwards, castles were no longer built (despite the naming of Hearst Castle in California in 1947, designed by Julia Morgan for Sir William Randolph Hearst, the newspaper magnate). Wars now took place between nations, and the homes of the rich took the form of grand palaces. Opulence was now exhibited on an unprecedented scale, as we can see from castles all over Europe. However, increased diversification in social classes combined with a transition from feudal society into the modern world meant that defense once again returned to the basic features required by personal security. Opulence continued and the castle gave way to the palace, as in the splendor of Chateau de Fontainebleau near Paris in France, Villa Aldobrandini near Frascati in Italy, Zwinger Palace in Dresden, and Buckingham Palace in London. While this still meant keeping out unwanted individuals, the number of typologies of home increased dramatically as urban life started to accelerate in its diversity of income classes and forms of labor.

Since home has always been caught up in human conflict in one form or another, it has had to provide its own defense, or to take part in some type of collective system, where social energy could be harnessed to provide what individuals could not. For example, the construction of defensive walls, moats and even houses was a collective effort from people in a society. Human belief systems and psychology also contribute to our understanding of home. For example, in Islamic cultures where women are not allowed out of the home unless accompanied by a male relative, balconies are designed so they can see out to the world of men, but they cannot be seen themselves. This is evident in Mughal or Rajput architecture in India, or in most cities in the Middle East. Home then becomes a defensive wall in terms of social and religious practices, where the entire form of the building, and indeed whole cities, are constructed to encompass religious dogma. There are, of course, many degrees of variation depending on the specific needs of the belief system.

In a much less extreme form, home everywhere is influenced by the cultural worldview of its occupants, in particular their protection from real or perceived threats, such as evil spirits and threatening gods. In many rural communities today, residents still do not feel the need to lock doors and windows when they leave the house. But in most modern urban areas, sophisticated electronics replace the friendly surveillance of community. Electrical devices provide internal surveillance, with direct connections to private security firms, and complex locking mechanisms on all the doors and windows, or even specially trained and selected dogs. At the biological level, the idea of defense is even built into our neurological systems, one-half dealing with fight and flight, or attack and escape, the other dealing with relaxation and rest. Therefore, the concept of defense is a primal part of our psychosomatic make-up, which has evolved along with the actual changes to our physical body over millions of years of evolution.

MODERN SURVEILLANCE

Defense applies not only to the simple physical act of keeping out unwanted people, it is also relevant to the virtual world, where electronic communication has become an invasive part of our home. Clearly, the idea of home as somewhere to be defended is increasing rather than decreasing in both its significance and cost. The burgeoning use of electronic communication for shopping, banking, education, and a plethora of other uses, also demands defensive networks and systems. The Internet is itself mutating into new and unexpected forms that require complex networks and strategies to protect its function. Previously unknown forms of defense such as "firewalls," "virus protection," "spam filters," "spyware" and so on, are now commonplace. Defense in the third millennium now requires highly sophisticated protection to ensure both personal and physical security at home, while at the same time it limits physical movement, replacing it with electronic communication. To use an extreme case, it is obvious that anyone who can work entirely from home – an increasing percentage of the population – need never leave unless they become sick, since other basic services such as banking, shopping, and entertainment can all be provided for electronically in a virtual world. Even money becomes irrelevant in this context. An evolving idea of home is therefore intimately linked to parallel defensive networks and systems.

So today's post-modern society also belongs to a parallel and virtual world of electronic communication and being. Here, a new and insidious process in the form of surveillance systems is now in place, which can be used for both defense, as well as encroachment into the home. There is no clear boundary between these two processes. Their use contains one of the great ethical problems of our times – the degree to which human rights should be sacrificed to individual and collective security.

TOP LEFT
Zwinger Palace, Dresden, Germany. Designed by the famous eighteenth-century architect, Matthaus Daniel Poppelmann, Zwinger Palace is one of Germany's most prominent landmarks. It was built on a site formerly used as a castle, whose inner and outer walls functioned as massive barriers from invasions.

FAR LEFT
Cliff dwellings of the Mesa Verde National Park, Colorado, USA. This is one of the most remarkable sites on Earth for any series of homes ever built. It is located near the top of a canyon wall under a huge overhang, offering supreme defensive qualities as well as protection from the elements.

ABOVE
A traditional home in Bahrain. This is an example of home in an Islamic society where women's activities must be invisible to the outside world. Balconies and terraces of these houses are designed to allow women to have views on events taking place outside the dwelling without anyone being able to see them.

RIGHT
Hill House, Helensburgh, Scotland. This house is the finest domestic building ever designed by the master architect, Charles Rennie Mackintosh. He borrowed its design features from Scottish baronial castles, and was a formative influence in the Art Nouveau movement. Simple, clean lines and natural colors characterize the house.

Chapter 3
Home as
Cloister

The concept of home as cloister opens up the question of typologies once again. The word "cloister" has a variety of possible interpretations: It immediately conjures up the idea of courtyard and the geometry of the square; something hidden, secretive, protected, internal, and private. In formal terms, the cloister or courtyard represents the square at the domestic level, but there is also a direct analogy with the square at the city level. Two great typologies have ruled the development of urban life: The street and the square. Roads are about points and lines and the movement between them. The street has been for centuries the key to transportation, and the words "shopping" and "street" have long been synonymous. Streets are conduits for commerce and communication, services and transport. Roads and streets have been important to civilized life from ancient times, and Roman roads are famous for setting in place many of the major trajectories of contemporary European transportation. Overall, the Romans built around 50,000 miles (80,500 km) of roads. The Fosse Way in England and the Appian Way in Italy are classic examples, and the construction method used lasted over 2,000 years before it was surpassed by modern technology.

THE SQUARE

The square on the other hand, even as a geometric concept, is not about movement but about rest and other associated activities, such as contemplation, reflection and discussion. At least since Hellenic times, over 2,500 years ago, the square has structured cities through the medium of a gridiron plan, and ancient Greek colonial towns in Asia Minor, such as Miletus, Priene and Pergamon, are famous as the predecessors of contemporary gridiron planning. However, gridiron planning was also a part of Asian urbanization. Japanese cities such as Kyoto and Nara, as well as the Chinese cities of Chang'an, Luoyang and Yangzhou, are all famous as early examples of gridiron planning. Today this is also evident in the United States of America where the entire country is based on cadastral gridiron planning; that is, the division of land into square or rectilinear sections, New York being a prime example. Therefore, the use of the grid as a fundamental geometric structure has been formative to urban development. But at that level, the grid remains a two-dimensional concept. Cities also demand the third dimension of height, as well as transformation in the fourth dimension – the space of time and history. This is the realm of urban design, where adapted spaces are generated for human use.

Squares have various uses when it comes to human interaction. The Greek square or agora was the archetypal urban form that encapsulated the concepts of discourse and philosophy, as well as that of commerce and the exchange of goods. The Greek home was built around the idea of a square or cloister, and was also the chosen form of the Romans who came after them. The agora – the central urban space of Greek cities – was the ultimate statement of urban life, where conversation was as important as commodities. Citizens gathered to exchange ideas, to gossip, or perhaps to listen to famous philosophers such as Socrates, Plato, Euripides, or Epicurus. The agora was usually constructed with generous colonnades, which encouraged dialog, debate, and conversation in all of its forms by providing a space which sequestered individuals from the often searing heat of summer. The reconstructed Stoa of Attalos is a perfect example of this and can be seen today in Athens. The agora gradually developed over history as the space around which western cities were built, and a space upon which the future development of democracy was predicated. It was the locus of military drills, festivals, elections, and spectacles, and was the place where the entire administration of the city was located. The great squares of the world owe their existence to the agora, and many European cities have a dominant "square" where the identity of the city and its social life circulates. We can name, for example, Trafalgar Square in London, St Mark's Square in Venice, Times Square in New York, and Place des Vosges in Paris. While Asian cities owe no allegiance to the Greeks, they are not immune from having their own important urban squares, such as Tiananmen Square in Beijing, Tugu Monas (Monas Square) in Jakarta and Sanam Luang in Bangkok. Each of these squares have also been associated with civil unrest, and it is clear that one of the functions of the square in urban life has been as a place where civil society has expressed its grievances against tyrannical states and governments of all kinds, in both eastern and western cultures.

How then does this translate at the level of domestic life? The idea of cloister is not limited to home, but is a form of home. In architecture, the term "cloister" applies to any square form that is centered on a colonnaded courtyard and which has a variety of spaces on the periphery. The use of that particular type of space in Europe evolved from monastic life to which it was eminently suited. In medieval times, the Guilds, which were the basis of organized labor, generated their own collective system to regulate working conditions and educate their members. This unified system was given the Latin name *universitas*, the original form of the

university in western culture. From cloister and *universitas*, the modern university was born as form and function. University quadrangles became the adopted symbol of higher learning. However, this was also repeated over time in government and other institutions, such as hospitals, prisons, and asylums. So when we look at the idea of home as cloister throughout history, we also see that its adopted form was not arbitrary. It was tailored to a variety of human needs such as safety, security, privacy, the isolation of domestic functions, and the capacity to adapt to a variety of different climatic conditions and materials. Examples include the wonderful Spanish colonial courtyard houses in Mexico with their cool interiors and large hammocks for siesta, to the Arab cities in the deserts of Yemen, and the delicately framed simplicity of traditional Japanese houses with enclosed Zen gardens. Even the British system of new towns adopted the courtyard house as part of their architectural vocabulary for public housing.

TOP
The Appian Way, Rome, Italy. The Romans depended on roads being built to link all parts of its empire. Roads and streets have been the key to commerce and transport for centuries and the words "shopping" and "street" have long been synonymous. The street is the most elementary urban form.

RIGHT
St Peter's Square, Vatican City, Italy. This is probably the most significant square in the Christian world as well as being an architectural and urban masterpiece. It is here that the Pope gives his annual blessing to Catholics all around the world.

TOP LEFT
Stoa of Attalos, Athens, Greece.
This restored cloister was
originally a two-story commercial
building and a precursor for many
contemporary architectural and
urban forms. The presence of
colonnades on both floors
promoted interaction, dialog, and
debate among visitors. There
were rooms on both floors for
commercial purposes.

TOP RIGHT
The Lion Court, Alhambra Palace,
Granada, Spain. The court is the
central feature of the Harem —
one section of the Alhambra
Palace that ties three rooms
together: The Hall of the Two
Sisters; the Hall of the Abencer-
rajes; and the Hall of the Kings.
The basin of the magnificent
Lion Fountain is supported by
12 marble lions.

FOLLOWING PAGES
Former hospital courtyard,
Mexico City, Mexico. The
courtyard is a basic domestic
and urban form that appears all
over the world. The central
fountain is a cooling device, and
the garden offers every room a
view of greenery and flowers.

THE COURTYARD HOUSE

The courtyard house as cloister has therefore had a huge range of applications throughout the world, and across the entire historical spectrum. In addition, certain cultures, such as that of Islam, have traditionally favored the courtyard form. The position of women in this society and the need for extreme privacy within the blank walls that the courtyard offers means that the cloister is tailor-made for people of the Muslim faith. The traditional Islamic courtyard house, particularly that of the wealthy, can frequently reach a height exceeding three or four stories, and can be found in cities such as Cairo, Fez, Aleppo, Damascus or Baghdad. For Islam, this type of housing contains at least three important features. First, the building height means that on the upper floors, balconies can be constructed that permit views out without anyone looking in, such as the mushrabiya shutters used in Egypt or the carved and ornate balconies of Mughal architecture. This also suggests social segregation of women to the upper floors, and men and the more public functions of storage and entertainment to the ground floor. Second, the courtyard house offers both an outside and an inside to its occupants. In those Islamic states where women cannot freely move about, the courtyard becomes a place that doubles for the public space of the city. It is an area where relatives and friends can meet in relative privacy and comfort within the acceptable norms of their culture. In addition, it offers a semi-public space whereby people may enter from the street, without directly intruding into the domestic space of the home. Third, the higher form of the courtyard house also allows a "chimney" effect to take place. With the careful integration of a fountain at ground level, the courtyard allows air to be cooled as it passes through the fountain or pond, also cooling the rooms at higher levels as the air rises up. In fact, this device serves the same function as a flue in a fire, except it is used for cooling rather than heating.

The courtyard is not limited to Islamic architecture in the Middle East, India, Africa and a few other locations. Its generic benefits have been widely adopted in many other regions. In China, at the urban level, the idea of cloister was also implicit, and it remained the dominant form for hundreds of years. Wealth was measured not by the height or grandeur of a building, but by the extent of its walls. The same form was used with great effect in the Heavenly City in Beijing, which is structured around two ceremonial squares. The traditional Chinese house in Beijing was bounded by lanes called *hutongs* with their internal courtyards called *si he yuan*. However, its existence has been widely threatened since the low-rise nature of the courtyard house represents a huge barrier to development. It is already being replaced by high-rise apartments and a process of importing western domestic typologies that the American scholar Tony King refers to as "villafication." China's extraordinary growth over the last 20 years and its expectations for the future suggest that the traditional courtyard house may soon be consigned to museum environments in designated conservation areas, and vast tracts of these beautiful old houses have already been extinguished from Chinese cities.

The traditional Balinese courtyard house is yet another application of the widespread use of the cloister as architectural form. Because of the prevalence of Balinese Hinduism, the courtyard has a somewhat different function from other locations. For example, in contrast to the Islamic courtyard which can be built over as many floors as construction methods and wealth will allow, in Bali, religious practices forbid construction that is higher than the average height of coconut trees (49 ft/15 m). In addition, the external wall does not denote the actual structure of the house, since the space it encloses is subdivided into nine squares called Sanga Mandala. Each square has a different function and may be occupied by a different building form. The family shrine occupies the northeast corner and the central space is usually an open courtyard. This space is usually quite large and is the common area used by the family on a daily basis, as well as the location for rituals and celebrations. Traditional Balinese society and cosmology also revolves around the principle that the prime function of home is that of a shrine for the ancestors. Family members are therefore custodians of home in perpetuity, but do not "own" it. For that reason, in contrast to materialistic societies elsewhere, Balinese homes have no value as commodities, and only have value in use. They are in a very real sense, religious cloisters.

The courtyard and the archetype of the cloister have had universal application across a wide range of climatic conditions, although the form has predominated in hot or warm temperate zones. Psychologically, this architectural structure is introspective, segregated, of limited horizon, self-centered, and concentrated on family life. These qualities are necessary to society and will continue to serve the world's inhabitants for centuries to come.

OPPOSITE
Interior of an Islamic school, Morocco. Courtyard design is favored in Muslim countries because it offers both closure and exposure – closure from the outside world and exposure within the family. The design also protects its occupants from hot, dry climatic conditions.

ABOVE
Casa de Montego, Mexico. A classic Mexican home for the wealthy. This courtyard house has a wide veranda that borders the courtyard. A large hammock and outside furniture demonstrate the use of the veranda as an extension of the living space, allowing residents to enjoy the interior landscape of the courtyard.

TOP
Summer Palace, Yiheyuan, China. In today's China, courtyard houses represent a huge barrier to development. Due to the rapid growth in both population and development over the last 20 years, these houses have been replaced by high-rise apartments.

Chapter 4
Home as Spirit

Home as spirit concerns the relationship between humanity and the unseen world in its many guises. The function of home under this ideology encompasses everything from organized religion and animistic beliefs, to the worlds of black magic or voodoo. Home as spirit focuses on safeguarding occupants from all manner of unseen forces, the representation of gods, and ceremonies in their worship or offerings to appease them. Overall, these practices seek to maintain equilibrium within the home, where health, wealth and happiness are commonly held aspirations. Also important is the position of home as a place where family beliefs are nourished. This notion incorporates believing in some kind of god in the form of organized religion, existence after death, particular ideologies and practices in life, as well as the power accorded to individuals within society such as those of seer, jro taksu, shaman, witchdoctor, medicine man or priest.

A PLACE OF PRAYER AND REMEMBRANCE

These meanings of home as spirit suggest two main concepts: Home as a place of worship, and home as a memoir. The notion of worship imbeds a devotion to natural spirits, deities, the idea of God and its manifestations. The spirit world is not homogeneous. Some spirits are good, some bad, and some relatively benign. Some protect health, some the environment, some food supplies, and some are harnessed in the interest of harming others. Such religious observance may ask for blessings in the manner of a good harvest, protection from accidents, physical strength, good weather, family success, abundant crops, forgiveness from wrongdoing, or healing for illnesses. Vernacular societies frequently have specific homes dedicated to their gods and healers in the form of spirit or medicine houses. Worship may also be directed to evil spirits not to bring any misfortune or disturbance to the household's living environment. People from the Ivory Coast, for example, implant a huge masked dancer doll on stilts in front of their homes for protection. Countless examples exist of this kind of practice.

The notion of home as a memoir first embraces the idea of remembrance where home remains a repository for the soul. The soul of every family member is to be perpetuated and respected, even though the person may no longer be in the physical world. Second, home also represents the locus for a commemoration of legendary figures, values, or memorable deeds embraced by communities and societies at a larger scale.

LEFT
Taj Mahal, Agra, India. The Taj Mahal, a symbol of eternal love, was built in 1631 by Shah Jahan, the fifth Mughal emperor, in reminiscence of his second wife, Mumtaz Mahal, a Muslim princess from Persia. The building was designed by the Iranian architect, Ustad Isa.

TOP
A house in Ivory Coast, Africa. A large-scale, masked dancer doll on stilts is installed in front of this dwelling to dispatch all invisible evil spirits. They are unwanted and deemed to possess powers that inflict hazards and harm to the home's residents.

Therefore, devotion to higher, invisible forces has been part of daily life, maintained from generation to generation in various societies across history and within every type of human group be it hunter-gatherer, nomadic, slave state, medieval, or modern. The Greeks believed that their ancient gods had been overthrown by the Titans: A group of 12 new gods (Zeus, Poseidon, Hades, Hestia, Hera, Ares, Athena, Apollo, Aphrodite, Hermes, Artemis, and Hephaestus), whose sacred home was Mount Olympus. In every home in ancient Greece, there was a shrine or shrines to these gods. The same was true of the Romans, who also worshiped a group of 12 different gods. Even at that time the great sages of China, Lao Tse and Confucius, had established Taoism (based on Buddhism) and Confucianism respectively, and shrines to these ideologies have been an integral part of home across the whole of Asia for over 2,500 years. To accommodate these practices and other forms of observance of spirit, home offers the most immediate space for private contemplation and prayer. In most places, this takes the shape of a family altar or shrine where, for example, a statue of Siddhartha Gautama, Lao Tan, or Kung-fu-tse sits, surrounded with incense, flowers, and other offerings. Similar practices are also common in Japanese families. Shinto, the indigenous faith of Japanese people has no founder, scriptures or sutras. Shinto gods are called Kami and are represented in the forces of nature. Amaterasu, the sun god, was the most important deity. Japan's other religion, Zen Buddhism, had similar forms of worship, but since it had no personified gods, objects were usually used for meditation in the form of a flower, a painting or even a hand-drawn circle representing the cosmos. In addition, a family altar may also be present in the home, which is specifically devoted to paying respect to a family's ancestors.

In communities of early peoples who still function today, life still takes place within the governing compass of the spirit world. For instance, The Abelam village situated between the Sepik River and the Prince Alexander Mountains in northern Papua New Guinea has a ceremonial spirit house referred as Haus Tambaran. This is an "all-roof" house. The whole structure slopes to the ground at the back and the frame is constructed by bamboo poles forming a high-peaked ridge at the front. The prominent role of ritual and spirit is demonstrated from the scale of the Haus Tambaran which can reach 82 ft (25 m) in height. This is five to six times higher than the height of houses built next to and opposite it. While ordinary dwellings do not have decorative elements, the Haus Tambaran has its upper front wall decorated with blue and red oval-shaped ornaments, symbolic faces, cassowaries, and flying foxes. Abelam people secure the lower part of the front facade of this ceremonial house with plaited mats with two entrances, whereas living houses have none of these securities.

RIGHT
Interior of a Haus Tambaran, Palambei Village, Papua New Guinea. These lively symbols in the forms of carvings or masks, used in a Haus Tambaran, are imbued with the religious beliefs of the people. Based on the principles of totenism and animism, these creations are made to drive out bad spirits.

TOP
Statues of Buddha, Bangkok, Thailand. In Thailand, where Buddhism is widely practiced, it is common to find an altar located at a prominent part of the house. A statue of Buddha is usually accompanied by offerings such as flowers.

ABOVE RIGHT
Graceland, Memphis, Tennessee, USA. The former home of rock legend Elvis Presley from the late 1950s until his death in 1973. It is now a museum showcasing his remarkable career and the site of his grave.

The significance of home as a medium for the spirit world, a space of transaction, meditation and prayer, is evident within the vernacular house of the Balinese in Indonesia. It exhibits singular generic qualities and demonstrates in great detail the extent to which home as spirit is defined by, and embedded within, family life. It is the locus where the macrocosmic forces of gods and nature determine the daily life of the people. The traditional Balinese courtyard house or compound is divided into nine zones, called Sanga Mandala. The family shrine is called Merajan or Sanggah and is located in the most sacred zone Utama-Utama – usually at the northeast corner of Tanah Sikut Satak (the site where the house is). Other domestic functions are located in relation to the family shrine and are not negotiable. Bathrooms, WCs, washing areas, kitchens etc. are already determined before anyone decides to build a traditional house. The Merajan has several smaller shrines each of which is devoted to a deva or deity, the god's manifestations, and the family's ancestors, whose souls have received further ceremonies following a cremation rite. In order to safeguard the house from "bad" spirits, there are also small shrines located at every corner of the house. For similar purposes, there is another shrine built just in front of the main entrance, as one enters the compound. While some shrines are built with stone foundations, timber structures, grass straw, or palm sugar husk roofing, most are wholly constructed from soft natural volcanic stone quarried close by or collected from adjacent rivers. Even the placing of floors has ritual significance, with the kitchen at the lowest level and the shrine having the highest elevation.

Thus spirit worship in the Balinese home infuses both behavior and architecture. A woman who is menstruating is not allowed to enter or even stand near the shrine. In this circumstance, she is also exempted from involvement in the preparation of offerings, ceremonies, and prayer. Family members and non-family members who are in mourning are also restricted from entering. All equipment used for ritual, including other matters relating to these shrines, is not usually mixed with those utilized for other purposes, despite the fact that their functions overlap. Some families even have an additional building and kitchen to support the operation of the family shrines. Offerings are made to the ancestors on a daily basis. Apart from a daily offering, each family holds a bigger ceremony to celebrate the day when the shrines were completed. It comes every 210 days (six Balinese months) – the day when family members and relatives coming from the same ancestral line meet, pray, and gather for meals. In a traditional family compound, a significant portion of the family's annual income can be spent on offerings and ceremonies.

Therefore, the observation of ritual complexity carried by home goes beyond mere physical experience. In Bali and other Indonesian societies, every stage of constructing a home involves a series of observances that may come in various forms of ceremony, offerings, and sacrifices. In order to invite "good" spirits and calm down "bad" forces, such rituals may have to take place on a specific day according to a particular calendar. Types of building materials used, the selection of site, and distinctive choices of symbolic and decorative forms are all part of the effort to deploy spiritual significance to home. Failing to fulfill any of these procedures may be regarded as a direct cause for insecurity, illness, bad luck, or psychological discomfort experienced by members of the household.

Measuring the Tanah Sikut Satak, site clearing, putting in foundations, fitting columns and beams, roofing, etc., are all commenced on a particular day. Each involves offerings and ceremony. Building materials used for shrines should be the finest available in terms of quality and durability. In circumstances where these practices cannot be performed, negligence may be excused by performing other special ritual ceremonies. Such ceremonies are also applied when the sacred value of a family shrine is disturbed or compromised by any means. At another level, even the spirit of the owner is incorporated into the home by constructing a special scale based on his actual physical being. Such measuring sticks form the basis for all elements in the construction process.

TOP LEFT
Animism-Hinduism practices in Balinese society. Balinese daily life is closely linked to this belief system. No day passes without offerings to the gods. The Balinese calendar dictates hundreds of special ceremonies and events every year.

HERO WORSHIP

In today's society, home as spirit is also represented in the process of conservation where homes of society's greatest representatives, good or bad, have been protected for posterity. These rise above the importance of individuals and are emblematic of entire histories – the rule of presidents, victory in war, the development of art and literature, and other accomplishments. In this context, houses are consciously preserved in order to commemorate and memorialize a past that is not only significant to a particular family but also to a wider audience, community, or country. In the United States of America, for example, the house of Thomas Jefferson at Monticello near Charlottesville, Virginia, is a wonderful piece of architecture that celebrates this famous president. Alternatively, the simple birthplace of Elvis Presley in Tupelo, Mississippi is also a form of shrine for millions of Americans, as is his house, Graceland, in Memphis.

Paradoxically, it would appear that as society has progressed, the relationship between home as spirit and its reflection in dwelling form has decreased with an overall increase in the complexity of social development. Expressions of home as spirit have been gradually simplified or even eliminated over time. In fact, societies wrongly labeled "primitive" are much closer to home as spirit than most homes today, which are largely bereft of spiritual content and expression. In the developed world, new gods such as Nike, Sony, and Chanel, have arisen to reflect today's Mount Olympus of consumer society and commodity fetishism.

TOP CENTRE
North lawn of the White House, Washington DC, USA. The official residence of the President of the United States of America, the White House was conceived by George Washington, who selected its actual location. Its development began in 1792 and it was completed in 1800 in the Classical style of architecture.

TOP RIGHT
10 Downing Street, London, England. The historic home and office of the Prime Minister of the United Kingdom, this building is of modest appearance and does not reflect the important activities held inside it. It symbolizes that the government remains close to the ordinary life of the people.

ABOVE
Home interior of a Shaker community. The spartan nature of Shaker religious beliefs is reflected in their whole environment. The design of artefacts is simple yet beautiful. The minimal use of furniture also reflects this philosophy. Simplicity is a widely acknowledged value of Shaker communities.

Chapter 5
Home as Journey

Home as journey has had a long history, from the trading caravans of the Great Silk Route to the space capsules that NASA has sent to the moon. While the nomad is central to our idea of home as an experience of movement, the concept also has many variations.

NOMADISM

In the strict sense of the word, "nomadism" only has two interpretations. Pastoral nomadic life was a symbiosis between humans and animals, where movement was demanded because animals of whatever kind had depleted the landscape of food. One theory of pastoral nomadism is that it grew out of the activities of hunter-gatherer people; another is that it evolved much later after mixed farming had developed. In any event, pastoral nomads were dependent on animal husbandry, and their lifestyle allowed them to exploit a variety of different landforms so, technically, it is a form of farming, replacing plants with animals. The domestication of goats, horses, sheep, cattle, and other creatures allowed this form of nomadism to evolve. The Mongols, Magyars and Moors were typical examples of this. Pastoral nomadism was also dictated by the seasons, where migration was imposed by the passage from one season to another.

True nomadism, however, required no justification for movement – it was just natural behavior, rather than staying in one place. Historic nomadic peoples populated all forms of landscape: the Bedouin and Tuareg of the desert, the Pygmies of the central African jungle, the Innu people of Quebec and Labrador, or the Moken sea gypsies of the Surin Islands in southern Thailand. Therefore, nomadism even included movement over water, and the nomadic Hakka boat people of southern China can be seen in anchorages in Hong Kong today.

TOP
Example of an Aboriginal wurley, Australia. This hut exemplifies the journeys of the largely nomadic lifestyle of the Australian Aborigines. Home is an endless journey following the myths and legends of the Dreamtime – their spiritual world. All forms of home were crude, temporary, and disposable.

LEFT
A hut of the Bambendjelle tribe, Makao, Democratic Republic of the Congo. The construction of this temporary hut coincides with the tribe's constant movement in search of food. This migration is also necessary to avoid disastrous damage potentially caused by bad weather conditions.

MOBILE "HOMES"

The development of home in these contexts also bred a variety of physical dwellings. Both true nomadism and pastoral nomadism led to the construction of an immense variety of structures that were sometimes fixed (to be revisited at the same time the following year), or that were transported by camel, horse or other animals such as the llama and guanaco of Peru. Many true nomads, such as the pygmy tribes of the Ituri Forest in the Democratic Republic of the Congo or the Australian Aborigines, only had the most minimal of temporary and disposable structures. Since nomadism took place in all kinds of climatic conditions, home had to be adapted accordingly. The Inuit built temporary ice huts called "igloos" whenever they needed refuge. The Mongols developed circular buildings called "yurts," which were suited to the high winds of the Steppe, which were also used by the Kirghiz people in the Gobi desert. In America the Plains Indians developed the "tepee," which was a superb adaptation to climatic conditions. It also satisfied the need for a demountable structure. The tepee could be transported as the tribe moved, being used predominantly during periods of hunting buffalo. It used a framework of long poles in a conical form, covered with animal skins as a protective membrane. Ventilation through the apex of the tepee allowed a central fire to be lit for heating and cooking. The outside was usually decorated with symbolic images. Today animal skins have been replaced by high quality canvas, and tepees built according to the original design are still in vogue and can now be purchased by mail order. The other structure used by the Plains Indians was the wigwam, which is often confused with the tepee. It was, however, an entirely different form, built in the shape of a dome from flexible tree branches covered with rush matting, and was usually used to store grain.

The Bedouin Arabs developed an altogether different form of tent home; a structure that could easily cover a large area and accommodate many people. The Bedouin account for 10 percent of the population of the central Middle East. Their nomadic lifestyle is based in the desert environments of Saudi Arabia, Yemen, Israel, Syria, as well as Egypt, Tunisia, and Libya in North Africa. It is estimated that in Saudi Arabia alone there are around 700,000 Bedouin people. Most are Sunni Muslims, but there are also a small number of Christians because any Bedouin who believed in Jesus Christ was put to death. The Bedouin tent was usually black in color and extremely lightweight, being made from wool strips and lightweight timbers in compression. Its shape is very like the advanced tent forms used today by contemporary architects, where steel and powerful synthetic materials parallel the Bedouin use of rope and canvas. The tent was nonetheless a simple affair, based on a series of vertical poles with a horizontal membrane stretched over them and fixed with ropes into the ground. Like most nomadic people, the concept of furniture was alien, and people sat, conversed, and slept on the floor.

The idea of nomad is by no means confined to early forms of social organization, and it has had many equivalents as society has evolved. The Romany people are one such example and are found throughout Europe and Asia. Originating from northwest India, they migrated through Persia and Turkey, and hence into Western Europe. The Romany have been given many names by local people, including the English "gypsy" and the French *tzigane*, and they have suffered serious persecution over their entire history, which originated 800 to 1000 years ago. This has continued right into the modern period, when they were declared "sub-human" by the Nazis and sent to concentration camps. One traditional form of Romany home recognized throughout Europe has been the highly decorated horse-drawn caravan or cart. These carts have been used for centuries and in many cases, have been superseded today by motor homes, often with air-conditioning, a bathroom and the usual amenities of modern homes. While many Romany remain nomadic, significant numbers have decided to live in fixed settlements, with some 70 percent of today's Romany population residing in small towns such as Hameau Tzigane in Grasse, France, or Shuto Orizari in Skopje, Macedonia.

ABOVE
A typical caravan used by the Romany people. A precursor of the mobile home, the caravan is one of the original features of gypsy life. Originally pulled by horses, most gypsies now use some kind of mechanical transport, such as cars or vans. Caravans were also moving art forms, using complex decorative features and bright colors.

TOP
Native American dwelling, Great Plains, USA. The tepee as a nomadic dwelling has two distinct features: It has a hole at the top that allows an open fire and cooking activities to take place inside; and it uses 10 poles as a basic frame, covered with animal skins, which is easily transportable on horseback.

FOLLOWING PAGES
Bedouin tents, the Sahara, Morocco. In Arabic, *bedouin* means "inhabitant of the desert." The bedouin build their tents to accommodate family members and to serve their guests. In the 1950s and 60s, however, the bedouin started to change their nomadic lifestyle to settle and work in cities across the Middle East.

Technology has also extended the concept of home into space, with space flights and space stations now transporting home out into the universe.

MODERN MIGRATION

In today's globalized world, home as journey has taken on new meanings as modern forms of conflict, disease, economic opportunity and lifestyle have taken place. The greatest of these is probably migration due to famine, persecution and unemployment. Legal migration to the United States of America is now approaching one million per annum. Since the system of registration as a resident of a particular village was abolished in China, 200 million people have left rural areas for cities, with 40 million on the move at any one time. The United Nations (UNHCR) currently estimates a total of approximately 175 million migrants worldwide. In addition to this, there are approximately 12 million refugees, which suggests about 200 million persons are moving home in some form or another at any one time. Today, for those who have suffered from political persecution, war, disease or natural disasters, home has taken on the forms of temporary tent settlements and other places of detention across the globe. This is most prevalent in Africa. Here, home as journey has become suspended until people can return to their original settlement, or be welcomed by some other country. Unfortunately, refugee camps have a habit of turning into semi-permanent forms of home as the world's capacity to absorb these populations is resisted.

Home as journey in the modern world is not, however, limited to migrants and refugees. Wealth and technology also manufacture their own forms of home as journey, as seen in the mobile home. Greater retirement incomes combined with advanced health care has allowed people in developed countries to chose mobility rather than belonging to a fixed settlement. In addition, it is a much cheaper form of home. Rather than having a huge percentage of one's savings locked up in fixed capital, home as journey can be bought for a tenth of the price. This form of home is on the increase. The mobile home is now ubiquitous, with many new models developing since the original and iconic Airstream Trailer of the United States, or the Volkswagen Microbus of Europe, both popular in the 1950s. Having worked for 40 or 50 years, many retirees enjoying good health now buy some form of mobile home that is self-contained or requires towing. Sometimes both are used together, where a self-powered mobile home also tows a car, offering a more flexible system of transportation. Mobile homes assemble into temporary settlements at designated sites for specified periods, and then move to the next destination. These are altogether different from what is called a trailer park, where homes are indeed mobile, but hardly ever move from an initial fixed location.

The mobile home phenomenon is predominantly limited to wealthy countries and/or those with large land masses, such as the United States of America or Australia. Since the formation of the European Economic Community (EEC), movement across national boundaries and the transfer of certain benefits has also opened up increased possibilities across the whole of Europe.

Technology has also extended the concept of home into space, with space flights and space stations now transporting home out into the universe. Oil rigs also represent home as journey, at least temporarily, for those who must work on location throughout the world. The same is true of ocean liners, and huge, floating settlements such as *The World*: a ship comprised of luxury private apartments, which travels to the four corners of the globe. As the world's population increases, it is expected that mobility for whatever reason is also likely to increase. An evolving trend is to combine home as journey with electronic communication, where people become what author Steven Roberts has called "technomads," with online nomadic living and support wherever home happens to be. The possible combination of electronic communication, flexible transport, and accommodation with the virtual world promises that new and unheralded forms of home as journey are on their way.

TOP LEFT
Trailers or caravans have been widely used as temporary homes for people who are traveling. This is especially true of many western countries where large distances are best covered by taking one's home along. Recreational vehicles provide people with the comfort of a moving home – a space to sleep, cook, dine in, wash, and relax.

ABOVE
An emergency shelter at Cape Hallett, Antarctica. Cape Hallett was the site for New Zealand and the United States of America's joint research base in Antarctica (1957–73). This type of shelter was commonly used to protect researchers who worked on the project from the constant cold weather conditions of Antarctica.

TOP RIGHT
Gemini Space Capsule docking in orbit. The ultimate mobile home traveling at thousands of miles per hour and providing every basic service necessary for survival. However, in contrast to other mobile forms of home, space capsules have highly limited performance specifications, with little room for errors of judgment.

Chapter 6
Home as
Art

Throughout history, home for people in every single topography and climate has always had a symbolic function. The reason for this is obvious: People live not only in the material world of their own physical requirements, but also in environments where societies express their collective history, beliefs, aspirations, emotions, the exhibition of power and authority, and even fears and tribulations. From the time humanity first came into consciousness, the imagination has been harnessed as the mechanism by which representation of other worlds could be realized. Today, we call this "art" and it is a concept of modernity to the extent that a small painting by the French impressionist Vincent Van Gogh can sell for upwards of US$50 million dollars. To this degree, art has simply become part of contemporary investment strategies for the wealthy, in the process changing art from any practical function into collector's items for state-controlled art galleries and private entrepreneurs.

AN IDEA OF BEAUTY

Although the word "art" is useful in describing certain functions of home, it can also be misleading. Art as a concept has little validity over history unless we consider both its context and practice. In ancient times, art did not exist as we know it today. As modernism was the first epoch to conceive of itself as a separate "bit" of history – a period apart, independent, and definable from the rest – so it was the first to reappropriate the function of art from the symbolic to the material, from the sacred to the profane, and from the world of the spirit to that of money, wealth, and power.

When examining home as art, it is important to consider the relationship between "art" and "aesthetics." While these terms are commonly tied together, there is no necessary relationship between them. In ancient Greek *aestheta* means "perceptible things" and it was not until the eighteenth century that aesthetics became related to the idea of beauty, first in German and then in English. Therefore, our concepts of beauty, art, and aesthetics are a direct product of our time and have little to do with how history has dealt with systems for representing consciousness. There is a famous Balinese saying: "We have no art, we simply do everything as well as we can." This indicates a condition that had existed for millennia, where the function of art was to support the daily life of people and where it had no exchange value.

Art was simply the best anyone could do in whatever activity they were undertaking. Without doubt, home was organized around material processes and was structured around these activities: Fire for cooking, animal skins and blankets for sleeping, space to tell stories and transmit the oral history of the people. However, the symbolic world was at least equal to the material, and was often more important. While there has always been a collective dimension to home where communities celebrated their relation to family life, home has always played its own important part in rituals and ceremonies, such as those associated with the birth of children, rites of passage, marriage, and the journey beyond life into the worlds of gods and spirits. In each case, home as art was fully integrated. It did not occupy a separate space of objectivity and contemplation, and the world of "otherness" was expressed both through the human body in trance, dance, or meditation, or through fetishes, painting, objects carved from wood, metal and stone, and even in the layout of space, both within the dwelling and its relationship to other buildings in the community. The ancient caves of Lascaux in France have highly decorated interiors, as do the Tassilli frescoes in cave dwellings of the Sahara desert. In contrast to the idea that art was dependent on a complex division of labor required to release labor from toil, in Lascaux we find that art celebrated life and was necessary to its success.

TOP
A prominent mural of the Gyantse Kumbum Monastery, Gyantse, Tibet. Being the largest stupa in Tibet, this monastery has four floors with chapels of different sizes and is filled with statues and murals. *Kumbum* in Tibetan means 100,000 images. This is one of the few monasteries surviving after the destruction caused by Chinese occupation.

LEFT
Lascaux cave painting, Lascaux, France. Some of the earliest forms of home – caves – were decorated with highly stylized and symbolic paintings. In contrast to the idea that art is dependant on a complex division of labor required to release labor from toil, the Lascaux painting in France demonstrates that the celebration of life was necessary to its success.

RIGHT
An example of Maori carving, New Zealand. Traditional Maori homes are works of art with carved and painted beams and lintels, highly woven tapestries made from reeds as well as elaborately sculpted and ornate panels and supporting columns.

TOP FAR RIGHT
Aboriginal hand painting, Australia. The Australian Aborigines had all manner of art totems, sculptures, fetishes, implements etc., which were frequently a representation of natural phenomena such as lightning, storms, animals, and vegetation of all kinds. This example demonstrates its use in cave painting.

FAR RIGHT
Tokyo Bay, Japan. This bathroom is built based on feng shui principles. It is designed to overlook the bay, which is considered to bring positive "chi" or energy not only to the house, but also to its occupants.

ART IS CULTURE

Home as art has many dimensions. One of the most basic is the relationship to the cosmos, where the positioning of home frequently reflected religious or spiritual dimensions. Positioning was often directly related to compass points, or the rising and setting of the sun. In the ancient Chinese practice of feng shui, particular geographic features and relationships are important, and elements called dragon lines help "chi" (the circulating life energy found in all things) flow naturally in the landscape. For example, having mountains behind and water in front of an abode was always desirable. The Cheyenne Indians always adopted a circular camp form with the entrance to the east, which was also the orientation for the doorway in all the tepees. Groupings of tents symbolized clan structures, human life cycles, and relationships to the Earth such as hunting and the production of crops.

The relationship between mythology and art was absolute in the life of Australia's Aborigines to the extent that the life of every individual was the perfect expression of a unity with every living creature and feature of the physical landscape. A film called *Where the Green Ants Dream* (1984) by the famous German director Wim Wenders personified the ongoing conflict between corporations and indigenous communities. In his film, the local Australian Aboriginal community refused to allow any disruption to the Earth, because that was the place "where the green ants dream." While the Aborigines had no dwellings, they had all manner of "art" totems, sculptures, fetishes, implements etc., which were frequently a representation of natural phenomena such as lightning, storms, animals, and vegetation of all kinds.

Home as art even has zoomorphic qualities where the actual form of the house or settlement mimics some kind of animal, as in the tortoise of the Lunda Kingdom of Angola or the village of Boum Massenia in Chad, which takes the form of a rhinoceros. The human body has also been used as art, as in the anthropomorphic plans of the Fali people in Cameroon. While early people frequently based the form of home on the representation of living creatures, all materials used to construct home also lent themselves to some manner of adornment, and the use of natural dyes and paints was widespread. No part of any building was immune to decoration or carving. Traditional Maori homes, for example, have carved and painted beams and lintels, highly woven tapestries made from reeds as wall panels, and elaborately sculpted and ornate supporting columns. The Haida Indians of British Columbia also erected huge carved totem poles as part of home, which had huge symbolic significance.

Even as long ago as the ancient Egyptians, architecture was still influenced by religion and ritual, as seen in the pyramids and mastabas constructed for the dead.

ABOVE
The Marble Court, Palace of Versailles, France. Commissioned by Louis XIV, development of the Palace of Versailles began in 1669 and was built over the next 25 years by architects Louis Le Vau and Jules Hardouin-Mansart, with the world-famous André Le Nôtre designing the landscape. After its construction, Versailles had a tremendous influence on French architecture and the arts.

TOP
The Great Temple of Ramses II, Abu Simbel, Egypt. This is one of the cut-rock temples located in the ancient Wawat in Nubia. The temple's giant facade is about 125 ft (38 m) long and 102 ft (31 m) high and is dedicated to the New Kingdom's most prominent gods: Ptah (god of creation), Amun-Re (god of greatness), Re-Harakhte (god of the sun), and Ramses II himself.

ALL IN THE DETAIL

It is clear that art as we know it today became increasingly detached from daily life as civilization evolved. Part of this was due to the progress of architecture as a discrete art form. Art was applied to home by experts rather than being created based on traditional rituals, conventions, and beliefs. Even as long ago as the ancient Egyptians, architecture was still influenced by religion and ritual, as seen in the pyramids and mastabas constructed for the dead, and the temples and other ritual places as homes for the gods. In ancient Greece and Rome, the courtyard house had been established as the standard art form. Apart from the building itself, experts were then used, as they have been until today, to create art in the form of murals, paintings, sculptures and landscape features using both plants and objects such as fountains to generate home as art. In many ways, this process reached its pinnacle during the Renaissance and Baroque periods, where the concentration of wealth into private hands combined with the ability to express this wealth through material means is unsurpassed even today. The homes of the world's greatest

billionaires such as Bill Gates, Warren Buffet, and Karl Albrecht fade into obscurity when compared to those of the last 500 years. For example, the Palace of Versailles near Paris, commissioned by Louis XIV, was started in 1669, and was built over the next 25 years by architects Louis Le Vau and Jules Hardouin-Mansart with the world-famous André Le Nôtre designing the landscape. Approximately 36,000 workers were employed in its construction. Later, Buckingham Palace in London was initiated by King George IV around 1820, and was designed and supervised by the architect John Nash. But such extravagant homes were by no means unique, and the whole of Europe and Asia are replete with the most incredible examples of home as art: The Chateau of Chambord in the Loire Valley (1519–47) designed by Domenico da Cortona, Belvedere Palace in Vienna (1714–22) by Johann Lucas von Hildebrandt, Blenheim Palace in England (1705–22) by Sir John Vanbrugh, and the Winter Palace in St Petersburg (1762) by Bartolomeo Rastrelli. All these palaces are consummate examples of home as art because they incorporate painting, sculpture, wood carving, landscaping, and architectural detailing.

Home as the art of architecture really came into being with the creation of modern professions and institutions: The Royal Institute of British Architects being the first such establishment to take concrete form in 1834. Since then, the development of home as the art of architecture has been influenced by recent history, social development, and technological advances. Many architects also continued the tradition of designing everything in the building including furniture and fittings, so they created an easily identifiable style. Prime examples were Frank Lloyd Wright (Fallingwater, Bear Run, Pennsylvania, 1935), Charles Rennie Mackintosh (Hill House, Helensburgh, Scotland, 1902–03), Antonio Gaudi (the Casa Mila, 1905–10, and Casa Batllo, 1905–07 in Barcelona), Ludwig Mies van der Rohe (The Farnsworth House, Plano, Illinois, 1951), and the Greene Brothers (Gamble House, Pasadena, California, 1908). Home as art is not, however, limited to individual buildings, and some remarkable housing complexes have also had a huge influence, such as Auguste Perret's apartment building on the Rue Franklin in Paris (1903), Le Corbusier's Unite d'Habitation in Marseilles (1947–52), Ralph Erskine's

Byker Redevelopment in Newcastle-upon-Tyne, England (1973–78), and the Palace of Abraxas by Ricardo Bofill in Marne-La-Vallée, France (1978–83). Overall, history has provided us with all the evidence we need to consider home as art in a multiplicity of dimensions, providing for material needs and raising the spirit in countless ways.

ABOVE
Casa Batllo, Barcelona, Spain. Translated as the "House of Bones," Casa Batllo is one of Antonio Gaudi's masterpieces. Gaudi pioneered the Art Nouveau movement and built this apartment building between 1905–07. His style has an organic, skeletal quality which clearly distinguishes his buildings from others in the city.

Chapter 7
Home as
Facade

The word "facade" is a French word meaning "front," but it also has another meaning of "false" or "illusory." When we say that a person is "putting on a facade," we mean that they are pretending to be something that they are not; they are hiding their true feelings or personality. However, "facade" is also used to describe the front of a building, usually facing the street. The idea of something "false" also applies to buildings, since a facade usually does not tell you much about what is going on inside. For all practical purposes a building usually has five surfaces. The facade seen from the street therefore only allows one of these surfaces to be seen. This also raises an interesting conundrum for architects, namely whether or not facades come into the realm of what we call "architecture" since only one surface is usually designed, and it is normally part of a continuous frontage stretching the entire length of a street.

AT FACE VALUE

Without doubt, the concepts "street" and "facade" are inseparably linked. Furthermore, facades are usually composed of many buildings, usually houses, and they all look the same. Facades are usually made up of a single repeated module. There may, however, be subtle variations either in each single unit or indeed over the entire surface where central or terminal features may act to unify the overall design, as in the famous terraces of John Nash in London. Facades also imply the idea of "front" and "back," a practice from which modern architecture has tried to escape, since buildings are supposed to be unified sculptural objects that do not place a premium on any single aspect. In this paradigm, there can be no fronts or backs, only buildings. Overall, this implies that the terrace is an urban form rather than an architectural one.

While it is possible to design a street without having it bounded by facades, it is not possible to design a continuous facade without making a street in the process. Similarly, it is highly unusual to use a continuous facade for homes without designing the basic unit from which the facade is composed. As a broad generalization, we can therefore say that the evolution of the contemporary city has been in many cases dependent on the application of the idea of facade to domestic purposes. In the process, this created streets that were the very foundation of urbanization. This fact can be evidenced in some of the great cities of the world, particularly in Europe. Paris is famous for its boulevards that are bounded by continuous facades around six stories high. In Britain, both Bath and Edinburgh are famous for their Georgian terraces usually around four to six stories high, and London is also well-known for its extensive Edwardian terraces.

Barcelona has magnificent *avenidas* bordered by extensive facades fringed with rows of street trees, and the Gran Via de les Corts Catalanes — truly one of the great streets of the world. New York is renowned for its "brownstone" terraces, which were the very basis for the development of Manhattan, extending north over the entire length of the island, from Battery Park to West 220th Street near the Cloisters Museum. Other examples abound, from Buenos Aires in Argentina to the medieval facades of Florence and Venice, or the magnificent terraces of the Ringstrasse in Vienna. In every case, facadism was the device that generally married middle class respectability to the public space of the street in the central city. Working class people in industrial areas usually occupied significantly poorer quality terraced housing close to their source of work.

Home as facade was used extensively in Europe, the Americas, and Russia, having singularly less application in the East. At least part of this had to do with how social class was defined, what construction materials and skills were available, and how the political economy of a country determined what constituted wealth. In addition, tradition and custom played a huge part. In China, for example, the conspicuous display of wealth was not socially acceptable, and the homes of the wealthy almost never rose above a single story in height. The preferred use of the courtyard form for domestic use meant that the homes of the wealthy were defined by the size of the compound, not how tall or elaborately decorated the building was. In essence, the traditional Chinese *hutong* or alley was in fact another type of facade, usually one that had no qualities at all other than a few gates, which allowed entry from the alley into the domestic space of home.

LEFT
Workers' houses, Fushun, China. Fushun is an industrialized city with almost 63 percent of its 2 million residents working in various industrial companies, mainly coal mining. Housing quality and environment in this city remains a serious concern.

TOP
Cumberland Terrace, Regent's Park, London, England. Completed in 1827, this residential unit was designed in the Neoclassical style by one of Britain's most famous architects, John Nash.

OPPOSITE
Brownstone houses, Brooklyn, New York City, USA. New York's "brownstones" typify the city's urban development. These elegant homes in the form of a continuous facade epitomize the cosmopolitan charm of the districts from 225th Street to lower Manhattan.

FOLLOWING PAGES
Hundertwasser House, Vienna, Austria. This apartment complex was designed by the Austrian artist, Friedensreich Hundertwasser. He tried to humanize the tendency to standardize units and is known for his riotous colors and unorthodox facades.

BIRTH OF THE TERRACE

One fine example of the use of the terrace in urbanization comes from Edinburgh in Scotland, referred to as "the Athens of the North." The clarity of Edinburgh's historical growth is a classic example of urban development due to the precision and visibility of its architecture, and seldom is history displayed so precisely in built form. The ancient city is prominent in a castle built on top of a volcanic plug, glaciation having determined the form of the medieval city that falls away from the ridgeline on both sides. The center of the medieval town runs down the ridge called "the Royal Mile" to the Palace of Holyroodhouse at the bottom, a spectacular and seldom used home for the British Royal Family. At the beginning of the eighteenth century, conditions in the medieval town (itself a series of facades or "closes") had become so bad and offensive to the rich that they decided to build another environment to escape what they termed "the smoky beehives of the unwashed." This has since been referred to as the "New Town," a bastion of middle class gentility, which it has maintained to the present time. The New Town was located roughly a kilometre away from the castle, on the other side of a small lake, and the competition for the master plan was won by James Craig in 1766, when he was only 22 years old. The New Town was laid out on a gridiron plan, using the device of the facade on every street to construct homes for the professional classes. Each part of the gridiron had a central garden held in common by adjacent properties. Although these gardens remain inaccessible to the public, they provided Edinburgh with significant open spaces in the very center of the city. Home as facade was therefore laid down over the last 250 years as the adopted form for the entire city center, through Georgian, and Victorian times, and into the modern period. Along with Bath, Edinburgh is one of the best examples of Georgian architecture and planning in Britain.

ABOVE
Victoria Street, Edinburgh, Scotland. This view of Victoria Street down towards West Bow and the Grassmarket — the oldest part of Edinburgh — showcases a continuous facade. The buildings contain both shops and apartments, and the street has been formed over centuries of development and redevelopment as the city grew.

While it is possible to design a street without having it bounded by facades, it is not possible to design a continuous facade without making a street in the process.

At the time they originated around 1750, similar terraces formed the heart of the bourgeois city throughout Europe. Homes such as these had never been seen before. They were bright, airy, and full of light; built from stone that would seldom age; secure from criminals; and maintained neighborliness and conversation through proximity and common front and back gardens. They had wide streets and sidewalks, street trees and clarity of purpose. Depending on the topography, at least one basement was built below ground, sometimes two. Behind the common facade, however, two basic forms of housing were deployed. The first was the division of the facade into a specified number of vertically organized homes over four to six stories, limited by height given that elevators had not yet been invented. Here, class structure was apparent with the servants occupying the basement and the attic, with family reception and dining rooms on the ground floor and bedrooms on the first and second floors. The other form of housing, sometimes referred to as the "tenement," used an entirely different structure with a common door to the street. Each separate unit of the facade was segregated horizontally into apartments that usually occupied opposite sides of the common stair. This form was much more prevalent in France than in Britain. Few of the immense facades created by Napoleon III and his architect Baron Hausmann hide homes over four or five stories. They feature direct access to the street and are singularly limited to apartment dwelling. Perhaps the collective memory of the French Revolution of 1789 inhibited the obvious demonstration of wealth represented in the vertical division of facade into home. In addition, since most terraces were built by speculative builders, as indeed are most homes today, there were significant variations within houses and apartments across all aspects of planning and construction. Homes seldom had fewer than three to four bedrooms, and the internal spaces had immense variation in layout. Homes built in the eighteenth century demonstrated

magnificent work by all trades, with complex plaster cornices and ceiling roses, huge skirting boards at floor level, beautifully carved doors and window details, and a widespread use of etched glass, handmade tiles, and other decorative elements. Even the stone and wrought iron work were art forms in themselves.

The use of the facade was not solely the purview of the middle classes. About the time that James Craig designed Edinburgh's New Town, one of the greatest events in human history was taking shape in the form of the Industrial Revolution. Not only did this generate the wealth that allowed a burgeoning middle class and its adopted form of housing, it also dramatically increased land values. With the need to house workers close to mines and factories, the row house – the working class equivalent of the bourgeois terrace – came into existence. All the great centers of production from Glasgow and Manchester to Pittsburgh, Lyons and Frankfurt had to accommodate workers in the smallest possible space in close proximity to work. The row house became a ubiquitous form of home, with standard housing units crushed together in narrow streets, with minimal facilities and little amenity. The heartland of the Industrial Revolution, the English Midlands, is still using row housing built at the end of the nineteenth century, many of which, like the mines and equipment used in production, are now conservation items for visiting tourists. These types of home as facade were also featured by the famous pop group the Beatles in a scene from the film *Yellow Submarine*. Here, a small external door on the outside (signifying poverty and hence identification with the community), has been converted into a single huge home by knocking out the internal partitions. Therefore, the facade is indeed an adaptable urban form that has served its purpose well under a diversity of circumstances. Nonetheless, while retaining its capacity for privacy and illusion at an individual level, it advertises, in no uncertain manner, the social purpose for which it was constructed.

ABOVE
Row houses, Back Bay, Boston, Massachusetts, USA. These apartments from Boston are the equivalent of the New York "brownstones" and give the area much of its character. Back Bay has always been an up-market area for wealthy professionals.

TOP LEFT
Homes built in the eighteenth century demonstrated a magnificent attention to detail with complex ceiling roses, plaster cornices, beautifully carved doors and windows, and a widespread use of etched glass, handmade tiles, and other decorative elements.

Chapter 8
Home as
Function

As we have seen, home has a diversity of functions. In different places and at different times, home has protected humans from nature, other people, gods, and evil spirits. It is a place for celebration and decoration, and a sanctuary for religious observance. At another level, home provides a place to work; make love; sleep or rest; to cook; to provide privacy, warmth or coolness; and perhaps somewhere to take care of washing and personal hygiene. In all of these cases, however, there are a plethora of ways in which these functions can be both performed and expressed. If we look at the astonishing variety of homes, we cannot even make general assumptions about how these various functions are incorporated, except perhaps in the developed world of today. Even there, huge cultural differences predominate.

DOMESTIC RITES AND RULES

We have already noted that some nomadic people, such as the Australian Aborigines or the Ituri pygmies of the Democratic Republic of the Congo, do not even possess a physical structure to call home. In these cultures, the overall functions of home exist as part of nature. Food does not come standardized, processed, canned, or frozen. Food is living nature, and is usually alive until just before it is eaten. The rain or river provides for washing, and even the spirits exist in plants and animals. In more settled times, many ancient cultures also provided for certain traditional domestic functions to take place in commonality, such as bathing, with the bath being a collective concept in both ancient Greece and Rome. The Romans, in particular, built baths wherever they had colonies,

which at that time was most of the known western world. Bath in England, named after its Roman baths, can still be seen today. Many Roman baths were also fed by huge aqueducts that transported water as far as 62 miles (100 km). Probably the greatest examples of these were the Baths of Diocletian and the Baths of Caracalla, remnants of which can also be seen today in modern Rome. (The Baths of Diocletian were the largest ever built, being completed in 305 CE, they functioned for 230 years until the Goths cut off the supply of water to the city.) One can also find collective parallels in all other domestic functions, such as eating, sleeping, and making love. All these functions have taken place collectively in one form or another, for example, in primitive rituals, ancient bacchanalian rites, Roman orgies, and various rites of solstice and celebrations during the Medieval period, while others related to witchcraft and Satanism.

Even these normally accepted functions of home have a huge variety of expression. Sleeping, for instance, can be practiced simply by lying down anywhere and going to sleep with no support for either head or body, to the use of immense and complicated structures either on, or raised above the ground, such as Victorian four-poster beds. In between we find beds made from a variety of materials, from straw and horsehair to solid cotton pads, as in the Japanese futon, or woven as in the Mexican hammock, which comes in all sizes up to the "matrimonio" that can hold an entire family. Even head supports have huge variation, from the solid wooden or reed pillows of the Chinese to luxurious pillows made from the wool of animals, breast feathers of geese, or today's synthetic fibers. After sleeping, home probably has the universal function of preparing and eating food. Anthropologists have for centuries studied the significance of both in the symbolic sense as well as the functional, although these usually overlap in complex ways.

LEFT
Roman Public Baths, Bath, England. Bath is one of the greatest Georgian cities in England. It is the site of historic Roman baths from which derives its name. Bathing was one of the most important leisure activities of the ancient Romans and was practiced as a communal activity.

TOP
One of the prime functions of home is the preparation of food, and each culture has its own very different customs. Traditional Japanese homes like this one do not use furniture in the western sense. Family meals are served on a table and enjoyed sitting on tatami-covered floors.

The famous French anthropologist Claude Levi-Strauss wrote two books entitled *The Raw and the Cooked* and *The Origin of Table Manners* which dealt with this subject – how and where food was prepared, for what purposes and locations, and the manners associated with time and place. Levi-Strauss and others have described in great detail the symbolic and ritual functions involved in eating and the entire panoply of associations that food has had over the centuries. More recently, Margaret Visser has written about *The Rituals of Dinner*, where table manners, eating rituals and food taboos are covered in detail. Visser explains that every human society has eating rules and from these rules, manners in deportment, behavior and speech have followed. Conforming to these rules creates harmony, orderliness and class distinctions and, in excess, snobbery. Even the technology of eating has evolved from simply eating with fingers to the use of wooden chopsticks and metal instruments. Where eating has risen to a high art, a dozen different implements, including glasses and plates, may be used for the same meal. Cutlery can also be used differently. For example, the spoon replaces the knife in certain Asian countries such as the Philippines or Indonesia, and is used for cutting as well as drinking. In some cultures, the knife is used to cut the food after it is placed between the teeth, rather than on the plate. Every object, function, and process dealing with food is culturally designated.

While all of the above considerations relate to the *functions* of home, we are also concerned here with home itself as *function*. Most early cultures have built extremely functional homes as far as their structure is concerned, such as the igloo, tepee, yurt, or mud-brick house. One can also argue that even the stark simplicity of Classical Greek architecture was still very functional, despite the fact that temples were painted in bright colors with all kinds of added decoration. The same can be said about the great cathedrals of the Medieval and Gothic periods; that the functions of the buildings were totally expressed in their form. Cathedrals were adorned with all types of art. While the stonework in many cases was elaborately sculpted and carved, the expression of structure dominated. Ross King's book *Brunelleschi's Dome* is a masterly account of the immense functional considerations that went into the erection of the great dome of Santa Maria del Fiore in Florence.

RIGHT
Basilica Santa Maria del Fiore, Florence, Italy. As shown, this cathedral has a distinctive 148 ft-wide (45 m-wide) dome resembling a lily flower – the symbol of Florence. It was designed by the famous architect, Arnolfo de Cambio in 1296, but took decades to complete due to the fact that the dome had to be invented as it was being built.

THE RISE OF ARCHITECTURE

By the twentieth century, however, architecture had become well established both as an art form and as a professional activity, and architectural history has classified particular styles in accordance with the periods which they occupied. Hence, students learn about the Assyrian, Babylonian, Greek, Roman, Medieval, Gothic, and Modern periods. If they are lucky, they will also learn about the immense complexity of Asian art and architecture in the Americas, China, India and other places. These periods are further subdivided into a huge diversity of other typologies. But by the end of the nineteenth century in Europe, a new movement in architecture had evolved which was called the Art Nouveau (or New Art), which in turn progressed into another period called Art Deco. All of this transpired over a period of around 40 years from 1890 to 1930. Both styles relied on using decorative features in building design and all associated elements such as furniture and furnishings. The Art Nouveau used extremely fluid organic forms, and architects Charles Plumet, Baron Victor Horta, Charles Rennie Mackintosh, Hector Guimard, and Antonio Gaudi are prime examples of this style of art. In Vienna at the *Fin De Siècle* (end of the nineteenth century), the Viennese Secession created its own adaptation in the work of architects Otto Wagner and Adolf Loos, and in the paintings of Gustav Klimt and Egon Schiele.

The Art Nouveau morphed into the Art Deco, where decorative arts were still of high priority, although by that time, around 1910, the fluid biotic forms of the Art Nouveau were giving way to the more geometric yet still stylized forms of the Art Deco. In contrast to earlier historical periods, both of these art forms were of relatively short duration, even when they are considered together. In many ways it is easier to think of them as facets of the same style, rather than two separate styles. Both in a very real sense heralded the advent of Functionalism that followed shortly after World War I. In many ways, both styles could be considered diversions to the central function of architecture. Functionalism became the architecture of Modernism and existed in its heyday for half a century (from approximately 1925 to 1975), although its principles have many adherents, even today.

LEFT
The main bedroom in Hill House, Helensburgh, Scotland. Designed by Scotland's most famous architect, Charles Rennie Mackintosh, Hill House contrasts a highly functional exterior with a more decorative yet spartan interior.

FUNCTIONALISM

Functionalism in architecture refers to home as well as other buildings in a particular way. In marked contrast to the decorative periods that preceded it, Functionalism believed that pursuing beauty by adding more and more decoration was both futile as well as false. It maintained that beauty in architecture could only be achieved if exactly the opposite position was adopted – the elimination of all decorative features throughout the entire building. The idea expressed by the famous architect Ludwig Mies van der Rohe that "less is more" became the aesthetic agenda for half of the twentieth century. This position has probably never had a more profound manifestation than his Barcelona Pavilion of 1929, a building which had no purpose at all other than expressing a new architectural philosophy. The domestic scale of the Pavilion resembles an up-market, contemporary home of today, even though it was built more than 75 years ago. The Pavilion's internal walls were independent to its structure and could be moved at will. Being a master of Functionalism, Mies van der Rohe still believed that "God is in the details." Clarity of function, beginning with structure, became the prime purpose of modern architecture. For the Functionalist, the idea that "beauty is truth, truth beauty," correlated truth to the surgical exposure of the inner workings of architecture, stripping away every unnecessary element until the "truth" of the building was revealed.

The constellation of ideas which surrounded Functionalism became crystallized in one of the most famous design institutions that the world has ever seen – the Bauhaus. Opened in Weimar, Germany, in 1919, under the direction of master architect Walter Gropius, the Bauhaus employed world-famous artists such as Paul Klee, Wassilly Kandinsky, and Laszlo Moholy-Nagy. Weimar was considered the ground of genius, with Johann Wolfgang von Goethe, Friedrich Christoph von Schiller and Franz Liszt also once calling it home. The Bauhaus moved to Dessau in 1930 under the tutelage of Mies van der Rohe at approximately the same time as the Barcelona Pavilion was being built. The Bauhaus philosophy undoubtedly had the most profound influence over the art of architecture in the twentieth century. While its basic design philosophy centered on function as beauty, the deeper meaning behind Functionalism was the concept that in harnessing mass production to Functionalist design, objects of beauty which until that time had only been afforded by the wealthy, could now be brought within the reach of ordinary citizens. Unfortunately, Functionalism in design was also pursued as functional social science and eugenics, a philosophy which we refer to as Fascism or National Socialism. The Third Reich closed down the Bauhaus in 1933, and the Diaspora of many Bauhaus staff spread Functionalism to many other countries, particularly the United States of America.

ABOVE
Rue Franklin Apartments, Paris, France. This wonderful block of apartments in the Art Deco style illustrates how even high-rises can provide beautiful homes. The detailing of the building is quite exceptional, having been designed by Auguste Perret, a famous French architect who pioneered the use of concrete in some of his other buildings.

TOP LEFT
Barcelona Pavilion, Barcelona, Spain. This house was designed by the world-famous architect, Ludwig Mies van der Rohe and was built for the 1929 World's Fair in Barcelona. Like many architects, he derived inspiration from traditional Japanese architecture. While this is not a "home" as such, it is an archetype of the homes he designed and a perfect model of his architectural philosophy.

ABOVE
Farnsworth House, Plano, Illinois, USA. This transparent glass house is the perfect embodiment of Mies van der Rohe's great passion for minimalism and Functionalism. Though it was claimed unliveable by its owner, Dr Farnsworth, this house has long been regarded as a symbol and true representation of modern architecture in the twentieth century.

TOP
Interior of the Glass House, New Canaan, Connecticut, USA. Designed by the famous American architect, Philip Johnson, this steel-framed glass house is a classic example of the International Style seen in America in the late 1940s. Johnson was clearly inspired by Mies van der Rohe's design of Farnsworth House.

Home played a central role in the expression of Functionalism, and for many of the Bauhaus architects and those who came after them, the domestic scale of home represented the smallest spatial unit where an entire philosophy or its variants could be rendered manifest. Indeed, many of the Modernists are as famous for their residences as they are for much larger projects. In 1929, Pierre Chareau built an apartment in Paris called La Maison de Verre (The Glass House) which remains today an archetype in the development of Functionalism. In exactly the same year, Mies van der Rohe was completing The Tugendhat home in Brno in the Czech Republic. Along with the Farnsworth House in the United States of America (1951), Mies van der Rohe built two icons in the domestic sphere of home, both masterpieces of contemporary architecture. Mies van der Rohe's concept in both houses took his basic philosophy to its ultimate conclusion, whereby every single element in the building was expressed in its uttermost simplicity, creating one continuous and endless flow of space out of minimal architectural elements. Indeed, the Farnsworth House actually constituted a single space subdivided by partitions. The great American architect, Philip Johnson, followed Mies van der Rohe's example by building a similar home in New Canaan, Connecticut, which was also called The Glass House (1949) because it had no external solid walls and for all practical purposes was very transparent.

Examples of Functionalism are therefore ubiquitous, and have adopted many differing forms of expression throughout the world. Other classics are Le Corbusier's Villa Savoye (1928–29) at Poissy in France (as well as his "domino" housing), and the Rietveld-Schroder House (1924–25) in Utrecht by Gerrit Rietveld. The latter example was part of The Netherlands' own unique contribution to Modernism. This came in the form of a movement called De Stijl (the Style) — one which was also seriously influenced by the artists Piet Mondrian and Theo van Doesburg. More recent examples are Richard Meier's Douglas House (1973) in Harbor Springs, Michigan, and Rem Koolhaas' house, the Villa Dall'Ava (1991) in Saint Cloud, France. Tragically, Functionalism, like many movements in art, made inflated claims for its own accomplishments. Many so-called Functionalist buildings were so dysfunctional in human terms that their owners refused to occupy them, as in Mies van der Rohe's Farnsworth House. People simply did not want to live in environments that were functional to the point of sterility. One might even argue that the Functionalists did not build homes, they built houses — and to what extent can one belong to a glass box? In addition, many such houses were unsustainable in today's terms, where huge expanses of glass turned them into refrigerators in the winter and ovens in the summer. In a book entitled *With Man in Mind*, Constance Perrin neatly sums up the core problem of Functionalism by quoting Mies van der

The idea that home is not a physical space but a space of meaning, association, history, and inheritance, became a central concern in Post-modernism.

Rohe: "If anyone will tell us architects what people need, we'll tell them how to build it." Perrin's reprise was that since no one apparently ever told him what they needed, he continued to build for himself. Functionalism's greatest error therefore was in assuming that the truth of home lay in the perfect use of materials in delineating space, rather than in the perfect satisfaction of needs – the emotional and psychological requirements of individuals; a problem that began to be addressed in the advent of Post-modernism around 1975.

THE HOME OF THE FUTURE

Post-modern architecture evolved out of the defects of Modernism. In concentrating on minimalism and the elimination of any extraneous detail, the Modernists also deprived culture of a vast range of meanings that had previously been expressed in architectural fea-tures. In a very real sense, the Modernists got as far away from the individual's needs for meaning in their environment as was possible. Over the last 40 years, Post-modernism has set about correcting this error by deliberately creating buildings that are rich in historical and cultural referents. The idea that home is not a physical space but a space of meaning, association, history, and inheritance, became of central concern. Post-modernism is also eclectic, in that it does not apply the same formula to every problem, as is the case in Functionalism. The result is a variety in design, rich in symbolic meaning, and expressive of human sentiment and emotion. Many of the most famous Post-modern architects have built "homes," including Frank Gehry, Coop Himmelblau, Bernard Tschumi, and Robert Venturi. The latter architect built a home called the Vanna Venturi House (1962) that is a prime example of the genre and contains a huge array of references to classical architecture in its construction.

While Post-modern architecture is not formulaic, a movement has evolved within it called New Urbanism, or alternatively, Traditional New Design (TND), Neo Traditionalism or Neo Eclecticism. This style heavily relies on certain common traditional features, such as doors, windows, picket fences, verandas, and wood shingles. New Urbanism is burdened by nostalgia for the lifestyles of the 1950s, along with images of Cape Cod villages and Prairie homes. Of prime concern is reinstating the traditional values and images of the past, characterized by small town USA, with walkable environments, front gardens, picket fences, town squares, village centers and the rest. The town of Seaside, Florida is a classic example, but literally hundreds of local authorities have now adopted New Urbanism as the chosen development model. It has also mutated into adaptations for sub-cultures, with cities like Santa Ana in California advertising Latino New Urbanism where houses have balconies and are painted bright yellows, blues and pinks, adapted to the Latino personality and culture. Like it or not, New Urbanism has precipitated a landslide of conservative values in urban design and it remains to be seen where its future lies.

Part 2

Home

Today

Chapter 9
In the
City

Living in compact spaces in close proximity to others requires a home that enhances social interaction – while also providing places for solitude and privacy.

Whether it is a dwelling in the depths of a metropolis, or a house on a sunny suburban block, city homes are characteristically governed by the constraints of urban density.

The city is a great place to live – vibrant with its diverse cultures, its history reflected in the architecture, and its network of road and rail a constant hum. But larger populations can create over-crowding, and more buildings and infrastructure result in less available space and limited access to the natural environment.

It is this dense urban context that informs our modern home design in the city.

PERSONAL RETREAT

The antidote to the complexity of the outside world is the simplicity of the interior environment. Clean lines in an ordered environment with simple, accessible forms are pleasing to the eye and relieve the mind.

Increasing population requires interaction with many people on a daily basis. As a result, people are becoming more inward focused to maintain a sense of personal space and their homes are a reflection of this. A high fence encloses the property, a drive-in garage eliminates chance interaction with neighbors and the front veranda, a place to sit and watch the world go by, has all but vanished.

Homes are now designed to meet the needs of the occupants: spaces to live, work, and play. There really is little need to leave.

COMPACT FOOTPRINT

Buildings have sprung up on much of the available land in the city, and construction space is at a premium. To avoid urban sprawl, homes are now constrained to a compact footprint. Designing a multi-level dwelling is a simple solution to getting the most out of a reduced spatial allotment.

A multi-functional room is also an efficient use of space. The kitchen and dining room is combined with the living room in an "open plan" concept, thus reducing the size of each area, but giving a feeling of increased overall space. Architecturally, there are several tricks to give the illusion of space. For example, the exterior environment becomes an extension of the interior space when full height windows are used.

CONTRIVED NATURE

As increased infrastructure erodes the natural environment, immediate access to nature has become limited. In response, design for the city dwelling has created purposeful touchstones to nature.

The built form of a dwelling can capitalize on the external environment. A strategically placed window frames the view to a garden, tree, or water feature, like a precious piece of artwork. A balcony steps out onto a lofty view overlooking the city below. A small courtyard becomes a private oasis.

THE CITY HOME

Living in the city has some very challenging design constraints. Space is limited in a densely built urban setting, which increases proximity to neighbors and often offers limited access to nature. As a result, a home within the city is characterized by a compact footprint, homes that optimize a sense of privacy and have revitalizing references to nature.

ABOVE
Orange Grove,
Pugh + Scarpa Architects

TOP RIGHT
Legal / Illegal House,
Manuel Herz Architecture
& Urbanism

OPPOSITE
1532 House,
Fougeron Architecture

11th Street House CALIFORNIA, USA
Koning Eizenberg Architecture

Constructed	2001
Home type	Two-story family home
Structure	Standard wood-framing

"The 11th Street house is very straightforward. A few simple overscaled moves are used to transcend expectations of the potential of cost-conscious conventional construction. The house is light-filled and organized around a big outdoor room."

Julie Eizenberg

ECONOMICAL CONTEMPORARY DESIGN

In 1998 the Shines bought a very small teardown single-family house in Santa Monica, California. After about a year they were ready to improve their living situation. Having happily lived in a speculative condominium designed by Koning Eizenberg Architects for another client, the Shines trusted them to build an economical contemporary design.

Money was always a key issue for the owners, who were nervous about over-extending their resources. The architects first looked at a remodel/addition, but as the economy continued to improve, the Shines felt more comfortable building a new home. By then the design was established.

The architects have always seen practical parameters as opportunities to reassess conventional outcomes, rather than as limitations. So, although they briefly flirted with a redesign, the original approach did not seem to them to be at all compromised. In fact, the limitations of accepting conventional layouts (the existing conditions) and construction approaches (cost), had pushed them to look at how to infuse ordinary construction with a contemporary sensibility.

OPEN PLAN, OPEN LIVING

The design was developed not so much as a custom house but more as a speculative contemporary house for design-savvy, middle-class families — something you could buy from a catalog with a few variations. The house has three bedrooms upstairs and a study/ guestroom as well as a home-office downstairs supplementing the usual living, dining, and family rooms.

ABOVE
The house has a quiet but evocative presence from the street with layers of tall grasses concealing a small outdoor patio that is reached by an oversized sliding door. The front door is located on the side.

OPPOSITE
A view from the outdoor room looking back toward the house where glazing sets up a strong indoor–outdoor connection. The stucco wall is detailed to appear to float above and provides a backdrop to the overscaled pop-out window to the main bedroom.

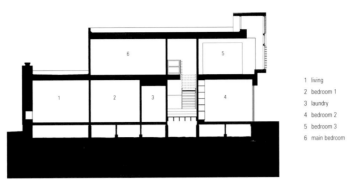

1 living
2 bedroom 1
3 laundry
4 bedroom 2
5 bedroom 3
6 main bedroom

EAST–WEST SECTION

GROUND FLOOR   FIRST FLOOR

The downstairs spaces spiral around the kitchen with a simple open plan that establishes strong connections to the outside. The building(s) are used to enhance the creation of a strong social outside space – an outdoor living room. Even the detached garage – the standard throwaway – is upgraded just a little (and painted a sky blue) as it forms the fourth wall to the outside space flanked by the house to the west and hedges to the north and south.

GIVING THE HOUSE AN IDENTITY

Koning Eizenberg Architecture also consciously included the oversized picture-frame doors that have become somewhat of a signature for their residential projects as a way of providing a "feature" trademark for the design. Houses, they believe, need identity and status-merchandising strategies, just like other design products such as cars or clothes. Otherwise, they tried to keep demanding detailing to a minimum, focusing on the large, dramatic pop-out window to the main bedroom and the glazing in the living areas that make the house feel so open.

The house, including the garage, at approximately 3,500 sq ft (325 sq m) was completed for about US$570,000 in 2001. On the west side of Los Angeles, this was "as cheap as you could get" using the conventional architect/general contractor approach. There was no "sweat-equity" or "nifty delivery" method involved here, just a tweaking of the system with a good contractor and a trusting client.

FAR LEFT
The living/dining areas face the street. Neither client nor architect liked shades, so tall grasses were used to screen the interior. The planting is supplemented by translucent rolldown shades to control the effects of the sun. It is a serene space that includes an oversized wood-framed sliding door, maple flooring, and a painted medium-density fiberboard (MDF) ceiling and feature wall.

TOP LEFT
The kitchen is a concentration of color and texture within the quiet colors and finishes that characterize the rest of the house. Kitchens are always energetic places and the green glass tile and orange painted cabinets heighten this characteristic. Glimpses of the kitchen contribute fragments of color to the adjacent living spaces.

ABOVE
The main bedroom has a small area of space with a high ceiling that draws light from glazing on two sides. The unexpected and exaggerated change of scale and texture (Douglas fir plywood) provides a dramatic effect for minimum expenditure. The bedroom windows have exterior wood slats to provide added pattern, as well as shade from the morning sun.

1532 House SAN FRANCISCO, USA
Fougeron Architecture

Constructed	2005
Home type	Three-level family home
Structure	Glass, steel, stucco, and wood

"This design expresses my commitment to true contextualism: relating the house to the natural forces of the steep site; integrating its spaces with land, light, and view; placing it firmly within its San Francisco slope rather than perched on stilts. The result is a contemporary restatement of the city's bold spirit in the artistic vocabulary of its owners."

Anne Fougeron

ABOVE
The demure facade playfully and respectfully reinterprets a familiar San Francisco building form with traditional materials, translating the bay window of the front-facing artist's studio into a monocle design. The house is integrated fully into the extra-deep lot, using the steep site's various levels of grade to interlock its complex spaces.

LEVEL THREE

LEVEL TWO

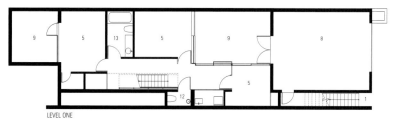

LEVEL ONE

1 entry
2 deck
3 bridge
4 living
5 bedroom
6 main bedroom
7 artist's studio
8 garage
9 courtyard
10 kitchen/dining
11 study
12 WC
13 bathroom
14 open to below

ABOVE AND LEFT
The living area's placement at
the rear of the house, level with
the backyard, creates the fluid
beauty and privacy of indoor/
outdoor California living. Flooding
the center of the house with
light. The middle courtyard (left)
transforms every inner space,
giving all rooms a gleaming
double aspect.

COURTYARDS AND LIGHT

This new house, in-filled on an existing 25-ft (7.5-m)
wide lot in San Francisco, includes two distinct
volumes that are separated by an interior courtyard.
The structure at the front has a garage at street level
with a painting studio above it. The back volume is
the main house, with the bedrooms on the lower
level, the living spaces in the middle, and an intimate
main bedroom suite situated on the top floor, facing
southwest onto the backyard garden.

The design of this project uses two sectional moves:
horizontal and vertical. The horizontal move creates
two courtyards – one in the middle and one at the
back of the house – while the vertical move digs the
lower bedrooms down to the garage and street level.
The combination of these two moves serves to interlock the house to the site as well as the surrounding
urban fabric, thus interweaving the inside and outside
spaces with a play of light and dark. The inspiration for
this weave of complex spatial relationships came
directly from the artist/owner's paintings, which are
abstractions based on fabrics and their many contextual relationships.

CONTROLLING NATURAL LIGHT

Throughout this sectional interplay, the floor-to-ceiling
windows, glass floors, and skylights manipulate the
natural light and allow it to penetrate deep into all
rooms. The house is transparent from the street to
the backyard, offering a rare glimpse into an intimate
world that is usually closed behind the doors and
facades of San Francisco homes.

The main floor of the house – an open floor plan with kitchen, dining, and living spaces – is punctuated by a two-story space for the staircase, and is on ground level with the rear yard. A setback of the building on the third floor opens the house to spectacular views of the bay and the Golden Gate Bridge.

OUTDOOR SPACES GALORE

The house has seven outdoor spaces, all with distinctive qualities and views: the front deck off the studio, the deck on top of the studio, the lower level courtyard, the entry level deck off the court-yard, the back courtyard, the glass and wood walkway, and the backyard. These seven decks and spaces unfurl right around the living areas of the house, thereby unlocking the visual complexity of the structure and its site. Sensitive landscaping by Ron Lutsko integrates the plan.

This house boldly introduces a new building typology to San Francisco. It is a house of courtyards and light that brings new life to the world of the city's residential architecture, and allows for new modes of indoor/outdoor living.

ABOVE
At the top of the house, in a garden-view glass bay, sits the quaint main bedroom suite. Scaled for intimacy, with a lowered ceiling, this floating retreat feels a world away from the city street at the opposite end of the site.

RIGHT
In a reference to the owner's engagement with fabric in her artworks, the glass railings on the custom steel staircase incorporate a pattern of woven strands. The design concept echoes throughout the house: two light courts interwoven with two distinct volumes in an innovative, complex rhythm.

The viewer's eye in this artist's home is kept in constant motion, exposing from a multitude of angles what and who is on display. This visual enticement, and the size and scale of the interior spaces, lend beautifully to the flow of life within and throughout the house.

LEFT
From all vantage points of the open-plan main floor, the sectional interplay of the house offers visual surprises. The glass and wood walkway (above right) yields yet another charm when accessed at rooftop level: breathtaking views of the San Francisco skyline and the Golden Gate Bridge.

Alamo Street Loft TEXAS, USA

Lake | Flato Architects

Constructed	2001
Home type	Urban loft/studio
Structure	Exposed steel framing inserted into existing brick shell building

"We took the burned-out shell of a building and transformed it into an 'industrial hacienda.' The open plan is filled with natural light from the saw-toothed roof, and with views of interior courtyards. The result is a home that screens out the urban environment and expresses the building's industrial past through the creative use of steel and concrete."

Lake | Flato Architects

OUT OF THE ASHES

A 1920s industrial building in inner city San Antonio, which was damaged in a devastating fire, was the palette upon which the architects worked to transform the remaining building into a comfortable living and studio space. The owner and architect had already begun working on creating a loft space to accommodate work and living when the fire gutted the inside of the building. Essentially, only the shell remained.

The "shell" set the scene for an open plan, airy new dwelling. The original wooden roof structure was replaced with a saw-toothed, steel-framed roof that secured the free-standing brick walls. This roof style, with its alternating clear glass and dark plywood, reflects the old factories in the San Antonio area and is a feature of the building. It also allows plenty of light into the interior and, even on the most overcast days, no other lighting is necessary. Ironically, if it hadn't been for the fire, the ceiling would have been much lower than its current 20 ft (6 m).

The fire also warped some steel walls in one of the factory's old rooms. The architect took advantage of this to create the dining area, giving it an artistic edginess. The walls, floor, and ceiling are covered with sheets of steel. The overall result is one of elegant minimalism.

TWO BUILDINGS, ONE UNIT

There are two buildings on the site that were once adjoining warehouses — one is now used for living and one for work. The main building offers wide volumes of space and contains the generous central living area, dining room, kitchen, and bedrooms. Barn-style doors separate the bedroom from the living area. The whole home has an open airy feel, not surprising, given the ceiling height. The other building contains studio space, living space, guest rooms, service areas, and a garage. The layout is reminiscent of a Spanish hacienda.

There is a narrow alley that runs between the two buildings and leads into a large central courtyard with a pool, which provides a tranquil interlude in an industrialized setting. The alley itself was transformed into the entry area.

MATERIALS MEANT TO LAST

The materials were chosen for their sturdy qualities — steel was used for the framing and railings, the brick walls were retained, and steel and translucent glass cladding was used for the facades. Concrete fiberboard (a mixture of cement, concrete, and recycled paper) was set into the exterior walls of the original brick structure. This not only preserves the historic character of the exterior of the building, it also offers privacy for the owner.

The cement floors were rubbed with old crank-case oil and finished with wax, an environmentally friendly alternative to chemical-based concrete stains.

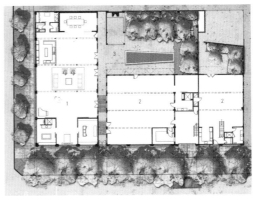

1 living loft
2 studio
3 pool and courtyard

N

ABOVE LEFT
A lap pool is the focal point
of the courtyard. This water
element helps to soften the
hard edges of the industrial
materials – concrete, steel,
and brick.

TOP LEFT
Stained concrete fiberboard
panels and high windows infill
between brick piers, providing
separation and privacy from
the street.

TOP
A structural steel frame was
inserted into the existing
masonry structure. Clerestory
windows allow light to fill
the living space, even on
cloudy days.

ABOVE
Stained concrete floors and
smooth plywood paneling on the
walls and ceiling provide warmth
to the industrial aesthetic.

Bellevue Hill House SYDNEY, AUSTRALIA

buzacottwebber

Constructed	2005
Home type	Single-story family home
Structure	Steel frame, concrete floor slab, timber framing, plasterboard, and corrugated steel roofing

"This house is all about allowing for a relaxed family lifestyle in Sydney's great climate, while taking advantage of its position high on a hillside with great city views. This is a house I would be happy to live in myself."

Stephen Buzacott

ABOVE RIGHT
Perched high above street level, entry to the house is via terraced gardens, paved patios, and grassed areas. Placed between the two wings, the western courtyard affords spectacular views of the city skyline and the Sydney Harbour Bridge. The western elevation is screened both for privacy and solar control with adjustable and retractable aluminum venetian blinds.

OPPOSITE
The burnished concrete paving of the rear eastern courtyard extends into the light and sunny kitchen/family room, giving flow and continuity between outdoor and indoor areas. The kitchen, with its uncluttered profle, is designed to integrate with the overall space. A walk-through pantry and laundry area is accessed via a joinery door beside the refrigerator.

DESIGNS ON OUTDOOR LIFESTYLE

This relatively large 3,000-sq-ft (280-sq-m) site is located in the rugged coastal landscape typical of much of eastern Sydney and its inland waterways. The site is steeply graded, exposed, elevated, and east–west in aspect on the western slope of Bellevue Hill. Reflecting Sydney's benign climate, this house is designed for an outdoor lifestyle, and is focused on the full enjoyment of the surrounding landscape and views.

The simple plan grew out of the brief for a single-level house and a request to retain the original 1920s cottage, by locating a new wing along the southern side of the site to form two outdoor spaces. The cost of retaining the cottage, however, far outweighed the benefit to the overall project. The H-shaped plan evolved from the original design – flipping the proposed bedroom wing to the overshadowed northern edge of the site and arranging the living spaces along the sunnier southern edge became the intelligent solution.

A VIEW TO PRIVACY

The H-shaped plan forms two courtyard spaces, which directly relate to the surrounding internal spaces. The larger eastern courtyard is shielded from cold winter and hot summer westerly winds, allowing a protected and private outdoor living space with a small lap pool extending into the garden. The smaller western courtyard opens to the western city skyline view and flows out to a small stepped terrace that connects to the terraced front garden. The dining room forms the link between the two side pavilions and opens up on both sides, allowing the courtyard spaces and view to flow through the entire house.

The entry is via long stairs which rise past the secluded side patios and the terraced gardens. This leads to a small stepped terrace; here, visitors can rest and take in the western view over the city skyline and Sydney Harbour Bridge. Entry to the house is through the western atrium, which then leads through to the rear

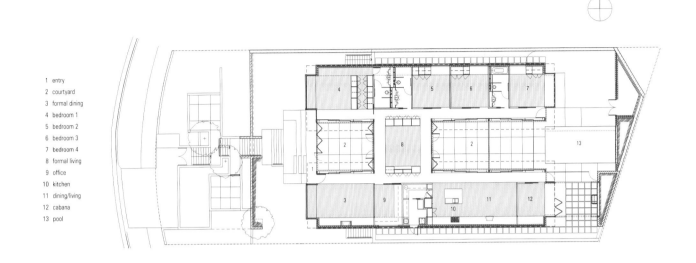

1 entry
2 courtyard
3 formal dining
4 bedroom 1
5 bedroom 2
6 bedroom 3
7 bedroom 4
8 formal living
9 office
10 kitchen
11 dining/living
12 cabana
13 pool

of the house along the edges of the atria. The extension of the exterior floor finish into the interior blurs the delineation between inside and outside.

LIGHT AND SPACE

The open design complements a close family lifestyle. The family entertains constantly and this house allows for a range of both formal and informal gatherings. Sliding and folding glass walls around the courtyards open up the interiors to the outside, making what is a modestly sized house feel larger and more spacious. In contrast, the side walls facing the boundary are masonry, acting as a container for the house and giving privacy to the interior. Highlight windows are located along both the northern and southern sides of

the home, maximizing flow-through ventilation and light, and giving a view of the sky from the interior. The resulting mono-pitched roof form gives the interior a heightened sense of airiness and space while focusing the eye on the atria.

MAXIMIZING LOW KEY MATERIALS

Materials are low key – off-white concrete, steel, timber floors, white-painted plasterboard walls and ceilings, blackbutt-veneered joinery with insets and highlights of Calacatta marble. The windows are 10 ft (3 m) high, clear anodized aluminum and solar glass with rendered masonry walls to the boundary walls and terraced gardens. The roof is finished in corrugated steel.

This house is designed for an outdoor lifestyle, and is focused on the full enjoyment of the surrounding landscape and views.

ABOVE
The dining room is a calming, timber-paneled space that is regularly used for family meals, quiet contemplation, and newspaper-reading. It also connects the two courtyards, linking the main areas and consolidating the spatial flow throughout the entire house.

RIGHT
All bedrooms have built-in wardrobes and desks. This light-filled child's room has a bay window facing the rear garden and swimming pool. The large cavity sliding doors give a direct connection to the central courtyard beyond.

Casa D'Água SÃO PAULO, BRAZIL

Isay Weinfeld

Construction	2002–2003
Home type	Four-level family dwelling
Structure	Poured concrete

"Our clients are people with a great regard for nature and a deep appreciation of outdoor living. With this in mind, we designed a house where they could feel closer to nature, and forget they live in São Paulo, an 18 million-strong metropolis. It seems that after moving into this house they don't go to their getaway spot in the countryside as often as they once did."

Isay Weinfeld

WATER FEATURE

A narrow pool runs alongside the house, from the entry to the back of the block. In the first section of the pool, large granite stones, which are anchored to the bottom slab, seem to skip across the water surface, forming a pathway to the central patio. A little further on, this pool becomes a lap pool that stretches to the back wall of the block.

LONG AND NARROW

The block's long and narrow shape inspired the architects to create a central patio that divides the building into two blocks. This allows for good insulation in all the rooms – they all face either north, east, or west. Outdoors, thick natural-twine ropes make a natural curtain that shades the patio and filters the sunlight, creating dappled patterns of light and shade.

The house is spread over four levels, and all the spaces are arranged according to their primary functions. For example, the garage and utility rooms are on level one, while the dining and living rooms, kitchen, and laundry areas are located on level two. Level three contains a family room and the bedrooms; and finally, level four comprises a small office and a terrace.

As they have three adult children, the owners wanted their bedroom to be private and set apart from the others. So on level three the three bedrooms with ensuites and a private living room are located in one wing, while the main bedroom is located in the other.

MERGING NEW AND OLD

It was the clients' wish that the house would not look, or feel, "new." So the architects proposed that it be built with some elements from the clients' farm. For instance, rough stones cover the boundary walls, and recycled timber was used for flooring in the bedrooms. The rust stains on the wood were retained, providing a link with times long past. These older elements are a reference to the family's lifestyle and history as well as their special relationship with nature.

GARDEN OF DELIGHTS

The landscaping around the house includes orchids, ferns, and bromeliads, many of which grow in the small crevices of the external wall. The back garden contains various types of underbrush, as well as flowering plants such as daisies and lilies, and a jabuticaba tree, a member of the myrtle family, with white flowers and blue-black berries. On the terrace on level four, there are several potted fruit trees, including pomegranate, tangerine, pitanga, and lemon trees.

TOP RIGHT
The office on level four is surrounded by glass, so the owner can enjoy the view while working. The treetops in the foreground give way to the city skyline in the distance.

RIGHT
The entry hallway is actually a narrow pool – in the first half, it is a stone path leading to the central patio; in the second half, it is a lap pool extending to the back of the block.

1 entry
2 ramp
3 dining
4 living
5 lap pool
6 kitchen
7 bedroom
8 main bedroom
9 family
10 office
11 roof terrace

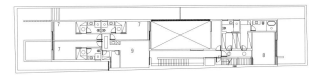

LEVEL TWO

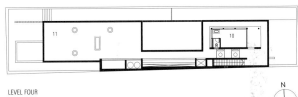

LEVEL THREE

LEVEL FOUR

N

TOP LEFT
This detail of the front facade shows the partition of bamboo canes separating the pedestrian entrance from the garage ramp.

LEFT
The stairway leading to level one is made of stone. A recess built into the ceiling allows daylight to illuminate the space. A bas relief sculpture set into the wall lends a historic note.

The older elements of the home are a reference to the family's lifestyle and history as well as their special relationship with nature.

ABOVE
The open wooden deck is integrated into the dining and living rooms via large sliding glass doors. A curtain of natural twine hangs down from a beam on level four, screening the patio from the sun.

LEFT
The entry path leads from the street to the central patio of wooden decking. Rough stones from the owners' country estate cover the side wall, where native orchids grow in small crevices.

Casa Perellos ZEJTUN, MALTA
Architecture Project

Construction	2001–2005
Home type	Two-story, single-family terraced palazzo
Structure	Traditional masonry, steel frame

"Here was a special and uniquely noble property, despite its size, which had regrettably lost much of its luster and, through generations of neglect, fallen into disrepair. Seeing the palazzo reborn was a joy. Restoring it to its former elegance and infusing it with its righteous status in the village was extremely satisfying."

Architecture Project

A LONG AND NOBLE HISTORY

During the late seventeenth and early eighteenth centuries, the eastern half of the island of Malta flourished. Having fortified the southern harbors against invasions by Mediterranean corsairs, the Knights of Malta ushered in a period of peace and prosperity.

Sitting on a strategic vantage point overlooking the harbors, the town of Zejtun was much sought after by the nobles and Knights of the island. Many built palaces and also contributed financially to the establishment of new churches, including the church of Saint Catherine of Alexandria, the town's patron.

Built during this period, Casa Perellos was the country residence of the Grand Master at the time, a Spaniard, Ramon Perellos y Rocafull (1697–1720). Perellos was a great lover of the arts and a benevolent administrator.

RESTORATION TO GLORY

Casa Perellos is located within the historic core of the village. It is an intimate retreat – not large, yet stately and noble. Together with much of the town, the property suffered damage during World War II, when it was converted to different uses. During the early phases of the refurbishment works, an air-raid shelter, cut from the rock, was uncovered adjacent to the cellar. Political turbulence during the latter half of the twentieth century resulted in the residence suffering severe neglect and abandonment.

LEFT
As with many Mediterranean buildings, the pool helps to cool the air within the shady walled garden of Casa Perellos. During the day, citrus trees provide shelter from the midday sun; on warm summer evenings, their fragrance wafts across the courtyard and throughout the palazzo.

The recent meticulous refurbishment of the property restores to the house its serene dignity and nobility, as well as its princely standing in the architectural and social fabric of the town. The works involved the complete restoration of the fabric and the redecoration of the interiors. With minimum intervention, the original spaces and volumes were recreated. In the interiors, contemporary interventions are grafted onto the simple volumes of the eighteenth-century spaces, the original details being retained and restored wherever possible.

DELICATE, DECORATIVE, DURABLE

To the rear of the building, two lateral wings of glass and steel emphasize the delicacy of the original decoration. These extend from the main volume, reaching out to the garden, parallel to the house's main axis. These extensions house the kitchen (set in the heart of the garden), a guest bedroom, bathrooms

for the two bedroom wings on the first floor, and additional service spaces. Faced in folding hardwood louvered shutters, the filtered daylight casts a gentle glow on the surfaces within, while the rooms become extensions of the garden beyond.

Between the wings, the courtyard and its attached garden becomes the central living room of the "palazzo," a tranquil and sheltered space for relaxation, overlooked by the balcony to the centrally placed family room at first-floor level.

Leading away from the courtyard, the original garden path had led to a small fountain and water bowl, set within a niche surmounted by the Grand Master's coat of arms. The remaining stretch of this path has been replaced by a linear pool of water set among a small number of preserved leafy citrus trees, which shade it from the harsh summer light and excessive heat.

ABOVE
This glass and steel extension houses the kitchen on the ground floor, a guest room above, and a main bedroom suite on top.

ABOVE LEFT
The original courtyard structures, including the arched screen and the well head, have been painstakingly restored to their former splendor.

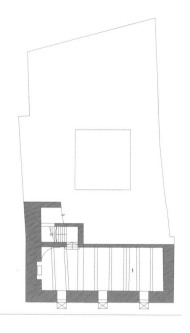

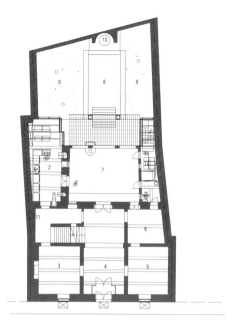

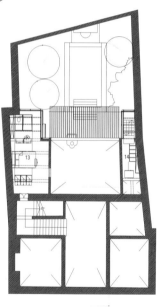

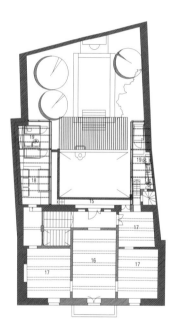

1 family	8 pool	15 terrace
2 kitchen	9 orange grove	16 family
3 dining	10 fountain	17 bedroom
4 hall	11 pantry	18 dressing
5 study	12 storage	19 bathroom
6 playroom	13 guest bedroom	
7 courtyard	14 laundry	

The recent meticulous refurbishment
of the property restores to the house its
serene nobility and dignity.

ABOVE
The elegant main bathroom is
located in one of the wings of
the new extension. It receives
abundant filtered light through
the wooden shutters.

FAR LEFT
Original details have been
retained and restored wherever
possible. The calming ambience
of the entrance hall opens to the
tranquil courtyard and garden.

LEFT
A glimpse through sliding glass
doors reveals the sleek steel
staircase that gives access to
the laundry. The understated
details of the new additions help
form this impressive restoration
project into a complementary
and coherent whole.

Charter House Apartments MELBOURNE, AUSTRALIA

Jackson Clements Burrows Architects

Constructed	2002
Home type	Office block and inner city apartments
Structure	Timber and steel frame, with zinc cladding placed on original brick building

> "This project attempts to demonstrate an appropriate contemporary response to architectural and cultural heritage considerations. The result is a distinct and identifiable contemporary extension, which complements the existing building through its conscious connections in form, reinforcing the verticality of the impressive Federation Warehouse style."
>
> **Jackson Clements Burrows Architects**

A NOBLE HERITAGE

The original Charter House was constructed in Melbourne during the commercial resurgence that followed the depression of the early 1890s. The house was commissioned in 1905 by a large Melbourne printing company, Charles Troedel & Co, to accommodate their burgeoning printing works and offices. Architect Nahum Barnet was engaged to design the premises, which have been described as an example of the Federation Warehouse style.

The printing company occupied the building until 1932 before moving to larger premises in South Melbourne. A well-known Melbourne architectural company, A & K Henderson, then bought the site and a year later made some major alterations, which included re-positioning the entry, building a large ground floor lobby and installing a passenger lift. All offices in the building were completely refurbished.

Today, Charter House is regarded as an important heritage building. It is located in Bank Place opposite the Mitre Tavern, which is the central business district's oldest building. There are a number of other significant heritage sites in the vicinity.

REDEVELOPING HISTORY

One of the major requests in the redevelopment brief was for a rooftop extension that incorporated residential apartments. Given the historical significance of the building, a sensitive approach was required. The architect considered the recommendations made by the planning department of the city council and their heritage advisers. This resulted in an evolutionary design process that allowed for the testing of opportunities for a more contemporary architecture that would not compromise the original building.

VERTICAL EXTENSION AND SEPARATION

The architectural styles in the rooftop extension have been separated, and the extension itself is a "wrapped extrusion." The lower level of the new work is limited to the space within the external walls of the original structure. The upper levels are not confined to this limitation and merge well with the outer limits of the original facade and the accompanying detail.

SWEEPING FORM

The sweep of the new built form has the effect of diminishing the visual volume from street level. It also connects in a formal way with the mansard roof of an adjacent rooftop extension (a favored solution in the city council's planning guidelines). Two balconies extrude through the new form, which further emphasizes the distortion. The zinc facade sweeps across the extension – the architect likens the effect to a piece of curling paper, an image that sits nicely with the history of the building and its early use as a printing works.

A MARRIAGE BETWEEN OLD AND NEW

Deep windows are like punctuation marks in the facade, and the standing seams have been strategically positioned in order to more closely reflect the heritage aspect and detail of the building. This also results in a strong visual connection between the two architectural styles, and ensures that the contrasting ideas sit well together and complement one another. The outcome is that the extension, while contemporary and distinctive, also balances the existing building through the use of connecting forms. The Federation Warehouse style is retained but given a modern flavor.

LEFT
The architecture of the new extension echoes the detailing and fenestration of the existing building. The form sweeps backwards from the corner to engage with the mansard roof beyond, while the changing geometry is subtly accentuated by the protruding balconies.

FAR LEFT
The apartment living spaces have generously proportioned decks, an abundance of natural light, and expansive views of the city.

ABOVE
Balconies provide much-needed private outdoor space for the apartments, which are nestled among the city towers of the central business district.

FOLLOWING PAGES
The modern rooftop extension complements the heritage fabric of Melbourne's Bank Place and provides a strong architectural identity for Charter House with the surrounding context.

Cremorne Street House AUCKLAND, NEW ZEALAND

Stevens Lawson Architects

Constructed	2004
Home type	Two-story family home
Structure	Concrete blocks, GRC, timber, and zinc

"Shapes and textures are contrasted and repeated throughout the house and landscape creating a sense of harmony, complexity, and visual delight. The triangular geometries repeated throughout establish an integrated theme that engenders a personal character to the house."

Gary Lawson and Nicholas Stevens

PUBLIC FACE, PRIVATE MASK

This family house is situated on a quiet street in the inner Auckland suburb of Herne Bay. Honed concrete blocks, dark stained timber, and white pre-cast concrete have been combined in an intensive sculptural composition. The cast concrete facade acts simultaneously as a public sculpture, and as a protective mask for the private spaces behind.

The living spaces are laid out in a linear progression along the length of the site, connecting the front courtyard to the rear courtyard. This continuous space steps down several levels, following the land's natural slope, defining distinct living and dining areas. The three bedrooms are on the upper floor along with the "sky lounge." The sky lounge functions as a private living space with separate stair access, or as an extension to the main bedroom suite.

The southern side houses garaging, service court, laundry, bathroom, and study. One unusual feature is the double staircase, one leading to the sky lounge and the other to the bedrooms. While it may not appear to make sense at first, it resolves a circulation dilemma and provides one of the most engaging moments in the house.

JOURNEY THROUGH THE HOUSE

The visitor enters through a slatted gate, alongside a block wall, passes by the front courtyard, slips under the sculpted facade, through the heavy crafted timber pivot door, into a dark gallery with a red velvet curtain, turns right to pass through a gap in the wall, and descends into an elongated living space, which steps down toward the rear courtyard, and has a sculpted ceiling and irregular spaced vertical slot windows down one side. From there ascend to the sky lounge.

FORMS AND MOTIFS

The sculpted front facade has a dual function – to provide privacy and protection, but also to give some-thing back to the street. The architects see it as a mask, its form reminiscent of Pacific tapa patterns, origami, and Modernist design. It is made of glass reinforced concrete (GRC) and formed in one large mold.

Thematic motifs recur throughout the house. One is of triangulated forms, a Pacific reference, which can be seen in the front facade, the front door, the living room ceilings, the kitchen bar, the Noguchi paper ceiling light, and the garden plan. The other is of irregular spacing and random patterns, which can be seen in the slot windows, driveway paving, the sliding timber

ABOVE
View from the front courtyard looking through to the rear lawn and lap pool. The main entry is positioned within the series of honed block walls, which slice through into the interior creating a strong interplay with the folded ceiling of the living, dining, and kitchen beyond.

RIGHT
Looking along the lap pool reveals the open-ended plan of the house, with living and kitchen contained between the parallel honed block walls. The sky lounge sits atop, within the end of the upper level, capturing great views of the harbor and the setting sun.

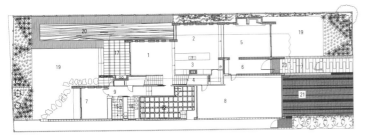

GROUND FLOOR

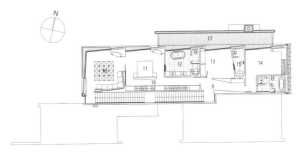

FIRST FLOOR

1	living	6	entry	11	bedroom 1	16	dressing	21	motorcourt
2	dining	7	study/guest	12	ensuite	17	terrace	22	service court
3	kitchen	8	garage	13	bedroom 2	18	laundry	23	entry court
4	store	9	hallway	14	bedroom 3	19	lawn		
5	lounge	10	sky lounge	15	bathroom	20	pool		

doors, the stairway screen, and the bathroom floor tiles. These variations on a theme give the house a particular resonance.

CRAFT AND QUALITY MATERIALS

Materials with texture and richness have been used: elongated honed concrete blocks, dark timber floors and joinery, velour carpets, velvet curtains, leather upholstery. There is a stark contrast between the earthiness of concrete and the plushness of velvet.

Although austere in one way, it is also a tactile and sensuous house, with a restrained sense of luxury.

The architects are practitioners of contemporary architecture, with its Modernist underpinnings, but are also interested in historic architecture, traditional Japanese architecture with its dark timber, sliding screens, asymmetry, level changes, and flowing spaces, and the New Zealand regionalism of John Scott. The aim is to create multiple readings.

ABOVE
The concrete terrazzo-topped island bench with honed block sides, provides another linear element to the kitchen and dining area. The pleated ceiling and the textured timber sliding door to the living space, combined with art and classic furniture, add a further layer of interest to the rich material palette used throughout the house.

Fabric Wall Residence FUKUOKA, JAPAN

Kazuhiko Oishi Architecture Atelier

Constructed	2004
Home type	Single dwelling
Structure	Polycarbonate slabs and polyester fabric walls on cement slabs

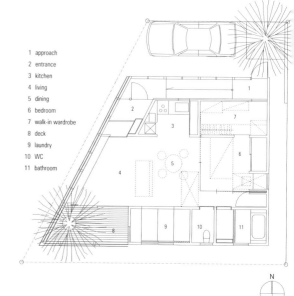

1 approach
2 entrance
3 kitchen
4 living
5 dining
6 bedroom
7 walk-in wardrobe
8 deck
9 laundry
10 WC
11 bathroom

N

ABOVE
The architect's use of polycarbonate cellular slabs provides the client with complete privacy; the fabric sheath adds warmth and mutes the exterior scenery and lights. In consideration of the client's stage in life, ramps for wheelchair access lead to the entry at the far right.

RIGHT
A narrow hallway leads to the entry of the home. The distinctive "fabric" walls acknowledge the client's association with dress design in her youth.

"This is a compact dwelling designed to accommodate the very basic needs of its ageing client for maintenance, security, and functionality."

Kazuhiko Oishi

MODERNIST ENCLAVE

The city of Fukuoka on Japan's southernmost island of Kyushu is developing a deserved reputation as a wellspring of Modernism. Isolated from the mainland, and also from the mainland's history and traditional approach to architecture, in recent years Fukuoka has attracted a wealth of creative artists who are catering to a new demographic of discerning, wealthy, and informed clients.

POLYCARBONATE SKIN

This renaissance is typified in Kazuhiko Oishi's Fabric Wall Residence. Located on a small 1,410-sq-ft- (131-sq-m-) corner site in a busy residential street, this compact dwelling is set on a series of concrete slabs, giving the house a raised appearance.

In response to the client's need for high-level security, coupled with the restrictions of the site, the home's exterior is composed of a double-skin of polycarbonate hollow cellular slabs with a blue and green polyester fiber cloth sheath. The "fabric," and the way it wraps around the home like a sash belt are an acknowledgment of the client's association with dress design in her youth.

The materials allows for thermal flow, and constantly changes appearance, depending upon the weather, lighting conditions, and the observer's perspective.

LIGHT FILTER

The light from the surrounding buildings becomes muted as it passes through the opaque polycarbonate skin. Providing privacy from the street, the thin walls are both a characteristic of traditional Japanese architecture and a response to the region's reasonably mild climate.

The interior of the house is a one-room space, set between a flat wooden ceiling and a timber floor, which is raised above the ground. The house is naturally ventilated – air enters the home through floor vents and exits via two elevated windows.

TRADITIONAL IDEA

The home has an open plan living, dining, sleeping, and tatami quarters but the single space can be divided and areas made private by mobile internal partitions that run in two directions. A private guest sleeping area can be created in this way.

Set within the external polycarbonate wall, an exterior deck is open to the sky and provides the interior's only view of a naturally lit environment.

ABOVE
The arrangement of space in this compact ultra-modern home recalls traditional Japanese design. The effect is accentated by the use of pale timbers and sliding screens.

TOP
The importance of the private terrace is seen in the amount of unfiltered light it admits to the interior and also in the way it frames the tree, giving the home an important reference to nature.

Horizon Apartments SYDNEY, AUSTRALIA
Harry Seidler & Associates

Construction	1996–1999
Home type	Forty-three story apartment building
Structure	Reinforced concrete columns and structural facade, toughened cantilevered glass balustrades, and pre-stressed concrete floors

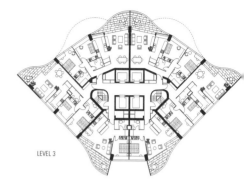

LEVEL 3

ABOVE
A quirk in local planning rules meant the site for the Horizon Apartments was exempt from height restrictions. In order to relate to the streetscape of the surrounding inner-city terrace houses, the height was lowered, and three, four-story terraces were built along street frontages.

> "From a distance, the curved balconies provide a scintillating, animated pattern, terminating with a cap of continuous balconies to the penthouse. The deliberate restricted palette of external materials reinforces the tower's sculptural, monolithic appearance."
>
> Harry Seidler & Associates

PENTHOUSE

Planning authorities in Sydney are not generally favorable to high-rise developments in designated suburban areas, so plans had to be considered carefully before submission and subsequent permission to build was granted. Horizon Apartments was designed so that visual obstructions to views were kept to a minimum. In addition, the slimness of the building meant that it would cast fewer shadows than larger, taller buildings.

This 43-level tower was designed to obtain the widest possible outlook over Sydney Harbour and across to the Opera House and the Sydney Harbour Bridge. To achieve this, the tower was shaped to expose the sweep of the view from north to west.

FANTASTIC FLEXIBILITY

The apartment tower consists of two penthouses, 18 three-bedroom apartments, 157 two-bedroom apartments and 45 one-bedroom apartments. In the townhouses, there is one three-bedroom apartment, eight two-bedroom apartments, and 22 one-bedroom/studio apartments.

Floor space in the apartment tower is divided evenly between living and bedroom areas, giving each apartment a high degree of flexibility of function.

The units on the first six floors have their living area in the center, so that the lower garden apartment building does not obstruct their views. There is a range of outlook choices on the next 24 levels depending on the position of living areas and terraces on successive levels. This gives residents a choice of views – either the city skyline or beautiful Sydney Harbour.

The views are even more expansive in the higher apartments, extending out to the Pacific Ocean. The orientation of the balconies also alters in the larger apartments, which are situated in the top quarter of the tower, permitting even more dramatic views.

SEEING WHAT'S OUTSIDE

The living areas and main bedrooms have full glass walls to capture views. Narrower horizontal windows are installed in the kitchens and other bedrooms. Terrace overhangs or exterior awnings provide effective protection from the heat of the sun, and also remove the need for venetian blinds, which would detract from the views.

All balconies have a distinct shape and are large enough to accommodate outdoor furniture and cooking facilities. Each apartment is also individually air-conditioned. The entire top floor of the tower is crowned with a lavish penthouse.

REST AND RECREATION

The site was excavated to accommodate a five-level, 500-car basement garage, with a centrally placed elevator providing access to the entrance lobby. There are extensive recreational facilities for the apartment-dwellers, with a barbecue area, swimming pool, and tennis court, which are visible from the terraces of the surrounding low-rise apartments. The remainder of the site has been extensively landscaped.

The split-level lower studio/garden units each have either a ground-floor private patio, or an upper-floor, or roof-level terrace.

LEFT
The combined living and dining areas have full glass walls to exploit the dramatic views of the city and harbor.

ABOVE
The higher the apartment, the more expansive the view. The spacious curved balconies can accommodate outdoor furniture and cooking facilities. The terrace overhangs provide protection from the weather and also eliminate the need for venetian blinds.

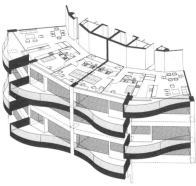

House C MEXICO CITY, MEXICO
TEN Arquitectos

Constructed	2004
Home type	Three-level residence
Structure	Reinforced concrete frames and concrete slabs

SOUTHWEST-NORTHEAST SECTION

"The clients' brief was for a multistory family home on a narrow, exposed site that would incorporate views, while at the same time providing security and privacy. The owners wanted an open-plan design with lots of light and a sense of space throughout the house, as well as privacy and quiet for the bedrooms on the upper level."

TEN Arquitectos

ABOVE
This view of the exterior of House C illustrates the high degree of privacy required by the clients because of the building's exposed corner location. The brutalist nature of the exterior eastern wall is softened by the presence of the skylight alongside a soaring "keep," and also by the overtly Modernist, angular form of the wall itself.

TOP RIGHT
Functionalism can be seen in the second-level family room — an expansive living area where every articulation between spaces has been erased. House C's L-shaped design provides a sense of inter-connectedness as one looks out out the window across the central courtyard to the kitchen and guest bedrooms beyond.

FAR RIGHT
Here the courtyard is showcased as the central focus of House C. A sense of privacy, if not intimacy, is achieved by the high wrap-around facades. The extensive use of glass helps to fuse the interior and exterior spaces.

The design of TEN Arquitectos' House C is representative of the range of cosmopolitan residential architecture that can be found throughout twenty-first century Mexico City today.

PRIVACY AND SECURITY

House C is a single-family residence situated on a difficult, sloping site of approximately 4,305 sq ft (400 sq m) in one of the most expensive and exclusive neighborhoods in the city — Lomas de Chapultepec, the Beverly Hills of Mexico City.

A hallmark of TEN Arquitectos' work is their insistence on an intimate dialogue with the client at every stage of development. The project team of Enrique Norten, Bernardo Gomez-Pimienta and Jorge Luis Perez devised the L-shaped plan, with the living areas oriented in a northerly aspect to maximize privacy from the busy streetscape to the building's south. Highly exposed due to its corner-site locale, the home's massive southern wall also provides a level of security highly sought after in a suburb where private security firms, and walls 10 ft (3 m) high or more, are not uncommon.

The L-shaped plan, coupled with House C's high parting wall enclosure, reinforce the interior/exterior spaces as the central focus of the home.

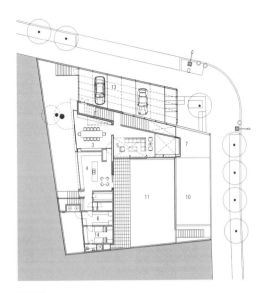

LEVEL TWO

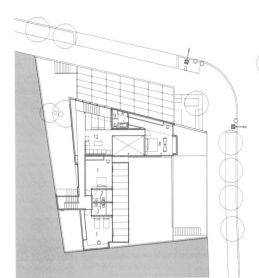

LEVEL THREE

1 bedroom
2 bathroom
3 dining
4 kitchen
5 living
6 laundry
7 reflective pool
8 main bedroom
9 main bathroom
10 terrace
11 garden
12 family
13 garage
14 service area

The L-shaped plan, coupled with House C's high
parting wall enclosure, reinforce the interior/exterior
spaces as the central focus of the house.

OPPOSITE
The horizontal limitations
imposed by the relatively small
size of the building site did not
prevent the architects from
achieving a vivid sense of space.
This openness was achieved by
incorporating large voids into the
design and building "up."
An external wall appears to
disappear into the interior,
enhancing the building's sense
of balance, while at the same
time providing continuity
between the interior and exterior.

ABOVE
The hallway connects the three
bedrooms and the family room
on the second floor. Despite its
narrowness, the hallway has
a sense of openness, provided
by diffused light from an elongated window in the building's
western wall, as well as by
downlights and a high ceiling.

TOP RIGHT
This view of the family room
demonstrates the architects'
minimalist approach and keen
sense of the practical – the
generously proportioned central
built-in serves as a work bench
and storage area.

LINKING THE LEVELS

The main entrance's double height strongly emphasizes
the horizontality of the courtyard reflecting pool, seen
beyond a window to the left of the entry, as well as
the verticality of the two flights of stairs on the right.
These stairs link the primary living spaces below, to
the main bedroom on the upper level, which is isolated
from noisy living areas by a hallway. The hallway is lit
from above by a vertical skylight on the building's
western wall.

Each of the two guest bedrooms, also on the upper
level, has its own bathroom and affords expansive
views over the central courtyard and beyond.

The primary living, dining, and outdoor/interior spaces
are located on the middle floor and linked by stairs on
the eastern side of the house to the bedrooms and
family room above, as well as to the library and stone-
paved courtyard below. The ground floor also contains
the home's six-car garage and a small storage area.

EXTERNAL AND INTERNAL VIEWS

Throughout the home there is an artful interplay
of space and view, enhanced by the continuity of
external and internal materials, which fuses interior
and exterior spaces.

Large, uncluttered living spaces allow a wide variety of
functions. The interplay effect reaches its peak in the
top-floor family room, which has extensive views of
the interior. From this vantage point, the double height
of the ground-floor library and living room weaves
these rooms into the panoramic skyline, lending the
distant city views a certain immediacy.

House for Art Collectors SYDNEY, AUSTRALIA

Marsh Cashman Koolloos Architects

Construction	2000–2001
Home type	Single dwelling, contemporary terrace house
Structure	Three level, concrete slab floor with load-bearing brickwork

"The terrace house type is identified and expressed with close reference to its predecessors, but is also re-evaluated and transformed into a more open, flowing and dynamic form and spatial experience...the spatial experience was most important to us in this project, with elements of surprise and drama, containment and modesty, serenity and enigma."

Mark Cashman

The House for Art Collectors is a residence to house art and books, the two great passions of its occupants. The house had to be spacious, with a central void space and a Modernist style. Both owners required a working space.

The project was part of a new subdivision and, co-incidentally, a redevelopment of a former art gallery in an urban part of Sydney. The subdivision created a row of long, narrow allotments. The client purchased one of the middle lots and although the home is freestanding, it is sandwiched between two other houses of similar scale and size. The surrounding context is predominantly residential with a mixture of house types and styles ranging from historic to contemporary.

EXPRESSIVE AND ENIGMATIC

The simple rectangular building form and structural system of concrete floors, with load-bearing brickwork and lightweight roof, combine harmoniously with generally simple finishes, such as cement-rendered walls and steel-troweled, tinted concrete floors.

The use of "floating rectangular boxes" both internally and externally are designed to break down any sense of division between the inside and outside. The design invites visitors to enter and journey through the sequence of spaces – areas that express elements of the occupants' personalities, while not giving too much away.

The entrance is through a narrow lobby into a double-height void with a 23-ft (7-m) ceiling over the main lounge area. This extends into the open-plan dining and kitchen area and on into the courtyard. Separate studios are located at each end of the house, with the occupants meeting in the middle to cook, dine, and lounge. The studio to the eastern end of the house is contained within the library walls, creating the sense of a structural wall of books.

The central outdoor area provides a private living space with a lap pool and garden. The upper level contains bedrooms for owners and guests and the basement level, to the rear, houses a garage and storage area.

THE CHALLENGES OF LIGHT AND HEAT

With the site's east–west orientation along a narrow site, moderating heat in the west-facing living area while maximizing light was a challenge. The central courtyard allows plenty of daylight and sunlight to penetrate the interior, while motorized blinds on the glazed walls screen the hot afternoon sun when necessary. A central roof light, equipped with motorized opening windows, lets in northern sunlight and southern daylight to the central interior on both levels, while also creating good air movement through stack-effect ventilation.

ABOVE
This view from the first floor bridge down into the central void looks like a series of "boxes," but each has a purpose. The suspended zinc clad box contains the main bedroom walk-in wardrobe. It drops down to become the ceiling over the kitchen area. The large concrete slab at ground level is the kitchen's island bench; the black box along the kitchen wall encloses cupboards; the pink strip is a cupboard light.

ABOVE RIGHT
The shelves housing the library are a space-saving dividing wall, separating the studio at the eastern end of the house from the dining and kitchen areas.

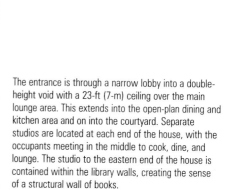

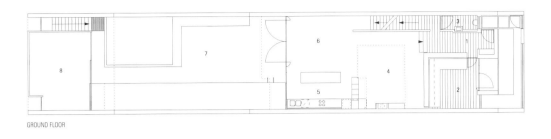

GROUND FLOOR

FIRST FLOOR

N

1 entry
2 study 1
3 wc
4 living
5 kitchen
6 dining
7 courtyard/pool
8 study 2
9 open to below
10 guests
11 bathroom
12 balcony
13 main bedroom
14 walk-in wardrobe
15 ensuite

LEFT
The simple hot-dip galvanized finish on the steel-framed windows creates a "barely there" separation between inside and out. Local views are possible at the upper level and can be enjoyed from a balcony off the main bedroom.

ABOVE
A lap pool and courtyard lie between one of the studies and the main living area. With the site's east–west orientation, the central courtyard maximizes penetration of the northern sun to the center of the living areas. The courtyard tree, which will grow large, provides both visual privacy to a neighboring apartment block and shading in summer. The high courtyard wall extends and encompasses the rear studio and the courtyard.

House Mongolia JOHANNESBURG, SOUTH AFRICA
Hugh Fraser

Constructed	2003
Home type	Free-standing, single-family residence
Structure	Single story with load-bearing brickwork; timber and corrugated iron roofing

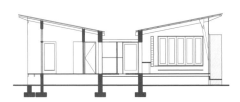

> "Johannesburg is not universally perceived as one of the world's beautiful cities. However, it probably has more trees than any other city on the planet. This house was positioned in a particularly sylvan setting and I sought to exploit the nature of the site."
>
> Hugh Fraser

ABOVE
The north orientation of House Mongolia helps maximize sunlight penetration, which in mid-winter lasts only a short time. In summer, light and heat are intense. Lush vegetation to the side of the main living area shields the house from the hot afternoon sun, offering cool respite when temperatures soar.

SPACE FOR LIFE AND WORK

Architect Hugh Fraser wanted to build a comfortable and practical home that blended in with the leafy surroundings of his urban Johannesburg home site. As a single practicing architect, he also wanted a separate office on the same property. As to the significance of the quirky appellation, the property had been registered under the name "Mongolian Properties." Fraser liked the name – and so it stayed.

The large, gently sloping site was already heavily landscaped with exotic and indigenous trees. Rather than remove them, Fraser decided to position the house among them.

CHOOSING MATERIALS

In some rooms, the floors are suspended timber (eucalypt) on concrete foundations, and in others, they are suspended concrete. This choice was made because the soil on the property is largely clay and prone to instability. Concrete serves to stabilize the foundations. Doors and windows are framed in meranti timber. South African pine was chosen for the roof, which is also covered with corrugated iron sheeting.

GREEN INTEGRATION

The abundance of trees on the site inspired Fraser to integrate them into the overall design. His prime consideration was to take advantage of what the site had to offer – in particular to make the most of the leafy views.

The house consists of two pavilions, with the living areas in the front, facing north, the sleeping areas at the back, and the entrance sitting in the middle. Because the house faces north, the strong summer sun may have posed a problem, therefore positioning the pavilions correctly on the site was an important consideration. However, the number of trees and their proximity to the house offers adequate protection, helping maintain a pleasant temperature year round.

A NATURAL ENTRANCE

The house is located deep within its forest setting, approximately 100 ft (30 m) away from car access and parking. Visitors make the journey to the house down a winding, tree-studded path. Once reached, the entrance area features a native tree growing up through the space, boxed in behind glass panels.

All rooms – living, dining and kitchen area, bedrooms and two bathrooms – are enveloped by the surrounding vegetation, helping to blur the boundaries between inside and out. Doors open out onto the garden, effectively increasing the size of the living areas.

FORM AND FUNCTION

Furniture and fittings form part of the architecture of House Mongolia. The kitchen is designed as a unit on wheels with open shelves. The shutters in the main bedroom open independently of the glass doors, and the shower is placed outside in the garden.

ABOVE
Much of the house opens out onto the garden. The outdoor environment essentially becomes part of the interior, adding to the available living space.

RIGHT
As winter approaches, the deciduous trees discard their protective canopy, exposing the exterior of the house to more intense light. As a result, the house becomes more sculptural, the starkness of the outside color blending well with the surrounding hues.

Jalan Tempinis KUALA LUMPUR, MALAYSIA
Seksan Design

Construction	1995–2000
Home type	Two-story family home
Structure	Overburnt bricks, steel, and exposed concrete

"The objective is a process designed to capture and imbed the passage of time into the fabric of the building, not unlike the natural changes that happen in a temporal landscape."

Seksan

A GARDEN HOUSE

Tucked away in a quaint neighborhood of Kuala Lumpur, this is a house undergoing the natural weathering and disintegration process of any organic structure, subtly incorporating this entropy into the additions and modifications made on the existing 1970s semi-detached building.

Conceptualized primarily as a "garden house" into which the visitor must first untangle themselves through the structured curtain of red-rooted *Cissus* creepers at the entrance, the house splits into a series of almost "accidental" living and garden spaces that begin to define the vocabulary of the dwelling.

LOCAL MATERIALS

The house, with a land area of 4,000 sq ft (370 sq m) was converted to a studio and home office in 1995, when most of the trees in the garden were planted. The brief was to both transform and convert it back into a home of 3,000 sq ft (280 sq m) to accommodate an expanding family with children and dogs. Further remodeling was carried out in 2001 and 2005.

It was important for the house to reflect and adapt to the fluctuating changes and needs of the family. The design had to reflect a personal reinterpretation of the working-class aesthetic, glorifying the use of local and cheap building materials and leaving things unfinished to let time, children, and dogs have their turn to make their mark on the surroundings.

LEFT
The cool, neutral palette, the display of traditional and contemporary artifacts, and the use of everyday materials helps tie the interior of the earthy and laid-back living area into its all-important surroundings.

ABOVE
A hammock takes pride of place in the living area, blurring the boundaries between inside and out. The vertical lines created by the palm trunks heightens the sense of a treetop retreat in the middle of the city.

FIRST FLOOR

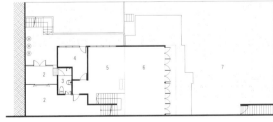

GROUND FLOOR

1 street
2 bedroom
3 bathroom
4 kitchen
5 dining
6 living
7 garden
8 meeting platform
9 study
10 reception
11 studio
12 tree-house
13 glasshouse

CAPTURING THE PASSAGE OF TIME

The layering of materials such as overburnt bricks, steel, and exposed concrete provide the perfect canvas for the garden to permeate the perforations of the architectural envelope. The aging of materials, and the patina of wear and tear is reflected back into the living spaces, diffusing the boundaries of interior and exterior, light and shadow, porous and solid.

WALK THROUGH THE HOUSE

Once through the lush entrance, a flight of stairs delivers the visitor into the wide living area that spills into a palm-shaded garden cooled by an adjacent water feature. The trees provide a canopy, filtering the sky and the external surroundings, creating dappled patches of light and shadow, which skim the surface of the brick-paved courtyard. The living space divides into the open kitchen and dining area and merges into the courtyard, which is accessible from the entrance level.

The sleeping space on the first level slips into a small tree-house extension that overlooks the paved courtyard below. The light-filled bathroom, overlooking the kitchen courtyard, opens out toward the sky.

An impressive collection of paintings, sculptures, and bric-a-brac adorn every corner of the house. Overlooking the spaces below is a roof garden that spills color, texture, and form to the surprised visitor climbing the ladder that accesses it.

Like a favorite chair, which through years of use and abuse has the indelible imprint of the owner, this house comes to root in a symbiotic relationship of family, plants, trees, and the land.

TOP LEFT
Large fold-back doors open onto the paved courtyard with its grove of palms and fountain.

OPPOSITE
A small tree-house extension overlooks the courtyard and provides a pleasant outdoor dining area.

TOP RIGHT
The small, multi-purpose courtyard is both a children's play area and an adult's retreat. Custom-built wire-mesh outdoor furniture is a testament to the resourcefulness encouraged by the architect. By using local and cheap building materials, the house is imbued with a sense of continual change, without forgoing concepts of style, longevity, and comfort.

ABOVE
"Reclining" on a purpose-built platform, this stainless steel sculpture makes a bold statement in the courtyard.

Legal / Illegal House COLOGNE, GERMANY

Manuel Herz Architecture & Urbanism

Constructed	2003
Home type	Mixed-use (two apartments, one office), five-level building
Structure	Concrete and glass

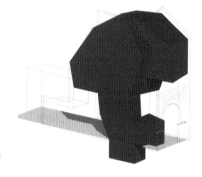

RIGHT
The building's "legal" volume (green) complies with the rules of the local building code, including that it be set back 3 ft (1 m) from the historic facade. The "illegal" volume (red) exceeds the maximum permitted floor area. It spans from street level upwards, through the legal volume, the upper levels curving back down to complete a partial loop around the historic front gate. There is no differentiation between walls, floors, and roof.

LEFT
The free-form, "goggle-eyed" illegal structure seems to jut out defiantly against the rules and regulations imposed by local planning authorities.

"To diagnose the psychosis of a suburb means working on the symptoms. These symptoms become apparent via both the built and non-built environments. They are made visible in the scale of the urban fabric as well as on the scale of a building. They are written into the local code and rules governing the development of that suburb."

Manuel Herz

A SUBURB IN DISCONTENT

Located south of the medieval border of Cologne, Bayenthal was founded in the middle of the nineteenth century and was incorporated into the district of Cologne in the 1880s in the wake of a large municipal reform. The founding of Bayenthal and its primary source of development goes back to its first discontent – "industrial discontent."

In other parts of the world, in the first half of the nineteenth century, industrial wheels were turning, but in Prussia things were slow. Germany had little of the new technology. Gustav Mevissen, a developer and financial speculator from Cologne, changed this when he founded Kölner Maschinenbau AG (the Cologne Machine Construction Company Ltd) in 1856, which soon grew to be a major player in Germany's steel market, gaining contracts to build bridges, cathedral roofs, and other buildings of cultural significance. The factory shaped Bayenthal's urban fabric enormously.

CITIZENS IN DISCONTENT

The gap between rich and poor was starkly evident in the housing of the time, with workers living in very congested and overcrowded conditions. Only meters away from these homes was a wasteland, originally intended to be used as an extension of the factory. The extension did not eventuate and the site remained an artificial wasteland. Adequate housing was lacking in the neighborhood and higher rent could be demanded of the tenants, most of whom were factory workers. The owners of the company discovered, as a secondary means of income, that the market value of the sites they owned increased once development plans had been set up for those sites. It was never intended that the "planned" developments be carried out, rather, the intention was to raise the market value. This combination of factors contributed to the general quality of the neighborhood, which is one of missing identity, or missing character.

POOR PLANNING

A large development was constructed in the 1960s with over 1,000 apartments on the site. In the 1970s an urban master plan was proposed for Bayenthal, to stem the flow of families moving to rural areas – the population had decreased by 25 percent at this time. The plan removed the tram line in the main street, the street width was doubled, and the density of construction was to be halved by building mainly fully detached buildings. Suburbia was to move in.

This development plan, which remains the binding by-law since that time, has never been applied, for two reasons. First, most houses on the main road were classed as historical landmarks so they could not be demolished, and as a consequence the road could not be widened. Second, the maximum density construction was so low that making a profit was impossible, so investors decided to stay away.

ABOVE
The windows and skylights of the illegal section of the building look toward the sky and onto the neighboring terraces. Every faceted surface throws a shadow across one of the adjoining sites, something forbidden by German planning law.

FOLLOWING PAGES
Illegal/Legal jauntily celebrates its individuality among the nineteeth-century facades of the landmark buildings, while still paying homage to their prestige and position in the streetscape. As foreign as the structure might seem in the area, it acts upon the history, the state of the urban fabric, and attempts to enrich the immediate context.

Not a single exterior wall is standing
upright and the differentiation between
wall, roof, and floor is dissolved.

COOL AND CALCULATING

The prerequisite of the project is based purely on a cost-benefit calculation. A developer decided that the only way to utilize what was considered a commercially unviable site in the main street was to invest in "architecture." That way, marketability would be increased and thus, also, profit on the investment.

LEGAL VOLUME

The 18-ft (5.5-m) wide and 82-ft (25-m) deep site, in combination with all rules, fire regulations, building laws, the municipal development plan, and the rules of "construction near landmark buildings" resulted in a clearly defined and non-ambiguous volume. Form follows the law. A transparent and orthogonal volume was devised, which steps back from the building's historic facade by 3 ft (1 m), and thereby complies with the municipal building line set out in the development plan. According to the plan, a construction is not allowed to cover the whole site, so a stepping down of the volume is created by making terraces on each level in the back part of the site. This volume of the building is formulated according to all laws and binds itself to the rules. This is the "legal" volume.

ILLEGAL VOLUME

The second volume is formed through different measures. It is the defiant volume. How many rules can be disregarded in a place dominated and strangled by rules? As a whole, this volume is not allowed to exist at all, because its complete floor area exceeds the maximum permitted. Hence, the volume in itself is illegal. Being a non-orthogonal, free-formed body, it is mainly opaque and traces a path from street level through the gate, moving up the floors, piercing through them, and facing with its main mass at the upper levels back down upon the street, thereby completing a loop around the historic gate.

Fire regulations are disregarded and the main mass encroaches the street again, crossing the municipal building line. Not a single exterior wall is standing upright and the differentiation between wall, roof, and floor – the main categories of building elements in architecture – is dissolved. It is covered with a bright-red polyurethane coating which allows for a "construction without details" and forms a continuous skin over all surfaces of the building. This is the "illegal" volume, being disrespectful as it is of the German building code and the laws and regulations of that site in particular.

VIEWING THE CONTEXT AS THE CAPITAL

The building is a reaction to the urbanization of this part of Cologne. It introduces a foreign body into the urban fabric, and moves right up to the limits of the site, or rather, exceeds them, in its ratio of mass, its measurement, its complexity, and its materials. It ruthlessly overloads the site. It may be an architectural intervention that is not in the best interest of the suburb, but on the other hand, maybe it has a self-sufficiency. It expresses the economic situation, the constellation of laws and rules to form, and the socio-cultural condition of the suburb in a built form.

LEFT AND ABOVE
The stairwell follows the angular, non-orthogonal structure of the exterior. It also functions as a light well, allowing shafts of sunlight from the numerous skylights above to penetrate the lower levels of the building.

TOP
The cantilevered staircase appears to float within the stairwell without dominating the space. The gaps between the stair treads enable light to flow throughout the space and also permit views through to the glass doors beyond.

The Lowe Apartment LONDON, ENGLAND
Brookes Stacey Randall Architects

Completed	1995
Home type	Apartment
Structure	Steel frame, concrete floor, steel and timber mezzanine level, steel and glass stair

"The project has been described as 'redefining high-tech,' which I think is because it is a very warm environment; it is comfortable to spend time in. The technology helps achieve this, keeping it calm, rather than dominating. The client trained as an architect so was able to quickly grasp our ideas and give clear feedback, which helped enormously."

Nik Randall (now of Space Craft Architects)

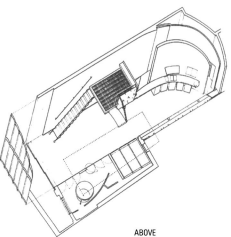

ABOVE
The existing curved ceiling of the apartment has been combined with two curved walls to accentuate the center of the main space. Three large pull-out "pods" transform the main space into a functional and flexible area – either a dressing room, recording room, or dining/kitchen space. The rooflight opens hydraulically, so that on warm nights the owner can lie in bed and gaze at the stars.

FLEXIBILITY OF USE

Chris Lowe of the UK band Pet Shop Boys requested a flexible living space to fit within the top floor of a converted warehouse. The challenge was to maximize the sense of space, while generating flexible accommodation choices. The main volume is designed as a single room, the function of which can change depending on the facilities brought into use.

The storage area is equipped with three large pull-out "pods," each providing a different facility for the main space. By pulling out a particular pod, the space changes from kitchen/dining room to dressing room to music and recording room. The pods were designed to be flexible – all storage boxes, shelves, clothes rails, and work surfaces are fully interchangeable. Their configuration can change as the owner's needs change. When concealed, there is no evidence of the pods' tracks or wheels. The development of the pods demonstrated a successful collaboration between architect, engineer, and contractor — an optimal mix of expertise for the realization of an innovative design.

SPACE, LIGHT, AND PRIVACY

Although diversity of use was a major consideration, the architect also aimed to maintain and enhance the sense of space. The stair, with its glass treads and risers, provides minimal visual interruption to the overall volume. This is achieved by using the glass structurally, forming a folded plate in one direction and a truss in the other. No other structure is then required to hold the treads in space.

The roof area is brought into everyday use by doubling as a terrace, accessed via a folded plate-glass stair and a hydraulically opening rooflight. In summer the owner can lie in bed beneath the stars with the rooflight open and enjoy views of London's skyline.

The glass in the kitchen and dining areas is held from behind by a stainless steel support. The frame of each pane pivots to maintain privacy and allows control over the view. Although the apartment is relatively small, the repeated connections to the external environment increase the generous sense of the space.

THE LIGHT SIDE OF LIVING

The lighting concept enhances the architecture rather than simply lighting the space. Window screens are lit from behind to allow a gentle transition from day to night. Downlights can be dimmed to provide soft light to the kitchen/dining area, and the birch-faced screens contain fluorescent tubes for an even light.

The main wall runs the entire length of the apartment, disappearing around the curve to the entrance. It is lit by flush rectangular ceiling downlights.

LEFT
Recessed ceiling downlights in the bathroom are directed onto the rear of the folding screens. The sleek fittings include a heated towel rack, stainless steel bath, and a shower head with a pressure switch linked to an integrated fiber-optic light.

ABOVE LEFT
The circulation of the apartment has been designed to maximize a sense of scale, concealing views and revealing them as the user moves through the space. Privacy in the main living area is provided by pivoting glass screens covered with a birch veneer; these also generate a warm, gentle radiance.

ABOVE
The glass treads and risers of the stairs provides minimal visual interruption, allowing light to flow throughout the entire volume. Daylight is modified through a combination of translucent screens, opaque blinds, and louvers, allowing total control over the degree of privacy and light.

McAssey House SYDNEY, AUSTRALIA
Ian Moore Architects

Constructed	2005
Home type	Four-level, four-bedroom family home
Structure	Steel frame, concrete floor slabs, and reinforced concrete block retaining walls

"The difficulties imposed by the steeply sloping site, height limits, and four large gum trees have driven the design to produce the stepped, two-pavilion form that breaks down the scale of this large house. The small, stone-cladding tiles, with their texture and minor color variations, further reduce the scale, and complement and contrast with the trunks of the large trees retained on the site."

Ian Moore

ABOVE
The home is split into two pavilions of differing heights, each orientated differently from the other, following the irregular boundaries of the site. The placement of the pavilions has allowed the four large gum trees that graced the original site to remain. The color and texture of the trees are reflected in the exterior surfaces of basalt stone cladding and bronze aluminum.

LEFT
From the street, the house reads as a modest two story structure, although it is actually four stories high. A steel and timber entry bridge slips between the two pavilions and through a frameless glass sliding entry door.

TOP RIGHT
The main living area, visible here, is linked by the exterior timber deck to the family living area. These two areas are the only spaces on the same level across the two pavilions.

APPEARANCES CAN BE DECEIVING

An irregular-shaped block of land on a slope above Sydney's Balmoral Beach is the site of this four-bedroom home. Topography and local council height restrictions were used to create the stepped, two-pavilion form. From the street, the house appears to be two stories, rather than its actual four stories.

An entry bridge slips into the wedge of space between the two pavilions, and tumbles down a long staircase to the deck and plunge pool below. Basalt cladding and hardwood decking flow through the frameless, sliding-glass door into this space, emphasizing its treatment as an exterior, rather than an interior space.

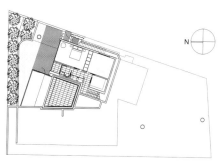

LOWEST LEVEL

A SENSUAL SKIN FOR THE HOME

Local council requirements that the house have a predominantly stone facade led to the choice of stone cladding. That the stonework is non-structural, is evident in the street facade of the two cantilevered pavilions – in the lack of grouting between the tiles and in the thickness of the tiles, visible at the corners and in the reveals. Also, thin sections of steel beam and column have been clad in bronze aluminum. Structural logic was not the driver here – rather, perfecting the shifting scales, textures, and colors of the skin.

PERFECT PAVILIONS

The main bedroom and ensuite are on the upper level of the western pavilion, and there is a roof terrace above the entry space. Immediately below are the music room/study, which overlook the double height dining area and from which there are stunning views of Sydney Harbour. Kitchen, dining, and living areas are located on the lower level, with the guest bathroom and utility room both within the kitchen "pod."

The children's bedrooms and bathrooms are on the upper level of the eastern pavilion, and a second living area and garage are on the level beneath. The lowest level of the home contains a wine cellar, gym, and self-contained guest accommodation.

The two living areas are the only spaces on the same level across the two pavilions. They are linked by a northeast facing timber deck. The plunge pool is set between these two areas.

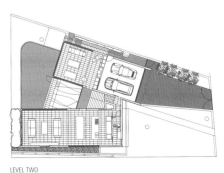

LEVEL TWO

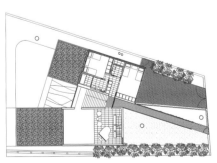

LEVEL THREE

TOP LEVEL

TOP LEFT
After entering from street level, the wedge-shaped main staircase, between the two pavilions, descends dramatically to a landing that looks over the plunge pool. The stone-clad walls of the stairwell continue the theme set by the exterior, also maintaining the separation between pavilions.

TOP RIGHT
The transition from exterior to interior occurs at the stone-clad portals at the base of the main staircase – visible here, the opening into the main living area. The glass louvers effectively moderate natural ventilation.

ABOVE
Stainless steel and American oak create the kitchen's pleasing clean lines. Behind the American oak-clad storage pod lies a bathroom and utility room.

MARVELLOUS MATERIALS

The house frame is lightweight steel, which serves two purposes: first, to allow the creation of large, clear spans to help sliding doors integrate inside and outside spaces; second, to keep excavation and construction of retaining walls on the slope to a minimum. The steel beams and columns that are not part of the continuous wall plane are clad in bronze-anodized aluminum, which matches the door, window frames, and louvers. Basalt slabs are used on the floors of all living areas and bathrooms. As well, basalt wall tiles are used in the bathroom.

American oak is used for air-conditioning grilles, and joinery units – in the kitchen the oak is complemented by stainless steel benchtops. The concrete roofs are covered in large, dark gray rock ballast, providing continuity with the texture and color of the basalt cladding.

ENERGY EFFICIENCY

To reduce energy consumption, numerous passive environmental principles were integrated into the design. All living areas and bedrooms enjoy a north-easterly aspect, with cross-ventilation provided through glass sliding doors and louvers. Floor to ceiling glass lets in plenty of natural light; outside aluminum louvers provide shade.

The stone-tiled concrete floor and the 12-in- (300-mm-) thick insulated external walls and roof have a high thermal mass, thus protecting the home from extremes of temperature. A water tank beneath the rear deck collects rainwater from the roof, which is then used in the garden.

An entry bridge slips into the wedge of space between the two pavilions, and tumbles down a long staircase to the deck and plunge pool below.

LEFT
The plunge pool, viewed from the roof terrace above the main staircase. The pool is lined with the same basalt stone as the exterior walls. This image clearly shows the divergent angles of the two pavilions.

ABOVE
The main living room is glazed on three sides with views to Sydney Harbour and Balmoral Beach, and to the plunge pool, visible at right. The fourth wall contains built-in storage and a fireplace. The simple material palette of American oak, basalt stone, and bronze aluminum throughout the home ties the various areas together.

Metro Hollywood Transit Village CALIFORNIA, USA

Kanner Architects

Completed	2003
Home type	Multi-level apartment block
Structure	Heavy steel moment frames for support over the subway station; and plaster, glass, and paint

"The project is more about social impact than its design aesthetic. The design was approached with the idea that high-density, transit-oriented development can be achieved within reasonable budgets and with architecturally interesting design and materials. The increasing need for multi-family housing in a city with so little open space means developers and architects have to be more creative and thoughtful to avoid creating uninteresting, unlivable, and unsafe structures that simply serve to warehouse people."

Kanner Architects

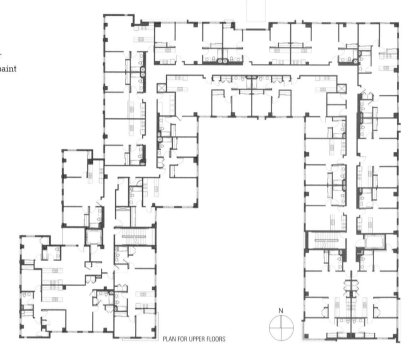

PLAN FOR UPPER FLOORS

N

STYLISH YET COMPLETELY AFFORDABLE

The corner of Hollywood Boulevard and Western Avenue in Hollywood is the site for this mixed-used development. Consisting of 60 mostly two- or three-bedroom home units, it sits above 10,000 sq ft (930 sq m) of retail space and a child care center. The development, designed for low-income families, is built above a subway station, so the challenge was to design a structurally sound building that came in on budget. Its central location means that the residents are easily able to commute into and around the city by subway and other public transport.

The interiors of the units are simple and spacious. The fixtures and appliances maintain the project's theme of being interesting without breaking the budget.

ABOVE
At a busy intersection in the heart of a revitalized Hollywood, Metro Hollywood Transit Village was designed with rooftop photovoltaic panels to reduce energy bills for residents.

OPPOSITE
Considering that the project sits on top of a subway station, the main design challenge was creating an inexpensive, yet structurally sound and interesting building, on a typically tight budget for "affordable" housing.

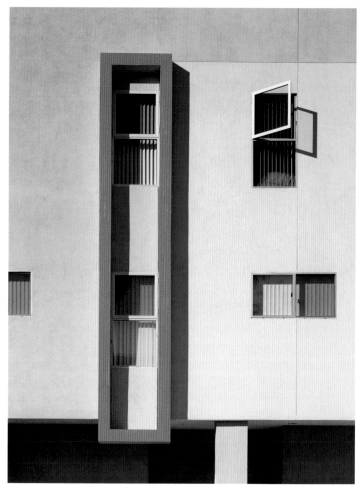

ENERGIZING BENEFITS

The architects designed Metro Hollywood as a model that exhibited social and environmental benefits for its residents, as well as being aesthetically pleasing. One area that was of particular concern for the architect was energy efficiency. Photovoltaic panels – the wing-like pieces on the roof – were placed there to lower energy usage. As a result this building performs at least 20 percent more efficiently than state codes require.

To maintain a sense of unity with the neighborhood, Metro Hollywood's large courtyard has been lined up with the existing courtyard of a nearby housing project. The effect of this is to create a large open space between the two developments. The colorful design with its modern features complements the design of the subway station that sits beneath the development.

SCHEDULING AND BUDGETARY CHALLENGES

A number of challenges confronted the architect on this project. The construction schedule was extremely tight, and had to be fast-tracked through approvals, in part because of deadlines to secure state funding for "affordable" housing.

The heavy steel frames needed to support the building above the subway station were expensive, which meant the architect had to devise cost-effective design elements elsewhere in the structure. One creative response was to reduce the number and size of the windows in the development, and to position them cleverly in both a vertical and horizontal configuration. This had the effect of limiting the noise from the street as well as the underground trains. The windows were also soundproofed.

Another strategy to stay within the constraints of the budget was to use painted plaster instead of more costly materials to replicate the colorful design of the Metro station.

Metro Hollywood Transit Village, built at the front-end of a focused revitalization of the east Hollywood community, puts people in affordable residences that they can be proud to call home and that are near to jobs and/or transportation to jobs and amenities.

TOP LEFT
In this typical top-floor corner unit, butt-glazed corner windows and simple bright interior colors effectively receive and spread light. Rooms feel spacious and bright as a result, and provide wide-angle views of the city.

FAR LEFT
Painted plaster panels on the building's exterior refer to the color scheme of the tiles in the existing subway station construction. Kanner Architects expanded on the original colors, which were basic primary hues, to develop a more dynamic and rich color scheme for the facade and finishes.

ABOVE
Strategic window orientations and protruding window details break up an otherwise simple and smooth north elevation. Touches of color and unexpected placement of routine items such as windows help bring the building to life without the need to spend money on extravagant materials or structural tricks.

RIGHT
The western elevation illustrates the raised deck upon which the project was designed. Stairs lead up to the main approach on Western Avenue and a ramp descends into the subterranean parking. The top floor isn't a floor at all, but a screen to hide the building's mechanical equipment. Strategically arranged venting grills perform a function similar to that of the windows on lower levels.

WESTERN ELEVATION

Mica House LONDON, ENGLAND
Stanton Williams Architects

Constructed	1997
Home type	Penthouse apartment
Structure	Steel frame top floor placed on existing warehouse building

"We tracked the path of the sun throughout the day and from season to season to make maximum use of light flowing into the apartment. The effect is a living space constantly changed by nature...the plan was to view the inside and outside as one space. We did this by careful use of glass, stainless steel, overlapping levels, screens, and sliding panels inside, with cedar decking outside."

Stanton Williams

ABOVE
The living and dining area, the studio, and the main bedroom all open onto the cedar-decked terrace. The minimal glazing structure and the continuity of timber allow the interior and exterior spaces to dissolve seamlessly into one another.

ABOVE RIGHT
The careful balance of structural form with the optimum amount of glass has enabled spectacular natural illumination and reflection within the penthouse. The spatial arrangement affords a large degree of multi-use — spaces feel united by using only a limited palette of materials.

FLEXIBILITY AND FREEDOM

This flexible, light-filled apartment on the top of a refurbished factory in north London's Islington district offers multi-purpose interiors that adapt to the living and working needs of the owner.

Rather than adhering to formally defined home and office environments, the space accommodates whatever is required at the time. To avoid the "working from home" elements, the client wanted a pared-back gallery ambience — a space that is open, light, white, and furnished sparingly. The L-shaped penthouse apartment opens along its entire length onto a spacious terrace with a full-height sliding glazed wall that makes it a natural extension of the interior.

FINDING THE PERFECT PLACE

The client discovered an existing warehouse boasting 360° views. This warehouse block had been granted a change of use from light industrial to residential. Architect Paul Williams then developed an open-plan design that would afford not only comfort for the owner, but also a stimulating and appropriate backdrop for meetings and creative work.

LOOKING AT LIGHT

Driven by the orchestration of light entering the building from morning to night, the concept focused upon the color shifts of daylight throughout the day. Hence, no color is used inside; abundant light and its changing hues constantly redefines the space.

The open-plan living and dining area doubles both as a flexible living space and an appropriate professional environment for meetings.

A private elevator delivers visitors directly to the lobby of the apartment. Here the eye is drawn to the full height glass doors with views over London. The living space opens to a large, roof terrace decked in cedar.

MOVEMENT THROUGH SPACE

Three sycamore timber planes define the sleeping spaces — one pivots and folds flush into the wall, another is a door cut within a panel, and the third slides straight out of a wall.

Sycamore flooring is used throughout the apartment, and within the main living space the floor is folded up to conceal the kitchen units.

DEFINING INTERIOR SPACES

By maintaining a limited palette of materials, the plaster walls define the internal volume and reflect light around the space. Design was meticulous, with flat radiators flushed into walls, underfloor heating below the engineered sycamore boards, and sun-shading blinds concealed within the ceiling.

Other than the custom-built furniture, all elements were designed by Stanton Williams as integral sculptural entities in the project. The fixed kitchen and sliding doors allow other internal elements to become individual items in their own right.

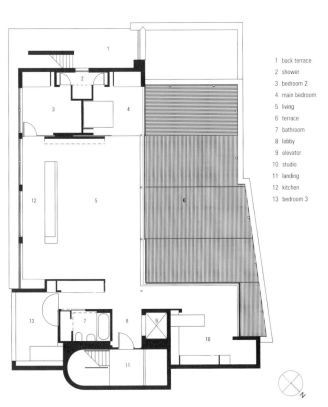

1 back terrace
2 shower
3 bedroom 2
4 main bedroom
5 living
6 terrace
7 bathroom
8 lobby
9 elevator
10 studio
11 landing
12 kitchen
13 bedroom 3

ABOVE
The simple, open-plan living and dining area doubles as both a meeting room for work and as after-hours space for the family. The kitchen is hidden by a timber screen, and a row of small windows provides a backdrop to the full-height glazing of the terrace-facing wall. The end wall is animated by natural light from the carefully carved roof light. A sycamore screen slides out of the wall creating privacy for the main bedroom.

Mitchinson Residence SYDNEY, AUSTRALIA

Stephen Varady Architecture

Construction	2003–2004
Home type	Two-story house, behind single-story historic terrace facade
Structure	Extensive alterations and additions

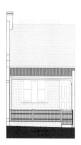

"For this project, the owner made a brave decision. She had already commissioned someone else for a design, with plans ready for council approval. She saw one of our projects and decided to start the design process again. The completed house is the outcome of a successful client/architect relationship"

Stephen Varady

ABOVE
The client desired parking but no garage and a garden, so the garage door motor is part of a mechanical sculpture that hangs over this open courtyard. To complete this ensemble, a concrete planter box hovers above. This screens views from the residential and office towers in the distance.

RIGHT
Stairway to Heaven. The stair has been used as a dramatic transition zone between the more open living areas downstairs and the private bedrooms upstairs, by focusing the view on the northern sky at the top. The transition has been further heightened through the use of red on the walls, ceiling, and floor.

WHITE AND LIGHT

This new design subverts the conventional terrace-house configuration by creating a spiral circulation path though the new house. With north to the front of the house, a courtyard was inserted into the center of the plan to draw natural light into the previously dark spaces at the rear. The staircase faces north so that it doubles as a lightshaft, bringing the low winter sunshine into the rear kitchen and dining spaces.

The client wanted a white house, as a backdrop for artworks and special personal items, but the staircase was to be a strong feature using a bright color. Red was chosen, creating a beautiful red tube, charging the senses each time one travels up or down the staircase. At different times of the day and during the different seasons, the quality of light passing through the stairwell shifts from subtle to dramatic, bathing the lower spaces in strong sunshine or soft light. The living, dining, and kitchen areas are all in one, reducing their overall size while maintaining a feeling of space, a feeling that is further heightened by "borrowing" space from the adjacent central courtyard and rear garden.

SLEEPING IN STYLE

The landing at the top of the staircase leads to the bedrooms. It has a glass floor – another method of drawing more light into the living spaces below. The bedrooms are large and private, and each has its own bathroom. To achieve a greater feeling of space, the main bedroom and ensuite "borrow" space and light

GROUND FLOOR

FIRST FLOOR

N

from each other through the use of a clear glass wall, allowing two modest-sized spaces to feel much bigger than they really are. The highlight windows around all four sides of the ensuite create a light-filled space that is totally private in a very constrained inner-city setting.

INTERSECTING ELEMENTS

The overall design is a sculptural composition of intersecting forms, and this is followed through with a composition of sculptural ceiling elements in the living/dining/kitchen space.

Finally, this project is the latest in an ongoing exploration of sculptural form. The architect is constantly searching for poetic sculptural forms that do not compromise the use of the spaces within. The composition of this project is a series of intersecting rectilinear elements – from the large scale to the small scale – from the overall form to the smaller sculptured ceiling of the living/dining/kitchen space.

SCREENING FROM THE OUTSIDE

The site has two street frontages. A sensitive facade was designed for the rear, which incorporates a garage door and gate. Local council insisted that some visibility be maintained from the street into the rear garden, so the garage door has a series of angled blades that give a greater sense of openness between the garden and the street, while totally blocking any view into the rear of the house.

TOP FAR LEFT
The clear glass floor landing at the top of the staircase allows for more natural light and sunshine to reach the ground floor, and also provides a dramatic transition from the staircase to the bedrooms.

LEFT
A view of the kitchen, dining, living area, and courtyard showing the composition of spaces with sculptured elements on the ceiling. The stairwell also doubles as a lightshaft, with the low winter northern sun shining right down onto the floor of the southern end of the house.

Mt Eden House AUCKLAND, NEW ZEALAND
South Pacific Architecture

Constructed	2006
Home type	Suburban, single dwelling
Structure	Two-and-a-half story concrete house

"I was very keen to work with the solidness of rock, which aside from its many attractive qualities, helped influence a decision toward a more affordable concrete construction."

Megan Rule

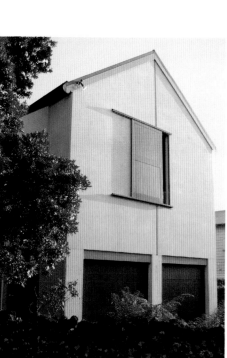

ABOVE
A single, cedar-paneled sliding door against a raw, prefabricated concrete panel exterior offers a simple gesture to the inner suburban street, while also disguising a third level of living space within the home.

TOP RIGHT
Glazed cedar-sliding doors open off the main living area onto a north-facing deck and a secluded back garden. A series of strip timber louvers, across the north-facing perimeter wall, offers secure cross-ventilation, while subtly connecting the two concrete panel structures.

PROBLEMS WITH THE SITE

Making maximum use of a small Auckland in-fill site, Mt Eden House is located on the rocky Mt Eden lava flow, with dry wall scoria boundaries. The surrounding housing is quite varied. In this part of Auckland, town planning regulations stipulated that new homes had to resemble villas, and this, along with a limited budget and a restrictive space of only 4,300 sq ft (400 sq m), posed something of a challenge for the architect.

The architect looked at the two-story buildings in the area, in particular the Martha Mine pumphouse in near-by Waihi, and applied its utilitarian qualities to her design, while keeping at the back of her mind some of the elements of thirteenth century monastic buildings — such as proportion, use of light, and solidity.

The size and location of the site made crane access and maneuverability difficult. The site also contained a sewer line junction and a stormwater soakpit (a chamber in the rock for natural drainage). Rock cutting was also required — rock and fertile soil were stockpiled for later landscaping of the site.

READY-MADE REMEDIES

The architect used prefabricated panel technology borrowed from commercial warehousing. This allowed for rapid construction and the bulk of the house went up over several days.

Another aspect of the design is that it offers a degree of adaptability, providing the potential for two independently operating or self-contained parts within a single residence, or perhaps, in the future, two separate residences.

Precast concrete panels were used in a further effort to economize. The panels were limited to two modular lengths of 10½ ft (3.2 m) and 4 ft (1.2 m). From these, there is a natural evolution into two major, equally sized "concrete containers," from which four minor, equally sized skylit bay windows protrude. These bay windows have wooden frames, which fit in well with older houses in the area. They provide visual relief to the exterior and interior edges of the house, while also disguising the concrete panel joints within mitered corners. In addition, they allow filtered light into both the north and south ends of the house.

LEVELS AND LIGHT

In between the two concrete containers, there is a central circulation staircase and entry space. The main living level sits above a basement entry and garage level. A deck opens off the first floor kitchen and living areas, giving a view of the rear north-facing garden.

CHARACTERISTIC FITTINGS

The double-hung windows in the bays are situated just above floor level, and when they are fully open are at handrail height. Setting them back into the rooms, as one would hang a picture frame, gives the striking effect of light and shade.

The finishing of Mt Eden House is notable for its simple use of raw materials, and the effective juxtaposition of timber and concrete. The fittings are generally inexpensive, with the joinery and interior cladding done in pine and plywood.

1 garage
2 entry
3 workshop
4 courtyard
5 studio
6 bedroom
7 bathroom
8 living/kitchen
9 deck
10 open to below

GARDEN LEVEL   GROUND FLOOR   FIRST FLOOR

LEFT
Two "concrete living containers" are divided by a central circulation staircase — constructed almost entirely of pine and plywood. Translucent sheet cladding filters light onto a raw interior of timber against concrete.

ABOVE
Viewed from the bedroom loft above, the skylit bay — and the distinct alcove of light-filled space it creates — modulates the exterior and interior edges of the home. At the same time, it provides a means to disguise concrete panel joints within mitered corners.

Orange Grove CALIFORNIA, USA
Pugh + Scarpa Architects

Constructed	2006
Home type	Multi-family loft condominiums
Structure	Cast-in-place concrete on the first floor; conventional wood framing above the concrete

"Charles Eames once said that ideas are not subject to ownership but exist in the world and are waiting to be snatched up and worked upon. In selecting an idea to develop or work upon, Eames described the responsibility that came with this. He said that a designer must treat the ideas with the utmost of care and invention, otherwise, the ideas would be ruined forever for all others."

Pugh + Scarpa Architects

CHANGING THE PALETTE

Orange Grove makes a bold new architectural statement in the City of West Hollywood. It is a sensitively designed building that blends in well with the neighborhood, which is characterized by traditional bungalow-style, single-family dwellings. What makes Orange Grove special, however, is the manner in which it diverges from the overwhelming mood of the area, and yet remains compatible with it. The material palette and scale is different – rather than use traditional pitched roof forms, Orange Grove has been designed using Modernist principles. So it is eclectic and unconventional, but still sits consistently in its surroundings.

The large balcony in the front facade gives the building a strong relationship to the streetscape, yet Orange Grove is certainly distinct from nearby houses and other buildings.

A SENSE OF SCULPTURE

The large-scale elements of the building instill it with drama, but it is also broken down into manageable human-scale parts, and then further divided into two different buildings. Because of its flaunting of convention, Orange Grove can, in a sense, be likened to the Schindler House, which is an icon of Californian Modernism located only a short distance away. As with the Schindler House, the windows, balcony and

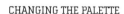

East elevation

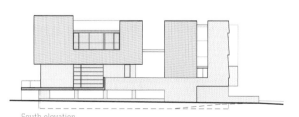

South elevation

ABOVE
The bedroom flows out to the terrace, which opens both spaces onto the street, connecting the whole structure to the neighborhood.

RIGHT
The building mass is broken into smaller elements that fit into the scale of the street and the neighboring structures of mainly bungalow-style homes.

SECOND FLOOR PLAN

MEZZANINE PLAN

N

GROUND FLOOR PLAN

UNIT 5	UNIT 4	UNIT 3
		UNIT 2	UNIT 1

1	living room	6	balcony
2	kitchen	7	courtyard
3	bathroom	8	driveway
4	mezzanine	9	open
5	bedroom		

other typical architectural elements of Orange Grove have a sculptural essence to them. The windows have been inserted into the spaces between different sections of the building.

BALANCING TENSIONS

One way to describe the design of Orange Grove is as a subtle balance of tensions. A three-dimensional composition is created by the strategic placement of windows, doors, balconies, and building volumes. This generates a feeling of fluidity to the building. Each part of the structure has a clearly defined shape – for example, the corrugated metal surround enclosing the second floor balcony in the north and east facades.

Another example of this demarcation can be seen in the two square-profile balcony surrounds in the front facade. One of them is small and open at the front, while the other is large and veiled with stainless steel

slats. Yet in spite of these contrasts, each balcony maintains a sense of overall balance and is closely related to other elements of the building.

LIGHT, SPACE, AND ART

The architects wanted all the elements of the building to be interpreted as abstract, so even though a window is a window, it also can be seen as a slit, or as a framed box.

Orange Grove encapsulates the notion – and reality – of large, simple interior volumes of space. It is a model whose foundations are space, light, and the industrial materials of the loft, which is the antithesis of the bungalow. In this regard, the building responds to the wishes of a burgeoning niche market of clients who want something distinctive and open, and which caters to their lifestyle choices.

Parnell House AUCKLAND, NEW ZEALAND
Crosson Clarke Carnachan Architects

Constructed	2002
Home type	Single dwelling
Structure	Concrete slab lower floor, timber upper floor and wall framing

"This is an exploration of the dichotomy between the architectural style of an 1870s Victorian cottage and a modern, minimalist design. The project was about combining and modifying a nineteenth-century building to fit a twenty-first century lifestyle."

Simon Carnachan

ABOVE
The facade of the house had to be retained due to local planning restrictions, which listed the home as a heritage building.

RADICAL REFORM

The original cottage on this site was built in the 1870s for a sea captain, and because of its history, the local planning authorities stipulated that the facade be retained in order to comply with the area's heritage zoning. The original cottage interior, however, has been completely replaced.

The brief for Parnell House was to remove the existing, badly constructed, sub-standard "lean-to" and replace it with a new double height addition. One of the most effective ways of reducing the bulk of the building was to locate the new kitchen, bathroom, and service areas underneath the existing house.

The architect decided to leave the existing cottage and its front veranda and to completely refurbish the rest of the exterior of the building, so that it was in the same style as other houses in the area, thus maintaining the character, scale, and appearance of the street.

The original chimney conceals a skylight to the guest bedroom, and a loft has been added in the roof space, which has views across to the adjacent reserve and the city beyond.

Another decision was to provide a negative detail/recess to isolate the new addition from the cottage. This meant that the simple cottage shape with its pyramidal roof was not only maintained, but accentuated.

VANISHING ACTS

The walls were removed from the original cottage layout, although the original hallway was kept. The main bedroom now opens to natural light and pleasing views. The sandblasted glass sliders can close off the bedroom for privacy. The ensuite and wardrobe are extensions of the main bedroom, rather than separate rooms, giving the feeling of openness.

MORE THAN JUST PARKING

Another consideration for the site was car parking. This was provided on site by disguising the front of the garages and then recessing them so that they resembled walls coming from the side of the house. As well, louvers were added to clad the garage doors – this kept the horizontal weatherboard look at the front of the house.

EAST ELEVATION

NORTH ELEVATION

1 garage
2 main bedroom
  and bathroom
3 bedroom
4 bathroom
5 open to below
6 kitchen
7 dining/living
8 library
9 veranda

GROUND FLOOR

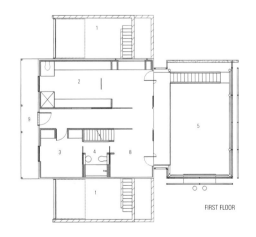

FIRST FLOOR

TOP
The rear courtyard features
grass with inlaid tile lines,
and yuccas, selected for their
dramatic foliage. The gas flares
and table are perfect for evening
outdoor dining.

ABOVE
The glass and steel stairs, and
the exterior louvers over the
glass box at the rear of the
house are functional, while
also adding a sleek charm to
the structure.

Louvers were also used over glazed areas to continue the horizontal weatherboard appearance. In fact, the garage performed another function – it disguised the building in the backyard and minimized the view from the street.

SMALL, SIMPLE, SUPER

The level of the new addition was constructed under the gutter line of the existing house, and the whole essence of the idea was to keep the addition simple and small.

Materials are also simple and minimalist. The timber floor is oiled tawa, a native New Zealand timber, and the appliances are stainless steel. The glass walkway and stairs are stylish and elegant, and the exterior louvers are aluminum. Colored halogen lights are recessed into the floor in the entry hall, providing a warm welcome.

The courtyard is the essence of simplicity. The lawn is inlaid with honed basalt tiles, which add warmth and texture, and four yuccas were planted to add a striking foliage feature to the area. The lap pool and jacuzzi are separated by glass.

ABOVE
Pivot doors are designed to look like part of the kitchen and also to provide access to the garages, which are located on either side of the house.

TOP LEFT
The kitchen is white and stainless steel, with a stainless-steel island bench. The glass walkway allows "borrowed" light from above into the kitchen below.

OPPOSITE
The exterior view looking from the rear courtyard. The exterior louvers are aluminum with aerofoil-shaped blades. They are adjustable in order to offer protection from the afternoon sun.

Skybox WELLINGTON, NEW ZEALAND
Melling:Morse Architects

Construction	2001–2002
Home type	City house, single dwelling
Structure	Three-level timber box bolted to steel frame

"The visible separation of the
Skybox from my office building
beneath is far more than an
architectural conceit. The
concept really works – aided
by the wind slapping against
its underbelly, there is no
awareness inside the box of the
sometimes stressful world it
seeks to escape."

Gerald Melling

ABOVE
The underbelly of the Skybox
is deliberately exposed to both
the eye and the elements.
An electric hoist is a valuable
conveyance for furniture,
appliances, boxes of groceries,
as well as bicycles.

RIGHT
Egmont Street is a narrow
mid-city alleyway of early
twentieth-century warehouses,
most of which have been
re-engineered and adapted
for apartments over the past
decade. On its lofty steel frame,
the Skybox is inserted into a gap
above the continuous wall of
brickwork that lines the west
side of the street.

LEFT
Heavily glazed on three of its four sides (east, north, and west), the Skybox is an effective solar heater. Its system of fenestration is a gentle satire on the archetypal Modernist curtain-wall of the commercial building, here constructed in natural timber with infill panels of fixed glazing, louvers, and flat colorsteel sheet glued to plywood. The vertical orange neon "Skybox" sign is a participatory gesture to the 24-hour life of the city.

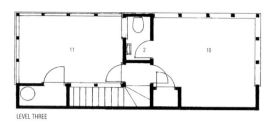

LEVEL THREE

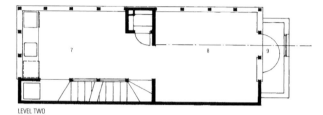

LEVEL TWO

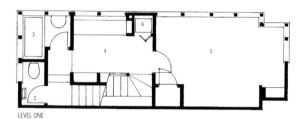

LEVEL ONE

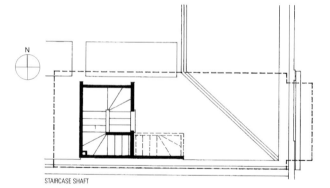

STAIRCASE SHAFT

1 staircase
2 WC
3 bathroom
4 study
5 main bedroom
6 laundry
7 kitchen/dining
8 living/sitting area
9 balcony
10 guest bedroom
11 loggia

TOP RIGHT
The east-facing nose of the sitting area (level 2) becomes a morning balcony, cantilevered over the street. The glazed gate in the balustrade wall opens to allow access for items lifted from the street on the electric hoist. All the internal timbers are environmentally-friendly macrocarpa, which does not require chemical treatment.

RIGHT
The staircase arrives at the study (level 1), running between a wall of bookshelves (the "library") and a wall of opal glass, which "borrows" and enhances sunlight into the staircase shaft. Wall and ceiling linings are predominantly colorsteel sheet on plywood or plasterboard.

REINVENTING WELLINGTON

Melling:Morse Architects are known for their small timber houses, which have been enlivening the hinterlands of Wellington (the capital city of New Zealand) for more than a decade. This pursuit of domestic architectural opportunity has now continued into the heart of the city, down a narrow lane lined with colonial brickwork and the ghosts of an early twentieth-century red-light district. Gerald Melling's Skybox, his own living accommodation above his office warehouse, suggests an architecture of limitless urban possibility.

In recent years, Wellington has been relentlessly reinventing itself through the inhabitation of its core. Along with new apartment blocks, domestically converted commercial and historic buildings have brought new life to the nation's cultural and administrative hub. Like most cities, however, the center of Wellington tends towards architectural chaos. Melling's response has been to bring order to his air space.

LIVING AND WORKING IN THE SAME – YET DIFFERENT – SPACE

The notion of live/work/play in the same location is the new urban paradigm. While endorsing this, Melling recognizes the sanity in an appropriate degree of segregation – hence the Skybox displays a physical, visual, and conceptual independence from the office building beneath it, connected only by the concealed umbilical cord of its staircase shaft. A lofty steel frame slung high over the roof of the existing building provides a platform for the box's apparent autonomy.

NARROW FOOTPRINT, WIDE VISION

The narrow footprint (11½ ft x 26 ft [3.5 m x 8 m]) of the Skybox is defined by its supporting steel frame. The box itself is made up of three layers of plywood-braced timber frame, using a 36 in (900 mm) planning grid and 9 ft (2.7 m) ceiling heights. The lowest level – with main bedroom, study, and bathroom – is deliberately reclusive, reflected in higher window-sill heights than those of the upper two layers. The intermediate level is an open space for kitchen, dining, and living, with a small, east-facing balcony cantilevered over the street. The top floor provides a guest room and a covered loggia.

Clad in vertical corrugated steel, the cold south face of the Skybox is completely closed. All other facades open to the warmth of the sun, the views, and the adjacent cityscape.

SUMPTUOUS SKIN

The Skybox's skin is a consistent, low-maintenance grid framed in macrocarpa and filled with direct glazing, glass louvers, colorsteel sheet, and plywood. While the external rough-sawn timber is allowed to weather to a natural silver-gray, internal timbers are dressed smooth and sealed against steel-clad linings – a sophisticated counterpoint of soft versus hard, warm versus cool, human versus slick.

Straddling an industrial warehouse of humble origin, the Skybox moves – quite literally, layer by layer – from the ordinary to the extraordinary. Planning approvals were only reluctantly granted by city fathers who imagined the Skybox as tilting at windmills. Certainly, it rocks in a gust of wind, but rarely has a New Zealand architect been so well-cradled under Pacific moons.

ABOVE
A macrocarpa and stainless-steel kitchen bench abuts the western end of level 2, overlooking an urban village of assorted apartments in adjacent buildings, both old and new. Window glass is direct-glazed into exposed structural framework (macrocarpa posts and lintels); the louvers are assembled kit-sets.

Solar Umbrella CALIFORNIA, USA
Pugh + Scarpa Architects

Constructed	2005
Home type	Single-family home renovation and addition
Structure	Tilt-up concrete, steel, and wood framing

"Kiesler once wrote, 'Our Western world has been overrun by masses of art objects. What we really need are not more and more objects, but an objective."

Pugh + Scarpa Architects

ABOVE
It was important to the clients to integrate principles of sustainability into the design, so the architects looked at the whole site and took advantage of as many opportunities as possible in order to create a sustainable living environment. This included reorienting the house 180º for better solar orientation.

RIGHT
The old backyard has been transformed into a new entry court. Instead of using concrete or stone when remodeling the home, the architects used decomposed granite and gravel hardscape, including a storm-water retention basin, which allows the ground to absorb water as well as alleviate urban run-off to the ocean – a vast improvement on less environmentally friendly alternatives. The landscaping is purposely low maintenance and is complemented by the use of drought-tolerant xeriscaping, which also sits well with the texture and colors of the house.

SUSTAINABLE LIVING

Venice, California is populated with mostly single-story bungalows, and the Solar Umbrella is a bold precedent for the area, its double-story, environmentally sensitive form setting a standard for a new generation of Mod–ernist architecture. The site is 41 ft (12.5 m) wide and 100 ft (30 m) long. The existing 650-sq-ft (60.5-sq-m) bungalow was transformed into a 1,900-sq-ft (176.5-sq-m) residence that proclaims itself ready for the challenges of the twenty-first century.

Inspired by Paul Rudolph's "Umbrella House" of 1953, the Solar Umbrella is a modern reinvention of the solar canopy, which provides thermal resistance to hot summers and protection against cold winters. Sustainability was important, so the architects looked at the whole site and took advantage of as many opportunities as possible to create a sustainable living environment.

CAPTURING THE SUN'S ENERGY

Using both active and passive solar design techniques, energy consumption is neutral. In addition, the majority of the materials used in the interior are made from recycled or renewable products. All materials used for the building itself and the landscaping around it were chosen because of their aesthetic and actual impact on the site. The result is an artistic sensory experience.

Another consideration the architects took into account was aspect – they rotated the residence 180º from its original orientation, so what used to be the front and main entry at the north became the back facing south. As well as allowing optimal exposure to the southern sunlight, this gave the architects more space, and a chance to create a more welcoming introduction to the building.

Solar panels are wrapped around the south elevation. They protect the building from the intensity of the sun, and also absorb and transform the captured sunlight into usable energy – in fact, all the electricity in the home is provided by this strategy. The solar canopy is functional, performing the role of energy collector, but also aesthetically pleasing, with an interesting experimental effect.

EXPANDING SPACES

One wall at the south was removed, and the primary layout of the existing dwelling retained. The original bungalow was quite compact, and now there is a large addition to the south – it includes a new entry, living area, main bedroom, and laundry and storage areas.

The kitchen, formerly at the back of the house, now opens up into a large living area, which in its turn, opens out to a generously sized front yard. A glass

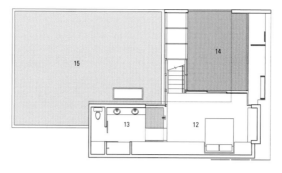

1 study
2 closet
3 bedroom
4 bathroom
5 dining room
6 kitchen
7 living room
8 utility closet
9 laundry
10 fish pond
11 jacuzzi
12 main bedroom
13 main bathroom
14 terrace
15 roof below

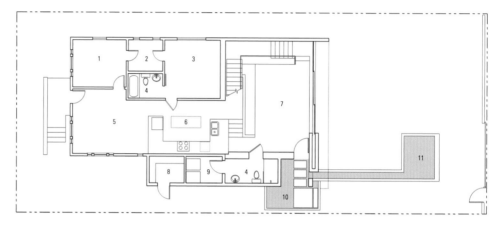

GROUND FLOOR

wall in the living area marks the boundary between inside and outside, and creates a visual walkway from one end of the site to the other.

EXTERIOR SPACES, INTERIOR FEEL

Exterior spaces are thought of as "outdoor rooms" and the architects have achieved this by creating strong visual and physical links between the interior and exterior, resulting in a more energetic relationship between the two.

This blurring of boundaries is further accentuated by the entry area along the western edge of the site. A concrete pool – a convincing landscape element in its own right – marks the route to the front door. At the entry, the pool cascades into a lower level of water. A variation on the concept of the welcome mat is provided by the stepping stones. They are immersed in water and create an exciting invitation to the inside of the home. Once again, the outside and the inside come together.

The main bedroom is on the second level and demonstrates the strategy of interlocking space. It is situated above the living area and accessed by a set of floating, folded-plate steel stairs. The room opens onto a covered terrace overlooking the garden, extending the bedroom space outside. The overall impression is of a loft exposed to the outside. The bedroom terrace not only brings the outside in, it also provides the front elevation with a view of the garden.

This deep terrace carves out an exterior space within the visual bounds of the building envelope and provides the front elevation with a unique character. The second level is not enclosed at all, but rather, it is protected by the planes that wrap around it.

LIGHT AND TRANSPARENCY

The design is given depth and richness through the composition of interlocking solid and open spaces. Views are visible from the front to the back, giving the house a transparent quality. These "visual corridors" contain the formal elements of the home, such as stairs, guardrails, bearing walls, structural columns, built-in furniture, and cabinetwork, but they vary in density, texture, and color.

Natural light is plentiful and the stepped roofs and clerestory windows emphasize the light and generate light and shadow at various times of the day, which serves to enliven the more permanent fixtures of the design. The outcome is a layered composition with plenty of interest, both formal and informal.

MATERIALS FOR BEAUTY AND PERFORMANCE

The materials used in the residence have been artfully used as design features, for example, an acoustic panel, made from recycled newspaper, was palm-sanded and employed as the finish material for the custom-made cabinets. Oriented strand board, a structural grade building material, became the main flooring material besides concrete.

FAR LEFT
The new living space flows unbroken into the entry court. Privacy screens made from steel and industrial brooms shield the main bedroom, on the second floor, from direct view.

ABOVE
In the kitchen/dining area the natural cherry dining table is complemented by the cabinets and flooring. Both of these are made from oriented strand board, which is both cost effective and meets with the owner's wishes of using long-lasting and environmentally responsible materials.

TOP RIGHT
An airy, light filled space is created by having the main bedroom opening out onto a covered terrace that overlooks the garden. The feeling of space is further accentuated as the bedroom flows seamlessly into the light filled main bathroom.

RIGHT
Detail of the floating, perforated steel staircase leading to the main bedroom. The medium and design of the staircase, off the main living area, continues with the theme of flooding the house in light, and is an architectural feature in its own right.

SOMA House SAN FRANCISCO, USA
Jim Jennings Architecture

Completed	1998
Home type	Two-story, single-family residence
Structure	Steel, translucent glass, concrete, and wood

"Every client desires some degree of invention from their architect. With this house, invention occurred not only in the design and physical making of the place, but in the infusion of a type and standard of living into a part of town where it hadn't previously existed."

Jim Jennings

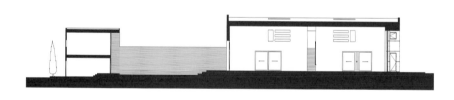

ABOVE
SOMA's street elevation is a modern graphic presence in a transitional urban neighborhood. Steel panels make up the bulk of the facade; a two-story, four-part grid of translucent glass, a smooth counterpoint to the hard metal, allows diffused light into the main interior.

TOP RIGHT
An interior courtyard is situated between the main house and the studio/guesthouse. The limestone-paved terrace is flanked by rows of black-trunk bamboo in pebbles. A wood screen wraps the courtyard and forms a contrasting element with the home's concrete rear wall.

ELUSIVE EDGE

Located in San Francisco's south of Market district (SOMA) — an industrial precinct with few single-family residences — SOMA House retains the foundations and concrete walls of its former function as an old commercial building, and presents a modern yet enigmatic face to the denizens of this gritty urban neighborhood.

ABSTRACTED FORMS

The house, courtyard, and separate studio/guesthouse span from the busy street frontage to the rear alley. The building's inscrutable facade features translucent glass and perforated steel. The steel is spaced away from the building wall so that small holes in each panel focus light inside. In a "camera obscura" effect, multiple images are projected onto the translucent glass interior walls, which when viewed from the inside display the abstracted motion of the exterior. Apart from this element of visual complexity, the spacious interiors are light-filled, minimally detailed, and serene.

The heart of the two-story house is a long and high living/dining area that runs along half the building and opens to the courtyard. This airy space, capped by a barrel-vaulted ceiling, features white walls, swaths of wood and steel, and a light-colored travertine floor. The other half contains a kitchen, pantry and study/office on the ground level and two bedrooms overhead, reached via a poured-concrete stairway.

The living area is mostly maintained as one open-plan space. However, sliding partitions of translucent glass, framed in mahogany and blued steel, are sometimes used to seal off the front area as an office conference room. The partitions can also divide the study and kitchen from the main area.

TRANSLUCENT ILLUMINATIONS

Natural light signifies the house. An abundance of diffused northern light, ushered through the translucent glass at the front, is balanced by bright sunlight from the south, streaming through the glass wall to the courtyard. Skylights are scattered above both floors.

Translucent glass bands, set in rectangular reliefs, bring copious light into the massive bedrooms and ensuite bathrooms. Although each bedroom has a lower, more intimate ceiling than the living area below, they are not identical; the southern bedroom has roof access, while the northern bedroom has a walk-in wardrobe and part of the "camera obscura" effect on its bathroom wall. Both bathrooms are sheathed in limestone.

The rectangular courtyard is lined in Alaskan yellow cedar planks, echoing the siding of the adjacent building. The minimalist look of the rest of the house continues with the use of limestone pavers, pebbles, and black-trunk bamboo for landscaping. With no transparent windows on the perimeter, the courtyard is the building's sole link to the natural environment.

ABOVE RIGHT
The glazed front door, largely hidden from the street, is tucked into a recess in the steel facade. The perforated steel transmits light to the interior through a translucent glass wall for a "camera obscura" effect.

RIGHT
The studio/guesthouse also incorporates an alley garage. Alaskan yellow cedar planks and floor-to-ceiling glass are the predominant materials of this secondary structure, whose upper level looks out over the private outdoor area.

GROUND FLOOR

FIRST FLOOR

1 living
2 office
3 bathroom
4 kitchen
5 pantry
6 courtyard
7 garage
8 bedroom
9 walk-in wardrobe

N

ABOVE
Sliding panels of mahogany, blued steel, and glass allow the main space to be subdivided for flexibility of use. Here, the panels close off the main living space to create a temporary meeting area. The front door is at center left; next to it is the translucent glass interior wall that is at the back of the exterior steel facade.

RIGHT
The vaulted ceiling of the main living area incorporates motorized skylights that ventilate the two-story volume. Multiple sources of natural light illuminate the space. Blued-steel panels define the fireplace wall and subtly contrast with the wood. Steel also surrounds the opening to the kitchen, at left.

OPPOSITE
Concrete sheer walls are left exposed in the stairway off the living area, the plugholes complementing the perforations of the exterior steel. A light sculpture by John Wigmore is predominant in the living area beyond. The mahogany stairs lead to the main bedrooms.

Urale Arapai House   AUCKLAND, NEW ZEALAND

Malcolm Walker Architects

Constructed	2004
Home type	Two-story family house
Structure	Masonry, concrete slab floors, and absorbent acoustic ceilings

> "My clients commented that up to 30 people have stayed for a week and there still seemed plenty of room. They said it had been designed for hard 'coconuts' and wild Samoan kids. The hallway takes a 'thrashing.' This is music to an architect, whose job it is to provide a place that complements and enhances their clients' way of living."
>
> **Malcolm Walker Architects**

ABOVE
In a heritage area occupied mainly by Victorian villas, the street elevation gives a nod to this predominant neighborhood form, and includes a backward salute to the traditional veranda. The entrance wall is clad in translucent fiberglass, giving a generous and unexpected sunlit introduction to the house.

TOP RIGHT
Within the simple plan of the house there remains a spatial complexity. The stairs and main circulation point pivots around the "big step." The translucent nature of the hall gives a sense of being connected with the outdoors. Large pivot and sliding doors facilitate the indoor/outdoor feel to the rooms.

PACIFIC ISLAND LIFESTYLE

Located on a tiny inner-city site, the Urale Arapai House needed to be a dwelling for a robust and social family of eight with an extended Pacific island family of playwrights, television producers, musicians, filmmakers, and sportspeople. With six children, a steady stream of visitors, and short- and long-term guests, the design had to provide space as well as privacy.

The owners have lived in the area for many years, in a suburb once home to many Pacific island families. These days, few remain. Real estate prices and lack of adequate space have forced them to relocate. Urale Arapai House is the owners' declaration that they intend to remain in the area and to bring their family up there.

ROBUST MATERIALS

The family's lifestyle includes a broad range of activities, from rugby in the hallway to the care of infants, from quiet homework assignments to band practice – many occurring at the same time. Careful planning was required in order to accommodate these pursuits.

A busy house requires resilient materials. The architect chose a strapped and lined concrete block with pre-stressed concrete floors. Absorbent acoustic ceilings were installed in the main living area.

FINDING FORM

Local planning authorities have strict regulations regarding special character requirements, so the architect drew on neighboring Victorian villas as a reference for form and context. Another reference – this time to the practicalities of Pacific living – inspired the deep veranda and the shaded outdoor areas.

The form is essentially that of a split villa. The traditional central hallway of the villa plan has now been set at one side. Instead of being used as merely a circulation device, the upper and lower hallways have been expanded and fenestrated as social spaces. These feed into simple rooms that provide a retreat from the energy of the household — essential in a house that is, by the owner's admission, the loudest in the street.

The rooms themselves are not fixed territory in the conventional sense; usage and occupation is fluid. Consistent with this, the upper bathroom is planned to be both ensuite to the parents' room and a general household bathroom. Large pivot and sliding doors are used between the circulation spaces and social rooms, to further include and manage the hallways as social areas and as integral areas of the house.

As owner Arnette Arapai comments, "Europeans have a sense of *this is my space*; Island families do not."

The downstairs living room has spaces adjoining it – the kitchen, hallway, window seat, auxiliary family room, and outdoor room all operate independently of each other. Dining is informal and usually happens outside or at the kitchen servery. The family room, adjacent to the living room, serves as a formal dining room, entertainment space, or adult refuge.

NATIVE LANDSCAPES

Landscaping is underway, using a mix of native New Zealand and Pacific island plants such as frangipanis, nikau palms, flaxes, and black bamboo, with black taros for ground cover. It is a clear reference to the Pacific origins of the residents, but the plants are also selected for hardiness and visual interest against the raw concrete of the walls.

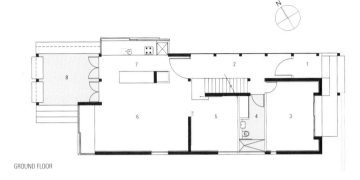

GROUND FLOOR

1 entry
2 hallway
3 bedroom
4 bathroom
5 bedroom/family
6 living
7 kitchen
8 deck
9 bedroom
10 bathroom
11 bedroom
12 living/bedroom

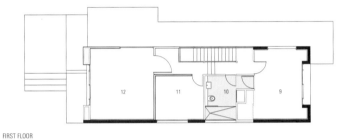

FIRST FLOOR

ABOVE
A hall runs down one side of the house and includes the kitchen on its journey from the front door to the backyard. The main living area is to the right.

LEFT
To the rear of the house, the outdoor room (on left) is perfectly suited to the maritime climate and Pacific lifestyle, and is an important and fully utilized space.

Weathering Steel House TORONTO, CANADA
Shim-Sutcliffe Architects

Constructed	2001
Home type	Single dwelling, residential house
Structure	Wood frame, steel columns, and beams clad with weathering steel on a plywood backing

"The design of this project is an emphatic critique of the material and spatial banality of the surrounding suburban neighborhood. We hope that the Weathering Steel House offers the possibility of a much richer physical experience – one that engages all the senses."

Brigitte Shim and Howard Sutcliffe

NORTH ELEVATION

TOP RIGHT
Winter view of the street elevation (facing north) showing the home's weathering steel cladding and the retaining wall in the foreground, also in weathering steel.

FAR RIGHT
View of the ravine-side of the house, showing the reflecting pool and adjoining swimming pool extending from the center of the structure into the wintry garden. The many windows facing south draw in the maximum amount of warmth from the sun, while also capturing views of the ravine and city skyline beyond.

CREATING A CONTRAST WITH THE EXISTING HOUSING

In the Toronto garden suburb of Don Mills, 1960s ranch bungalows and their surrounding landscaping are being levelled to be replaced by substantial, clumsy, historically referential monster houses. Constructed of beige brick, taupe-colored stucco and reconstituted stone, these new houses form the new ideal suburban dream house. Complemented by decorative and ornamental landscaping, they are the antithesis of their Modernist predecessors.

Weathering Steel House sits in direct contrast to this context. Materially rich, dark, and abstract, it creates a clear threshold to the world within, to the site it creates, and to the ravine edge over which it looks. The L-shaped house frames a reconfigured landscape created around shaped, tree-covered mounds and

a sweeping meadow. Imbedding itself into the center of the house, the reflecting pool and swimming pool beyond form the intermediary between building and landscape, weaving reflected light, motion, and sound into the heart of the project.

LIGHT AND MOVEMENT

From the street this house is seemingly much more opaque than adjacent buildings; meanwhile, sculptural cut-outs in the elevation offer precise transparent glimpses of the ravine beyond. Upon entering the home, a circulation space parallel to the front elevation connects the garage entry, front entry, basement courtyard, and second level in one continuous slice of vertical and horizontal space. From the entry, one catches a glimpse of the ravine treetops beyond, before rising up a few steps to the main living level. From here the landscape and the house unfold, with the linear watercourse weaving internal and external space together.

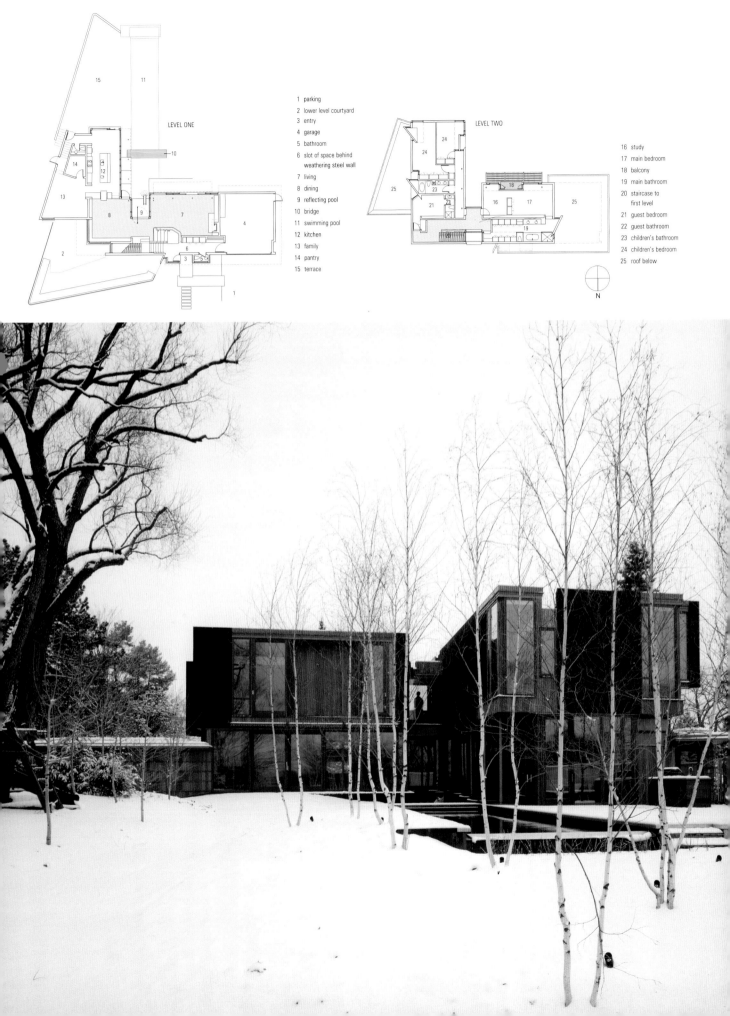

LEVEL ONE

15
11
14
12
13
8
9
7
4
10
2
6
3 5
1

1 parking
2 lower level courtyard
3 entry
4 garage
5 bathroom
6 slot of space behind
  weathering steel wall
7 living
8 dining
9 reflecting pool
10 bridge
11 swimming pool
12 kitchen
13 family
14 pantry
15 terrace

LEVEL TWO

24
24
25
23
21
16
17
25
18
19
22
20

16 study
17 main bedroom
18 balcony
19 main bathroom
20 staircase to
   first level
21 guest bedroom
22 guest bathroom
23 children's bathroom
24 children's bedroom
25 roof below

N

TOP LEFT
Imbedding itself into the center of the house, the reflecting pool connects the building with the exterior landscape, while also bringing reflected light, motion, and sound into the heart of the home.

LEFT
View of the entry with the staircase to the second level and the staircase to the lower level visible. The lower level courtyard is beyond the door. The main living level is a few steps up from the entry.

ABOVE
A skylight and inverted bay window drops a pool of light on the landing of the staircase to the second level, terminating at the end of the reflecting pool axis. The rich chocolate walls tie together the natural finishes of timber and concrete.

A skylight and inverted bay window drops a pool of light on the landing of the staircase to the second level, terminating at the end of the reflecting pool axis. On the second level, this inverted bay window and large window on the south side of the house help to form a "bridge" between the main bedroom and the children's wing.

THE CHALLENGE OF CLIMATE

Toronto is situated on the northern shore of Lake Ontario, and is part of a large freshwater system known as the Great Lakes. The site's adjacency to this body of water creates a technically challenging climatic condition ranging from –40°F to 104°F (–40°C to 40°C). The passive solar design of the project responds directly to this challenge – with few windows and much of the service and circulation

on the north side and the public rooms on the south side, where there is maximum solar gain, as well as views of the verdant ravine and city skyline beyond.

CREATING TEXTURES

The building cladding is weathering steel, which was selected because of its direct interaction with nature, allowing, as it does, the richly textured skin to darken slowly. Because weathering steel is usually fabricated in large sections for bridges and other civil engineering works, the channels and all the fixed components of this cladding system were break-formed from weathering steel plate.

Westcliff Estate JOHANNESBURG, SOUTH AFRICA
studioMAS architects + urban designers

Construction	2001–2002
Home type	Three-story family home
Structure	Off-shutter concrete carcass with stone and aluminum cladding

ABOVE
As the afternoon light fades, owners enjoy views from the entertainment/living area looking across the swimming pool. Two glass sliding doors open from the internal living space to the patio.

> "Our goal was to design a twenty-first century African house that embodies the 'new values' of modern South Africa — respect for the land, for its setting, and for the people."
>
> Pierre Swanepoel

MODERNISM IN AN AFRICAN CONTEXT

Considered by some to be a seminal work of Johannesburg Modernism, Westcliff Estate was designed to sit on a steep site, partially submerged into the slope at the back. The site was originally subdivided from the 100-year-old Rand Lord property, now a school for disabled children. The school could not use this part of the site owing to the extreme slope, and the home's location is in an area where much of the natural vegetation had been destroyed.

The expansive views, the breathtaking landscape, and the tempered Highveld weather demanded a building that was open to its surroundings; one that invites the landscape inside. The raised pool and wide patio obscure views of neighboring houses at the front of the property, while the structural columns frame the more distant vistas.

TREE MOTIFS

The tree-like columns hold the bedrooms high in the "treetops," while the open-plan living area is under the tree-trunks next to the "river" — the pool. This narrative reflects very literally how many South Africans choose to live their lives — close to nature. The roof opens to invite in the winter sun, its rays also warming the dark slate wall in the windless colder months. To further support the tree analogy, the structures that guide the automated roof resemble the long, dramatic leaves of the bird of paradise plant (*Strelitzia*).

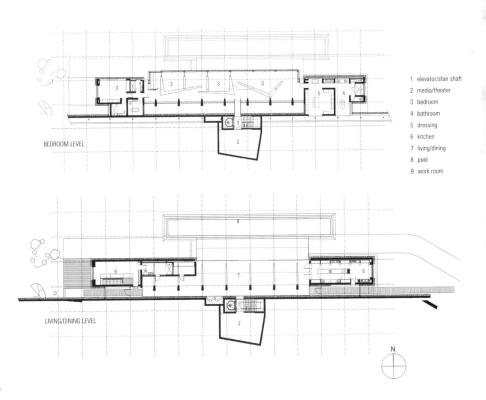

1 elevator/stair shaft
2 media/theater
3 bedroom
4 bathroom
5 dressing
6 kitchen
7 living/dining
8 pool
9 work room

BEDROOM LEVEL

LIVING/DINING LEVEL

N

TOP LEFT
An aerial view of Westcliff Estate showing the roof, pool, and patio area. Most of the landscape in front of the building was rehabilitated using only indigenous trees and grasses.

ABOVE
Looking east from the garden, across the deck toward the study. The shutters and glass fold and slide down respectively to expose the inside to the surrounding gardens.

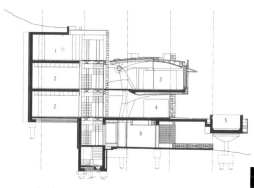

1 study
2 theater/media
3 bedroom
4 living/dining
5 pool
6 parking

LETTING IN THE LANDSCAPE

Visitors to this impressive home park in front of the retaining wall under the trees. They then approach from the east via a narrow, boarded ramp that is complete with an electrically operated, vertically sliding steel gate. Entry to the house is bordered by a retaining wall and two rubble dry stone walls contained by wire cages. Views to the northern landscape are hidden until the living space is entered, when the spectacular scene is revealed. Large glass doors slide away into the two flanking structures to integrate the patio, swimming pool, and the living space.

Seven tree-like columns support the bedrooms above and create a spacious living area underneath, with no obstruction between the pool, terrace, and magnificent panorama beyond. The impression is of sitting under a tree with one's back leaning against the trunk. The interplay between the organic and the rectilinear forms is a reflection of a desire to be part of nature, but also to be protected from it.

Furnishings are sparse; there is a deliberate feeling of emptiness, which allows the surrounding landscape to become the protagonist.

The main bedroom is the farthest east of the home's four bedrooms; it has an ensuite bathroom and a dressing room in the flanking structure. Thorn-shaped, removable cupboards delineate the other bedrooms, ensuring privacy and flexible storage for each space.

Stone from the site, in conjunction with concrete, was used in the construction of the house, affirming the building's connection with its surroundings.

The house is fully automated, allowing the family to change the internal environment in response to the climate outside. The notion of door, window, and roof is questioned in the design – the roof opens, the doors and windows disappear to give access to the outside landscape, inviting it to become part of the interior. Some believe Westcliff Estate heralds the emergence of the new African house, or at least offers an alternative to the typical Eurocentric notion of building.

ABOVE
The imposing glass-floored elevator delivers occupants and visitors speedily to their desired level within the house.

LEFT
A view from the living room looking north across the entertainment area, pool, and beyond to leafy Johannesburg, a city considered to be part of the biggest urban forest in the world.

RIGHT
The automated roof opens over the living space, allowing the family to control the internal environment in response to the conditions outside.

Wind House SINGAPORE
WOHA

Construction	2004–2006
Home type	Two-story detached dwelling
Structure	Reinforced concrete with steelwork, and pad footings

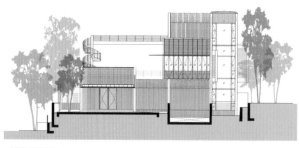

NORTH ELEVATION

"This private family residence was designed as a 'machine' to capture Singapore's light breezes ... in order to avoid the need for air-conditioning as much as possible."

Richard Hassell

LEFT
A steel bridge links the pool on level one to a roof terrace and roof garden, complete with overflow bathtub, on level two. Passive cooling methods figure prominently in the house design – breezes are directed over the swimming pool and water features to produce evaporatively cooled air, which then enters the house through open windows and doors.

LIFE IS A BREEZE

The clients requested a home that not only took advantage of Singapore's breezes and the extensive views of the nearby Botanic Gardens, but one that also delivered privacy and seclusion. The design process involved in-depth research into local wind patterns. Although Singapore has an equatorial climate with light breezes, comfort in the sometimes oppressive heat can be increased substantially by small increases in wind velocity and, in turn, by directing wind to activity locations in and around the home.

HARVESTING THE WIND

A series of devices was selected to act as wind "harvesters." Walls are extended beyond the building envelope to capture wind and thus increase the air pressure on openings. Selected blocks in the wall are omitted to form openings, light recesses, or service penetrations. Deflectors direct passing air into the home to increase air volume, and large overhangs deflect wind traveling up the hill slopes and direct it down into rooms and terraces.

Wind "towers" create air movement throughout the house. At each end of the circulation void, the two highest points of the house have electrically operated louvers. These can be opened on the leeward side of the prevailing wind to create a negative pressure, drawing warm air up and out of the home.

Inside the home, sliding doors stack to reduce the barrier to air movement; pocket doors slide out of the way when in use; bathroom walls move out from the main walls to create cross-ventilated louvered slots; and bedroom doors incorporate sliding joinery, which can be opened for ventilation while still maintaining privacy.

MINIMAL BARRIERS AND WIND-COOLING

The architectural envelope is minimized where possible to create a secure perimeter without blocking the wind. Vertical aluminum screens, constructed using angles that repeat the deflection strategy at a much smaller scale, present a minimal barrier to breezes. Internal openings allow breezes to permeate the house from end to end and back to front. The classically traditional device of "enfilade" – a series of aligned doors or openings – facilitates air flow throughout the house from one room to another.

Other environmental measures employed included both passive and active devices: wind is directed over water as it enters the house from different directions to create evaporative cooling; large overhangs keep out direct light; roof gardens shade the structure, and absorb both light energy and carbon; and water is heated by pumps on the roof for use in the home.

PATTERN AND TEXTURE

Extensive layering of diverse architectural "surfaces" – water, metal mesh, grass, concrete, plaster and paint, timber, fabric, aluminum, screens, walls – make a textural statement in the landscape. These are visually weightless, suspended in three dimensions throughout the site.

LIFESTYLE AND ART

The house is designed around the lifestyle of the owner. Gardens and water elements are everywhere, from the basement to the roof, and the main bedroom features an overflow bathtub adjoining a water garden. Entertaining is of great importance – the house has a Western and a Chinese dining room, an outdoor Asian kitchen, a barbecue, pool, and pavilion.

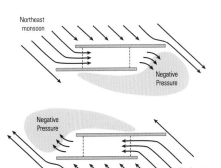

Northeast monsoon

Negative Pressure

Negative Pressure

Southwest monsoon

ABOVE
This diagram shows how the walls of the house extend beyond the building envelope to capture the air movement created by the southeast and northwest monsoons. This generates areas of negative pressure that then draw cool breezes through the house.

TOP
In order to keep the wind "harvesting" potential at a premium, the house is enclosed with aluminum screen walls, creating a secure perimeter and a visually pleasing facade without blocking the breezes.

ABOVE RIGHT
Walls, overflow spout, and roof eaves protrude from the main walls to form a striking graphic pattern on the house exterior. The window overhangs are important in providing much-needed summer shade and a cooler internal temperature.

FOLLOWING PAGES
Entertainment areas are given prominence in the design, reflecting their importance in the owners' lifestyle. Careful placement of the house on the site allows all rooms to engage with the outdoor areas, the pool, and the tropical vegetation.

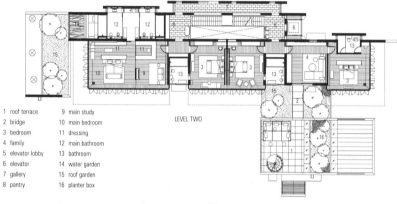

1	elevator
2	elevator lobby
3	gym
4	billiard room
5	gallery
6	roof
7	roof terrace
8	store
9	pantry
10	bathroom
11	bridge

ATTIC

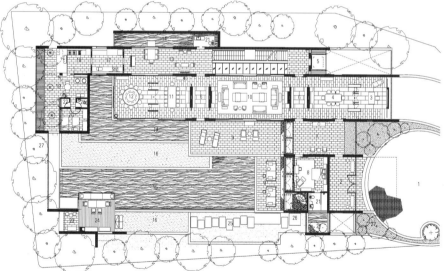

1	roof terrace	9	main study
2	bridge	10	main bedroom
3	bedroom	11	dressing
4	family	12	main bathroom
5	elevator lobby	13	bathroom
6	elevator	14	water garden
7	gallery	15	roof garden
8	pantry	16	planter box

LEVEL TWO

LEVEL ONE

1	port-cochere	15	swimming pool
2	entry	16	lawn
3	study	17	dry kitchen
4	meeting	18	wet kitchen
5	elevator	19	utility
6	passage	20	maid
7	foyer	21	bath
8	guest room	22	shower
9	terrace	23	barbecue
10	living	24	pavilion
11	Western dining	25	stepping stones
12	Chinese dining	26	outdoor shower
13	gallery	27	garden
14	water gallery		

N

BASEMENT LEVEL

1	garage
2	garden
3	reflection pool
4	pool pump
5	store
6	household shelter
7	powder room
8	shoe rack
9	entry
10	elevator
11	elevator lobby
12	wine dining
13	wine cellar

ABOVE
Looking across the water gallery from the Chinese dining area toward the pavilion and swimming pool. A "layering" of spaces creates an understated opulence, and emphasizes the connection between the interior and the surrounding gardens.

RIGHT
A wall of windows maximizes the views. They open out fully, providing minimal barrier to the light breezes. Translucent fine aluminum mesh affords privacy without impeding the dappled light that filters through from the tropical gardens.

LEFT
The entrance screen was created using angled, vertical aluminum panes, which repeats the wind deflection strategy integrated into the house design but on a micro scale. Behind the screen, the entrance features a sky-lit cast-concrete mural by Australian artist, Bruce Reynolds. The mural weaves together Chinese symbolic icons, family memories, and local elements.

ABOVE
The interior openings link the areas between the deflector walls. A series of aligned doors allows the breeze to flow through the house from one room to another – spaces are connected by staircases and a glass-floored bridge.

Chapter 10
Outer
City

Despite the commute and the influence of neighboring properties, a home on the city fringe has both rural serenity and access to urban amenity.

A short drive past the city limits, turn off the highway onto a quiet road and approach a house partially concealed from view by tall trees. This is the perfect setting for a home on the city fringe, and it has the best of both worlds – an urban lifestyle within a rural setting.

The city fringe is an area of transition between the city and the country, with many of the homes built on large blocks of remnant farmland, or virgin land. Homes here generally have a relatively large footprint and are more aesthetically diverse compared with their generic cousins in the sprawling subdivisions nearby. While the city is close, it is not immediately accessible, and this semi-rural setting still requires home design to loosely fit within the existing context.

ACCESSIBILITY

Appealing to a variety of lifestyles, the outer city home's location takes advantage of both rural and urban environments, although neither area is instantly available. As a result, there is a lot of time spent away from the home, both for work and play.

Reliance on the car is a key feature in the design of houses in the outer city. Arrival at the home is rarely on foot. The once proud and welcoming front door is often consigned to an inferior location, tucked behind a large garage that dominates the front of the house. And the garage houses more than a vehicle, it is frequently a storehouse of props for an array of outdoor activities.

SPACIOUS FOOTPRINT

A home on a subtsantial area of land has the luxury of a spacious footprint. However, the outer city location does not have the actual seclusion found in the rural setting, and the sense of space is limited by distinct property boundaries, and the possibility of being overlooked by neighbors.

Large interior spaces that are clearly defined are a design feature for this type of home. Specialist areas create a sense of privacy within the home – a playroom for children, or a parents' retreat.

A sizeable backyard is a feature of the outer city home's environment, and access to it is an essential element for the lifestyle of the homeowners. A private open area, the backyard may be an extension of the home's interior space, or simply the transition between internal and external space.

CONTEXTUAL INFLUENCE

The aesthetic diversity of the city fringe is not without limitations, and a home designed for this location is influenced by its context, and must complement the neighborhood.

A free-standing, detached dwelling is typical of the outer city location. The scale of the home and the type of building materials used, will ideally fit in with the proximate buildings. The aesthetic must also be sensitive to the surroundings – the home integrating with the texture of the landscape in which it is sited.

THE OUTER CITY HOME

This location gives the best of both worlds – a serene, semi-rural environment, but also one that is close enough to the city to take advantage of all that it has to offer.

ABOVE
Oshry Residence,
Studio Pali Fekete Architects
(SPF:a)

TOP RIGHT
Floating House,
Ngiom Partnership

OPPOSITE
Hill House,
Johnston Marklee & Associates

Amy Loh House SUNGEI BOLAH, MALAYSIA
Jimmy Lim (CSL Associates)

Constructed	2002
Home type	Multi-level home
Structure	Concrete frame with brick infill

"In architecture, nothing is more important than listening to the client and creating an environment for them that effortlessly caters to their needs and maximizes their happiness."

Jimmy Lim

ABOVE
The swimming pool is seen here extending from double doors. The area provides the occupants with an outdoor lounging and swimming area, with the gazebo (in partial view to the right) providing shade from the harsh tropical sun.

THE LOCATION

Amy Loh House is situated in a gated golf course community in the western suburbs of Kuala Lumpur.

Located along a narrow 8,000-sq-ft (750-sq-m) block on a steep incline that slopes away from the street, the home has been constructed diagonally across the site on a 45° axis due to the peculiarities of the site's topography. This axis increases the home's sense of space, resulting in a multi-level structure partially raised on stilts to minimize environmental impact and eliminate the need for the "cut and fill" approach so common in developments of this type.

OPEN SPACES

For this design the architect was interested in pursuing a theory of openness made possible by an absence of internal walls, thus creating vast, separate areas visually connected to one another. Large spaces such as the living room, the central focus of the house, are spanned by a network of beams, with massive columns that support the roof structure in the absence of internal walls.

The home's roof is a blend of traditionally spreading eaves and pitched terracotta tiles. Metal sheeting was also required to provide the curvature necessary to follow the unorthodox parabolic double axis that takes the Amy Loh house in two different directions.

NATURAL AIR-CONDITIONING

The home has no air-conditioning, instead relying upon air wells and cross-ventilation to encourage wind movement. The home's interior is lavishly decorated with carved doorways and high windows that permit rising warm air to escape, thus creating a natural flow and movement of air.

Decorative windows in the living areas use recycled stained glass from Indonesia and are framed in local Chengal hardwood, one of the densest species of timber and highly resistant to white ants.

The main bedroom is situated near to an outdoor swimming pool on the upper level that is accessed through sliding doors. Water from the pool cascades through a void to the ground floor between the downstairs living and dining rooms and into a reflecting pool.

TOP LEFT
Pitched roofs with spreading eaves and white plaster-rendered exteriors are a Jimmy Lim signature, both effective means of temperature control in the harsh tropical climate.

TOP RIGHT
Recycled stained glass from Indonesia provides an ornamental touch to this side panel in the home's lobby. Timber is a practical building element in the tropics due to its ability to absorb and dissipate heat without transferring it to the interior.

ABOVE
The rich color of the Chengal hardwood combined with the intricate patterning of the window design create an ever-changing interplay of light and shade in the living area.

Beau Constance CAPE TOWN, SOUTH AFRICA
Metropolis

Construction	2003–2004
Home type	Two level, free-standing residence
Structure	Steel and concrete

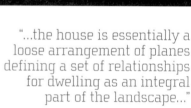

> "...the house is essentially a loose arrangement of planes defining a set of relationships for dwelling as an integral part of the landscape..."
>
> Jon Jacobson

ABOVE
Architecturally speaking, Beau Constance is a collection of cubic forms made up of individual planes, which are nestled into a wild and mountainous landscape.

ABOVE RIGHT
Walls of glass in the living room connect the main home to a variety of outside entertainment areas for different seasonal use. Wrap-around timber slats provide sun-control and a sense of enclosure.

Beau Constance is located in a rural strip between leafy suburban Constantia and the rugged slopes of the Vlakkenberg mountains. A newly developed wine farm, it enjoys an unspoilt natural setting, with spectacular views of the Cape Peninsula below, and pristine forested mountain slopes all around.

The design of Beau Constance was developed so as not to compromise the unique site, while at the same time departing from the solid white walls and pitched roofs of traditional Cape wineland architecture. In its place, the architects pursued an architecture of generous voids, floating horizontal planes, and natural materials that would completely merge with its surroundings.

THE RESIDENCE

The residence and its associated spa pavilion are sited on an elongated platform tucked into a fold in the steep mountainside, completely isolated from surrounding neighbors. The house does not have a specific orientation. It was conceived as a filter through which the landscape could enter from all directions.

The accommodation is therefore organized around a system of outdoor courtyards, simultaneously shaping and being shaped by the building. The courtyards allow shelter from strong southeasterly winds in summer, allow views from all parts of the building, and create an unimpeded flow of space from inside to outside.

SEPARATE SCULPTURAL ELEMENTS

The house touches lightly on the landscape. It is arranged into two "boxes," formed by floating concrete flat roofs and turned-down timber screen walls. All the elements of the house — suspended floors, stairs, and external and internal walls, are expressed as separate sculptural elements, floating in a loose composition, under the "sheltering sky" of the overarching forms.

The accommodation is organized into three interlocking volumes, with services in one single-story block, the double-volume kitchen/dining/family room in another, and the living room, study, and bedrooms in a third slightly higher block, with an underground wine cellar and entertainment area beneath.

The farm folds itself around a natural gully, incorporating rolling vineyards on its lower slopes, and a steep craggy mountainside higher up.

ABOVE
The house hovers above the ground plane, flowing through to the landscape beyond.

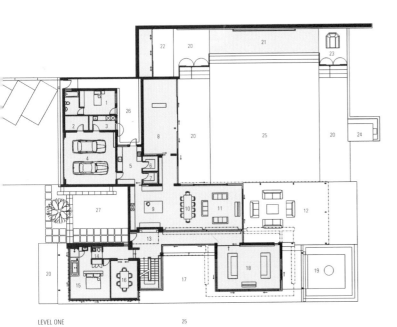

LEVEL ONE

LEVEL TWO

1 staff quarters	6 pantry	11 family	16 study	21 pool	26 courtyard	31 bedroom
2 office	7 cold room	12 north terrace	17 east terrace	22 pool seating	27 entrance court	32 bathroom
3 utility	8 playroom	13 entry	18 living	23 jacuzzi	28 main bedroom	33 TV room
4 garage	9 kitchen	14 guest WC	19 outside seating	24 barbecue	29 main bathroom	
5 scullery	10 dining	15 guest suite	20 deck	25 lawn	30 bedroom	

ABOVE
Transparency and volume allow an easy flow of inside-outside space in all directions.

OPPOSITE
A continuous membrane of glass under a concrete canopy emphasizes the experience of the sweeping views beyond.

Entry is from the south into a formal courtyard. An axial movement spine from the front door to the north patio defines circulation on both levels, and structures a progressive series of views of the landscape. The living level is designed for regular entertainment and an extroverted outdoor lifestyle.

By contrast, the bedrooms are entirely private. They float over the living level in a self-contained "capsule" linked to the central volume by narrow slot windows. They are less "bed rooms" and more shelves in the landscape. The ensuite has been recast as a sculptural object within the space of the main bedroom, which responds to the necessities and pleasures of bathing.

UNION OF ARCHITECTURE AND NATURE

Structurally, the house is essentially a series of thin concrete slabs, supported on slim steel columns, and stabilized by a number of free-standing concrete walls and columns. The lightness and delicacy of the structure contributes to the lack of materiality required by the architectural concept.

Materials themselves are chosen for their resonance with the colors of the site: stone, raw concrete, and sun-bleached balau.

At Beau Constance, shelter and enclosure have been reduced to an essence, to create a union between architecture and nature. It is simultaneously about making place and about finding a place in the landscape.

RIGHT
Stone, timber, and off-shutter concrete are the primary materials, integrating the home with the color tones and textures of the surrounding landscape. A separate recreational building, containing the spa, shown here, demonstrates the beauty and functionality of these materials.

FOLLOWING PAGES
The physical and conceptual center of the house is the double-volume kitchen/dining/family room, from which courtyards and living spaces radiate in all directions. It is at once the farm kitchen, the center of family life, and the "center of the landscape" – a vantage point from which the entire farm and its surrounding context can be experienced and appreciated. The focus of the kitchen is the framed view of the summit of the Vlakkenberg.

Belmont House CALIFORNIA, USA
Hariri & Hariri - Architecture

Construction	1999–2002
Home type	Single family residence
Structure	Concrete and lightweight steel frame

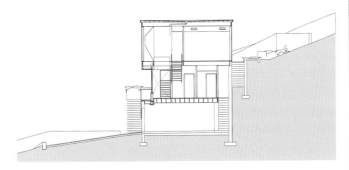

"What is expressed here is this paradoxical human desire to be part of the new and the old, the heavy and the light, the earth and the sky, the rooted and the mobile simultaneously."

Gisue Hariri

CREATING A HYBRID

This deceptively simple house is built straight into a hill in Belmont, near San Francisco. The New York architects wanted to explore the synthesis between the two dominant types of architecture in the region, namely the mobile-trailer home and the Mexican pueblo style of housing. The owners, who work in Silicon Valley, are a young couple with a child, and are representative of the new demographic that is emerging in the area.

To gain access to the house, the visitor follows a curved concrete retaining wall that edges the long driveway up to the entry. Concrete steps lead to the mid-entry level, where a long veranda with a blue stucco wall leads to the extra-large rusted steel front door – a dramatic statement in the overall design. This takes the visitor into the entrance hall, where a sculptural staircase invites one to the upper main floor.

PUEBLO INFLUENCES

The Mexican pueblo influence is evident in the lower level of the house, the heavy, stuccoed concrete walls providing texture, color, and warmth. The east side of the house contains the entry and gallery area, while the generously sized children's area sits on the west side.

The upper level of the home contains the main bedroom and ensuite at one end, with open loft living at the other. This part of the house contains the open-plan living room, dining area, and kitchen, a library in the center, and a home office at the other end. All these spaces open to a terrace and hillside at the back of the house.

TOP RIGHT
The rectangular volume of the upper floors floats over its solid concrete base, as if ready to "move on." A series of concrete steps takes one from the driveway to the mid-entry level.

RIGHT
Reminiscent of Mexican pueblo architecture, the heavy blue stucco walls ground the structure, anchoring the seemingly lightweight metal-wrapped upper floors.

OPPOSITE
Inspired equally by the iconic mobile-trailer home and Mexican pueblo architecture, the home is an expression of the old and the new, the heavy and the light. A curved concrete retaining wall directs the way uphill into the driveway.

MOBILE-HOME INFLUENCES

The influence of the mobile-trailer home can be seen in the upper level of the house, which is a large rectangular volume wrapped in metal sitting atop a solid base. It appears to hover over the lower level. Natural light and cross-ventilation come from the large openings in this rectangle, which also allow sweeping views of both the hill and valley.

SUCCESSFUL MERGING OF STYLES

The architects saw the marriage of the two styles as an expression of the human desire to be part of the new and the old, the heavy and the light – it is something of a paradox to be rooted to the ground and yet presenting a "mobile" vision.

One of the considerations the architects took into account was a comment by the editor of the *New York Times*, Blaine Harden, who said, "The American house has been swelling for decades. It has swollen even though a smaller family lives in it. Even the hulking and ostentatious suburban McMansion is bulking up, as mega-houses pop up across the United States."

Belmont House attempts to reverse this trend and show that "less is more." What is important to these architects is to connect to the culture and landscape that one builds on. In their opinion, to be original one has to understand and interpret the architecture of both the old and the new.

TOP LEFT
The interplay of old and new, evident in Belmont House's exterior, enters the interior of the home, with the aged steel door giving way to a stark and sculptural staircase.

CENTER
The oversized rusted steel door creates a dramatic entrance door, pivoting into the entrance hall. Its obvious weight and strength are in sharp contrast to the sparse decoration and lightweight fixtures beyond.

ABOVE
The airy main upper level contains the living, dining, and kitchen areas, as well as a library at the center, and the main bedroom and home-office at either end. All open onto a terrace and hillside views.

LOWER LEVEL

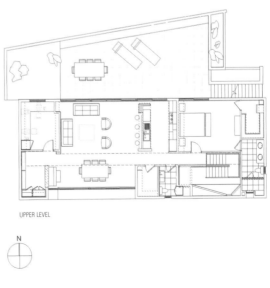

UPPER LEVEL

N

Benedict Canyon Residence CALIFORNIA, USA
Griffin Enright Architects

Constructed	2005
Home type	Single-dwelling contemporary house
Structure	Single-level concrete slab floor, wood, and steel frame

"The orchestration of both natural and artificial light creates ever-changing lighting conditions throughout the day, while the reflective quality of the floor and ceiling creates a dynamic spatial condition, blurring inside and out and up and down."

Griffin Enright Architects

TOP RIGHT
The exploded view of the home shows the interrelationship between the light boxes, the skylight, and the interior areas and view beyond.

ABOVE
The family room and living room, both with expansive views of the garden, are separated by a floating shelf. Steel columns hold and support the birch veneer timber divider that functions as an attractive book or display case.

A MODERNIST RENOVATION

For the extensive renovation of this 2,600-sq-ft (240-sq-m) mid-century house on a hillside site in Los Angeles, the client desired a transformation to make the house more true to the spirit of its Modernist origins, including bringing more natural light inside and exploiting and extending the dazzling views of the canyon setting and its indigenous wildlife.

A portion of the original gabled roof was replaced with an extended plane of the same angle, yielding a continuous upwardly sweeping surface. This new roof element was folded up and after replacing a stucco wall with a 50-ft (15-m) wide wall of glass, the rear facade became a large glazed surface that opened up the house. From the inside, there are now unobstructed views of the landscape and pool, and from the outside, the house is completely transparent in daylight and transforms into a glowing box in the dark.

INFUSING SPACES WITH LIGHT

In the interior, nearly all of the existing finishes were demolished and four interior walls were eliminated to create open, airy, light-infused public spaces. Within the new loft-like space, discrete functional areas are defined through changes in the ceiling, placement of furniture, custom-designed built-ins, and lighting. For example, a custom piece was designed – made of wood and supported by steel columns – that appears to float between the living area and den, and functions as both a bookcase and room divider. Similarly, a custom-made, cherry-veneered and stainless steel island defines the kitchen.

A FOCUS ON THE CEILING

The ceiling became a significant component of the overall design. It was designed to slope with a plywood panel system housing seemingly randomly placed track light fixtures. This system is punctuated by the intersection of two light boxes and a skylight. The light boxes are composed of resin panels with imbedded sea grass, creating a soft, glowing, filtered lighting effect. The light boxes are oriented to provide visual connections to the entry and the backyard. In an analogous fashion, the long, narrow skylight is positioned to mirror the main circulation of the house, casting striking patterns of shadows.

FINE FINISHING

To give visual interest to the floor, the concrete was stained and finished with an epoxy resin that has an almost liquid quality. The sloping ceiling, reflective surfaces, and the play of light and shadow make the space dynamic and full of energy, blurring distinctions between floor and ceiling and interior and exterior.

TOP RIGHT
The view from the rear of the house creates a somewhat voyeuristic feeling about the glazed wall, sitting, as it does, against the clear pool reflection. The nearly transparent rear wall is visually extended by its mirror image in the water; a design feature recognized by Venetian architects for hundreds of years.

RIGHT
A view from the centrally located living area looking up to the intersecting skylight and light boxes. The uplifting effect is achieved by literally raising the roof. This juxtaposition of the natural environment (the sky) with materials that incorporate nature underscores the desire to blend exterior and interior.

1 entry   8 bedroom
2 dining   9 garage
3 living   10 bedroom
4 family   11 WC
5 kitchen   12 main bedroom
6 bathroom   13 main bathroom
7 bedroom

CH House BARCELONA, SPAIN

BAAS Jordi Badia/Mercé Sangenís

Constructed	2000
Home type	Two-story family home
Structure	Concrete walls, metallic pillars

"The house was conceived as a small matchbox gently dropped on the grass, closed on the southern side because of the close proximity of the neighbors, and open on the northern side where the garden is wider."

BAAS Jordi Badia/Mercé Sangenís

ABOVE
The kitchen protrudes from the northern side, providing a "window" to this part of the garden. This side of the house is relatively closed as it is overlooked by a neighboring property. The use of white concrete and wood inside and outside creates a unified theme.

TOP RIGHT
The living areas of the house are one large space connected on a diagonal section. The interior of the house is organized around an internal patio that separates the living spaces from the children's and guest bedrooms, illuminating the interior and controlling the temperature.

INDIVIDUAL STYLE AND FORM

La Garriga is a popular holiday destination, located close to Barcelona, between the plain of the Vallès and the foothills of Montseny Mountain.

CH House is situated on a trapezoid-shaped block of land and can be accessed from two streets, each on a different level. The main entry is on the upper level while the other sits on the lower level, along with the garage and swimming pool. The inside of the house is arranged around two major spaces that are clearly delineated, according to their function.

The exterior of the house makes a strong individual statement, which is somewhat out of context with the neighborhood. Constructed in white concrete and wood, CH House resembles a rectangular box neatly placed on the site. This provides privacy without compromising the volume of the interior.

THE CENTRAL NUCLEUS

With its small courtyard, the entry is the focal point of the interior. Leading off from this area are the children's and guest bedrooms, positioned along the eastern facade. The rest of the house has been designed as a single space, with strategically placed furniture creating three separate spaces, all of which open out to the western facade.

The living room is part of the central space and close to the entry, while the dining room adjoins the living room and the kitchen. The stairs lead to the top floor of the house, their layout strengthening the axis that crosses the dwelling over much of its length.

PRIVATE SPACES

The bedrooms are hidden behind a slatted wall. An interior courtyard flows through an anteroom to the children's bedrooms, and the guest room is quite separate from the private family areas.

The main bedroom opens out to the house's western facade and the dressing room leads to the interior courtyard. The ensuite is primarily timber, with natural light provided by a skylight in the shower area. The walls of the ensuite blend with the garden and have been placed at an angle to both provide privacy and admit filtered light to the entry.

EXCITING EXTERIORS

The back street entrance functions as an outdoor foyer or porch. From this point, visitors enter the house by walking along an interior cobbled path to the interior courtyard, which is paved to complement the rest of the streetscape. The intoxicating perfumes of a lemon tree and lavender permeate the interior of the house.

LEVEL ONE

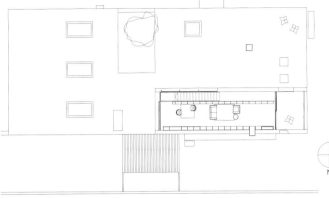

LEVEL TWO

N

LEFT
Both the children's and guest bedrooms are behind a wooden slatted wall, which protects this part of the house from noise while lending it some privacy.

FAR LEFT
The open stairway acts as an axis running east–west, allowing views of the whole house. Open shelving on the upper level to the right of the stairway doubles as a low wall or partition.

ABOVE
The house was conceived as a small matchbox that has been gently dropped on the grass. It is closed on the lateral side to provide privacy from the neighboring property but open where the garden is deeper.

Cliff House CAPE TOWN, SOUTH AFRICA
Van der Merwe Miszewski Architects

Construction	1999–2001
Home type	Three-level family home
Structure	Concrete frame with glass infill panels; timber and lightweight steel frame decks and timber shutters

> "The site is heavily wooded with poplars and pines that are common to the area, and it has spectacular views toward Table Mountain, the city, and the sea."
>
> Van der Merwe Miszewski Architects

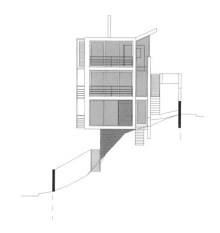

RESPECTING THE LAND

Cliff House is built on a long narrow site that is 45 ft (14 m) wide by 228 ft (70 m) long. Located in a heavily wooded area in a suburb of Cape Town, it has panoramic views toward Table Mountain, the cityscape, and the ocean. Two considerations early in the design process were to maximize access to the views and to retain as many of the trees on the site as possible in order to provide privacy, noise reduction, and protection from the sun.

The architects were asked to come up with a design that accommodated the usual living spaces – living room, dining room, kitchen, three bedrooms, bathrooms, and a study area – as well as a self-contained flat that could be used for visitors or staff, plenty of storage space, and a double garage.

The site configuration influenced the form of the house, a rectangular building sitting parallel to the natural contours of the land. This approach reduced the need for extensive excavation. There is a strong reference to nature in the design, as the modular arrangement admits plenty of light and ventilation, even to the lower parts of the house.

CLIFFTOP VIEWS TO THE SEA

In the middle of the three levels, the main entrance to the house leads directly into the living and dining areas. These are bound by a terrace that extends the living area to the outside and immediately draws the

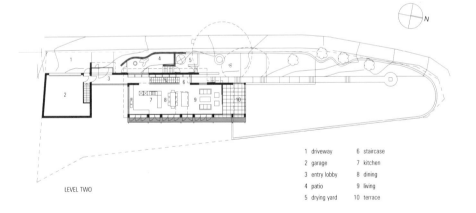

eye to the ocean views. A fireplace in the center of this area warms the house. This level also contains the garage as well as private access to the flat and laundry below.

A suspended staircase connects this level to the bedrooms and bathrooms on the one below, and to the upper level, which contains the study, the study terrace, and the rooftop terrace, all of which boast fine views of the mountains and the sea. The location of the stair allows uninterrupted views through the "view-facing" facades.

LAYERED AND SURPRISING

The northwestern facade is a solid wall with strategically placed openings that afford particular views, such as to the mountains. There are also doors leading to the garage and main entry. The northeastern facade is primarily a gallery structure, and timber decks provide protection from the sun in the hottest part of the day. The timber and supporting lightweight steel frame structure were chosen to contrast with the concrete finish on the rest of the house, and to give it a warm, textured ambience. The window shutters are also timber.

A central entry court, planted with native and exotic plants, is set in the middle of the rectangle of the house. The overall impression is that the home has a number of layers that provide the visitor with a variety of experiences.

LEVEL TWO

1	driveway	6	staircase
2	garage	7	kitchen
3	entry lobby	8	dining
4	patio	9	living
5	drying yard	10	terrace

FAR LEFT
The western facade shows the main entrance on the middle level. Pivoting timber screens control the amount of sunlight to the study on the upper level, while the roof slab tilts up along its western and southern edges to allow extensive views toward Table Mountain.

TOP LEFT
In contrast to the western facade, the eastern facade comprises an elevated and modulated concrete grid structure. Timber shutters screen the in-fill glazing, and a lightweight steel and timber balcony echoes the primary structural grid.

ABOVE
On the middle level, the kitchen can be seen beyond the living room. Sliding doors to the left open onto the east-facing balconies with their views toward the city and the sea. The stairs to the right link this level with the study above and the bedrooms below.

Exploded House BODRUM, TURKEY

GAD-Gokhan Avcioglu NEW YORK, USA

Constructed	2005
Home type	Three-story family house
Structure	Glass, steel, concrete, and local natural stone

"The house successfully reflects GAD Architecture's working principles, which are sustainability, eco-friendliness, and micro-climate. This project is also very successful in terms of combining geographical and local conditions with today's contemporary technology."

GAD Architecture

TOP
The natural cooling system for the house consists of a pool on the roof of the main building. Rainwater collects here, then cascades onto the next roof before being recirculated.

ABOVE
On the southeastern side of the house are the study, the unit on the left, and the main bedroom, on the right. A glass atrium connects these two separate buildings.

HISTORIC SETTING

Bodrum is a Mediterranean port and trade settlement in the southwest of Turkey. The area boasts a rich 3,000-year history, which includes the Hellenistic, Roman, and Ottoman periods. The venerated scientist Heredot was born here, and sculptures by renowned artists such as Leochares, Bryaxis, and Timotheos were once exhibited here. These works are now held in museum collections around the world.

METAPHOR FOR A SINGLE BUILDING

The owners have a vast antique collection reflecting the rich history of the area. They wanted a home that would complement and display their collection without making them feel as if they were living in a museum.

The local outdated building codes restricted new forms of architecture being introduced. To overcome this and to create a more flexible building type, the architects created a house with three separate buildings linked by a glass atrium – a metaphor for a single building that has been "exploded" into many parts.

Each unit, which complies with the regulation size of 800 sq ft (75 sq m), has a separate function. There is a main bedroom and ensuite; a kitchen and dining room; and a guesthouse with an adjacent study.

The central glass atrium has a dual function – it is the entry to the building as well as the main living area. Floor to ceiling windows allow 180° vistas of the stunning landscape and bay.

The electronically operated windows in the living room slide open flush to the ground, allowing sea breezes to cool the interior. This innermost space is the focal point of the home, and is connected to the three separate buildings or units by a series of concrete ramps that reconcile the building with the landscape.

The living and dining rooms look out onto the sun deck and swimming pool. From here, the ramp leads down the hillside to a guest unit (an additional self-contained apartment), which is nestled in the landscape and hidden from the house above.

PART OF THE LANDSCAPE

The open plan of the main house ensures that it is light and airy, a must in summer. As a secondary precaution, the roof of the building is covered with pools that collect rainwater. The water cascades from one roof to another and then recirculates, thus creating a natural cooling system for a hot climate.

The "Exploded House" harmonizes with the natural environment. When observed from above, the pools mirror the surrounding landscape and the panoramic views of the bay, helping to mask the presence of the building on the hill.

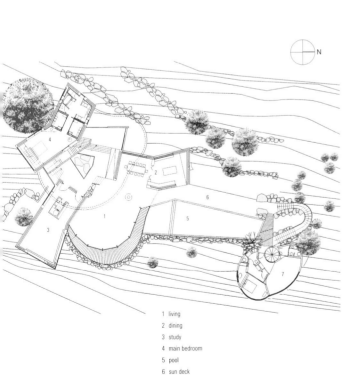

1 living
2 dining
3 study
4 main bedroom
5 pool
6 sun deck
7 guest unit

TOP
The home comprises three separate buildings, each with a separate function. The kitchen and dining room unit, seen here, look out over the swimming pool and sun deck. The structure itself forms a low-profile against the rising rocky terrain behind.

ABOVE
The neutral color palette of the living room, together with the indoor garden, and rough-texture, natural finishes, connect the interior with the sun-bleached terrain outside, at the same time providing the perfect backdrop for the owners' art collection.

Floating House SUNGAI BULOH, MALAYSIA
Ngiom Partnership

Constructed	2005
Home type	Two-level family home
Structure	Concrete, glass, and aluminum

FRONT

> "Water – and the floating qualities it possesses – was the inspiration for this dramatic home. The ambience of Floating House is completely determined by the overriding motif of water."
>
> Teng-Ngiom Lim

A "FLOATING" HOUSE

Sierramas, a gated community in Sungai Buloh, about 12 miles (20 km) from Kuala Lumpur, is the site for this dramatic house. Situated on the edge of a cliff, the house appears to float on water. It is this dazzling point of reference that dominates the overall impression of the structure.

MELDING OUTSIDE AND INSIDE

The formal responses to the setting are complemented by both lyrical and metaphysical responses, and the surrounding environment is integrated into the design of the house. The walls have been purposefully designed with a transparent quality, to make the boundaries between the inside and the outside appear somewhat ephemeral. The architect sees this as a desirable facet of the home. As the trees and other plants reach maturity, the distinction between exterior and interior spaces will be reduced further, uniting the built environment with the natural surroundings.

This blurring of boundaries between outside and inside is again accentuated when the glass louvers are opened. As the outside world enters the house, the sound of water quite naturally becomes integral to the inside spaces. Water is an important element of the design – it unites the house with the landscape.

ABOVE
The understated front of the house is expressed only by a carport and a water tower. Light streams through glass panels in the carport roof, separating it from the main house, and flooding the back wall in light. The water tower anchors the carport to the main house.

TOP RIGHT
The pathways along the side of the house leading to the main entrance mirror each other in form and structure; the one on the right, steps over water, and launches the "floating house".

OPPOSITE
The house floats over a pool of water and over the edge of the cliff, pointing toward the horizon. While the rest of the house is open and accessible, the balcony is private, and can be reached only from the bedrooms, ensuring that it remains a secluded retreat.

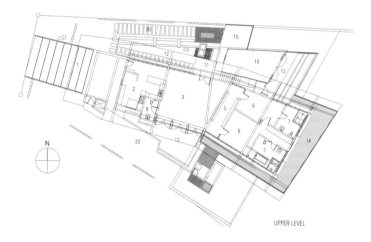

UPPER LEVEL

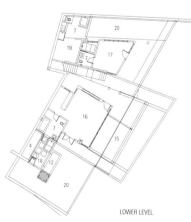

LOWER LEVEL

1 carport
2 kitchen
3 main hall
4 services
5 library
6 main bedroom
7 bathroom
8 bedroom
9 WC
10 dining
11 entry
12 water feature
13 pool
14 balcony
15 terrace
16 guest bedroom
17 maid's room
18 outdoor shower
19 laundry
20 garden

WATER IS THE KEY

The owner's love for water is expressed in the style of the bathrooms. On the ground floor, they are located in areas with the highest ceilings, and the walls are glazed almost from floor to ceiling, washing the rooms with natural light during the day. To accentuate the invitation of light, the main bathroom has an additional skylight. Part of the bathroom is extended over the main pool, so that glass, light, and water come together through their fluidity, lightness, and visual permeability.

Each of the larger bedrooms is visibly connected to a distinct water body – the main bedroom flows out to the main pool, and the second bedroom on the ground floor is linked to a water feature. The ground floor main bedroom is connected to both a garden and water feature. The various pools create a tranquil environment throughout the home, bringing the external environment inside.

The kitchen, too, looks out on water. The room has its own skylight, connecting the blue of the water with the blue of the sky, creating a serene indoor/outdoor flow.

The terrace on the ground floor faces the back of the slope and is accessible only from the bedrooms, connecting this part of the house to the environment.

The roof of the carport is joined to the main building by a row of glass panels that allow natural light to wash the back wall. The carport itself is a single thin concrete slab anchored by the water tower.

FAR TOP LEFT
The principal part of the house and deck floats over the lower garden. The edge of the main pool is visible in the foreground.

TOP RIGHT
The home's tapering walls result in a large roof overhang, which effectively shades the interior – a decided asset in a tropical climate. The deck looks back toward the main pool.

TOP LEFT
The main bathroom is spacious and well lit. A combination of light, glass, glazed tiles, and water makes the bathroom a liquid and sensual place.

RIGHT
The walls have a transparent quality, blurring the boundary between inside and outside, The interplay between glass, light, and water creates an ambience of cool serenity.

Heise House SYDNEY, AUSTRALIA
Peter Downes Designs

Completed	2002
Home type	Single family dwelling
Structure	Steel and timber

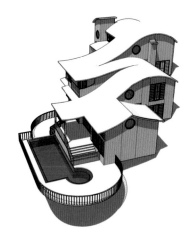

"I have a deep and lifelong love of the Australian landscape, and one of the ways I express this emotion is by designing houses on unspoilt bush sites. And the challenge becomes even more interesting when the site is steep, as the design inevitably becomes a three-dimensional exercise. So this project for me is close to being perfect."

Peter Downes

ABOVE
This computer image shows the swooping and diving roof lines of the house as it cascades down the steep site. The articulated plan shape meant that many of the significant trees on the original site were retained.

LEFT
The convoluted roof lines produced many geometrically interesting ceiling shapes, highlighted by the use of bold, contrasting colors throughout the home. Australian hardwoods were used extensively to capture the bush spirit.

TOP RIGHT
Exposed steel was used as a design element to emphasize the curved roof lines, and to visually link the indoors and outdoors. Multifold doors connect the family room to the covered outdoor entertaining area, which leads to the lower level deck and pool via wide timber stairs.

FAR RIGHT
Nestled amongst the gum trees, and perched on the edge of the precipitous slope, the modest entry gives little hint of the size of the structure below.

BUSH RETREAT

The owners needed a large family home to accommodate their three daughters and one son, with sufficient living spaces to help preserve a sense of order. The family includes several musicians, so space was needed in the living area for a grand piano. The house was also to take maximum advantage of the uninterrupted bush views from as many of the rooms as possible, to provide a respite from the owners' busy professional lives.

Because the house is located on a steep block with no usable outdoor areas, the owners wanted a pool surrounded by large decks, all connected to the living areas. And they also wanted something unique.

DESIGN SOLUTIONS

Twenty minutes drive from the Sydney CBD, the site was 360 sq ft (4,000 sq m) of indigenous forest in Beecroft, with a fall of 52 ft (16 m) – the equivalent of five stories – over the building area. The clients had already had a previous unsympathetic design rejected by the local council and were anxious to get it right the second time around.

The first step in the design process was to identify all the significant trees, and then to try to fit a house between them. A zigzag outline was sketched up that saved all but one tree, and at the same time produced

a sunny northeast aspect for the house, as well as uninterrupted bush views from all the living areas and the main bedroom.

Three main floor levels were needed to compensate for the slope and to provide sufficient floor space (some 4,000 sq ft [360 sq m] in total), with the lowest (living) level further split by a 3-ft (1-m) drop, and then another 3-ft (1-m) drop to the pool and associated decks.

The top level contains the garage, a large utility room, and the entry. The middle level contains all the bedrooms while all three separate living areas are on the lowest level.

The main living areas open via multifold doors onto a covered entertaining deck, with wide steps leading to the pool decks.

CURVES AND SWOOPS

The swooping, curved rooflines ensured compliance with the overall height limit, while disguising the bulk and scale of the building as it steps down the site. An additional benefit of the curved rooflines was varied and interesting ceiling geometry, artfully highlighted by bold color selections.

Lightweight construction with minimum excavation was chosen as the most cost effective and environmentally friendly building methodology.

Further interest was added to the design by mixing painted weatherboards and corrugated steel cladding, both with vertical shadow lines to complement the design.

LIGHT AND PRIVACY

The use of obscure glass and glass bricks solved potential privacy issues for some of the secondary rooms that look out on adjoining dwellings. Skylights and carefully positioned highlight windows bathe the interior with natural light and provide views of the tree canopy and sky.

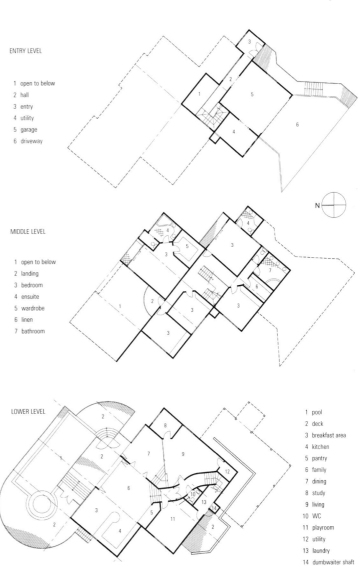

ENTRY LEVEL

1 open to below
2 hall
3 entry
4 utility
5 garage
6 driveway

N

MIDDLE LEVEL

1 open to below
2 landing
3 bedroom
4 ensuite
5 wardrobe
6 linen
7 bathroom

LOWER LEVEL

1 pool
2 deck
3 breakfast area
4 kitchen
5 pantry
6 family
7 dining
8 study
9 living
10 WC
11 playroom
12 utility
13 laundry
14 dumbwaiter shaft

Hill House CALIFORNIA, USA
Johnston Marklee and Associates

Constructed	2004
Home type	Three-level, single-family home
Structure	Concrete, steel, and timber

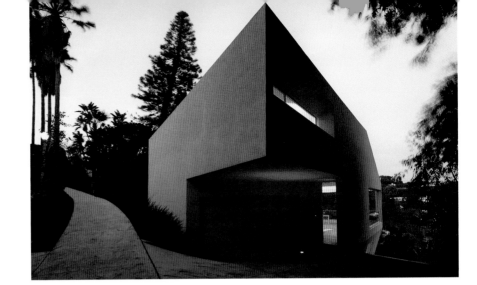

The site is an irregular-shaped block of land on a sloping hillside that has sweeping views across Rustic and Sullivan canyons to Santa Monica Bay. Local planning authorities have placed stringent restrictions on hillside construction so that the natural terrain is not compromised. The architects of Hill House used these restrictions to advantage, by incorporating them into the design and blending the house into the hillside.

PUSHING THE ENVELOPE

The fixed zoning envelope was the basis for the design, and the architect compressed the home's individual components into specific patterns. Non-structural walls and partitions were kept to a minimum. The upper level contains a semi-private loft space; the lower level contains the main bedroom, and between these two levels sits the central living and dining spaces. The levels are connected by a steel and glass staircase. The walls and ceiling of the interior have been shaped to emphasize the geometric feel of the house. They also double as storage spaces.

WONDERFUL WINDOWS

The windows have been strategically installed to get the most from views, and to allow plenty of light and air circulation. The lie of the land, with its impressive views of the canyon and ocean in three directions, means that the rear of the house actually appears as if it were the front. Sliding glass doors merge the inside with the outside. The windows to the bedrooms are recessed, permitting views to the outside, but preventing outsiders from looking in. Skylights have been placed both in the flat and sloped roofs, and create a three-dimensional ambience.

PICTURE PERFECT MATERIALS

The elastomeric cement exterior coating gives the house a continuity with its surroundings, as the roof and walls appear as a unified expression. The lavender color was inspired by the color of the bark of local eucalyptus trees and serves to merge the house with the landscape. As the day lengthens, the light changes and creates an interplay with the colors of the spectrum. Inside the house, polished Carrara marble and glossy countertops contribute to a seamless feeling. Coupled with the enameled steel and lacquered wood finishes, and the dark walnut flooring and cabinetry, the effect is complete.

Native California grasses have been planted in the garden, softening the slope. These are counterbalanced with dramatic succulent plants, well suited to the temperate climate of California.

STURDINESS AND STRENGTH

The home's challenging location demanded a strong assembly and the architects chose concrete, steel, and timber as their major construction materials. Nine 35 ft (10.5 m) deep, reinforced concrete piles form the foundation for the house; these are held together by a system of grade beams. From the foundation, the concrete walls are set at a slope, rather than vertically. A steel frame comes out of the concrete base to create the central core of the house and the cantilevered overhang at the home's entrance.

TOP LEFT AND ABOVE
Three-dimensional models illustrate the different requirements of the Hillside Zoning Ordinance as applied to the site to generate the maximum allowable building volume.

LEFT
The geometric shape of the house, as seen from across Santa Monica Canyon, is the zoning ordinance made visible on the hillside, with each inflection of the mass registering the topographic nuances of the site. The resulting sculptural design seamlessly engages with the surrounding site.

TOP
To express the continuity of the building skin and to minimize the conventional distinctions between roof and wall planes, an elastomeric cement exterior coating material was used. Oversized openings, which are oriented away from the street in favor of canyon and ocean views, puncture through the seamless skin.

ABOVE
The inclined walls rise perpendicularly from the grade instead of vertically, giving the house the figure of a "prevented fall" against the landscape.

TOP LEFT
Clerestory windows above the bookshelves draw light into the study from a skylight above, which brings direct light into the mezzanine-level bathroom and closet.

TOP RIGHT
The placement of a skylight window on the sloped roof further blurs the conventional differentiation between roof and wall. Indirect light sources and unanticipated views from these openings further enhance the three-dimensional quality of the space.

ABOVE
An open floor plan, high ceilings, and lofted upper level allow for dramatic views and natural light to be experienced throughout the house. With few interior partitions, the living spaces are flexible and able to accommodate contemporary lifestyles.

Public and private living areas are arranged within the fixed building envelope; thus the setbacks of the irregularly formed lot result in "shaped" living spaces.

1 entry
2 garage
3 living and dining
4 kitchen
5 library
6 bedroom
7 bathroom
8 study
9 sunroom
10 utility
11 main closet
12 main bedroom
13 main bathroom

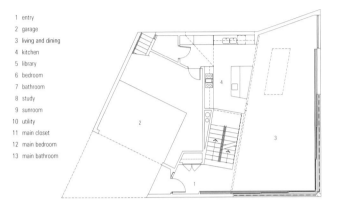

ENTRY LEVEL

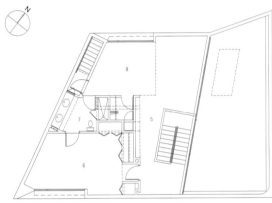

LOWER LEVEL

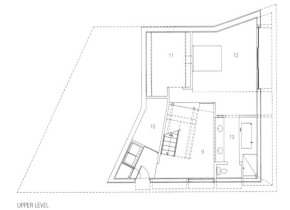

UPPER LEVEL

ABOVE
Light from the upper levels of the home cascades down the folded steel staircase into the sitting room of the more secluded main bedroom. The sculptural open staircase stitches together the three levels of the house.

Hofbauer House VIENNA, AUSTRIA
Pichler & Traupmann Architects

Construction	2000–2001
Home type	Three-story family home
Structure	Concrete slab floor and walls with steel columns

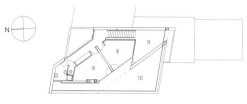

SECOND FLOOR

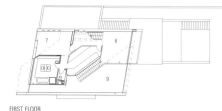

FIRST FLOOR

GROUND FLOOR

1	hall	6	library/study
2	office	7	main bedroom
3	garage	8	bedroom
4	living	9	open to below
5	dining	10	terrace

"Not only should space be capable of flowing from the inside out and the outside in, the spatial shell should also awaken from its autonomous state and architecturally merge inside and out in an analogous, flowing gesture. In addition, we go beyond classical Modernisms, 'Platonic solids,' and structural homogeneity in the direction of dynamic duality."

Pichler & Traupmann

A CITY SUBURB

In the northern part of Vienna-Floridsdorf, between the Old Danube (an old, cut-off branch of the river used as a recreational area) and the "New" Danube (a popular bathing place built as flood protection), there has been a dramatic increase in the price of building sites over recent years. This is one of the few remaining urban areas with loosely scattered single-family housing developments that lies close to the city center. Two nearby underground railway lines connect it to the rest of the city and surrounding urban areas.

Building only started in this area in the 1920s. It had once been a gravel bank, also serving for a time as a garbage tip. As no large-scale housing complexes had been built here, a plot size of about 10,800 sq ft (1,000 sq m) – the standard elsewhere – developed, and the permitted built area was set at 1,600 sq ft (150 sq m). This is the most common house size, and it is much in demand.

FLOWING SPACES

The clients' brief for a family home required the architects to maximize the area of the house, so a multilevel design utilizing various volumes was the solution.

An indoor pool and garage are at basement and ground floor level, automatically raising the living and private spaces. Typical of Pichler & Traupmann's design strategy is the diagonal axis at the center of the house, formed by staircases that open up broad views of the city. For example, the nearby Donauturm (Danube Tower), the symbol of the district, can be clearly seen from the upper levels.

The two-story living hall is linked with the upper levels by a library/study on the landing. That work area also functions as a kind of punctuation mark, leading to the bedrooms on the upper floors.

On several sides of the house, exterior platforms have been built, so as to link the internal spaces with the outdoor environment.

"FOLDED" SURFACES

Viennese building regulations allow for a certain leeway. For instance, the permitted height of eaves can be exceeded in some parts of the building as long as other parts are below the permitted height. The architects exploited this regulation by creating a complex composition.

The signature of the architects is the interlocking of various volumes. Within the house, it can be seen in the continuous surface that is "folded" back and forth a number of times – from wall to ceiling and back – creating a sense of continuity inside and out.

The architects have consistently used white render, metal sheeting, slate, and wood to give the house a harmonious but defined look.

FAR LEFT
The diagonal flight of wooden stairs links the two-story living hall with the double-height library/study above. The stairs also bridge the gap between the white plastered structural walls and the wooden lining.

ABOVE
This night view shows the spatial concept of the design: two intertwined double-story volumes are wrapped by a continuously "folded" surface. The furnishings and fittings lend the house a sleek, minimalist look.

TOP
The spaces are layered so that the floor of the library/study hovers above the dining area. White plaster has been used for the main surfaces, wood for the secondary elements, and gray paint for the structural elements.

ABOVE
The pool area was devised as a Modernist interpretation of a wellspring in a cave. Slate has been used on the walls and floor to connect the pool to the earth. Light shines only from the pool and floors, creating a warm and seductive ambience.

House and Atelier Lang-Kröll BAVARIA, GERMANY
Florian Nagler Architekten

Construction	2000–2002
Home type	Family residence with atelier
Structure	Two-story, timber construction on a basement of fairfaced concrete cladding; polycarbonate elements

"Our philosophy is to concentrate our attention on the project's local conditions – topography, urban structure, and social environment – and to unite function, construction, and design. Moreover, on this project the very small budget was an important criterion, which influenced our design."

Florian Nagler

TOP
The view from the northern side of the house shows the town of Gleissenberg in the distance. The house nestles into the hillside so that the entrance to the upper level is at ground level.

ABOVE
The southern side shows the home's traditional shape, which helps it to harmonize with the neighborhood. The large studio window on the upper level provides scenic views.

HOME AND STUDIO IN ONE

Gabriele Lang-Kröll and Peter Lang wanted to build a house for themselves and their four children near Cham, a small town in Bavaria, in a transition area between the Bavarian and the Bohemian forests. An artist who mainly works with large-sized woodcuts, Lang required a studio that could accommodate both a painting area and some machines for printing. On the one hand the project was determined by the small budget, on the other by both the clients and the public authority's open-minded attitude toward architecture.

PREFABRICATED UNITS

The house was built in a more or less marginal development area on the outskirts of Gleissenberg. Such is the form of the roof and the position of the house that it fits in with the neighboring buildings.

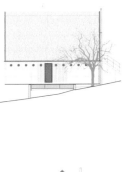

LEFT
Here the house is shown from
the southwestern side. The
sheltered entrance is nestled
under a deep overhang and
flanked by stacks of firewood,
which is used to heat the house
in winter.

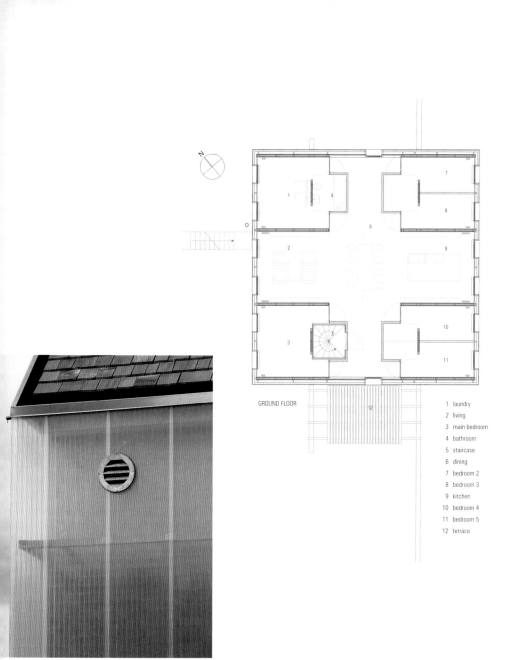

GROUND FLOOR

1 laundry
2 living
3 main bedroom
4 bathroom
5 staircase
6 dining
7 bedroom 2
8 bedroom 3
9 kitchen
10 bedroom 4
11 bedroom 5
12 terrace

ABOVE
A detail of the transparent double-wall facade, featuring the polycarbonate cladding and one of the ventilation holes, which are left open in the warmer months and closed during winter.

The timber construction stands on a basement, formed by two walls of fairfaced concrete that run parallel to the contour lines. Assembled from 14 prefabricated floor and wall units of different sizes, the house is a maximum size of 13½ x 41 feet (4.1 x 12.48 m). The overhang is created by beams that form walls in the ground floor. The floor units bear on these walls and are bolted together. Some short walls above the concrete walls in the basement take over the cross-bracing.

MAXIMIZING SPACES

The entrance, heating installation, and a workshop are located in the basement. The area is used as a roofed access, a carport, and storage area for firewood. The ground floor contains all the living areas. The studio is located in the first floor under the self-supporting roof.

The house has a neutral floor plan, so the young family can be flexible with their living space. One big room for the family is surrounded by several small rooms.

NATURAL LIGHT AND VENTILATION

A transparent double-wall facade creates a bright atmosphere both in the living area and in the light-flooded studio, so there is no need for artificial light in the daytime. The space between the inner and outer facade can be turned from summer to winter mode by simply covering the ventilation holes.

SIMPLE MATERIALS, STYLISH RESULT

The ceiling is made of rough fir wood, and all the cladding is made of polycarbonate, so there is no timber left exposed to the weather.

The clapboard roof and the simple connector system for the polycarbonate elements allowed the owners to participate in the building process. With the help of friends, the couple mounted the roof covering and the cladding. Moreover, Gabriele Lang-Kröll, who is a carpenter, built the wooden spiral staircase according to the architect's plans.

LEFT
The family's living space is a flexible area that can be changed over time to suit the growing family's needs. One of the ventilation holes can be seen in the transparent wall behind the dining area.

ABOVE
The top floor of the house contains Peter Lang's studio, which faces north and overlooks a picturesque view. Filled with natural light, it has its own entrance through a sliding glass door.

House of Courts TEXAS, USA

Lake | Flato Architects

Constructed   1997
Home type   Suburban villa
Structure   One-story steel frame with limestone walls and metal roofs

"The goal was to create a private haven that was friendly to the owner's art collection. We pushed the buildings to the outer edges of the lot, creating three internal courtyards. The stone walls are the defining element. They are about creating space internally rather than making a connection to the site."

Lake | Flato Architects

ABOVE
The house turns its back to the street and focuses inward toward the courtyards. The front door is reached by following a path that zigzags between large rough-cut boulders.

LEFT
A steel and glass gallery wraps around the perimeter of the primary courtyard, creating the transition from indoors to outdoors. White oak floors are banded with Colorado sandstone. The ceilings are exposed, acoustic-metal decking.

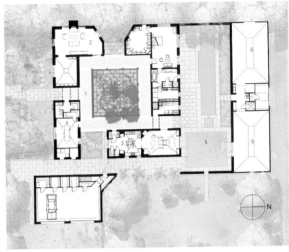

1 gallery   4 dining
2 living   5 pool courtyard
3 kitchen   6 studio

ART FOR ART'S SAKE

The architects were asked to design a house that would accommodate the impressive art collection of the owner. They took some inspiration from the essential simplicity of Texan architecture, seen in the warehouses, missions, and early stone houses that are part of the Texan landscape. The house is located in a "well-to-do suburb" populated with spacious homes, and the idea was to create an unassuming haven in the midst of the surrounding affluence.

The house is 12,580 sq ft (1,169 sq m) and has three internal courtyards, one of which has a pool. The center of the house – a large hall with high clerestory windows – contains the bulk of the owner's art collection. In the middle of this is a sculpture courtyard measuring 30 sq ft (2.8 sq m). Metal-and-glass windows and doors create a spacious gallery feeling.

PODS FOR PRIVACY

At the corners of the house sit the private and functional spaces – the bedrooms, living and dining areas, a study, and a kitchen. There is a careful delineation between the public and private areas. The private areas, called "pods" by the architect, resemble small pavilions. The wide doorways lead directly to the courtyards and garden, almost bringing nature inside the house. A row of oak trees provides shade in the courtyard garden.

PROTECTION FROM THE SUN

The roofs are metal, and those on the "pods" are topped with shaded glass lanterns that reduce the effects of the sun. This was an intentional move in order to protect the works of art from the sun, while simultaneously showing them to advantage. In the gallery area, the windows are tinted glass, filtering the potentially damaging ultraviolet rays from works by artists as varied as Picasso and de Kooning.

Another consideration in the design was ventilation. All the doors and windows open fully and breezeways are created by the positioning of the courtyards. This is critical in the hot climate of San Antonio.

STONE FOR SOLIDITY

The facade of the house is constructed of large slabs of local limestone, called "Old Yella," cut by local masons into 3 ft (90 cm) blocks and interwoven with Texan gray stone. Entry is through a recessed door built into a low wall at the front of the home. Internal walls are clad with limestone, and the floors are white oak banded in Colorado sandstone, which offers a warm contrast to the preponderance of stone in the house.

DECORATING WITH FLAIR

The high ceilings gave the owner more freedom in choosing the interior design and furnishings. Installation art sits comfortably with tall dressers and large antique candlesticks. The house, both inside and outside, is a statement of individuality in a suburban locale.

TOP LEFT
A pool courtyard separates the main house from the studio, grounded by its heavy limestone walls but lightened by the steel, lantern-like roofs that float above.

ABOVE
This rooftop view illustrates the concept of separate pods for separate functions, such as living, dining, and sleeping.

House on Blue Jay Way LOS ANGELES, USA
Studio Pali Fekete architects (SPF:a)

Construction	2002–2004
Home type	Single dwelling
Structure	Four-level steel and glass structure with teak plywood skin on top level

"This house is very special to me. You feel as if you are floating in space...a great sensation. You also get to feel the connection with all levels of the home at one time. It was quite a task to get it just right – building on a 45° angle isn't that simple, but the end result made it all worthwhile."

Zoltan E. Pali

NORTHEAST PERSPECTIVE

RENOVATING WITH VISION

Although technically a renovation project, only the foundation of the original Blue Jay Way house remains standing in this West Hollywood architectural icon. Although he is known for his spectacular historic preservation work, architect Zoltan Pali found nothing in the home's original design worth preserving. However, in order to maintain city entitlements on the land from the 1980s, the new design had to maintain some of the existing structure or it would lose up to half its height and size. The solution, which maintains the exact footprint of the original house for legal reasons, actually increased the square footage by almost 20 percent. As is often the case, constraints provided a catalyst for a uniquely beautiful architectural solution.

EXPANDING HORIZONS

The existing structure was inefficient and unsuccessful architecturally, minimizing rather than maximizing the home's greatest asset – its extravagant 180° views. New building and safety requirements enforced after the 1994 Northridge earthquake made it easier to

maintain the appearance of remodeling, under the pretext of shoring up the foundation. In actuality, however, the architect replaced the original design with an entirely new structure.

"INSERTING" SPACE AND CREATING LEVELS

Perched on a steep, nearly 45° grade, the house appears to be a three-level structure from the street. Were it possible to approach from the rear, however, one would see four distinct levels, jutting vertically from the slope. Without increasing the building envelope, a lower floor was created in the unique 20-ft (6-m) tall "crawlspace," which had existed underneath the floor of the original home due to the steep hillside. The architect dug underneath the house to "insert" the extra level of living space, in much the same way that architects in New York insert pocket theaters into historic building envelopes.

The homeowner enters a three-car garage on the second level, and once inside is greeted by a narrow, 22-ft (6.7-m) long window at car's eye level. Guests enter through the outer gate, serenaded by a water

TOP FAR LEFT
Initial elevation drawings put the "Miesian box" on the canyon side of the home, but building requirements and future design revisions moved the glass-walled sitting room to the opposite side of the home, where it doubles as a canopy for the home's entry door.

ABOVE
Sun sets over the home's private pool area. The pool is equipped with extra features, such as color LED lighting and special fountain elements to enhance the ambience.

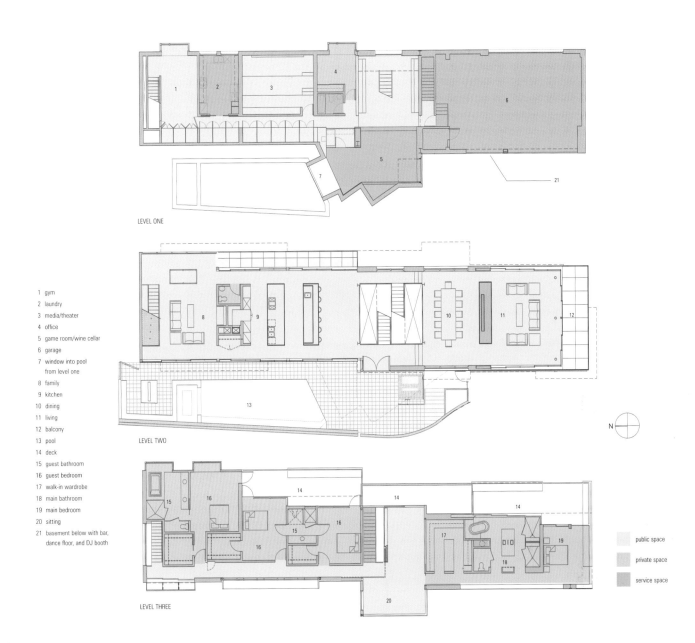

LEVEL ONE

1 gym
2 laundry
3 media/theater
4 office
5 game room/wine cellar
6 garage
7 window into pool
   from level one
8 family
9 kitchen
10 dining
11 living
12 balcony
13 pool
14 deck
15 guest bathroom
16 guest bedroom
17 walk-in wardrobe
18 main bathroom
19 main bedroom
20 sitting
21 basement below with bar,
   dance floor, and DJ booth

LEVEL TWO

N

LEVEL THREE

public space

private space

service space

feature that doubles as a privacy screen to the game room on the second floor. Guests ascend an outer stair past the 42-ft (12.8-m) fountain/swimming pool and enter the home on a clean, transparent level surrounded by glass. The long glass plinth cuts horizontally through the building's mass at the center, offering the home's public areas — living, dining, and kitchen — the most open view and floor plan. The main elements are located centrally and low to the walnut floor so that the views to the outside are not impeded.

A PLACE FOR WORK AND PLAY

The main floor's circulation plan flows around the perimeter, promoting changing vistas and connection with the outdoors as one moves freely between living room, dining room, and kitchen. A limestone water feature doubles as a bench and provides low separation between living and dining areas. Below, two concrete levels house entertainment and work spaces, including a media/home theater room with

LEFT
The kitchen has two island benches, helping to provide unbroken visual contact between the dining and living areas.

FAR LEFT
An imposing main stairwell connects all levels of the house and assists in creating the illusion of higher ceilings.

All four bedrooms open to an east-facing terrace to enjoy the radiant Los Angeles sunshine, predictable for most of the year.

stadium seating, glass-ceiling wine cellar (visible through the floor of the kitchen), pool table lounge, exercise room with windows overlooking the canyon, laundry room, and home office. The entire structure revolves around a generously cut 16-ft (4.8-m) main stairwell, making the home's standard ceiling heights feel higher and lighter.

THE HEIGHT OF HOME ENTERTAINMENT

Descending lower into the hillside, along a wood-paneled interior stair, one is transported to another place and time. A seductive 800-sq-ft (74-sq-m) night club with full bar offers guests all the pleasures of the Sunset Strip without the cover charge or drive down the hill. The lounge is equipped with a dual turntable DJ mix station and top-of-the-line sound system. Clad in teak wall panels of varying size and grain orientation, the lounge's rounded mirrors and white leather sofas efficiently transport the visitor to Soho in the 1970s. A mirrored ball, colored lights, and fog machine complete the mood, and a smoking terrace showcases breathtaking views of the Los Angeles basin at night.

MAXIMIZING VISTAS

The home's living quarters sit on the highest level, offering respite from ambient sound and vistas that seem to touch the sky above. The architect clad the upper residential level of the home in warm teak plywood panels. A main suite sits directly above the living room, sharing equally magnificent 180° vistas through 4-ft (1.2-m) high windows visible from the bed. Only steps from the bedside, a sitting lounge eases the journey to wakefulness with Barcelona chairs and a window-side view for morning coffee and a glance at the morning paper. A flat screen television inconspicuously awaits those who prefer "broadcast" news, mounted flush with the western wall and invisible to those who enter the room.

TRANSPARENT DESIGN, SUBTLE RESULT

Behind the master bed, a transparent shower "partitions" the bedroom from its luxurious bathroom, featuring limestone floors, an "overflow" bath, two pedestal sinks and an oversized walk-in wardrobe with two separate entry doors. A toilet and bidet are tucked away behind blue translucent glass.

A PLACE IN THE SUN

Three other bedrooms occupy the home's teak level, one with its own bathroom, the other two sharing a Jack-and-Jill style bathroom. All four bedrooms open to a shared east-facing terrace to enjoy the radiant Los Angeles sunshine, predictable for most of the year. The terrace is minimally landscaped with native plants and lined with a comfortable, cushioned bench for lounging. West of the bedrooms, a long and narrow eye-level window spans the entire entry corridor.

Perforating the smooth, marine-grade teak on the upper level, a Miesian steel-and-glass reading room juts out over the front entry, paying tribute to the legendary Modernist, while also offering western sun to the main suite, and conveniently providing shelter over the home's front entry.

ABOVE
Upon entry into the home, visitors are immediately greeted by expansive views across the Los Angeles basin.

LEFT
A long, low limestone water feature creates an elegant and understated separation between the dining area and living room.

FAR LEFT
The bed in the main suite faces the home's most spectacular views. A glass shower behind the bed separates the sleeping area from the main bathroom.

House X1 SUNGAI BULOH, MALAYSIA
Ngiom Partnership

Constructed	2003
Home type	Five-level, single-family residence
Structure	Steel, concrete, and glass

"Site terrains often have poetic
values and provide limits
within which the architect
must work. Other constraints
include budgets and planning
authorities. The architect
naturally must always have a
design agenda, and in the case
of House X1, this is related to
both spatial and formal qualities,
as well as a certain lyricism,
all the while mindful of the
restrictions imposed by site
conditions and climate."

Teng-Ngiom Lim

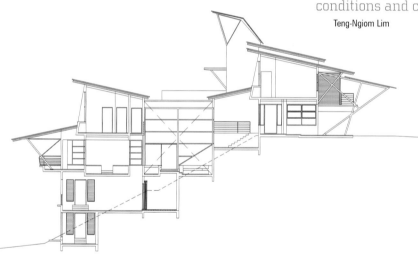

STEEP SITE CHALLENGES

Sungai Buloh is located about 12 miles (20 km) from Kuala Lumpur. The steep site, with an incline of 29°, was densely vegetated and had a small brook running across it. The house was purposely orientated toward the back of the site because it afforded the best views over the vegetation and beyond. This posed some difficulties, however, particularly as the site was quite narrow and flared at the back.

The architect wanted to keep the house as close to the slope as possible. To achieve this, a central courtyard breaks the house into two distinct parts. The courtyard space, conceived as a cubic void, is the link with all parts of the house. There is a visual link between the top and bottom of the slope, and a spatial link, which allows the passage of air to travel from the bottom to the top of the house. This breeze-way is emphasized by the formation of a wind shaft, which terminates at the rooftop.

MAXIMIZING TERRAIN

The line of slope of the site dictated the planes of the house, which slowly open and flare out toward the back. The lower part of the house is set into the incline, and so it maintains an even temperature. The upper part of the house sits on top, giving the effect of a minimal barrier between the interior and exterior. Prominent roof overhangs help to moderate temperatures.

TOP
The turret at the top of the house holds the water tank, which is warmed by the sun's rays. The turret also functions as a wind funnel, discharging rising warm air from the main house. Access to the observation deck is underneath the turret.

ABOVE
The street elevation is on the cliff's edge and possesses an austere simplicity. The main spaces of the house open toward the woods at the back. The slender struts supporting the roof echo the tall bamboos flourishing along the sides of the house.

The slope of the site dictates
the various planes of the house,
which closely follow the same
orientation. The spaces that are
sandwiched between the line of
the roof and the line of the land
flare open toward the back.

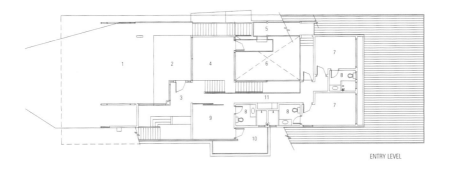

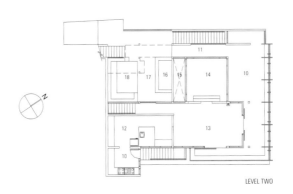

ENTRY LEVEL

LEVEL TWO

1 carport
2 entrance
3 foyer
4 family
5 bridge
6 void over courtyard
7 bedroom
8 bathroom
9 study
10 terrace
11 gallery
12 kitchen
13 dining
14 living
15 open to below
16 water feature
17 courtyard
18 sunken sitting area

USING LYRICISM

The architect considered the notion of lyricism in his design – something that is achieved when space, form, and materials react favorably with the light. He believes that architecture is successful when the climatic conditions are also taken into account. The natural landscape plays an important role – in fact, it should be considered as integral to the project. In House X1, the interior and the landscape blend, the walls becoming a transparent skin, blurring the visual barrier between the outside and inside spaces.

THE HOUSE AS ART

The architect believes that architecture should be a work of art. The canvas consists of the materials used; the backdrop is the surrounding landscape. The quality of light is a major criterion upon which art is judged – and so it is with architecture. Light also accentuates the natural qualities of solids, voids, and other textural spaces. Where light is soft and gentle, then space takes over; where light is weak, space takes on a dreamlike ambience. There is no internal decoration – the house is considered a work of art in itself. It also interacts with the natural environment – the wind, the rain, the sunlight. The sculptural poetry of the dwelling depends on the quality of light, so the house is kept white – a badge of purity and sincerity.

SIGNIFICANT FORM AND FUNCTION

Form is a critical element of the design, with the abstract preferred to the ordinary. Any deviation comes from the requirements of function, once again, emanating from the essence of natural light.

FAR LEFT
The house is visually connected throughout, with minimal barriers between the internal and external spaces. The courtyard, with its lush garden, is located in the middle of the house – this central location allows shafts of light to penetrate and illuminate all internal areas.

LEFT
Bathed in light throughout the day, the staircase leads to the bedrooms. The act of moving up and down through the light has a lyrical quality to it. The bench at the foot of the stairs is crafted from black-pigmented concrete and is yet another area to sit and contemplate the changing patterns of light during the day.

ABOVE
Viewed from the upper entrance, the house has an obvious synergy, with no distinguishable barrier between the various internal spaces and the external environment. The bridge integrates the inside with the outside; the courtyard brings the outside to the inside.

Jayasundere House COLOMBO, SRI LANKA
Varuna de Silva

Constructed	2001
Home type	Three-level family home
Structure	Brick, concrete, steel, glass, and timber

"The house is located just outside Colombo's inner city limits, in a densely populated urban setting, sandwiched between two houses. The challenge was to maximize the available space yet provide comfort and functionality."

Varuna de Silva

WHEN SIZE MATTERS

Small plot sizes are common in Colombo, so house design must always take this into account. Measuring 25 x 94 ft (7.5 x 28.5 m) and facing a busy street, Jayasundere House is located in a narrow side garden belonging to the client's parents' home. The house is built to the boundaries in front and on either side, but local regulations insist that a rear space be left open to the sky: This space has become the garden.

TRADITIONAL BUT CONTEMPORARY

The clients wanted a comfortable but unconventional three-bedroom home with separate work areas.

Because of the narrowness of the site, the architect was inspired by the traditional Sri Lankan courtyard house, so the middle of this house was opened to the sky in the traditional manner to admit plenty of natural light and ventilation. This design has the added benefit of keeping the house cool, a critical factor in this hot tropical location.

By keeping partition walls to a minimum, the house seems larger than it is, and the interior spaces flow into one another. Light materials were used in the design of the stairs to maintain this fluid ambience.

On the ground level, the office, storeroom, and powder room have walls. All the other spaces flow into one another and also open out into the garden, thus blurring the division between outside and inside.

LIGHT AND MOVEMENT

The husband's home office is connected to the carport, which is part of the house. The central triple-height void, which opens to the sky, provides light and air. A reflecting pool between the office and the living areas provides a quiet serenity in the middle of the house.

The owners love to entertain, so the kitchen area was placed in the center of the living and dining rooms. The reflecting pool is on one side, the veranda on the other, and the garden sits beyond.

UP ON THE ROOF

On level two, there is a family area and main bedroom with walk-in dressing room and ensuite. The two other bedrooms share a bathroom. The main bedroom and bathroom look over the garden; the other rooms, each with a timber mezzanine deck, look over the street.

Cantilevered concrete steps provide access to the roof terrace of the house. The wife's home office is also on the third level, with access to the roof terraces – an entertainment and play space.

SIMPLICITY AND STYLE

A cut and polished cement floor is just one of the basic finishes in the house. Aluminium French windows open to the garden and the roof terrace. The interior doors have been recycled from an old building. An orange-colored feature wall runs along the length of the house, providing a fascinating interplay of light and shadow as the day grows longer.

TOP LEFT

The shallow reflecting pool in the middle of the house acts as a buffer between the office and the living area, which includes the kitchen, and living and dining rooms. It also brings much needed light and ventilation into the long narrow plot. The glass walls to the garden beyond create a feeling of spaciousness.

ABOVE

The rear of the house becomes the "front," as it opens out to the mandatory rear space – the garden. The orange wall, which runs along the length of the house, ends with the double-height veranda outside the living room, complementing the "greenness" of the garden.

TOP

A steep steel checker plate and C purlin (roof beam) "ladder" provides access to the mezzanine deck.

TOP RIGHT

The middle of the house becomes its "heart," where the whole structure opens out vertically. The top is protected from the weather by a steel and glass roof, and the thin steel grilles and handrails make the building seem lighter.

1 study
2 main bedroom
3 family lounge
4 bedroom 2
5 bedroom 3
6 kitchen
7 living & dining
8 office
9 garage
10 veranda
11 open to below
12 garden
13 reflecting pool
14 open-air terrace

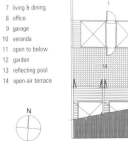

ROOF TERRACE

LEVEL TWO

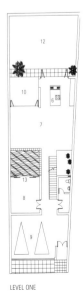

LEVEL ONE

The Mews VALLETTA, MALTA
Architecture Project

Construction	1994–1998
Home type	Four single-family residences
Structure	Stone-clad concrete frame base with load-bearing masonry above

> "The project sought to fuse the current Maltese preference for the detached villa and garden with the vernacular, cubic, Mediterranean-village farmhouse structure to create an updated idiom for the suburban residence. The villas were arranged to promote opportunities for social interaction through an array of private, semi-private, and public spaces; these external spaces becoming the fulcrum of the complex."
>
> **Architecture Project**

A CLUSTER OF UNITS

"The Mews" in Kappara, a charming suburb of Malta's capital city Valletta, is a condominium consisting of four homes located on a corner suburban site. The units are clustered around a spacious, central courtyard. This shared courtyard area is elevated above street level in order to accommodate a lower level of private parking – a cool, well-ventilated undercroft.

COMBINING TRADITIONAL FORMS WITH MODERN IDEAS

The project takes its cue from the Mediterranean *ortus clauses*, meaning "closed garden," and the local vernacular dwelling type – the two-story, Maltese-village farmhouse, with its solid external facades and central courtyard. The built fabric has been organized to create a balance between solid and void, and light and shade. The result is a natural equilibrium, where outside and inside merge without ever losing their definition. While the cubic massing echoes the local style, the solid podium walls are suggestive of Malta's historic fortifications.

The raised ground floor is dedicated to landscaping, with the central courtyard acting as the first in a series of threshold spaces that mediate between the street and the interiors of the homes. The main living spaces, in turn, lead out onto the surrounding private gardens. Each home has been designed as an extension of the central courtyard and the garden spaces creating a complex spatial and social environment – comprising private, semi-private, and public domains in a friendly, village-like setting.

The kitchen area, located in a corner of each unit, has been glazed in order to eliminate any feelings of enclosure and solidity – also providing a pleasant view from the kitchen out over the garden, which separates the homes from the perimeter wall.

WARM AND COOL AIR

Through the careful juxtaposition of open and closed spaces, the reservoir of cool air that accumulates in the sheltered court is evenly distributed throughout the four homes. Airflow occurs through slatted wooden openings, which were inspired by the traditional multi-layered Maltese windows with their practical louvered shutters. Warmer air, which rises unobstructed through the vertical voids within the homes themselves, is then extracted at the roof level.

PRIVATE SPACES

Each apartment has three bedrooms, the main with an ensuite. The homes extend from the lower parking level within the podium through to the family room and roof terraces. These are elevated above the surrounding suburbs to catch glimpses of Valletta and its beautiful harbors.

LEFT
The transition from the central courtyard to the staircase in each apartment is through a multi-layered door and screen. The white exterior walls with panels of blue mosaic tiles give The Mews a Mediterranean feel.

TOP RIGHT
Clean lines and simple interior finishes complement the light-filled homes. The timber finishes provide sophistication and warmth.

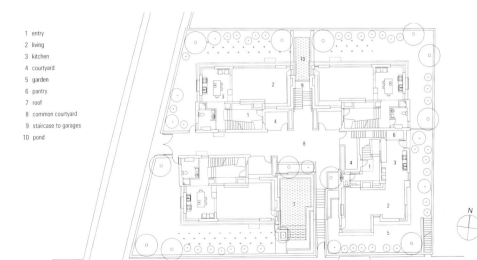

1 entry
2 living
3 kitchen
4 courtyard
5 garden
6 pantry
7 roof
8 common courtyard
9 staircase to garages
10 pond

The Mews apartments sit above street level, on top of a private parking area. The elevated dwellings enjoy glimpses of Valletta city and its surrounding harbors.

Mosewich House
BRITISH COLUMBIA, CANADA
D'Arcy Jones Design

Construction	2003–2004
Home type	Single-family dwelling
Structure	Wood-frame construction, finished in stucco

"This design expands on themes of asymmetry, continuity of form, and subtraction; the house's proportions were exaggerated and carved, transforming conventional wood frame construction into something substantial and dense. My preoccupation with section as a key determiner of how spaces feel is articulated through a range of interior and exterior spaces that are both simple and complex."

D'Arcy Jones

ABOVE
Glowing like a lantern in the trees, the house appears to be extruded from its rocky site. A muted stucco "brow" provides visual compression: a blunt form that exaggerates the fine linear detailing of the glass openings and scales down the height of the three-level house.

LEFT
Set back from the street, the house is nestled in a desert landscape. Shadowy window recesses protect the interior from the hot summer sun. A south-facing private courtyard is hinted at through five narrow slots in the wall.

VALLEY VIEWS, DEEP ROOTS

Perched on the edge of a steep slope in a natural setting, this pragmatic suburban home is surrounded by a variety of house types. Although formally different from the neighboring houses, the house is sensitive to the neighborhood's scale and materiality, while deferring to its immediate site and the desert landscape of the Thompson River valley.

Native vegetation was retained to provide a landscape buffer between the house and road — the front exterior is dotted with existing Ponderosa pines, sagebrush, and bunch-grass, in-filled with new indigenous plantings. To merge interior spaces with the landscape, a private courtyard unites the kitchen and dining areas. Intimate views of rock outcroppings contrast with long views to the river valley below.

STRONG MATERIALS

To meet budgetary constraints, no structural steel was used in the construction of the house. Rather, the house was built using conventional North American wood-frame construction, finished with conventional stucco. The structural capabilities of engineered lumber create the airy feel of the house, with its open spaces and generous overhangs.

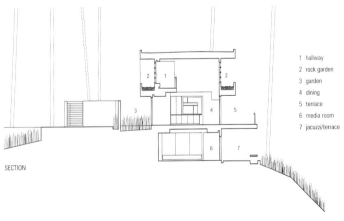

1 hallway
2 rock garden
3 garden
4 dining
5 terrace
6 media room
7 jacuzzi/terrace

SECTION

ABOVE
Overlooking the Thompson River valley at sunset, the muted stucco mass folds down to become an abstract floating plane. Separated from the dark mass of the chimney by transparent glass openings, it frames 270° views from the living area's corner windows.

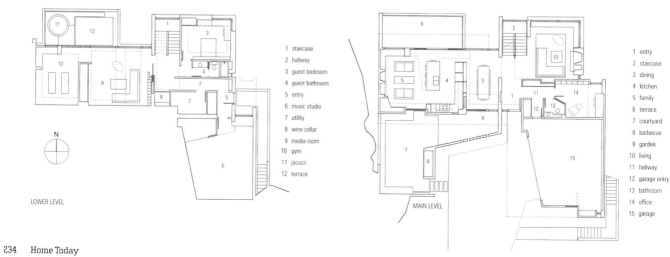

1 staircase
2 hallway
3 guest bedroom
4 guest bathroom
5 entry
6 music studio
7 utility
8 wine cellar
9 media room
10 gym
11 jacuzzi
12 terrace

N

LOWER LEVEL

1 entry
2 staircase
3 dining
4 kitchen
5 family
6 terrace
7 courtyard
8 barbecue
9 garden
10 living
11 hallway
12 garage entry
13 bathroom
14 office
15 garage

MAIN LEVEL

FAR LEFT
The double-height living area is dominated by a large chimney and open fireplace. The recessed stone panels mirror the rock outcroppings in the courtyard, while the chunky cherry mantle repeats the L-shaped asymmetry that occurs throughout the house.

TOP LEFT
A steel and maple staircase plunges through the core of the house, linking all three levels. The stairs' steel enclosure frames cropped internal views through the house, from the living area to the kitchen. A skylight over the stairs acts like a sundial through the day, constantly changing the steel mesh's level of transparency.

LEFT
The living area's mullions and floating stucco planes give human scale to a double-height space. The cherry storage ledge provides a sense of containment and security, to counter any feelings of vertigo.

INTERIOR VOIDS

The design and form of the house was primarily considered from the interior. A dark-tinted stucco mass grounds the house, visually linking courtyard walls, terraces, chimneys, and shear walls, thereby giving the impression of one continuous solid. In contrast is a muted stucco mass that wraps asymmetrically to frame panoramic views. Interior spaces are defined by modulating the voids between these two contrasting stucco masses. When the stucco masses extend inside the house, the threshold is defined with floor-to-ceiling glass, translucent in some locations for light and privacy. Windows were not considered as punched openings, but rather as voids between the two contrasting stucco masses.

SEEING AND HEARING

The clients are a young couple with two children. Upper level bedroom areas are separated for privacy with double-height dining and living areas, creating a voluminous central space naturally lit from the north and south. In the middle of this open space, a sculptural maple and steel staircase connects the home's three levels.

One of the clients is a drummer. A hidden feature of the lower level is a sound-proof recording studio tucked under the garage.

The client's comprehensive collection of Canadian art is strategically displayed throughout the home's circulation routes.

SHADE AND CONTRAST

Shade is provided by deep cantilevered overhangs. Cross-ventilation comes from carefully located operable windows, reducing reliance on air-conditioning. The largest glass openings in the house take advantage of north and east light, with the south-facing openings shaded from the strong summer sun. To keep the interior shaded during the hottest part of the day, the southwest walls of the house are blank.

The balance of dark and light, an abstraction of the immediate landscape, was realized by providing a small area of dark stucco in all the main living spaces, to reduce interior glare during hot summer days and foggy winters. This theme of contrast is carried to all the interior finishes; floors are maple and slate, with dark cherry built-in ledges functioning as storage chests and extra seating.

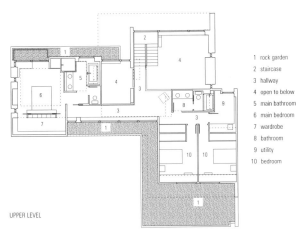

1 rock garden
2 staircase
3 hallway
4 open to below
5 main bathroom
6 main bedroom
7 wardrobe
8 bathroom
9 utility
10 bedroom

UPPER LEVEL

Oshry Residence CALIFORNIA, USA
Studio Pali Fekete architects (SPF:a)

Construction	2002–2004
Home type	Single-family dwelling
Structure	Concrete friction pile foundation, steel frame superstructure, plaster, glass, and limestone

"The glass bridge is more than a hallway – it is one of many places in the home that bid one a momentary pause, overlooking the profound beauty of the canyon."

Zoltan E. Pali

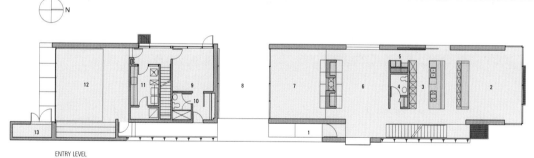

ENTRY LEVEL

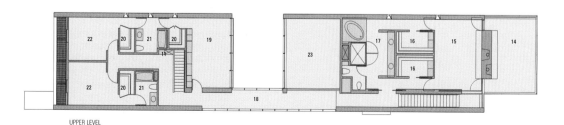

UPPER LEVEL

1 entry
2 family
3 kitchen
4 WC
5 pantry
6 dining
7 living
8 courtyard
9 maid
10 bathroom
11 utility
12 garage
13 storage
14 deck
15 main bedroom
16 walk-in wardrobe
17 main bathroom
18 bridge
19 study
20 closet
21 bathroom
22 bedroom
23 open to below

LEFT
On the outward side of the
home, the two volumes are
connected by a glass bridge
which overlooks a courtyard.
The eastern elevation is
shielded from direct sunlight
on the ground floor by a
series of limestone louvers.

ABOVE
A steep canyon below the
home's eastern elevation
provides a dramatic vista to
the entry corridor. The facade
is straightforwardly minimalist.

BEAUTIFUL, WHITE, MINIMALIST

The client's request was for a "white house" with minimalist beauty to be set on a narrow pad of land in the
upmarket Stone Canyon region of Bel Air, blessed with
spectacular views. The client, a designer by trade,
wanted the freedom to work from home periodically
without his workspace interfering with his home life.
Overall, the structure is designed to minimize the
geological impact (and hence the cost) of construction
on the precipitous site, while maximizing the variety of
views offered as one moves through the home.

A CHALLENGING SITE

Not only was the land a steep grade, the soil was not
suitable for residential development with a standard
foundation, so the structure needed to be rooted with
concrete friction piles dug 90 ft (27 m) below the
surface. The cost of this, and the challenge of staging

construction on a 45° grade, was a fundamental
aspect of the project's design. Strict zoning guidelines
for hillside lots, as well as the client's requirements,
created a tapestry of challenges that invigorated
Zoltan E. Pali, who sees architecture as the "art" of
solving such problems poetically.

BRIDGING CONNECTION

Organizing the home along a narrow floor plan and
incorporating an outdoor courtyard as livable space
minimized the number of foundation piles needed for
a sound structure; it also provided an answer to the
client's request for indoor/outdoor connection. The
design explores new expressions of transparency and
connectivity; two distinct volumes are connected by an
iconic glass bridge on the upper level with a central
courtyard on the ground floor. The layout juxtaposes
notions of private and public separation against this

indoor/outdoor connection. Traveling across the bridge from private to public living areas, floor-to-ceiling glass reveals exceptional views. The impact of direct sun is mitigated through a series of limestone louvers. These fixed white planes, spaced at intervals along the first floor, provide shading without obstructing views; they also cast shadow patterns throughout the day.

FINE-TUNING FOR COMFORT

Pali fine-tuned a plan to maximize both comfort and connection to the outdoors. Kitchen, dining, and sitting rooms face southeast, each space flowing into the next. Perched discreetly atop the kitchen and family room, the main suite and private terrace share a similar southeastern orientation. The kitchen's single rear wall is centrally placed and circulation around its perimeter leads to formal dining and living rooms.

The dining room is punctuated at its northwestern end by a long, narrow window, which frames the lush greenery of the backyard. The western edge of the living room backs up to a glass wall looking out to the central courtyard. The western volume contains a garage, two guest bedrooms, and the office. Canyon views can be enjoyed through the transparent bridge.

ABOVE
The minimalist wood-burning fireplace offers glowing evening warmth during winter and a clean, space-saving solution to fuel storage in the living room.

RIGHT
The striking glass bridge provides a dreamlike meeting space between the private and public areas. Windows across the bridge slide open to allow warmer air to escape during hot days.

ABOVE
A light-filled formal living room features double-height ceilings and a connection with the paved courtyard via sliding glass doors.

LEFT
The spacious main bathroom displays clean lines, minimal fuss-free finishes, and plenty of practical storage.

Pacaembu House SÃO PAULO, BRAZIL

Marcio Kogan Arquiteto

Construction	2003-2005
Home type	Two-level family home
Structure	Concrete and wood

> "With Pacaembu House, we aimed for the sort of architectural synthesis spoken of by the abstract painter Vassily Kandinsky in his studies on the relationship between movement and tension that exists in design. Each element in Pacaembu House adds to the clarity of the visual composition."
>
> Marcio Kogan & Gabriel Kogan

MODEL OF MODERNITY

Pacaembu House, named in honor of São Paulo's monument to football, Pacaembu Stadium, is the product of one of Brazil's leading lights of Modernism, Marcio Kogan.

Located in one of the city's most affluent neighborhoods, the home is an unashamed model of Modernity – its elongated box-like shape achieves visual synthesis through the architect's boldly sparing use of architectural elements.

The orderly instincts of the designer are expressed in his use of vast longitudinal concrete walls, which purposefully define the home's perimeters, provide security, and give form to its open living spaces.

The home's northern elevation is dominated by its double-fronted, white concrete facade, which ties the structure together, supporting the upper level and forming a false balcony for the bedrooms.

Although two-story, the exterior presents three horizontal layers. Concrete dominates the outer two layers with a middle recessed layer alternately glazed and lined with dark timber slats.

INTERPLAY OF MATERIALS

The living area extends onto a wooden deck in seamless transition.

Here, the dynamic between exterior and interior is that of a single space. From inside looking out, the color, texture, and design proportion of the perimeter wall form part of the interior decoration, playing in perfect harmony with the interior furnishings.

Similarly, the carefully positioned trees relate to the wall behind, as do sketchlines on a canvas, while at the same time their sketchy forms are in sharp contrast with two richly colored, sculpted chairs in the living room. The effect as a whole is that of looking at an abstract painting.

A pool lies between the wall and wooden deck and a pebbled garden extends from the eastern end of the deck, where more mature trees grow.

THE INTERIOR

The heart of Pacaembu House is its massive living room, decorated in the style of the 1950s with low-slung modular furniture and an elongated console along its southern wall.

A dining room, galley-style kitchen, and employee quarters complete the downstairs area, while upstairs the main bedroom and children's bedrooms, all with ensuites, face north with views into the courtyard.

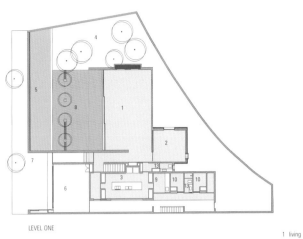

LEVEL ONE

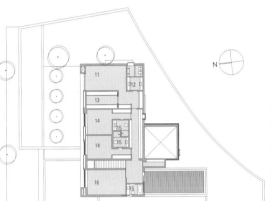

LEVEL TWO

1 living
2 dining
3 kitchen
4 garden
5 pool
6 garage
7 entry
8 deck
9 laundry
10 employee quarters
11 main bedroom
12 ensuite
13 dressing
14 bedroom
15 bathroom
16 TV room

N

TOP LEFT
The minimalist simplicity of the living room, with its low-slung console and modular furniture, is reinforced by the absence of internal partitions. The owners are able to indulge completely in the large expanse.

LEFT
An understated interplay of colors and textures. The deck and pool are nicely framed by the broad concrete overhang, which softens the transition between the indoor and outdoor spaces while also filtering light into the living room.

ABOVE
Nightfall brings a sense of intimacy and warmth. On the deck, the restrained, sensitive lighting illuminates the trees and draws the eye upward through the foliage.

FOLLOWING PAGES
Here the exterior deck and living room are seen as one complete whole – a clean, seamless union of indoor and outdoor spaces unencumbered by frames or columns. Despite the enormity of the space, it is completely private.

Rokko Housing I, II, and III
KOBE, JAPAN
Tadao Ando Architect and Associates

Construction	1981–2002
Home type	Nine-story low-rise apartment housing
Structure	Reinforced concrete

"The planning of Rokko Housing I began with a struggle over terrain and a dialogue with nature. In Rokko II this evolved into communicating more actively with nature, bringing nature inside the architecture. In Rokko III special attention was placed on the public spaces, which are the source of ventilation and lighting, and serve as devices to promote dialogues among people, and with nature. Through them I wished to express the wonderful richness and joy of living together."

Tadao Ando

ROKKO I – A VIEW TO COLLECTIVE HOUSING

Set on the edge of the Rokko Mountains in Kobe, the plan of this new collective housing concept takes advantage of the 60° slope of the land and the lush natural surroundings. Rokko Housing is located in the residential area of Hyogo, the south-facing site offering a panoramic view from Osaka Bay to Kobe. The architect's intention was to create a new style of communal living — one which reinforced a relationship between nature, and public and private space. An integral factor in achieving this goal was to employ a grid system to control the overall structure.

NATURAL INCLINATIONS

The architect wanted to plan this development keeping nature firmly in mind, noting that building projects in Japan have not always been developed in an environmentally sound manner. There was no plan to make radical changes to the topography, but rather to make use of the natural inclinations of the land. The building is, in fact, built right into the landscape, stepping down as the slope descends. To amalgamate the building into its surroundings the structure was sunk into the ground to keep the height down.

The building consists of a group of units that measure 17½ x 15¾ ft (5.3 x 4.8 m). Each unit has a terrace, and there is a range of views available depending on the unit's location within the development. The symmetrical plan allows for intentional gaps, which function as plaza areas and have the effect of uniting the building. Ventilation and insulation is promoted by the dry areas at the edges of the building.

Because the topography is irregular, there is a naturally occurring asymmetry in the structure of the development. One of the results of this is that the outdoor walkway has become the center of the project. The landscaping is designed to interact directly with the building. The geometric shapes accentuate the architecture's artificiality, with the consequence that the beauty of the natural surroundings is heightened.

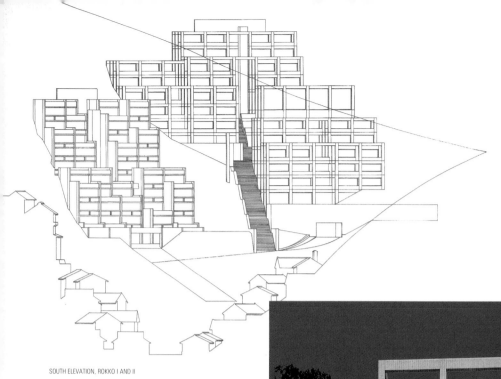

SOUTH ELEVATION, ROKKO I AND II

ROKKO II – AMALGAMATE WITH NATURE

The site for Rokko Housing II is four times bigger than that of Rokko Housing I. It also sits on a 60° slope, the steep incline leading the architect to further explore his desire to integrate the structure with the natural landscape. There was an interesting advantage in this regard – the site is located in a ravine, making it easier to merge the building with its surroundings.

A uniform grid of 17 x 17 ft (5.2 x 5.2 m) was adopted for this building, which consists of three complexes. Although all three are connected, they are quite individual in form. An asymmetric plan was generated when the grid was applied to the complexes, creating an authentic architectural order overall.

FACILITIES FOR EVERYONE

The architect strongly believes that a new building should contribute a level of meaning to its surroundings and its occupants, so an indoor pool was included, a facility that could be accessed by both Rokko Housing I and II residents. Another benefit was the addition of a peaceful rooftop plaza on the intermediate level, which allows magnificent views of the ocean and provides a pleasant communal space for social interaction among the residents.

Further expanding on his plan, the architect envisaged a third project for another nearby site, combining not only residences for older people, but also a kindergarten. There is a particular harmony between children and senior citizens, and their proximity in the plan further demonstrates the importance of communal space and social connection in the Rokko Housing II concept.

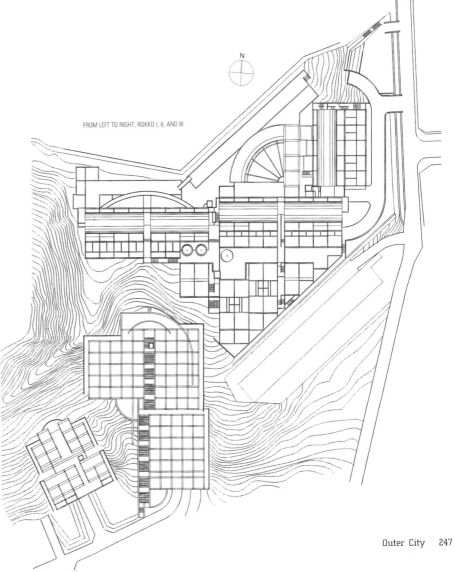

FROM LEFT TO RIGHT, ROKKO I, II, AND III

LEFT
The central stairway of Rokko II
provides an axis point for the
architecture as a whole.
Although a rigid grid system
was applied to the project, it
did not sacrifice flexibility of
layout or choice of vistas in
the modular design.

ABOVE
The three-dimensional alley
space of Rokko II links the public
and private areas of the housing.

TOP
Spectacular views toward Kobe
city are available from the high-
rise units, looking across the
rooftop greenery of Rokko III.

ROKKO III – A LIFESTYLE CHOICE

With the construction of the third housing complex in this development, the architect wanted to offer a lifestyle that closely reflected the location. He began thinking about the project before completing Rokko Housing II and had already put ideas on paper before he was asked to realize the concept as part of the recovery housing implemented for people whose homes had been destroyed in the Great Hanshin earthquake of 1995. In keeping with the ambience of the first two developments, the new site also offered beautiful views across the sea and the port of Kobe.

The structure of Rokko Housing III is once again arranged on a grid, this time measuring 22½ x 24½ ft (6.9 x 7.5 m), stepped over an elevation of 50 ft (15 m). Two of the blocks face south, right into the central axis of Rokko Housing II. One block faces east into the main walkway, and on the south side of the site there is a group of courtyard dwellings. The northern section of the site faces onto a garden. The parking area is hidden at a lower point.

LOOKING OUT AND IN

Each unit in Rokko Housing III has its own individual vista, affording residents a sense of individuality sometimes lacking in larger communal developments of this type.

One of the important community facilities open to all residents in Rokko Housing III is a swimming pool, which also has a view across the extensive gardens. There are other significant community considerations – one block of homes is specifically designed for the needs of senior citizens and also caters for residents with disabilities.

REAL INTERACTION

Walkways link the landscaped garden areas in the lower-level courtyard homes. This was an intentional exercise, the idea being that the path functions as communal space, as it did in the earlier projects. The hillside, which rises around the garden spaces, expands the communal areas by association.

The expanded communal areas, coupled with the housing complex, makes it easy for a real interaction between people and the natural environment. It also makes it easy for people to meet and enjoy one another's company, thus reinforcing and promoting the perception of living together in harmony.

The architect has been planning a fourth development in the Rokko Housing project, where he hopes to elaborate on the notion of close communal living intermingled with the pleasures of inhabiting the natural world.

The architect's intention was to create a new style of communal living – one which reinforced a relationship between nature, and public and private space.

ABOVE
The amphitheater-like quality of the central plaza in Rokko II creates a stately gathering place for residents.

LEFT
The individual dwellings within Rokko II complex retain a close relationship with nature and possess wonderful views toward Kobe city. Abundant natural light and a high degree of privacy add to the relaxed and inviting ambience of the homes.

TOP LEFT
The design of each apartment in Rokko II took into consideration the spatial qualities that best suited the stepped composition of the project.

Santa Monica House CALIFORNIA, USA

Chun Studio

Construction	2000–2002
Home type	Single dwelling, contemporary courtyard house
Structure	Two-level, concrete slab and raised floor construction with poured-in-place concrete walls and wood siding

"The genesis of the house was sub-dividing a standard rectangular lot into a series of exterior gardens and interior rooms by overlaying a grid. The house is an aggregation of these separate spaces – the design priority was establishing interesting spatial relationships to each part. The matrix of these relationships establishes a rich texture of stimulating adjacencies between interior rooms, and between interior rooms and exterior gardens."

David Chun

TOP RIGHT
Wooden screens surround the courtyard side of the family room. This sitting area faces the open courtyard toward the living room and the rock garden beyond. Views from this perspective capture the porosity and transparency of being in between the private and public rooms of the house.

PRIORITY: PRIVACY

The house was designed for the architect's parents, who requested a garden retreat away from the public realm, so privacy was a high priority. The context is a suburban neighborhood with an eclectic style of homes, all subdivided in rows of standard rectangular lots. The expansive openness of the interior spaces is modern in quality, and the finished materials are left to express their natural beauty, providing a sense of warmth and permanence to the house.

LAYERING THE EFFECT

Santa Monica House is H-shaped and is structured by three principal layers of space as one moves from the street to the rear garden. The first is the opaque layer (front of the building or street facade); the second is a transparent layer (central courtyard); and the third is the semi-transparent layer (rear of building).

The opaque layer is the two-story bar facing the street. It establishes a clear division between what is "in" and what is "out." In a sense, this buffer sets up the house to be able to invent its own separate private environment. The symmetrical street facade draws the visitor to its center by a two-story void that serves as an entry vestibule. This void space is a moment of transition from the opacity of the exterior wall to the transparency of its interior spaces. The 21-ft (6.4-m) wall is a statement of privacy that overwhelms the passerby, but dematerializes for the entering visitor.

EVEN WHEN OUTSIDE, YOU'RE INSIDE

The home is entered via 9-ft (2.7-m), pivoting, stainless steel doors – the home is exposed (transparent layer). The central courtyard and outdoor gardens can be viewed simultaneously through large floor to ceiling windows. The living room is flanked by two outdoor gardens: the central courtyard and the rock garden.

LEFT

The opaque layer is the two-story bar facing the street. It establishes a clear division between what is "in" and what is "out." In a sense, this buffer sets up the home to be able to invent its own separate private environment. The symmetrical street facade draws the visitor to its center by a two-story void that serves as an entry vestibule.

ABOVE

The living room is flanked by two outdoor gardens: the central courtyard and the rock garden. The room opens out onto the central courtyard via large accordion doors, When the doors are open the interior and exterior spaces are seamless.

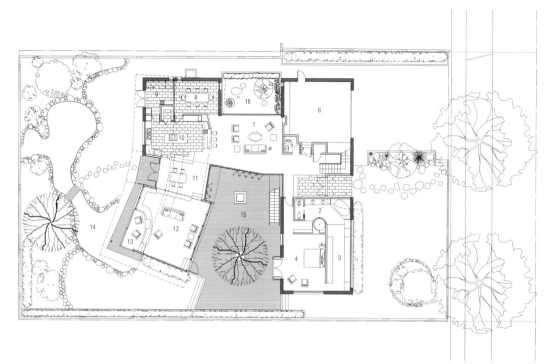

1 entry
2 main bathroom
3 closet
4 main bedroom
5 WC
6 garage
7 living
8 dining
9 utility
10 kitchen
11 breakfast
12 family
13 study
14 koi pond
15 central courtyard
16 rock garden

The living room opens onto the central courtyard by large accordion doors where the interior and the exterior can be made seamless. The sense of inside and outside is further challenged not just by the physical openings, but by the relationship to the outer opaque layer. Independent of the living room, the exterior courtyard space still feels very much inside the domestic compound.

The last semi-transparent layer is the rear one-story bar facing the back garden. It is composed of all the everyday domestic spaces (family room, kitchen, breakfast, and dining). This bar bends toward the rear and engages the garden with a covered viewing deck that hovers over the garden pond. In the family room, wooden screens direct the focus toward the rear garden by subtly veiling the central courtyard. The kitchen has direct access to all adjacent spaces. Its floor level is at the highest elevation, from which one steps down to the breakfast room, and from there down again into the family room. The relationship of these three rooms together creates a theater-like atmosphere.

CREATING LAYERS OF MEANING

The playful relationships of adjacent and overlapping spaces creates a constantly changing perception when moving through different layers of the home. The openness of the plan, and the large sheets of glass that dominate the perimeter walls of the home, create space that rhythmically expand and contract; first within the home, then out to the gardens and beyond.

LEFT
Looking out toward the courtyard from the kitchen, the foreground shows a fire pit (for warmth and barbecues) that is a focal point at the center of the property. It is a social gathering place for casual outdoor dining and conversation, and a place of interaction as all the rooms of the home have visual access to this central location.

ABOVE
The family room is a sunken, glass pavilion surrounded by lush gardens. The sunken floor and its dark color palette create intimacy and ground the room, while the surrounding glass walls allow commanding views to the perimeter of the property. Inside the room, the focal point is an open fireplace with a stainless-steel-clad flue suspended from the ceiling. Just beyond the fireplace is a small study area that opens out to the rear garden through floor to ceiling sliding glass doors.

TOP RIGHT
The living room is flanked by two outdoor gardens: the central courtyard and the rock garden. The rock garden is a "viewing garden," seen here from the living room. It is a careful and deliberately composed garden of rocks and small plantings that mimic larger gardens by way of proportion.

RIGHT
The semi-transparent layer is the rear, one-story bar facing the rear garden. It comprises the family room, kitchen, breakfast, and dining – the everyday domestic spaces. This bar bends toward the rear and engages the garden with a covered viewing deck that hovers over the koi pond.

The School House   LONDON, ENGLAND
Brookes Stacey Randall Architects

Constructed	1996
Home type	Apartment within refurbished school
Structure	Load-bearing brickwork, structural steel mezzanine level, steel and glass stair and mezzanine

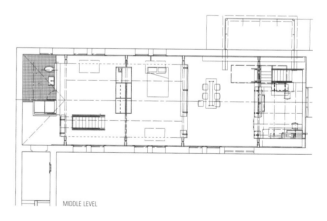

"The design approach was to make a distinction between the old and the new, allowing the original building to read clearly, with the new insertions touching the original fabric as lightly as possible. The design is not fixed but has the inherent flexibility to change, on both a daily and long-term basis. We love living there; especially Louis, who plays cricket in the main space."

Nik Randall (now of Space Craft Architects)

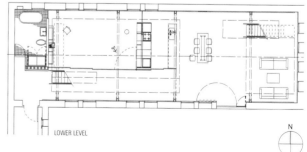

MIDDLE LEVEL

LOWER LEVEL

N

ABOVE
Clever use of sliding screens and custom-built storage units transform the main area into kitchen, dining, living, office, and play spaces. The glass-floored studio houses textile designer Suzsi Corio's materials.

BACK TO SCHOOL

Architect Nik Randall converted a Victorian school, built in 1871, into a private apartment for himself and his family. The large space, which originally housed two classrooms, perfectly suited Randall's desire for adaptability – where areas changed their function depending on the needs of the moment. An innovative approach to space and cleverly designed storage units made these transformations possible.

A LESSON IN SPACE

The height of the interior (some 24½ ft [7.5 m]) allowed plenty of space for three levels. The main family area is located on the lower level, as are the kitchen, living, dining, and office areas. There are no walls, and hence no defined rooms, with all spaces merging into one another. Where necessary, sliding screens are used to delineate areas within the volume. Randall's young son, Louis, has a large free area to play in; this same area can be used as an office, or it converts easily into a comfortable sleeping space for guests. This flexibility is achieved by using custom-built storage units, which can accommodate a range of functions, including a roll-out futon mattress.

The middle level of the apartment contains the bedrooms and dressing areas, and a studio for Randall's partner, textile designer Suzsi Corio. Large platforms are the focal point here, creating a sense of space, while still retaining the ambience of the original building. These platforms, which sit above the main living space beneath, define this level.

The floor of the larger platform is birch-faced plywood and coir matting. The floor of the studio is glass, which dramatically opens the area to the spaces below. A skylight lets in plenty of natural light. There are only two spaces on the top level, serving as sleeping areas, play space, or storage space, as required.

LIGHT AND COLOR

Lighting has been designed to suit the apartment's flexible floor plan. It is possible to evenly light the entire home. The architect also wanted the lighting to complement the style of the building, and to be discreet – the light fittings are flush, thus emphasizing the light, not the light fitting.

The color scheme also enhances the architectural purpose. A lime-yellow wall separates the main sitting area from the rest of the lower space. Kitchen and storage units are in soft shades of gray-green, and side walls and ceilings are off-white. The overall effect is subdued, yet it permits distinction between the home's different spaces. Creative use of color and light have resulted in a warm, flexible, modern home that manages to preserve its link with the past.

ABOVE
The kitchen is generally open to the living area but can also be closed off with retractable screens. The apartment's middle level is defined by large platforms – this one above the kitchen is covered in birch plywood and coir matting – which tie in with the original timber trusses and help sustain a sense of vertical space. Efficient heating for the apartment is provided by a pressurized hot water system. Radiators are recessed into the wall linings and a strong fan pushes the warm air into the volume of the house.

Casa Serrano SANTIAGO, CHILE

Felipe Assadi and Christophe Rousselle

Constructed	2006
Home type	Three-level residence
Structure	Concrete and steel frame on concrete slab

"The objective was to create a house that maximized the 180° views of Santiago and the surrounding mountains. The living areas are transparent spaces enclosed in glass, regulating light into the interior and set alongside a framework of concrete that is supported by steel columns."

Felipe Assadi

A DOMINANT PRESENCE

An imposing design dominating its surroundings, Casa Serrano comprises three living areas contained within a cocoon of reinforced concrete over a steel frame.

The living areas on the lower levels are organized around a central tower, which tie the building together while facilitating the movement of cooling breezes. Internal steel columns support the northern and southern facades and make a strong visual statement. A central fireplace acts as a partition between the dining and living areas, which lead to a ground-level, north-facing courtyard, where the koi pond points like a finger toward the panoramic views.

The middle level contains the main bedroom and a second bedroom, which open onto a common west-facing balcony. Two other bedrooms open onto a walled, north-facing, inner courtyard accessed by a series of sliding glass doors. A large glazed exterior affords views into the adjacent living room below. There are two more bedrooms, both of which open onto balconies. All four bedrooms have ensuites.

EXOTIC SKIN

Almendrillo, an exotic hardwood from the Amazon rain-forest, is used for the west-facing decking on the middle level. The upper level houses the study, where the north-facing, reinforced-concrete exterior is sheathed in a second skin of almendrillo. This lends the concrete exterior warmth, texture, and human scale. Light filters through a series of tiny, randomly placed windows.

CELEBRATION OF CUBISM

Casa Serrano deliberately confronts its surroundings rather than seamlessly blending with them. The result is a bold, formal statement that brings an international voice to the city of Santiago.

ABOVE
The void above the hallway neatly sets off the otherwise elongated floor plan. Downlights and hardwood floors bring a softness and intimacy to a living area that is flooded with views of Santiago city.

TOP RIGHT
The elegant almendrillo skin on the north-facing wall provides both continuity and contrast with the west-facing deck and inner courtyard below. Randomly placed windows in the wall introduce an intricate interplay of light into the upper level study.

RIGHT
The streetscape view of the house is an unashamedly Modernist statement. The home's domineering mass is accentuated by enclosing the two west-facing bedrooms in timber-clad, reinforced concrete.

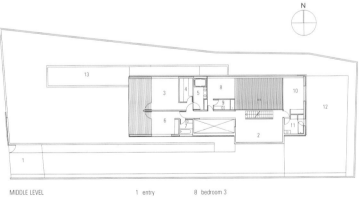

MIDDLE LEVEL

1 entry	8 bedroom 3
2 family	9 bathroom
3 main bedroom	10 bedroom 4
4 wardrobe	11 bathroom
5 main bathroom	12 garage
6 bedroom 2	13 lower level
7 bathroom	koi pond

ABOVE
A centrally placed fireplace in the living space on the lower level provides the room's focal point, its flue soaring through the ceiling into the courtyard above. Glass exterior walls on three sides flood the room with light.

Studio and Apartment House Huber LUCERNE, SWITZERLAND
Graser Architekten

Construction	2002–2003
Home type	Two apartments and two studios with an open staircase between
Structure	Wooden frame for the inner structure, cloth for the outer cover

"Our design work focuses on flexibility and the capacity to alter things along the way – and we apply our technical knowledge to the use of prefabricated materials. There are no right or wrong materials or forms for us, and to a certain extent we renounce ostentation. Under no circumstances must the 'form' of the project arise from our personal preferences – rather from the personal preferences of the client."

Jürg Graser

ABOVE
Viewed from the northeastern side of the building, House Huber sits lightly on the landscape, tucking into a curve of the road. The parking area is under the box-like front of the house.

RIGHT
A transitional space housing the lightweight staircase links the three levels as well as the two buildings. This connecting space acts as both a balcony and a terrace.

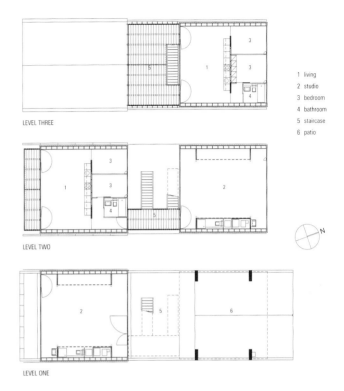

LEVEL THREE

LEVEL TWO

LEVEL ONE

1 living
2 studio
3 bedroom
4 bathroom
5 staircase
6 patio

MODERN INTERPRETATION

House Huber is situated in one of the oldest areas of Emmenbrücke in Lucerne, Switzerland. The house lies between a southern slope in the east, dotted with villas dating from the end of the nineteenth century, and a plain in the west, which contains single-family houses dating from the post-World War II period. The building site was once part of an old farm that extended over the whole area. The last farm building was torn down in 2002.

The new building reacts to the uniqueness of its location in two ways. First, it assumes the geometry of the old house, hinting at the original building complex. It also allows for the curve in the adjacent road, so the house sits comfortably in its surroundings. Second, the height and the number of stories in the new building are a kind of reinterpretation of a typical farmhouse – traditionally both a working and a living space – but with a modern twist.

MULTIFUNCTIONAL SPACE

Like all forms of design, architecture is subject to various trends, and these days, a minimalist formal expression – where architecture can be reduced to a two-dimensional plane – seems to be the fashion. Yet in spite of the move away from the structurally "self-contained" buildings of the recent past, there is no doubt that we are still fascinated by the relationship between structure and space.

In House Huber, there are two completely closed supporting longitudinal walls, which serve to frame the dual functions of working and living areas. Large transverse windows allow the free flow of light into these rooms. There is also a double height void situated between the two building apartments, which is used by both of them. This spatial element is a transitional space between the homes. Combined with the entry and the parking area under the second apartment, the area becomes a larger L-shaped multifunctional space.

ADDING VALUE

For the architects designing this project, budgetary constraints gave rise to creative solutions, encouraging the production of a structure with a style all its own. The architects were interested in looking at the basic space and then "adding value" to it. This meant that extra funds were allocated to a few specific elements that architecturally enhanced the project.

HIGH-TECH MATERIALS

The outer cover of the building is made of cloth – an efficient, high-tech material that adds an aesthetic dimension to the project, setting the building apart from its conventional setting. The durable cloth is multifunctional, serving as a sunshade, weather barrier, and air cushion. All these factors add to the passive energy balance of the project.

TOP LEFT
The cloth roof covering admits lots of natural light to the triple-height space between the two modules, while the large surface windows allow discreet views between the interiors of the two living areas.

ABOVE
The transparent effect of the cloth outer cover, which protects the interior from sun and glare, is echoed in the perforated metal plates on the stair treads. The whole building has a light, and light-filled, feel.

Ward Residence CALIFORNIA, USA

Marmol Radziner + Associates

Construction	2000–2003
Home type	Two-level house, single-family residence
Structure	Concrete block, steel, and glass

"The Ward Residence introduces a series of contrasts into the site: the solid volumes and the light glass pavilions, the rough structural nature of the concrete block with the burnished finish of the blocks, the light colored walls and the dark stained oak floors. These contrasts create a simple yet sensitive solution to the steep site."

Marmol Radziner + Associates

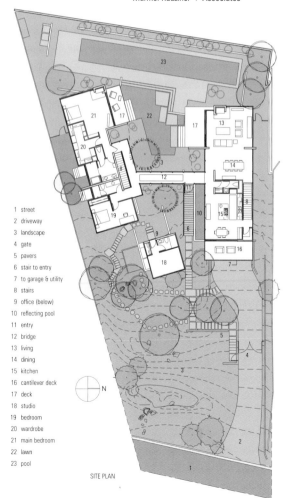

1 street
2 driveway
3 landscape
4 gate
5 pavers
6 stair to entry
7 to garage & utility
8 stairs
9 office (below)
10 reflecting pool
11 entry
12 bridge
13 living
14 dining
15 kitchen
16 cantilever deck
17 deck
18 studio
19 bedroom
20 wardrobe
21 main bedroom
22 lawn
23 pool

SITE PLAN

SEPARATE YET INTEGRATED

Situated in Rustic Canyon, one of the most serene areas in Los Angeles, this new residence offers views of the canyon and gently sloping hillsides to the east. The neighborhood has a rich architectural history, including residences by Ray Kappe, Pierre Koenig, and A. Quincy Jones, and provides local precedents for the ideals of Modernism. The Ward Residence takes lessons from these Modern neighbors, including the natural material palette and resolve for indoor/outdoor living, while making new design and material innovations.

Keeping with the notion of establishing a serene garden-like environment, the home's 4,000-sq-ft (370-sq-m) mass appears smaller because of the organization of the living and working spaces within three seemingly separate pavilions. Arranged according to the requirements of public use, private domains, and functional work areas, the separate volumes perch delicately atop solid masses of burnished concrete blocks imbedded in the hillside. A glass-enclosed walkway bridges the two masses, taking optimal advantage of the location and surrounding landscape. The landscape flows below and past the glazed entry hall as it bridges the public and private volumes of the home.

ABOVE
The Ward Residence is set in a steep hillside peppered with numerous large trees. During construction, much effort was spent protecting the original trees on the land, since the indoor/outdoor interaction is so important to the concept of the home.

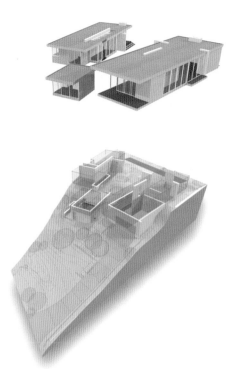

ABOVE
The house reveals itself as a progression from the solid masonry walls imbedded in the hillside, up into the lighter steel and glass pavilions above. The main approach to the house flows between the skewed positioning of the double cantilevered guest pavilion, on the left, and the cantilevered deck off the kitchen, on the right.

TOP RIGHT
"Volumes," made from stacked concrete masonry, sit within the steep hillside and provide the base for the steel and glass pavilions to float above. The three glass pavilions divide the house into public, private, and functional work areas. The contrast between the visual weight of the masonry volumes and the lightness of the upper pavilions create different experiences throughout the site.

EXPLOITING TOPOGRAPHY

Materials of burnished concrete block, galvanized steel paneling, and glass complement the openness of the design and the careful integration of the object-like forms on the site. Filtering in the landscape, the site introduces a skewed procession upon entry that leads up to the pavilions and provides glimpses of additional structures beyond.

A double cantilevered guest house rests on top of the studio, accentuating the breezeway and creating an intimate arrival area. Working with the landscape into one pictorial image, the simple lap pool lines the back of the property.

The design utilizes the opportunities of the site's natural topography and foliage to provide privacy and separation from neighboring lots. By shifting the home forward and away from the neighboring yards, the design exploits the steep site and builds within the hillside, allowing for additional stories. By keeping the structures below tree level, the home's focus becomes more introverted – a retreat within a lush hillside garden. During construction, a great deal of effort was spent ensuring the safety of the trees native to the site.

ABOVE
Looking back at the home from the cantilevered deck off the kitchen, the view reveals the close interaction of indoor and outdoor spaces. The steel structure provides the support necessary to create the large expanses of glass.

RIGHT
The water feature outside the kitchen directly connects natural elements to the interior of the home.

BLURRING BOUNDARIES

The home consistently blurs the distinction between interior and exterior spaces through the use of exposed natural materials, large expanses of glass, and significant outdoor living spaces. The living room and main bedroom each have direct access to the backyard, while a separate cantilevered balcony opens up the kitchen to surrounding treetops. A large window in the main bathroom provides protected views that can be enjoyed from the Japanese cedar hot tub.

A SOLID MOTIF

The concrete block is a defining motif in the home, for the masonry flows between the inside and outside of the home, acting both as a structural material and an exposed finished surface. All textures, from the craggy "split-faced" to sandblasted precision, and colors, from pale white to warm gray, were considered during the material selection process. The final choice, a custom fabricated block of white concrete with burnished faces was selected for its unique beauty and its ability to play off the rustic nature of the site.

ABOVE
The burnished concrete block is a central motif in both the interior and exterior of the home – seen here, in the fireplace surround and engaged column.

LEFT
The master bathroom combines a material palette of cedar casework, burnished concrete block, and stainless steel to create an intimate feel in this private space. The cedar hot tub reveals the Japanese influence on the design.

FOLLOWING PAGES
A lap pool runs the length of the backyard, emphasizing the horizontality of the steel and glass pavilions. Running almost parallel to the pool, a glass-enclosed walkway bridges the public and private areas of the home.

Chapter 11
Future
City

A new era of home design is unfolding. Homes of the future will maximize our limited resources, and use new techniques and materials that will be more sensitive to the environment.

Consider living in a home made of glass, where a voice-activated electric current turns the walls opaque on command. Or perhaps your home will be made of cardboard, plastic, or even rubber. Whatever your vision of the future might be, one thing is certain – home design in the city of the future will be motivated by the limited availability of resources.

With natural resources dwindling, homes will be designed for more efficient use of space, using innovative new materials that reduce the impact of humans on the environment. Technology will revolutionize conventional design, and traditional building methods will be replaced as home design becomes more complex.

INGENUITY OF FORM

Complex design and more efficient use of space will result in ingenious forms. Computer-3D modelling, one of the new technologies, allows architects to study their designs dynamically, examining them from every angle to resolve problems. This results in much more creative freedom, and organic forms are beginning to emerge as possible design solutions.

One innovation is to manipulate space: Rooms can now expand or contract as walls are moved along a track in the ceiling. These wall panels can be hidden away in a wall cavity, giving the illusion of more space, or turned at different angles to totally reconfigure the space.

CONSTRUCTION TECHNOLOGY

The burden on our natural resources is being reduced by both innovative design and the development of new building materials, such as composite materials and those that can be dismantled and reused. Such materials demand the development of compatible building techniques.

Modular home design is a novel construction technology. The prefabricated modular components are designed once and then manufactured with computer assistance, with services included, and reconfigured for each site. This process reduces product waste and makes construction on site more efficient.

SUSTAINABILITY

Limited access to resources and an increasing awareness of the environment has created an ethos of conservation that has unleashed a flood of invention in the areas of renewable energy and recycled materials.

We can power our homes by harnessing wind energy, and we can also use the sun to heat water simply and effectively. We are already recycling paper and plastics to make items such as carpet, insulation, and structural elements for the home. Floors need not be made of hardwood. Instead, a photograph of real wood can be laminated onto recycled plastic sheets.

ABOVE
Shanghai Star Mei Hwa Estate,
Ben Wood Studio Shanghai

TOP RIGHT
Moriyama House,
Ryue Nishizawa

OPPOSITE
Living Tomorrow Pavilion,
UN Studio

INNOVATIVE DESIGN

The city of the future will see the emergence of a new, innovative design movement that will embrace new materials and building techniques, resulting in new shapes and organic forms. This shift will require us to re-examine our understanding of what home is and will make us redefine ourselves, our lifestyles, and our relationships in response to our new surroundings.

Gardner 1050 LOS ANGELES, USA

Lorcan O'Herlihy Architects

Constructed	2006
Home type	Three-story apartment building
Structure	Steel and wood frame with cement-board cladding, timber, and glass

"Density is a critical issue in Los Angeles. This project represents an inventive way of dealing with housing for the masses. By creating a central light well and wrapping the building around this space, the central void becomes the heart of the project, providing circulation, light, and a place for social interaction."

Lorcan O'Herlihy

A NEW ARCHITECTURAL LANDSCAPE

West Hollywood has become increasingly urbanized over recent years, and the Gardner 1050 project of 10 housing units, south of the famous Santa Monica Boulevard, has made a significant contribution to the architectural landscape of the district. The architects used various approaches, such as incorporating courtyards into the design of the building, to give the units a distinctive appearance, thus distinguishing them from more commonplace styles in the area.

A CENTRAL COURTYARD

A major design consideration was to connect the indoor and outdoor spaces to maximize flexibility for the residents. Individual units are essentially wrapped around a courtyard in the center of the project, which measures 15,000 sq ft (about 4,600 sq m). The architects' strategic use of a simple form and refined materials has allowed variations in how the scale and facade of the building are perceived.

On the western facade, cedar slats placed around the cut-away box have been used to create a translucent exterior "skin." The courtyard sits inside this area. A glass-clad staircase makes a dramatic statement, immediately drawing the eye to this stark vertical exclamation mark. The staircase also marks the entry to the building and provides a subdued light in the evenings, enhancing the exterior.

MASTERFUL MATERIALS

For appearance and durability, the architects chose a painted cement-board cladding system as one of the main materials. The other primary materials used are transparent glass panels, horizontal cedar slats, and painted aluminum window frames.

The cedar slats cover the whole second level and also double as a screen for the entry to the garage and the third level's outside community area. Wood has also been used on the first and third levels to extend the wood theme.

EXCITING EXTERIOR, INTIMATE INTERIOR

The courtyard and interior of the project truly define it. Simultaneously spacious and intimate, the courtyard features drought-tolerant native shrubs, perfectly offset by the integral seating. A fountain close to the entry provides a tranquil ambience, and also contributes to the open feeling of the space.

Stainless steel cables run up to the level three walkways, providing the foundations for a hanging garden from that level. The steel gratings here also create a pattern of light and shadow on the courtyard below. The paving is a green-tinted concrete that complements the glass at the front entry.

SETTING A HIGH QUALITY BENCHMARK

One of the project's most successful attributes is its provision of medium-density housing within an esthetically pleasing structure.

LEFT
Wood is used as a feature on the fireplace wall, extending the exterior "skin" into the interior. The expansive windows and glass door fill the room with light and create an esthetic rarely evident in medium-density housing.

ABOVE
Cedar slats frame an exterior deck, providing both shade and privacy. The slats on the exterior walls not only unify the whole structure but also help break up the different elements.

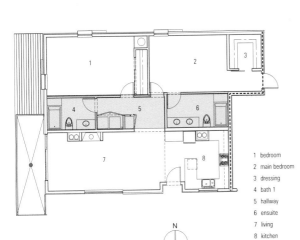

1 bedroom
2 main bedroom
3 dressing
4 bath 1
5 hallway
6 ensuite
7 living
8 kitchen

N

ABOVE
The architects see the Gardner 1050 project as establishing an innovative precedent for this part of West Hollywood's architectural environment. The translucent glass stairwell is a feature of the eye-catching facade. It also provides a strong vertical element in an otherwise horizontal composition.

LEFT
Bold color in the hallway provides a dynamic contrast with the pale-themed living room beyond.

Living Tomorrow
UNStudio

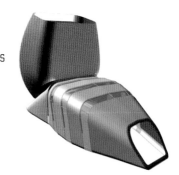

Constructed	2002
Home type	Future-oriented living and working prototype, temporary building (5 years) – showroom
Structure	Stucco and corrugated iron over concrete

"Living Tomorrow is a temporary building designed to raise people's awareness of future trends in housing and business. We needed to demonstrate that cutting-edge technology need not be too complex and can still be made to serve people's needs."

UNStudio

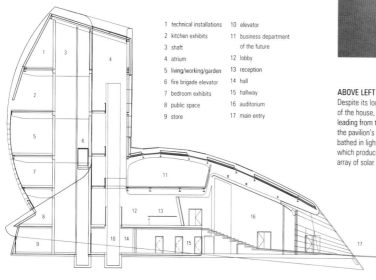

1	technical installations	10	elevator
2	kitchen exhibits	11	business department of the future
3	shaft	12	lobby
4	atrium	13	reception
5	living/working/garden	14	hall
6	fire brigade elevator	15	hallway
7	bedroom exhibits	16	auditorium
8	public space	17	main entry
9	store		

ABOVE LEFT
Despite its location in the middle of the house, this staircase – leading from the auditorium to the pavilion's reception area – is bathed in light from a glass roof, which produces electricity via an array of solar energy panels.

TOP
UNStudio's vision of what the future may hold – a curvaceously shaped combined office and living space.

ABOVE
Multi-tasked, wall-mounted LCD screens adjust lights, operate blinds, fill rooms with soft music, and even ignite the living area's gas fireplace.

TOP RIGHT
This view of the exterior is an assault on the senses, with its stucco over concrete blocks, load-bearing concrete panels, corrugated metal, and enormous expanses of 40-ft- (12-m-) high glass. Air voids in the concrete blocks beneath the stucco provide ample insulation and require minimal maintenance.

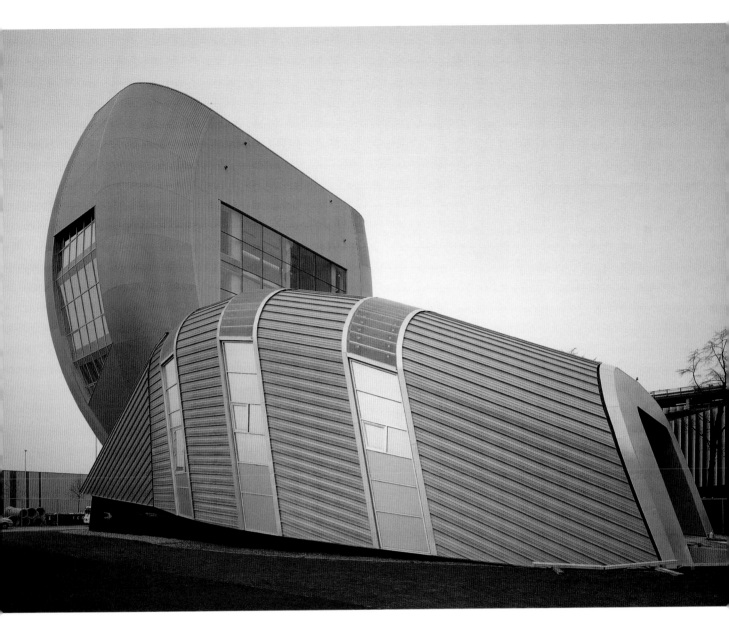

SHOWCASE FOR THE FUTURE

The Living Tomorrow Pavilion, on Arena Boulevard in Amsterdam, is a futuristic building designed by UNStudio, a network of architects, graphic designers, builders, and quantity surveyors headed by architect Ben van Berkel and art historian Caroline Bos. The building and its contents have an exhibition life of five years. After that, another Living Tomorrow Pavilion featuring new technologies will be constructed.

The building is designed to raise awareness of future trends in housing and in the workplace, and to nurture a spirit of innovation among professionals and the general public. It showcases cutting-edge technology while researchers develop and demonstrate concepts that may be integrated into the homes of the future.

CORPORATE SUPPORT

The project is supported by companies such as Bose, Microsoft, and Unilever, who provide prototypes of their products. In this way it serves as a platform for some of the world's most innovative corporations, who can discuss their products with the consumer.

A LIGHT FOOTPRINT

UNStudio's radical design gives a glimpse of what the future may hold. Fluid and curvaceous exterior walls achieve continuity between the horizontal and vertical planes as well as the internal and external spaces. The design triumphantly mimics the helicoidal system of DNA – its two spiral circuits intersect with each other over all levels.

All the materials used in the pavilion's construction are either recyclable or have a low impact on the environment. The building's own footprint is minimal, with less than half the lot assigned to it being used for the building. The remainder is used for staging various bi-annual open-air events.

BOOT SHAPE

Although the layout varies, the pavilion consists of two spaces – one horizontal, and the other vertical, much like a boot. The "foot" usually contains the office of the future, a meeting room, an auditorium and event hall, while the "leg" usually houses the kitchen exhibits and living quarters. Some spaces are reserved for the public.

The building is heated and cooled using solar energy and extensive natural ventilation systems. As an alternative to designated bedrooms, occupants may choose to sleep in "cocoons" within the living area. These circle-shaped beds can close up, and each has its own integrated multimedia system.

Communications and connectivity are paramount. The websites have speech technology, and electricity is supplied via transparent solar cells. A computer in the kitchen even provides recipes to help you lose weight, while ambient lighting in soft, muted shades of blue, green, and gray adjust to your mood.

In the pavilion, ideas are shelved if they fail to meet expectations. For example, the refrigerator that reordered food was discarded for being too clumsy and complicated to operate.

Longlands Mill CHESHIRE, ENGLAND

Space Craft Architects

Construction	2007–2008
Home type	Apartments, offices, studios, and shops
Structure	Steel frame with pre-cast concrete floors

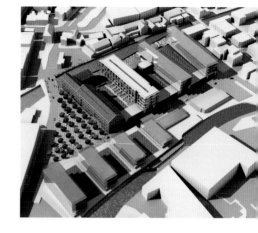

"We are very excited by the ideas we have developed for this project, especially the spaces to be opened up alongside the Canal and the River Tame. Our design will allow views through the site from the river to the canal, and beyond. It will also generate new routes to link the area together and help revitalize the town center."

Nik Randall

AN EYE ON HISTORY

Between the River Tame and the Huddersfield Narrow Canal in the center of Stalybridge, Cheshire, sits the 4.5 acre (1.8 ha) Longlands Mill site. Space Craft Architects won a recent competition to decide who would design a mixed-use scheme for the site. Space Craft was selected because they were seen to epitomize a design-led approach and also because of their inspired body of work to date. The company's ideas for the mixed-use development, incorporating the old with the new, were the most sympathetic to the site's history — there are some surviving mill buildings from centuries gone by.

A THREE-PRONGED FOCUS

Space Craft put forward three primary objectives for the development. First, they wanted to guarantee the future of the surviving mill buildings by performing appropriate alterations, giving them practical new uses, and constructing new buildings that were complementary to the existing ones. Second, they wanted to revitalize Stalybridge by amalgamating the original site with the surrounding semi-urban environment. Third, Space Craft wanted to design and build a broad range of both commercial and residential accommodation.

LOOKING TO THE FUTURE

The Space Craft proposal looks to the future, beyond the requirements of the site itself. They have the big picture in mind, and have identified possible retail prospects and the creation of more public space and transport infrastructure. Architect Nik Randall, a director of the company, sees their proposal as a way of rejuvenating the town center.

The proposal includes more than 250 new homes, offices, cafés, and restaurants, as well as a range of retail and other commercial spaces. As the town of Stalybridge sits at the foot of the Pennines, there is also a proposal for a hotel in the master plan.

Space Craft are spending time at the site with Urban Splash, the developer for the project, to finalize the design ideas, and also to restore those parts of the Mill complex that have been heritage-listed. This will set the scene for the proposed refurbishment of the site into residential apartments and commercial space.

The conversion of the Longlands Mill building has been designed to express the original cast-iron columns and timber roof trusses in such a way that they harmonize with the character of the apartments and shared spaces. The new buildings will comprise spacious, interlocking double-height apartments, maximizing the sense of space while keeping them affordable.

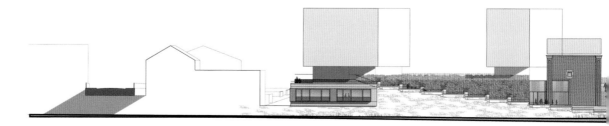

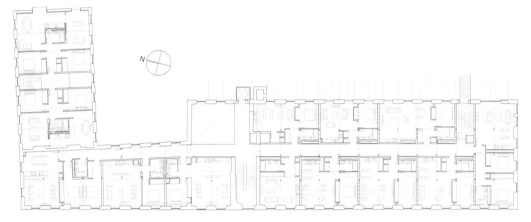

SECOND LEVEL

TOP LEFT
An aerial view of the proposed development, which is designed to enhance the commercial and economic life of Stalybridge, shows how the entire site is flanked by the canal and the river.

LEFT
The town's history is bound up with the heritage-listed mill buildings, so Space Craft wanted to restore these as well as incorporate modern architectural ideas.

ABOVE
The development will provide public access to the River Tame and the Huddersfield Narrow Canal, creating new parklands along these waterways and rejuvenating the entire site.

Moriyama House TOKYO, JAPAN

Ryue Nishizawa

Constructed	2005
Home type	Single dwelling (owner's house) and five apartments
Structure	Three levels and basement, concrete, plated steel, and glass

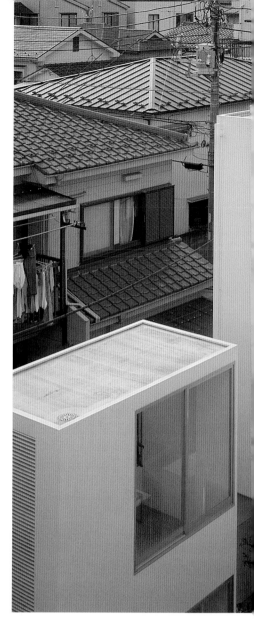

"Moriyama House is a community in miniature, composed of individually proportioned buildings on a small parcel of land in a typically urban setting. Its ten separate volumes cater to the varying needs of its occupants, as well as creating a series of connected individual gardens all open to the surroundings."

Ryue Nishizawa

In a densely populated area of Tokyo, the architect Ryue Nishizawa, and his associates, Ippei Takahashi and Kimihiko Okada, took a modest 3,000-sq-ft (290-sq-m) site and constructed a cluster of subterranean and aboveground two- and three-story towers. These fit in perfectly with their surrounding urban environment, while at the same time providing an innovative solution to the specific needs of the client.

ALTERNATIVE MODEL OF HABITATION

Although technically a single dwelling for its owner, Moriyama House is in fact a collection of ten separate self-contained buildings — exploring the theory of fragmenting a structure into its constituent parts. The result is an alternative model of habitation, which gives the owner the flexibility of living in any one of the spaces or moving between them as his mood or needs dictate.

The interior of each of the ten buildings contains varying combinations of kitchens, living rooms, and bedrooms, so the owner also has the option to rent any of the spaces for an additional income source.

SHARED GARDENS

Tiny landscaped areas weave in and out of the structures, designed by the architect to create a series of "Schreber Gardens," (a German tradition of leasing people small, allotted public spaces in which to grow vegetables, fruit, and flowers). In addition these spaces function as common areas where people can interact.

ABOVE
Variations in the footprint, floor plan, and height of each of the Moriyama buildings convey the impression of a town in miniature, full of harmoniously contrasting forms and pleasantly differing perspectives for its inhabitants. Common structural elements and styles provide a sense of community and shared values.

The walls of Moriyama House have been prefabricated out of plated steel so as to be as thin as possible — and to maximize the living and outdoor areas, on what is a typically small parcel of Tokyo real estate.

TURNING PRIVACY ON ITS HEAD

The buildings reflect an unorthodox approach to the issue of privacy: One bathroom is located outside, and cannot be accessed from within; another home includes an uncurtained glass wall, which faces the public courtyard. The architect hopes to cultivate openness among the occupants.

COMMUNITY AND HARMONY

Flung across the site in perfect proportion and harmony, Moriyama House's collection of towers, landscaped areas, and intricate network of pathways and alleyways follows the Japanese tradition of small residential dwellings, creating a community unto itself.

Moriyama House's many white concrete facades create a minimalist maze of Cubism, reminiscent of the paintings of Piet Mondrian and of the purity of Modernism in the 1920s.

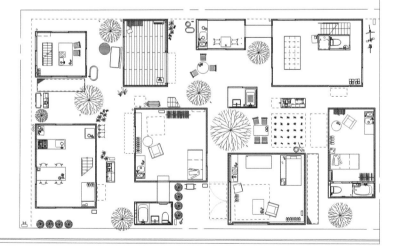

ABOVE LEFT
Large picture windows give a sense of openness and warmth to the small rooms, while also embracing expansive city views. Minimal ornamentation, characteristic of the project, is accentuated by the almost "invisible" window frames.

ABOVE
A myriad of open spaces is created from the location of Moriyama House's buildings – ranging from long, narrow alleyways to broader landscaped spaces such as the one pictured here. Ornamental trees and shrubs provide texture to spaces where the focus of the inhabitants is directed inwards through glass areas that face each other.

LEFT
Despite the close proximity of the separate buildings, there is no sense of clutter or density. Rather, the Moriyama buildings together have a sense of wholeness, each element part of a beautifully crafted entity. Narrow alleyways provide access points to entryways and connect the outdoor spaces.

ABOVE
In such compact living space, staircases are necessarily functional – narrow with minimal balustrading, shallow treads, and high angles. Their design typifies the architect's approach of maximizing internal spaces without compromising functionality.

One Room, Three Ways

John Aspinall C3D INTERACTIVE

> "To have imagined, 20 years ago, that an architect would have the opportunity to observe a digital representation of a design proposal in context would have pushed the limits of credibility. However, the current reality is exactly that, and more."
>
> John Aspinall

ABOVE AND RIGHT
The same basic shell can take on a series of quite different characters reflecting the owner's tastes. CAD technology permits a visual assessment of the impact of various furniture styles, even down to the choice of artwork.

TOP RIGHT
By utilizing computer visualization programs, with their extensive libraries of "modeled" furniture, clients can consider a vast range of design options.

COMPUTER AIDED DESIGN

It is now within the technical capabilities of most architectural practices to generate photo realistic images and even animations of design proposals. For architects, the arrival of Computer Aided Design (CAD) promised a radical alternative to existing design solutions. However, for the majority of architectural practices, CAD represents little more than computer-aided drafting, reducing documentation production times dramatically. At the other extreme, stand the pioneers of CAD, who recognize the huge potential at their fingertips.

STATE OF THE ART COMPUTER TECHNOLOGY

Frank Gehry's current work represents the "state of the art" in terms of pushing computer technology to its limits within the field of architecture. By searching for ways to help contractors better understand highly complex geometrical forms, Gehry's office began to develop its own specific software. This was based upon an existing package, CATIA, a purely three-

dimensional modeling program, originally created in France to design jet fighters and adapted by Boeing for commercial aircraft. This has now evolved to a point where physical models, still Gehry's preferred methods of schematic design, can be digitally scanned into the computer. From here, the design is further refined and developed to a point where exact quantities and geometries can be fed directly to the building contractor from the CAD model.

A further benefit of this approach is an increased dialogue between the architect and sub-contractor at the design development stage, which will lead to considerable cost and time saving and, perhaps, an even greater involvement from, and respect for, the architect beyond the production of documentation.

INTERACTIVE DESIGN PROCESSES

At a more practical level, many architectural practices are beginning to see the advantages of a more interactive design process, using currently available CAD technology.

Architecturally, the interactive model's greatest strength still remains within the design development stage and its ability to evolve and respond with the speed and accuracy necessary to produce an optimal design solution.

Specialized visualization studios now utilize software originally developed within the film industry, where speed is essential, to encourage all members of building design teams to assess the impact of new developments in context – internally and externally – from the earliest stages of concept design.

EFFECTIVE RESOLUTION

The progression of the three-dimensional model follows several defined stages that reflect the iterative process of design, from geometric considerations into compositional concerns involving material, surface texture, colors, and lighting. The visual portrayal of any potentially contentious areas of the design facilitates rapid and effective resolution of any issues.

It is the intention of interactive visualization studios to continue developing and enhancing these ideas, permitting a far more streamlined and effective design process.

This will lead to considerable time and cost savings for all members of the design team. More importantly, in creating an environment in which architectural design can be more critically and objectively assessed, standards of design, both in terms of resolution and quality, will inevitably improve.

ABOVE
The same room takes on a completely different identity in this rendering. The starkness of the 1990s apartment is softened by the inclusion of rich textures and materials.

Parque Espana MEXICO CITY, MEXICO
TEN Arquitectos

Constructed	2001
Home type	Multilevel residence with underground garage
Structure	Concrete frames and waffled slabs

WEST FACADE

ABOVE
This exterior view of the building from the Parque Espana across the street reveals the Modernist simplicity and angular form of the ground-floor concrete facade, as well as the cavernous entrance to the art gallery. Its straight lines and classical form typify TEN Arquitectos' approach to design – buildings that derive their character less from their shape than from the way they were built.

"Our clients wanted a modern building that would house family apartments and a penthouse above an art gallery and garage. The site is very exposed, so we wanted to give each apartment privacy without sacrificing either light or the views to the Parque Espana across the street."

TEN Arquitectos

With its innovative, grid-like exterior of aluminum and glass, TEN Arquitectos' multilevel residential building on a tight corner site is ideally located in one of Mexico City's densest urban environments.

A MODERN OUTLOOK

Situated in the Colonia Condesa district opposite the Parque Espana, a lovely city park built in 1921 to celebrate Mexico's victory in the War of Independence, the building consists of six single-family apartments and one two-story rooftop penthouse, all set above a contemporary art gallery on the ground floor. There is also an adjacent residents' garage with parking for 14 cars.

The clean modern lines of the building's facade of aluminum and glass reflect the changing face of Mexico City's most modern district, which blends traditional colonial architecture with splendid examples of Modernity, all set among tree-lined streets with alfresco restaurants.

The building's design is characterized by immaculate proportions and a considered layering of elements and materials. The external stairs and balconies provide a lively composition for streetscape views of the building.

ROOFTOP GARDEN

Each apartment contains two bedrooms that are centrally located along a narrow floor plan, with living areas on either side and services such as laundry, pantry, and storage placed along the eastern side.

ABOVE
The building's western facade shows an extensive use of glass, which seems to welcome the passerby into the project. Sliding, transparent fabric screens reinvent expansive, framed views of the surrounding neighborhood from the building's interior. Generous balconies provide ample space for entertaining.

TOP RIGHT
This ground level view illustrates the building's exquisite sense of proportion and how neatly it fits into the surrounding streetscape. Ornamentation is non-existent in a building where functionality and the pursuit of Modernism — as seen in the repetitious nature of the partitioning — is regarded as paramount.

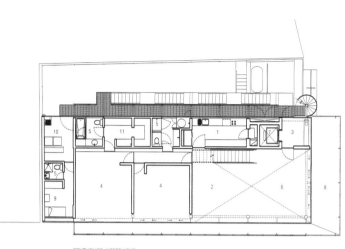

PENTHOUSE, UPPER LEVEL

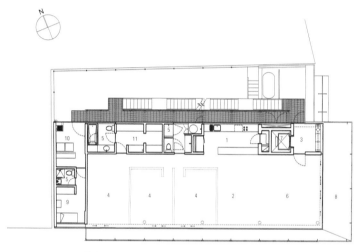

TYPICAL FLOOR PLAN

1 kitchen
2 dining
3 hallway
4 bedroom
5 bathroom
6 living
7 elevator
8 terrace
9 service area
10 utility
11 dressing room

The building's southern elevation provides views to Parque Espana by means of a cantilevered terrace. The bedrooms above the street on the western side are sheltered by an elegant, slim balcony set in the foreground of elaborate, continuously sliding partitions of translucent fabric, all contained within an intricate framework of aluminum. In addition to filtering out ultraviolet rays and harsh sunlight, they provide privacy and a random order that is constantly changing.

All residents share a roof garden, complete with lap pool and wood-decking surround. These elements assist in the "rediscovery of the rooftop" in a city where rooftops are normally occupied by nothing more than building machinery and clotheslines.

Service stairs connect every level, allowing access to each apartment via bridges. An external spiral staircase leading to the roof garden is recessed into the building's eastern corner. The two-story penthouse consists of an upper level loft containing a main bedroom, a guest suite, two bathrooms, and a

family room. Its lower level is a massive, functional open space, flooded with light from the 15-ft- (5-m-) high windows on its western facade. The kitchen, laundry, and a downstairs bathroom are located behind a large partition that anchors the stairs leading to the rooms above.

DESIGN AWARD

In Parque Espana, the principal designer, Enrique Norten, has demonstrated his ability to produce a building that is both technically innovative, in its use of complex industrial materials, and sensitive to the surrounding streetscape.

The Parque Espana development received the Design Excellence in Housing Award from the Boston Society of Architects in 2004.

The clean modern lines of the building's facade of aluminum and glass reflect the changing face of Mexico City's most modern district...

ABOVE
This interior view of the living area is taken from the second level of the penthouse. The importance of the "void" in architecture is seen in the designer's refusal to extend the loft further into the living area simply in order to gain more space.

SECTION VIEW

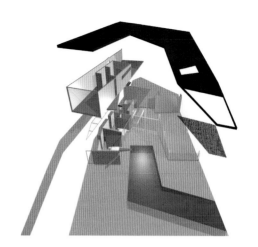

Ramp House BODRUM, TURKEY

GAD-Gokhan Avcioglu NEW YORK, USA

Construction	Yet to be completed
Home type	Multi-level family home
Structure	Steel core and fibrous concrete

"The 'Ramp House' reinterprets traditional dwellings in the area, yet its angular structure...fits into the clefts in the hillside and remains in keeping with the natural environment..."

GAD Architecture

BUILDING REGULATIONS

Bodrum is a seaside resort in southwestern Turkey, overlooking the blue Aegean Sea. The area has a long history, going back some 3,000 years, and as a result local planning authorities impose strict regulations on new building developments. In order to gain approval to build here, the architects had to either devise an innovative interpretation of the traditional villa-style home that predominates in the area or relate the design in some way to the town's ancient roots.

ANCIENT INSPIRATION

And so they did. The design of Ramp House was inspired by the Mausoleum of Halicarnassus, one of the Seven Wonders of the Ancient World. Built in about 350 BCE and renowned for its unique design, the Mausoleum had four steep staircases, one on each side. The distinctive "ramps" in Ramp House are a modern interpretation of this design.

Still at the planning stage, the home is 4000 sq ft (370 sq m) and will be built from a steel core and covered in fibrous concrete. The design blends with the undulating landscape and incorporates a multi-

functional rooftop terrace. Conveniently, the ramp access to the roof provides a neat solution to accommodating the owner's collection of motor cycles – the parking area is on top of the house. This way too, the first level, with its courtyard and pool area, will be kept clear of vehicles, allowing unimpeded views of the water and the valley.

There is also a roof terrace at the top of the house, which serves as an observation deck and entertaining area. In the hotter months, this will also be an inviting space, where one can sleep under the stars.

OPEN LIVING

Overlapping floor planes in the house adapt to the shape of the land. A ramp leading to a roof terrace can be accessed by both foot and bike, and expansive views of the valley and the bay can be enjoyed from all areas of the house.

The design of the house is very open, and the living spaces are generously proportioned. Because the climate in this part of Turkey is very hot, it is vital to create a flexible connection between the interior and exterior spaces. Floor to ceiling glass windows help to create this connection, allowing plenty of fresh air to circulate around the house. Their other function is to give sweeping views from every room.

TOP
An exploded view of the "Ramp House" showing how the rooms relate to each other.

LEFT
Defying the traditional style of the area, yet remaining in harmony with it, the architects found inspiration for the angles and "ramps" in the ancient Mausoleum of Halicarnassus.

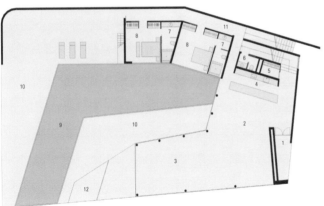

LEVEL ONE

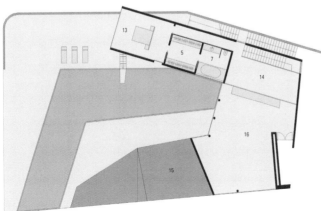

LEVEL TWO

1 entry
2 dining
3 living
4 kitchen
5 dressing
6 toilet
7 ensuite
8 bedroom
9 pool
10 courtyard
11 rooftop terrace entry
12 ramp to roof
13 main bedroom
14 mezzanine
15 roof
16 roof terrace

TOP
Defined by angles, the living room and the pool beyond become part of the landscape, tucked into the cleft of the hillside. One of the architects' signatures is the use of a neutral palette for interior finishes – easy on the eye and reflective of the natural landscape outside.

ABOVE
The roof ramp of the elongated living and dining room section almost collapses into the pool, which like everything else is both streamlined and angular.

Shanghai Star Mei Hwa Estate   SHANGHAI, CHINA

Ben Wood Studio Shanghai

Construction	In progress
Home type	Restored historic villas and contemporary villas; high-rise apartments with panoramic views
Structure	Villas: brickwork. Apartments: beam-free, flat plate tubular structural system

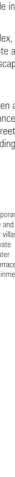

"The goal of this project is to create the most unique and prestigious residential address in Shanghai, and, indeed, in China. The generous amount of land in the Mei Hwa Estate allows the creation of many amenities usually not found in densely populated Shanghai. Here people live, entertain, and enjoy the things that mean the most to them."

Ben Wood

LIVING AN EXCLUSIVE LIFESTYLE

The villas, apartments, and gardens of Mei Hwa Estate form a secluded and tranquil living space for the residents, protected from the outside by a bamboo screen wall and dense shrubbery. In Shanghai, no other residential complex so close to the city enjoys such a large expanse of landscaped gardens.

There are 20 existing villas within the site, of English, French, and German styles. Of these, seven will be retained, and nine new villas constructed in a contemporary style, compatible in scale and size with the historic villas. Each villa will have a private garden featuring a south-facing lawn and a water feature. Both old and new villas will be located on existing landscaped roads – the old and new, side by side in a country landscape.

There are four high-rise towers within the complex, each positioned artfully on the site so as to create a particular relationship with the surrounding landscape.

PRIVATE GARDENS, HIDDEN DELIGHTS

The gardens of the estate are designed to be seen and enjoyed only from inside the estate. At the entrance to the estate, a low stone and copper gatehouse greets visitors, and overhead a trellis connects this building to the screen wall surrounding the complex.

LEFT
Lakeside villas are to be constructed in a contemporary style compatible in scale and size with the existing historic villas. Each villa will have a private garden with a unique water feature. Large outdoor terraces provide areas for entertainment and relaxation.

A country lane meanders from one end of the site to the other, passing through a lush landscape of lawns, lakes, and gardens. Unlike the world outside the walls, no radios play, no horns honk, and no trucks rumble.

The recreational facilities in the complex are situated at the southern end of the site, so the north gardens, with small curved lake and undulating beds of ornamental grasses and fragrant flowers, remain the more tranquil space. The southern gardens are the setting for the South Lake Towers. Also in the area are small pavilions, covered arbors, rose gardens, playgrounds, tennis courts, and a band shell for live concerts.

PANORAMIC PLEASURES

Outlook is important for all the residences. The northern garden apartments look out on the north lake and gardens, framed by the foliage of mature trees, many more than 75 years old. Each villa by the south lake comprises two duplex apartments, both of which enjoy ground level views of the lake and common gardens from their living and dining areas.

Panoramic views of the district can be enjoyed from the living and dining areas of the tower apartments. Like the large trees that surround the towers, the cladding of the building is predominantly green – green stone panels alternate with bands of glass, which reflect the surroundings.

MASTERFUL MATERIALS

The tower structure is tubular, comprising a reinforced concrete core that forms shear walls, with reinforced concrete columns providing the outer ring at the building edge. To minimize the thickness of flat plate, inner columns are incorporated between the core and outer-ring columns. The outer-ring columns are set back from the building edge so that the curtain wall is supported by the cantilever flat plate.

THE ORGANIZATION OF SPACES

There are two apartments per level in the towers – half are three bedroom, and the remainder are either four bedroom or two bedroom.

All units have a small maid's room, bath, and balcony adjacent the kitchen. A separate elevator connecting to a service lobby at the ground floor provides direct access to each kitchen and maid's area.

Two garden or sky penthouses share an entire floor of each tower. There is a great deal of flexibility in the size and configuration of these luxury homes. The penthouses have an area of approximately 4,140 sq ft (385 sq m), but can be made smaller or larger depending on the arrangement and size of the balconies and roof terraces.

ABOVE
Apartments in the towers have floor areas ranging from 1,980 sq ft (184 sq m) to 4,150 sq ft (385 sq m): Floors two to eight are garden apartments; floors nine to 10, garden penthouses, boasting extensive balconies and outdoor terraces; floors 11 to 30, sky apartments; and floors 31 to 32 sky penthouses.

RIGHT
A contemporary lifestyle is accommodated in residences that range in character from a restored mid-twentieth century villa to a modern penthouse apartment atop one of the 32-story South Lake Towers.

GU YANG LU 古羊路

Skyhouse, London
LONDON, ENGLAND

Marks Barfield Architects

Home type	Apartment tower block, 30–50 stories high
Structure	180 homes per 2.5 acres (1 hectare); concrete, steel, and glass

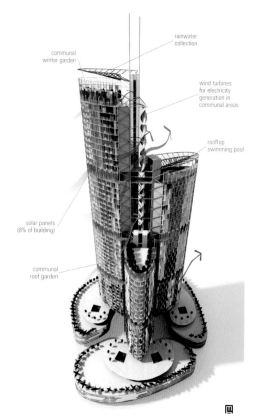

communal
winter garden

rainwater
collection

wind turbines
for electricity
generation in
communal areas

rooftop
swimming pool

solar panels
(8% of building)

communal
roof garden

"These aren't the old tower blocks that everyone loathes. Skyhouse has learnt from the past. We have designed buildings that look beautiful, set them in wonderful landscapes, focused heavily on quality of life and sought to meet commercial, environmental, political, and social housing requirements. In short, we think we have created a future way to live – a symbol of modern Britain."

Julia Barfield and David Marks

Architects David Marks and Julia Barfield set themselves a challenge – to redress a paucity of housing options for key sector workers in London by creating high-density, affordable, and aesthetically pleasing apartments that make clever use of light and space, and also offer fantastic views. The emphasis is on building an environment where people want to live, rather than a place where they have to live.

The project integrates within its tall exterior a wide range of housing choices and sizes, including shops, health clubs, and gardens. It uses green technology, including the renewable energy sources of solar and wind, as well as the latest insulation and recycling systems.

PRACTICALLY UNCONVENTIONAL

The aim of Skyhouse is to offer affordable apartment living to teachers, nurses, and police – key sector workers that sometimes have difficulty purchasing a home in an expensive city. Clusters of Skyhouses can be built within the setting of a new urban parkland, without disturbing London's historic sightlines – close to places of employment yet a world away from city hustle and bustle.

HIGH-RISE WITH HEART

Skyhouse takes a fresh look at the concept of residential tower blocks, making them places where people actually want to live. This is reflected in the provision of communal amenities: a rooftop swimming pool and double-height "skygardens" and "skylobbies," all with spectacular city views. The ground level is set in a pleasing, landscaped, or mixed-use urban context. Security is maintained via secure underground parking and a 24-hour concierge. Proximity to shopping and transport are other community positives.

THE GREEN SCENE

Integral to the project is the use of sustainable green technologies, which are cost-saving: Eight percent of the building is covered in solar panels; floor to ceiling glazing affords not only panoramic views but passive solar heating; high insulation and a resultant low demand for heating; wind turbines generate electricity for communal areas; and rainwater is collected from the rooftop and stored for use in skygarden areas.

LEFT
Enormous glass panels and a louvered glass roof envelop the teardrop rooftop pool. The pool is an important inclusion in the Skyhouse design concept – it helps create a focal point and meeting place for residents.

TOP
Double-height communal skygardens are a key feature of the project. The architects believe these areas, with their expansive city views and relaxed "green" environments, are a crucial part of creating places where people actually want to live. There is also an emphasis on security, convenience, and sustainability. "Green" initiatives, such as rainwater collection systems, recycling, wind-generated electricity, and solar panels are integrated into the structure.

ABOVE
A range of homes, from affordable one- or two-bedroom apartments to more expensive three- or four-bedroom duplexes can be accommodated within the structure. Extensive use of glass and high quality contemporary finishes add to the relaxed, urban appeal.

Tyson Street House MELBOURNE, AUSTRALIA

Jackson Clements Burrows Architects

Constructed	2005
Home type	Two-story family home
Structure	Timber frame, glass, steel, and polycarbonate cladding

"This project involved the replacement of a weatherboard cottage that was covered by a heritage overlay with a new two-story home. On the basis that the local council recommends retaining such buildings, the project called for an innovative response. The house is concealed behind a photographic image of the original cottage, which has been applied as a graphic overlay to a three-dimensional facade. Could this ironic gesture be an example of the streetscape ultimately preserved by the problem itself?"

Jackson Clements Burrows Architects

CONTEXT, DECAY, AND HERITAGE

Located in a narrow back street in inner-city Melbourne, the original single-fronted weatherboard cottage on the site was in a state of decay. The client's brief to the architects was to replace the existing house with a new two-story family residence. In the architects' opinion, the decrepit dwelling had little or no heritage significance – the council heritage adviser disagreed, however, suggesting that the house made a significant contribution to the character of streetscape. A compromise had to be reached.

The client was keen to avoid the time and cost implications of possible planning tribunal hearings. Predictably, they were told that the council's heritage advice would be to replace the existing structure with a building similar in form, scale, and detail to that of the surrounding buildings.

IDEAS AND EXPLORATION

The architects accepted the notion of appropriate form and scale for a property bound by heritage constraints, but questioned the validity of designing yet another "polite" contextual building as a means of commemorating the existing streetscape. They took a lateral approach to the vexing problem, formulating an innovative and workable solution. They explored the idea of context and memory by making it "virtual" – in essence, they attempted to immerse the new house into an image of the old house.

VIRTUALITY OR REALITY?

The architects worked on creating a new form – one that was of a scale and proportion appropriate to the small site (just 3,000 sq ft [280 sq m]) and to the neighboring buildings. The new facade was then clad in glazed panels and superimposed with a photographic image of the original single-story house at 1:1 scale. The image was printed on adhesive film and applied to the inside face of the glass panels, where it would be protected from sun and rain exposure. The image wraps itself around the panels, complementing the roof forms of the neighboring houses and reflecting the sky above. This configuration also helped to diminish the scale of the upper story. In this way, the single-story streetscape could be preserved by concealing the larger and higher form of the new house.

RIGHT
Employing inventive "smoke and mirror" tactics to satisfy the council's heritage requirements, the modern facade of the new house preserves the history and appearance of the single-story streetscape by concealing it behind an photo-realistic image of the original dwelling.

GROUND FLOOR

FIRST FLOOR

ROOF

INTERIOR RELATIONSHIPS

The living area, kitchen, bathrooms, bedrooms, roof decks, and double lock-up garage are concealed behind the photographic facade of the original dwelling. The house unfolds as a series of protected private spaces, opening out to interact with the garden and city views at the rear. A large lemon-scented gum tree is the only physical remnant of the original site. It was retained as a focal point for the garden, and its importance is recognized throughout the house interior by the use of colored laminate panels, sampled from the tones of the tree's seasonal bark and leaves.

COMMENTARY THROUGH ARCHITECTURE

This project is a response to the difficulties that may be encountered when required to create architectural solutions within heritage zones. It attempts to give rise to further debate about the sometimes conflicting aims of preservation and innovation within an architectural framework. In this sense, it is both a critique of the process and a surreal architectural solution.

PREVIOUS PAGES
The first floor roof deck provides a sculptural outdoor space to enjoy the expansive city views. Environmentally responsible principles were adopted during construction of the house, including the use of sustainable regrowth timber throughout.

RIGHT
Cost and energy efficiencies were integral to the project — external cladding materials are low maintenance, and glazing areas are limited and appropriately orientated to utilize their passive heating and cooling properties.

TOP
The multicolored laminate panels used in the kitchen echo the changing hues of the garden's lemon-scented gum tree. Two layers of polycarbonate cladding provide filtered natural daylight from the roof deck into the main entry area of the house.

ABOVE
An elegant choice of interior finishes imbues the light-filled and relaxed living/dining area with warmth and sophistication. The adjoining brick side fence, visible through the large window, pays homage to the cottage that originally stood on the site.

Voler House SAN DIEGO, USA

Wallace E Cunningham

Construction	2006–2008
Home type	"Two-level" residence
Structure	Post-tensioned concrete floor slabs, steel frame superstructure, and structural glazing system

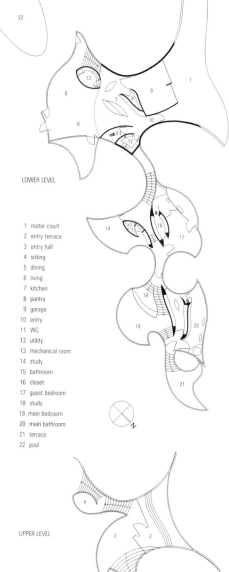

LOWER LEVEL

1 motor court
2 entry terrace
3 entry hall
4 sitting
5 dining
6 living
7 kitchen
8 pantry
9 garage
10 entry
11 WC
12 utility
13 mechanical room
14 study
15 bathroom
16 closet
17 guest bedroom
18 study
19 main bedroom
20 main bathroom
21 terrace
22 pool

UPPER LEVEL

> "Houses should be portraits of their owners, not the architect. Although each project is driven by the site and program, the design should be triggered by some poetic quality of the person who will live there."
>
> Wallace E Cunningham

ABOVE
The building has a sense of "movement" – the inert structure seemingly trying to free itself from its earthly restraints. Slender structural supports provide minimal distraction, allowing one to enjoy the sheer audacity of it all.

RIGHT
The scale and complexity of the roof is apparent here, with each section corresponding to a living area below and designed to maximize views to the north, east, and west. The driveway and motor court can be seen in the upper right of the picture.

Descending along a rocky escarpment overlooking beautiful Lake Hodges, 31 miles (50 km) north of San Diego on the San Dieguito River, is the site for Voler House.

The home's dynamic roofline resembles the pattern generated by the blades of a helicopter slowly coming to a halt – already it is an emblematic icon of organic architecture.

VERSATILE MATERIALS

Designed in titanium, which is 30 percent lighter than steel and 50 percent stronger, the roof has a bronze patina (a thin greenish layer of copper sulfate with anti-corrosive properties), adding durability and virtually eliminating maintenance.

The home's curvaceous design permits light to enter it at varying angles throughout the day creating an intricate interplay of angles and shapes. Walls become palettes for abstract patterns of shadow and reflection that constantly alter the mood of the home, giving inanimate, inert surfaces a sense of movement.

The scarf-like roof triumphantly demonstrates the philosophy of its designer – that buildings are not merely visual objects, but that they also need to radiate emotion. The titanium-clad covering is seemingly suspended above the site with its structural elements situated outside the bounds of the building envelope.

The versatility of concrete is evident in the many sculptured internal spaces, resulting in an expression of character that is difficult to obtain with more traditional materials, such as stone or steel.

The practicality of architectural grade cast-in-place concrete is reflected in its ability to withstand earthquakes, in its energy gain that reduces heating and cooling costs, and its ability to resist pest and water damage.

HARMONIZING WITH THE ENVIRONMENT

A sculptural reflection of the clients, the home's design is governed by the need to maintain a constant physical and visual connection to the landscape. It tumbles and cascades down a rocky escarpment always in harmony with the environment, its directions determined by pre-existing granite outcrops and the site's topography.

Internal and external spaces are obliquely defined due to large expanses of frameless glass that permit the penetration of light throughout. Undulating ceilings climb skyward to maximize the vistas beyond.

Transitional stairways spiral their way through the interior following the contours of the ground below. Kitchen benchtops, bathroom vanities, and closets are designed to mimic the curved contours of the house.

Access to the home is via an upper level terrace that descends into the living/dining area. A central hallway curls its way through the interior providing a sense of discovery, with fresh spaces constantly revealing themselves. Beyond the guest bedroom with attached bathroom and study lie the main bedroom with its study and main bathroom. Next to this sleeping area, a private north-facing terrace provides views over Lake Hodges and beyond.

ABOVE
The combination of Voler House's titanium and cast-in-place concrete perfectly complements the home's granite surrounds. Terraced living areas make full use of the site's natural topography in a design that harmonizes with, rather than dominates, the environment.

Wall House AUROVILLE, INDIA

Anupama Kundoo BERLIN, GERMANY

Constructed	2000
Home type	Three-level family home
Structure	Brick masonry, RCC frame structure, timber, terracotta

> "I believe that given the environmental crises facing us today, architects need to find appropriate technologies to build permanent buildings with the least possible impact. I don't think we need to keep inventing new materials, but rather to find innovative ways of using the same old healthy materials from the local area to suit our modern needs. This has been my quest."
>
> Anupama Kundoo

ECOLOGICAL EMPATHY

This residence is remarkable in a number of ways: First, it uses environmentally friendly building materials and alternative technologies; second, it is energy efficient; and third, it suits both its climate and its surroundings. The architects and owners explored ways to maximize these qualities, so the house is eco-friendly in the way it handles water and waste.

In order to optimize the amount of air circulation, the house is oriented to the southeast. The plan is linear, and the house contains a long rectangular space within the brick masonry shell. The areas of the house are organized into a long row, with a hallway separating the various indoor spaces. Each area has been strategically positioned so that there is a fluidity between the alcoves and projections, which sit on the northeastern side of the house, and the large 14-ft (4.3-m) overhang of the main vaulted roof on the southwestern side.

TRANSPARENCY AND PRIVACY

The large living areas are open, while the more private spaces of the bedrooms are isolated from the rest of the house without being apart from it. The house essentially follows a simple design: There are clear delineations between the interior spaces, but the volume is designed so that the divisions between the inside and the outside are somewhat blurred.

These spaces flow out into the garden, reached by a long flight of steps. Timber is one of the main elements of the southwestern facade, and the use of mesh gives an impression of transparency. This allows views to the outside but also offers shade from the sun, protecting the interior from heat and glare.

DERIVING NEW FROM OLD

The facades of the house are exposed brick, and have been scaled back to the smaller proportions of traditional bricks. They have been set in a lime mortar with 10 percent cement added for strength. The walls are either 4, 8, or 12 in (10, 20, or 30 cm) thick, and as they deviate from the normal 1:2 proportion, bonds were specifically designed for them. These "achakal" bricks also play a structural role in the ground floor.

The house is double height, which boosts the cross-ventilation in the interior. Catenary vaults with hollow clay tubes provide insulation and have the added bonus of reducing the use of steel in the building. The guest bedroom features a flat terraced roof, which comprises extruded clay modules over partly pre-cast beams. These are quite common in the neighborhood, as they offer effective insulation for houses with flat roofs.

EARTHY RESPONSES

On the middle level, terracotta pots were used as fillers. This strategy increased the depth of the concrete while simultaneously reducing the amount of concrete and steel required. It is interesting to note that this area did not require insulation. Overall, this has led to lower energy demands. In addition, solar photovoltaics supply electricity. Solar energy also powers a water heater and a water pump.

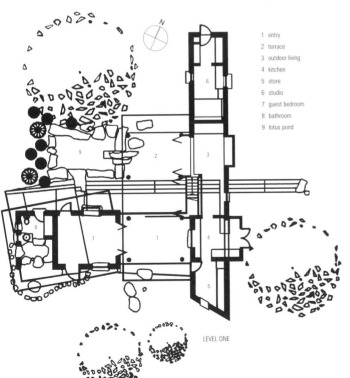

LEVEL ONE

1 entry
2 terrace
3 outdoor living
4 kitchen
5 store
6 studio
7 guest bedroom
8 bathroom
9 lotus pond

FAR LEFT
Supported by concrete columns, the vault shelters the house from the southwestern sun while also creating a transition space for various activities, such as outdoor living and dining – a must in a hot, humid climate.

TOP
The bedroom alcove projects out of the "wall" beneath the rain tree. Mesh screens keep mosquitoes at bay while also controlling the amount of glare from the southwestern sun during the late afternoon.

ABOVE
The lotus pond on the upper level lends an atmosphere of quiet contemplation to the terrace, which projects from the southwestern side of the building. The stairs lead down to the garden.

Zhujiajiao Cambridge Water Town SHANGHAI, CHINA
Ben Wood Studio

Constructed	2005
Home type	Contemporary style villas, townhouses, combining the traditional Chinese courtyard house style
Structure	Two–four level, load-bearing brickwork

"In modern China, we want both the old and the new. Using the age-old principles of water town planning, this master plan connects us with our history. At the same time a community of new homes with contemporary amenities provides us with a modern lifestyle."

Ben Wood

THE BEAUTY OF WATER

The beauty of a water town comes from an organic relationship between mankind and nature, and this relationship gives form to the built environment: The architect sees it as DNA expressed in the art of architecture.

The layout for this modern-day water town was derived from historic patterns of settlement. The physical relationship between buildings and water and public access to both water and buildings were the key organizing principles. Water is within walking distance of every home. Following a more than one-thousand-year-old tradition, the village center is located in the middle of the site, at the intersection of several canals.

TRADITION MEETS MODERNITY

As well as tradition, the project had to embrace a modern lifestyle, so the architect's challenge was to effectively blend new and old, innovation and tradition, change and continuity.

RIGHT
Inspired by the adjacent Zhujiajiao Old Water Town, the architect created new canals and built the villas around them. The architect's vision was to create a complex for families with a modern lifestyle, who also wished to be connected to nature and tradition.

TOP RIGHT
The vertical composition of the three-story villas is a reinterpation of the traditional Chinese architectural style. It retains the quality of intimacy of the older style, but unlike its predecessors it has plenty of light and natural air circulation.

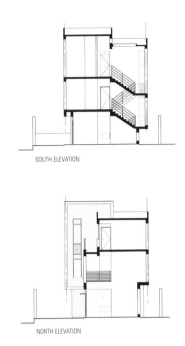

SOUTH ELEVATION

NORTH ELEVATION

THREE-STORY VILLA

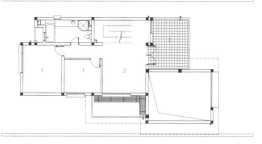

ROOF LEVEL

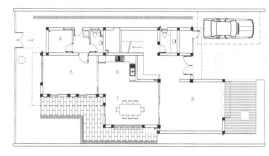

LEVEL TWO

1 guest
2 family
3 terrace
4 employee quarters
5 breakfast
6 kitchen
7 dining
8 living
9 main bedroom

LEVEL THREE

LEVEL ONE

N

ABOVE
Glass doors in the dining room open out to the home's court-yard, making it an extension of the living area.

RIGHT
Each three-story villa contains a spacious double-height sitting room with a glazed wall on one side and a folding glass door on the other, ensuring ample light and cross ventilation.

HISTORIC TIES

The historic Zhujiajiao Old Water Town is adjacent to the current site. Known as the "Venice of Shanghai," the old town is one of four famous old "cultural towns" in Shanghai. The new site works with the old.

Three sides of the current site are surrounded by water, and a river goes through it from the northwest corner. To emphasize the town's character, new canals were built around old ones. This also meant that the village center and townhouses could be situated around the water.

"Water alleys" and "street alleys" are the fabric of a traditional water town, both with specific functions. Water alleys were the main channels for traffic, commodity transportation, and connections to neighboring villages; street alleys were filled with necessary supply stores, side-by-side for ease of shopping and communication.

COURTYARD STYLE

The vertical composition of the courtyard houses is a new interpretation of a traditional Chinese architectural style. It achieves the essence of intimacy of traditional courtyard houses, while at the same time resolving the disadvantages of poor air circulation and lack of natural light.

The courtyard extends the living area from the dining room via glass doors.

SOMETHING FOR EVERYONE

About 55 percent of the town's homes are villas with two to three floors. The main bedroom of the three-story house is on the third floor with private bathroom and balcony. The first floor, with a fixed glass wall on one side and a folding glass door on the other, functions as the main sitting room. Large glass windows allow a connection to the outdoor yards. Each house has its own parking and an employee's room adjacent to the breakfast room and kitchen.

About 45 percent of the homes are townhouses with three to four floors. Two townhouses are linked by bridges on the second and third floors. They share an inner courtyard with a public staircase, which creates the feeling of being in a garden before entering the home. The upper unit entrance is on the third floor.

Gray bricks and roof tiles are the main materials for traditional houses in southeast China and these were the inspiration for Zhujiajiao Cambridge Water Town. Large glass walls on the first floors let in plenty of natural light, and connect the interiors visually and spatially with the exterior.

ABOVE
Surrounded by a lotus lake, the community center is the focal point of the water town. The large terrace on the top floor overlooks the whole of Zhujiajiao Cambridge Water Town.

Chapter 12

In the
Country

A home in the country embraces the natural environment, inviting designs that capture views of the landscape while at the same time harmonizing with it.

The main design intent of a home beyond the city limits – perhaps a farmhouse surrounded by pasture or a cottage tucked among the trees – is to exploit the intimate relationship it has with the natural landscape.

Living in a rural setting has the advantage of being in a vast private space with nature right at the doorstep. This can foster a desire to protect the existing vegetation, so homes are often built with a greater sensitivity to the landscape.

But the remote location may mean there are no existing infrastructure and utilities. There may also be less community contact, with reduced access to amenities. Despite its disadvantages, a home in the country serves to cultivate a relationship with nature that cannot be found in the city.

UNLIMITED VIEWS

The private space of a rural property provides unlimited access to the natural landscape, affording the home the greatest potential for views. And without the rigid constraints of designing a home in the city – blending into a streetscape or orienting toward a particular view – the location of a home on a rural block is ultimately flexible. It can capture views from anywhere.

Before the design process begins, the architect may identify particular views as focal points to be exploited once the home is built. A glimpse of a grove of trees might suggest the location of the bedrooms, while a vista that stretches cross the landscape would suit a living room. Taking advantage of such views could necessitate locating the home on a higher contour or building it on two levels.

LIGHT FOOTPRINT

If the site has no infrastructure and utilities in place, there may be an imperative to leave the existing landscape undisturbed, resulting in a home with a light footprint.

The home should merge with the landscape without unsettling the existing environment. A series of pavilions could be nestled into the descent of a steep incline, or an internal courtyard could be designed around an existing tree. Using solar energy or rainwater tanks instead of town supply further reduces the impact of the home on the environment.

A home in harmony with its natural surroundings still makes a statement on the landscape. This separateness can be expressed architecturally by raising the structure off the ground, making the lightest footprint of all.

NATURAL INFLUENCE

Ideally, the architect should borrow forms from the environment and replicate or reinterpret them in the design of the country home. If a home is built in a forested area, an exposed post and beam method of construction could echo the tall trees outside. A stone walkway could mimic a rocky outcrop, or an indoor plunge pool could be designed to look as if it is a natural part of the landscape.

PART OF THE ENVIRONMENT

A home in the country offers access to the natural environment, a private retreat from the outside world. Such a home should be designed to have a light footprint, with architectural details that echo the surrounding landscape.

ABOVE
Bowral House,
Glenn Murcutt

TOP RIGHT
Möbius House,
UN Studio

OPPOSITE
Chameleon House,
Anderson Anderson Architecture

Berman House JOADJA, AUSTRALIA
Harry Seidler & Associates

Constructed	2000
Home type	One-story, split-level home
Structure	Floors: concrete on steel support system. Walls: sandstone collected from the site and concrete blocks. Roof: steel framed with corrugated steel roofing

"The location was resolved after hours of exploring the many acres available. The final location was chosen because it combined magnificent views with generous, safe play areas for children, proximity to power, and a deep recess for a natural pool. This house is a culmination of Seidler's Modernist work, shaped as much by a global culture and technology as by the rugged Australian landscape and climate that it inhabits so compellingly."

Harry Seidler & Associates

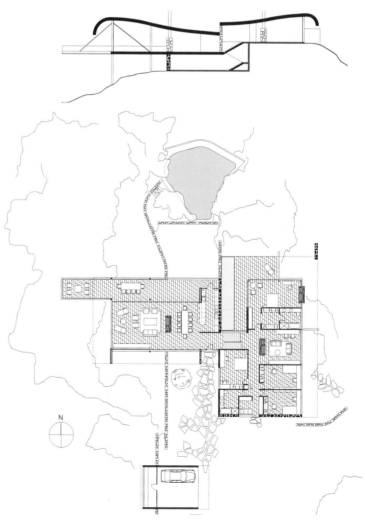

A HAVEN IN THE WILDERNESS

Berman House is situated in country New South Wales, on the crest of a rugged escarpment surrounded by a vast area of natural wilderness and overlooking a meandering river far below. The house itself is positioned against a large rock platform, so the living area is suspended and the balcony projects out from the home dramatically, taking full advantage of the beautiful natural setting. The vista from the living area is quite breathtaking.

The house is organized on two levels, with the enclosed bedroom area strategically placed above the generous living area. The living area is essentially a large pavilion with a preponderance of glass.

The main bedroom has been deliberately located on the northern end of the bedroom wing in order to take full advantage of sunlight, not to mention the splendid views to the northwest. An intimate view of a peaceful reflecting pool between the living and sleeping areas adds a dramatic contrast.

There are three other bedrooms, for children and for visitors. These are separated from the main bedroom area by a cosy living room that has its own fireplace. These three rooms share the main bathroom, while the main bedroom has its own large ensuite bathroom.

Following the natural topography of the site, the living room, kitchen, and dining areas are located half a level below the bedrooms. In order to suit the clients' casual lifestyle, and to maximize exposure to the spectacular outlook, these rooms are open plan, with a free-standing sandstone fireplace separating the living room from the dining room and kitchen.

TOP LEFT
Berman House with its swimming pool is seen here in its natural bushland setting. The pool is not just for cooling off and having fun, it is also a source of extra water when bushfires threaten.

FAR LEFT
Seen from below the cliff face, the home's protruding balcony looks like a springboard from which one might dive into the river below.

ABOVE
Diagonal braces and steel columns from the roof support the home's gravity-defying balcony, which is suspended over bushland and the Wingecarribee River.

FOLLOWING PAGES
The unique curved roofs, offset from one another, make the home a sculptural presence in the bushland surroundings. This view of the home's north elevation and pool shows the sleeping pavilion on the left and living pavilion on the right.

ABOVE
Floor to ceiling glazing on three sides of the living room gives spectacular panoramic views of the rugged Australian terrain and river below.

LEFT
View from the main entrance looking toward the dining and living areas. In an otherwise open plan space, the sandstone fireplace between the rooms gives some definition to the specific areas.

BOTTOM LEFT
Berman House's living and sleeping pavilions are separated by this stone paved courtyard and reflecting pool. The wall behind the pool is faced in sandstone hewn from the site.

STRUCTURE AND STYLE

The floor is constructed of concrete, and there are curved steel beams framing the extensively profiled roofs of the living area, the bedroom wing, and the garage. New developments in technology have made it possible to create these interesting profiles using a series of different radii.

The long balcony protrudes out over the edge of the cliff, making a stunning architectural and gravity-defying statement. It is hung from the steel columns of the roof and held in place with diagonal braces. The straight lines of the balcony complement the offset curved roofs of the dwelling.

ON THE GROUND AND IN THE POOL

To create a contrast with the suspended roof structure, the house itself is fixed to the ground – a very rugged landscape – by projecting rubble stone screen walls placed randomly on the site, as well as support piers and retaining walls. All of these have been built from sandstone, which is present in quite large quantities on the site. A welcome sense of continuity between the house and the garage is established by the unbroken sandstone retaining wall.

The long balcony protrudes out over
the edge of the cliff, making a stunning
architectural and gravity-defying statement.

The sandstone wall also embraces the swimming pool, which is located and maintained between two big rocky outcrops to the north of the house. Energy collectors have been positioned on the north-facing hillside right below the pool, allowing the water in the pool to be solar heated. As the area is also very susceptible to bushfires during the summer months, the pool has another very important function – it doubles as a water reservoir.

When the pool is switched to bushfire mode, water is pumped to sprinklers that are hidden under the eaves and projecting living areas. The house itself is bushfire resistant, built entirely of fireproof materials, including reinforced concrete floors, white block, stone walls, and a steel roof structure.

WATER FROM THE HEAVENS

The difficult site means that there is no access to the town water or the sewerage system. To counter this, rainwater is collected from the roofs and stored under the house in a large central storage tank. Waste water is recycled – it is chemically treated and then used for irrigation.

ENERGY RESPONSES

Stone fireplaces have been placed throughout the house, providing a means of energy self-sufficiency. The house is mostly open plan, so the fireplaces also function as effective dividers between specific areas. To further heat the house, radiant floor heating has been installed underneath the stone paving stones.

The landscaping around the home has been designed to recreate the natural bush environment. There are two grassed areas to provide play space for the owners' young children. The entry courtyard was sensitively designed by the owners using indigenous plants and stone paving collected from the site, all harmoniously relating to the pristine bushland surroundings.

ABOVE
Glazed walls and the curved roof "floating" over the 23-ft (7-m) ceiling in the main lounge area, create the impression of a graceful bird in flight.

Bowral House BOWRAL, AUSTRALIA

Glenn Murcutt

Construction	1997–2001
House type	Country house, single dwelling
Structure	Single level, reinforced concrete, timber frame, and structural steel on concrete slab

"The public and work entries of this house are both protected by a courtyard and a sloping wind-deflecting wall that houses the main access gallery serving all rooms. This wind deflector is a response to my observations and experience with pressure differential."

Glenn Murcutt

ABOVE
Viewed from the north, Bowral House's three major functional zones can be easily read: garage/tractor shed to the left, entry courtyard, and the main residential wing, with, at the extreme right, the veranda roof extending out over the terrace.

ABOVE RIGHT
The main facing of the house for walls and roof is corrugated galvanized steel. On the garage/tractor shed, there is a further layer of photovoltaic cells and inverter, which provides electric underfloor heating. The north face of the bedrooms is modulated by reinforced concrete blade columns.

RIGHT
At the western end of the house, beneath the Dutch gable roof, are two bedrooms that have external sliding timber screens for sun protection. To the right, behind a wind-protecting wall clad in slate, is the formal entry court and the homestead's front door.

THREE LINEAR ZONES

Layers and lines define many of Glenn Murcutt's houses – not just his approach to climate. In Bowral House, one of his largest designs, Murcutt separated the house into three linear zones defined by the section, with each differentiated by its roof shape, and hence by a different internal volume.

RURAL IDYLL

Located at Bowral in the Southern Highlands of New South Wales, 125 miles (200 km) southwest of Sydney, the home is set amidst undulating and prosperous farmland, hedgerows, and expanses of green pasture. It is a beautiful place, but winter can be very cold. Winds from the southwest can be particularly fierce. At the same time, summers can be very hot. The design had to respond to these competing demands – to provide warmth and shelter, to open up to the sun and air, and at all times to maximize the dramatic panorama of an Arcadian rural landscape.

SILVER WINDBREAK

From afar, the house looks like a long silver windbreak. There are no windows in the west wall, which folds up and over toward the north sky. It encloses an entry gallery that shields the three major forms of the house: the garage/tractor shed; a small courtyard; and a large residential wing of five bedrooms and two living rooms.

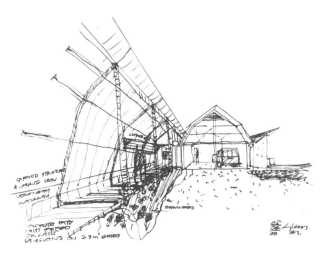

FOLLOWING PAGES
From the south, the Bowral House appears as a giant silver windbreak, or a low-lying cloud that might be reflected in the reservoir pond. The only vertical line is that of the fireplace flue.

The main living/dining/kitchen space has an internal volume that rises 15 ft (4.6 m). This big airy volume is grand, almost baronial in scale; it's rather like occupying the nave of a church.

HALL AS CATHEDRAL AISLE, HOME AS NAVE

The most extraordinary space of Bowral House is the 230-ft- (70-m-) long entry hall, an aisle-like space of cathedral proportions with sunlight bouncing off curving plaster. It's this gallery-like space which gives access to every room of the home. Murcutt has observed that "the form of the main access gallery suggests the wind-shaped trees" outside. The main living/dining/kitchen space, by contrast, has an internal volume that rises 15 ft (4.6 m) and reflects the wind-deflecting Dutch gable profile of the main roof. This big airy volume is grand, almost baronial in scale; it's rather like occupying the nave of a church. To the north, in this same space, windows overlook a broad terrace and it's here that the roof profile changes again, lifting up like the brim of a hat to the sky, and broadening at its end to form the third linear zone, a cantilevering veranda roof to the terrace. Along this north face, there are sliding insect screens, timber slatted screens, and glazed doors, all part of Murcutt's tripartite system of climate, light, and ventilation control.

FADE TO GRAY

The materials palette is consistently gray throughout. Floors are insulated reinforced concrete and finished in porfido stone or carpet. Externally, walls are either lined with gray slate, or where concrete, they are painted dark warm gray. Reinforced concrete columns and all corrugated galvanized steel wall linings and roofs are left in their natural state. Structural steel elements are painted in a natural gray, protective metallic. Paving is gray slate and porfido stone. Inside, plaster walls and ceilings are painted white and joinery is lined in clear finish timber veneer.

ABOVE
From a distance, the north face of the house at sunset highlights the dramatic upturned sun-catching eaves. Emphasized also is the mass of the terrace and the line of concrete blade columns, which indicate the module of bedrooms within.

RIGHT
The largest interior space is the living/dining/kitchen space, separated from the main access gallery by a wall of storage cupboards and joinery units. This is a grand space, a magical barn made into an elegant living space, or the nave of a church made into home.

OPPOSITE PAGE
The view from the front down the 230-m- (70-m-) long access gallery is dramatic. It's like looking down the aisle of a cathedral. Light spills down the curved profile of the wind-deflecting south wall. On the floor is the warm porfido stone, which grounds this ethereal, other-worldly space.

BR House RIO DE JANEIRO, BRAZIL

Marcio Kogan Arquiteto

Constructed	2004
Home type	Two-story house
Structure	Concrete construction with timber stilts

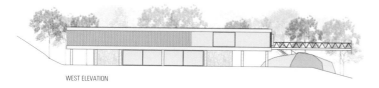

WEST ELEVATION

"In terms of an architectural proposition, BR House, located in the countryside, could not be more intriguing – the way the dense and impressive rainforest circumscribes and penetrates the area, and dominates all the senses. From the project's inception, the circumstances forced fundamental questions for our architecture: How can architecture present itself and how can it deliberately show itself as construction?"

Marcio Kogan & Gabriel Kogan

A RAINFOREST RETREAT

BR House is situated in a mountainous region of Rio de Janeiro – a particularly beautiful location. The challenge for the architect was to integrate the house with the forest landscape of creeks, towering trees, and brightly colored flowers. The architect wanted to create something that was not only in harmony with its surroundings, but was also comfortable and functional, stamped with his own particular style.

One source of inspiration for BR House came from another Brazilian house, Casa de Vidro (Glass House), designed by Lina de Bardi. That home is raised on stilts, seeking the same visual perspective as the crowns of trees; the use of glass blurring the distinction between the interior and exterior worlds.

Constructed as two monolithic cement blocks, BR House also stands on stilts. Raising the house in this way helps it to blend into its surroundings. The horizontal lines are visually distinct, while the vertical ones are designed to merge with the environment.

The thick wooden stilts or pillars of BR House are reminiscent of the trunks of the great trees in the rainforest, and give the effect of dimming the vertical lines, so the house seems to hover above the treetops. The beams and flagstones provide a contrast with the exposed raw concrete. In this way, the house proclaims its presence – it is not trying to hide in the forest; instead it affirms itself as a product of human endeavor and also as a place of shelter.

FILTERING THE LIGHT

The use of so much glass has created a transparent effect, and the house easily merges with the forest. This is because there are no frames – the glass is inlaid into the floor and the ceiling, creating an open, harmonious ambience.

The facade of the house is covered with a "skin" of vertical wooden laths or slats that create a light filter. When these slats are opened, they unfurl, turning outward as they open. A striking effect of the wooden facade is that in the evenings, the "skin" looks as if it is lit up.

SPACE FOR RELAXATION

The first level contains a heated swimming pool and a dry sauna, which has a large fixed glass wall, allowing an uninterrupted view of the landscape, the beautiful Atlantic rainforest. This area has been designed so that when one looks toward the pool, the glass wall acts as a frame to the scenery in the background. There is more than 70 ft (20 m) of door space on this first level, and a large rock sits half in and half out of the area, thus providing a link between the interior and the exterior.

The second level contains four bedroom suites, a guest bathroom, the kitchen, and the living and dining rooms. In the living room, the huge glass windows frame views of the surrounding forest, reducing to a minimum any visual barriers between the interior and exterior. Conversely, in the private part of the house, the wooden slats provide privacy for the bedrooms.

ABOVE
This view of the home's western facade shows how the bedrooms and kitchen on the upper level are faced with vertical wooden slats, which can be turned to admit more light. On the lower level is the leisure area, which includes a sauna, heated pool, and two bathrooms.

CENTER RIGHT
The inlaid floor to ceiling glass wall adjacent to the deck is virtually invisible, giving the illusion that one might step straight out into the forest. On the floor inside, the brown aluminum grid is the central heating duct.

RIGHT
This interior view shows the hallway that links the bedrooms with the living room. To the left, the entry deck "floats" among the rainforest trees. The thick wooden columns running alongside the glass wall are designed to echo the tree trunks outside.

FAR LEFT
A recycled wooden coffee table sits in front of the living room fireplace, which is faced with cinder limestone and topped by a stainless steel flue. The fireplace is flanked by a low wooden and cinder limestone closet housing the audiovisual system, designed by Marcio Kogan.

GETTING INSIDE

The terrain of the site made it possible to create something special. The house can be approached on both levels, but the formal entry is actually located on the second level, where the living areas are situated. (The first level houses the pool, jacuzzi, and sauna, and utility area.)

Instead of going up and down a staircase inside the house, one must go outside. On the second level, a bridge, or elevated walkway, passes over a small stream in the woods, and arrives at a wooden, tree-covered deck close to the entry door. Interestingly, this entry was built before the interior.

As night falls over the rainforest, the relationship between the interior and exterior of BR House acquires a completely new dimension. Once the trees disappear into the darkness, the house functions as a sort of flashlight. The interior light, filtered through the vertical slats in the private part of the house, or refracted through the expanses of glass in the living room, illuminates the surrounding forest, once again showcasing a house that is both a shelter and a form of artistic expression.

TOP
The elevated steel bridge connecting the parking area with the deck emerges out of the forest and leads to the second-level formal entry. The minimalist furnishings take nothing away from the breathtaking rainforest that surrounds the space.

ABOVE
Established rainforest trees "push" through the wooden deck, enhancing the impression that the house itself is part of the rainforest.

ABOVE RIGHT
A night view of the western facade of the house. On the lower level, the pool is lined with green glass pastilles. The pool area seems open to the elements but in fact it is protected by a glass wall.

FAR RIGHT
This view of the pool area is taken from the sauna. All the stone used for the wall facing comes from the property itself. To the left of the back wall is the end of an aluminum screen, which recedes into the wall.

FOLLOWING PAGES
Another view of the western facade of the house shows the mountainous terrain. The leisure area on the first level is inserted between two stone walls, while the second level houses the living areas and bedrooms.

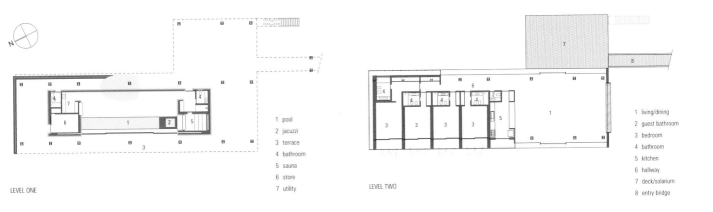

LEVEL ONE

1 pool
2 jacuzzi
3 terrace
4 bathroom
5 sauna
6 store
7 utility

LEVEL TWO

1 living/dining
2 guest bathroom
3 bedroom
4 bathroom
5 kitchen
6 hallway
7 deck/solarium
8 entry bridge

Chameleon House MICHIGAN, USA
Anderson Anderson Architecture

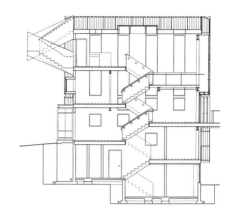

Constructed	2002
Home type	Family residence
Structure	Steel frame, prefabricated SIP panels

"A house would appear as an unsympathetic intrusion in this pure landscape, and with its singular vertical presence rising above the orchard, the tower is intended to reflect the austere, scaleless non-particularity of the occasional metal farm buildings dotted elsewhere on the hills."

Anderson Anderson Architecture

OPPOSITE
An exterior view in winter showing varied reflective surfaces of acrylic slats, glazing, aluminum window frames, and galvanized steel skin and stairs. This visual feast of textures extends into the steel-blue winter sky.

ABOVE
The cantilevered steel staircase that leads to the roof juts out from the main footprint of the building. This perspective is seen from the ground.

ABOVE LEFT
This view from the driveway approach shows the side of the house where the main entry is. Taken in spring, the surrounding grasses and rocks provide a lively contrast to the more subdued tones of the pre-fabricated materials.

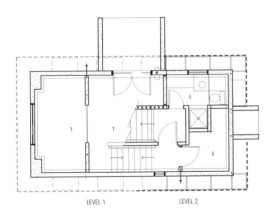

LEVEL 1   LEVEL 2

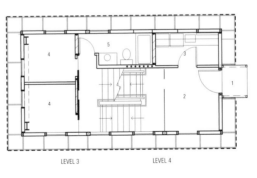

LEVEL 3   LEVEL 4

1   entry
2   playroom
3   laundry/pantry
4   bedroom
5   bathroom
6   work
7   storage
8   kitchen/dining
9   deck
10 main bedroom
11 main bathroom
12 living
13 guest/study
14 open to below

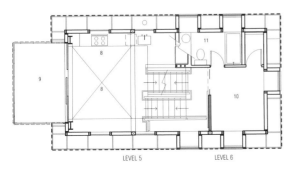

LEVEL 5   LEVEL 6

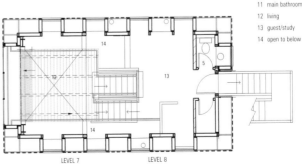

LEVEL 7   LEVEL 8

LAKESIDE LIVING

Chameleon House is designed as a tower, standing tall in the beautiful rugged landscape on a peninsula that extends into Lake Michigan. The clients, a couple and their three children, wanted to use the house at weekends and during vacations, and they were keen to maximize the views across the lake and the nearby cherry orchards.

There were a number of challenges faced by the architects in designing the house. First, the site is environmentally sensitive, and the terrain imposed its own restrictions. As a result, the foundations of the house take up less space than would otherwise be expected, stepping up into the natural slope of the land. This reduces the footprint while simultaneously allowing for more expansive lake and orchard views.

LIVING LARGE

It may not look it, but the house is small – 1,650 sq ft (149 sq m) – comprising nine different levels, with a roof deck. The deck is accessed by a cantilevered staircase that hangs from the outside of the structure.

The natural inclination of the site means that the entry is on level four of the house. The children's bedrooms and bathroom are located downstairs, and the main bedroom with ensuite is on the sixth level. The spacious living area is on the top level to optimize the sweeping views. The owners wanted large, open, family living spaces and smaller bedrooms, to encourage more communal gatherings, both inside and outside.

THE RIGHT MATERIALS

The architects decided to use some low-cost, quality prefabricated materials in the construction of the house, because of their adaptability. These materials are suitable for a range of site conditions and have minimal impact on the surrounding environment. The decision had a positive effect on the budget, but also meant that the house could be built quickly. Prefabricated panels were used for the exterior walls, floors, and roof. The steel frame and narrow height created volumes of space in the main living area, encouraging plenty of natural light and cross-ventilation.

The home's energy-efficient materials include solar heating, incorporating photovoltaic collection, and water catchment on the roof. Corrugated acrylic slats form the outer skin of the house, giving it a unique "chameleon" effect. The inner skin is reflective galvanized siding, which reflects the differing seasonal colors of the landscape. The overall effect is that the house completely merges with its surroundings at some times of the year, while standing out like a beacon at others – a true statement of originality. The inner skin also permits privacy, and screens out the worst effects of the sun and wind. It also creates a cooling effect for the house, as the heated air moves upward, drawing cool air into the interior, and eliminating the need for air-conditioning.

With such innovative design, it is not hard to see why Chameleon House is an award-winning construction.

Desert House CALIFORNIA, USA

Marmol Radziner + Associates

Constructed	2005
Home type	One-level single family residence
Structure	Prefabricated steel modules

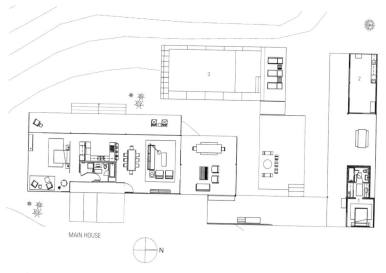

MAIN HOUSE

N

1 guest quarters
2 studio
3 pool

"The Desert House prototype home provided us the opportunity to explore the possibilities of developing eco-friendly modern prefabricated custom houses. We hope we will be able to help more people live a modern lifestyle, with the ideal beautiful spaces that enable indoor/outdoor living."

Marmol Radziner + Associates

BELOW
The Desert House stretches across the desert landscape in a series of enclosed spaces, covered walkways, and decks. The walls of windows and glass doors face the open environment and provide views to the San Jacinto Mountains.

AN OASIS IN THE DESERT

The Desert House prototype prefabricated home is oriented to best capture views of beautiful San Jacinto peak and the surrounding mountains. Located on a 5-acre (2-ha) site in Desert Hot Springs, California, the house extends through the landscape with covered outdoor living areas, which more than double the 2,100 sq ft (195 sq m) of interior space. A detached carport allows the owners to "leave the car behind" as they approach their home.

Designed for principal architect Leo Marmol and his partner Alisa Becket, the house employs four prefabricated house modules and six prefabricated deck modules. Sheltered living spaces blend the indoors with the outdoors, simultaneously extending and connecting the house to the north wing, which holds the guest quarters and studio space. By forming an L-shape, the home creates a protected environment that includes a pool, fire pit, and open terrace area.

AN ORGANIC APPROACH

While the walls facing the public dirt road are clad in metal siding to provide privacy for the owners, the walls facing the open terrace area are floor to ceiling windows and doors. This glazing floods the house with natural light, as well as providing extended views to the mountains beyond. The material palette of the home seeks to blend in with the surrounding natural

environment. The zincalum metal siding provides both durable protection and a weathered finish color that recedes into the landscape. The use of vertical grain cedar siding on the front entry and guest quarters introduces a rustic brown color to the home.

Seeking to complement the modern esthetic of the architecture and the organic beauty of the desert surroundings, the interior design reflects great esteem for nature and obscures distinctions between indoor and outdoor living spaces. By combining vintage, contemporary, and custom pieces, the home has a feel of understated elegance that highlights a genuine connection to the earth.

USING PREFABRICATION TECHNOLOGY

The home was built in a factory with prefabrication technologies, out of two basic types of modules: interior modules comprising the living spaces, and exterior modules that define covered outdoor living areas and provide protection from the sun. Using steel framing, the 12-ft- (3.5-m-) wide modules extend up to 64 ft (19.5 m) in length. The modules employ different types of cladding, including metal, wood, or glass, or are simply left open to the surrounding landscape. The modular steel frame construction is sustainable and durable, while allowing for maximum flexibility in creating large expanses of open space and glass.

The modules were shipped to the site, as were many "pre-installed" finishes, such as the custom wood cabinets and concrete floors. First, the steel floors and

roof frames of each of the modules were independently welded. Then, the floors and roofs were connected with steel columns. Once the full steel frame was prepared, the interior wall framing, plumbing, and electrical and mechanical components were completed. The finishes, cabinetry, appliances, and fixtures had been installed before the modules were shrink-wrapped for delivery. After being trucked to the project site, a crane then placed the modules onto the foundation, leaving minimal work left to complete the installation.

ABOVE
The Desert House is composed of ten prefabricated steel-frame modules. The design of the home places great emphasis on the merging of indoor and outdoor living spaces to create a modern retreat in the desert.

RIGHT
A long deck module runs the length of the main house, providing both outdoor living space and shade protection from the desert sun. The pool and studio, in the background, provide spaces for recreation at this weekend home.

FOLLOWING PAGES
Acting as a breezeway, a covered deck module connects the main house to the guest quarters and studio. Situated behind the vertical grain cedar siding, the guest quarters comprise kitchenette and full bathroom. As part of the prefabrication process, the concrete floors throughout the house were poured in the factory.

The wide concrete entry steps provide views to the deck module that connects to the guest quarters. In one day, a large crane placed all ten prefabricated modules on their concrete block foundation.

TOP RIGHT
Along the approach from the prefabricated carport to the front entry, a cutout section provides framed views of the San Jacinto Mountains and the guest quarters and studio wing of the house.

Since the house is located in the desert, the use of prefabrication provided an ideal way to ensure the high level of detail and precision for the less-developed location. In more remote locations, it can often be difficult finding a local contractor with the ability or the desire to build according to the exacting standards required by a Modernist design. Because the home's modules were constructed in a factory, it allowed for greater control over the details and finishes.

SUSTAINABLE DESIGN, SUSTAINABLE LIVING

Just as the spaces of the home embrace nature, so too do the designs and methods of fabrication. Because factory construction provides greater precision in cutting materials and increases the ability to save and reuse excess material, the construction of this home created significantly less waste than a home built on-site.

The factory-made modules employ renewable and environmentally friendly materials. For its primary structural system, the home is made from recycled steel rather than non-sustainable wood framing. Steel framing produces less waste because, unlike wood, the pieces are uniform in cut and quality. Steel also promises long-term endurance against natural elements, insects, and mold without requiring the chemical treatments necessary for wood framing.

To minimize energy consumption, the Desert House uses efficient materials and careful "green design." The home derives its electrical power from solar panels located on the roof above the bedroom, thus maximizing the benefits of the desert location. Deep overhangs shade the house from the harsh summer sun, and hidden pockets hold window shades that provide additional protection from the sun. In colder months, the concrete floors absorb solar energy during the day and release the stored heat at night, helping to make the home energy efficient. To increase insulation from the extensive use of windows and doors, triple-pane, low-emissivity (low-e), argon-filled insulating glass is used, which provides superior protection to standard glass. The floor to ceiling windows and doors supply ample natural night, thus eliminating the need for artificial light during the day.

As a prototype home, this house provided valuable design, fabrication, and installation lessons for the development of the architect's line of modern prefabricated homes. By combining Modernist esthetics, prefabrication technologies, and sustainable materials and design, the Desert House encapsulates a new potential for embracing a modern lifestyle that encourages indoor/outdoor living.

LEFT
The main house was prefabricated from two interior modules that are each 64 ft (19.5 m) long and 12 ft (3.5 m) wide. In the open plan, the living room, dining room, and kitchen all share a communal space, bound by the long wall of sliding glass doors.

ABOVE
The kitchen features custom-made teak cabinetry with cantilevered shelves and wall paneling – all constructed and installed in the modules prior to them being delivered to the site.

Gradman House CALIFORNIA, USA
Swatt Architects

Construction	2002–2005
Home type	Single dwelling, vacation retreat
Structure	Five-level, wood frame

"This design is a response to a near impossible site – a steep uphill parcel within a forest of towering cedar trees. The driveway switches back and forth, almost like threading a needle, to protect as many trees as possible, while the house has been designed with five ground-floor levels which 'tiptoe' on the land, providing access to the outdoors from every major space."

Robert Swatt

A FOREST LOCATION

The Gradman House is located on a steep up-sloping lot in Inverness Park, California, near the Point Reyes National Seashore. The site contains large mature cedar trees, and has beautiful filtered views of Tomales Bay to the northwest and the wetlands to the northeast.

LONG-TERM LIVING

The owners, a couple with grown children, currently live in Palo Alto, California, where they have been for more than 25 years. Through the years, the family vacationed in the area where the home is now located, and over time fell in love with the northern California coast. The new home is a vacation retreat for the short term, but will eventually become a permanent residence after the owners reach retirement.

The goals of the project are common to West Coast residential living – promoting enjoyment of the outdoors, maximizing views, and sensitively knitting the house to the land. It was important to provide access to the outdoors from all the major spaces in the home. The house and access road have been carefully situated to protect as many existing trees, most of them indigenous cedar, as possible.

USING TOPOGRAPHY

The house has been designed with multiple levels that "tiptoe on the land," minimizing grading and adverse effects on existing vegetation.

The dwelling includes five floor levels which gently step with the topography and create distinct zones for living. The entry and circulation space, located at the middle level, is designed as a light-infused central spine. It joins the "public" living and dining spaces at the lower level with the "private" bedroom areas at the upper levels. Each bedroom meets a natural grade and opens to its own private hillside terrace at the top of the site, whereas the living and dining areas open to expansive terraces with magnificent views to the bay and wetlands below.

ECONOMY AND STRENGTH

The building is a standard wood frame over a cast-in-place concrete pier and grade construction. The main living and dining area includes two levels of Douglas fir framing. The lower level includes glue-laminated beams that penetrate the space to create a low, wide overhang at the main terrace. Steel columns and beams have been kept to a minimum to keep the project economical.

1 main bedroom
2 ensuite
3 wardrobe
4 WC
5 bedroom
6 laundry
7 living
8 dining
9 entry
10 kitchen

ABOVE FAR LEFT
The front elevation, which shows the carport at the left and the kitchen at the right, features a stunning junction of textures including wood, glass, concrete, and stone. The construction is a standard wood frame over a cast-in-place concrete pier. Steel columns and beams have been minimized to help keep the project economical.

LEFT
Clean simple lines are the order of the day in this space with a color scheme to match. The openness of the upstairs corridor creates a connection with the living space below, ensuring one level of the house harmonizes with another.

ABOVE LEFT
The multi-level retreat features extensive floor to ceiling glass surfaces to maximize the surrounding woodland views. Warm natural timbers work hand in hand with sleek manufactured materials to create a perfectly balanced exterior.

The house includes five floor levels
which gently step with the topography and
create distinct zones for living.

ABOVE
From the glassed corner of the
kitchen and breakfast space
there are filtered views,
through the large cedar trees
that surround the site, of the
wetlands to the northeast.

LEFT
The living and dining area
features two levels of Douglas fir
framing. The lower-level, glue-
laminated beams penetrate the
space to create a low, wide
overhang across the entance.

FAR LEFT
In the bedroom wing, each
bedroom opens out to its
own private hillside garden at
the top of the site, complete
with viewing area to sit and
contemplate the superb
woodland vista.

House Lina LINZ, AUSTRIA
Caramel Architekten

Constructed	2004
Home type	Single-story family home
Structure	Timber, glass and steel, with fiberglass reinforced PVC-membrane

> "The question here was how to build a fully functioning home, with an inadequate budget and only a few weeks in which to complete the construction. We had a small space and were building a small house, but wanted to create the appearance of much bigger home."
>
> Caramel Architekten

SMALL SPACE, BIG PLANS

The biggest challenge for this project was how to build a practical, functional, self-sufficient home in a very short space of time and with very limited funds. Another consideration was that even though the house was small, the architect wanted to give the home the appearance of looking bigger by providing different rooms for different functions. This posed a number of problems because the house size is just 743 sq ft (69 sq m) and the budget was very small.

WHEN AN EXTENSION IS MORE THAN AN EXTENSION

The house is officially classified as an extension, but in reality it is an autonomous separate dwelling, for a mother and her child. The house is situated on family land in a pretty, partly wooded area on the south-western slope of Pöstlingberg, in the city of Linz. The design of the house takes full advantage of the beautiful panoramic views on offer, with extensive use of floor to ceiling glass. This also means the interior is bathed with natural light.

Though infrastructurally "docked" onto the extant building, the new unit includes all the necessary primary facilities, such as a full bathroom, kitchen, a heating system, and hot water. There is also a bedroom, a nursery, and a living room.

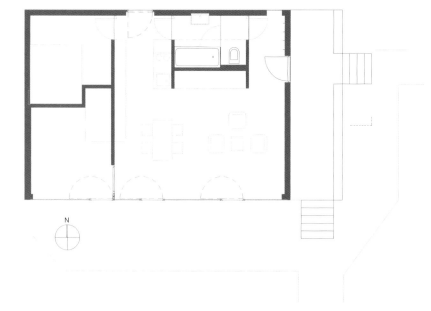

ABOVE LEFT
White walls and a cleverly placed floor to ceiling mirror give the small bedroom a spacious feel.

ABOVE
A glazed wall runs along the southern face of the home, flooding the interior with natural light. It also creates the illusion of a much larger home by making the room part of the wooded landscape.

N

STRETCHING RESOURCES

Because the architect was constrained both on a budgetary level and also because of the shortage of available construction space, the building's dimensions had to be very carefully determined. Through consistently rational planning, it was possible to reduce the duration and cost of construction. The proportions and the construction grid of the unit, for example, were designed in order to correspond with standard particleboard dimensions; and the building as a whole was planned using simple lightweight construction methods. The latter had the added bonus of providing an efficient system of thermal insulation.

Finally, it took only a few days to mount the partially prefabricated elements onto the completed steel framework, which is attached at regular intervals to the strip foundations of the dwelling. Because of the position of the building on the plot, it was not possible to use large prefabricated elements, so the architect decided to produce small elements, determined according to the size of the timber boards. These could easily be handled by two people.

A FLEXIBLE INTENTION

The dwelling is not intended to last forever, and this was a deliberate decision taken by the architect. It was designed so that it could be easily removed or extended, depending on the future living situation and differing requirements of the inhabitants.

ABOVE
Despite having a built area of just 743 sq ft (69 sq m), this compact home has all necessary primary facilities, including kitchen, living/dining, bathroom, and bedroom.

RIGHT
The veranda pulls out like a drawer from the main structure, the floor-level window representing the space left by the open drawer.

Jackson Family Retreat CALIFORNIA, USA
Fougeron Architecture

Constructed	2004
Home type	Two-story family home
Structure	Wood, copper, stucco, steel, and glass

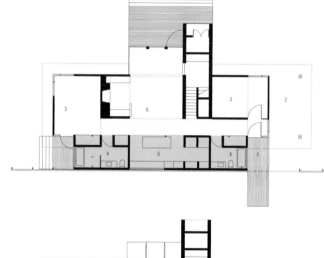

LEVEL ONE
1. entry
2. carport
3. bedroom
4. bathroom
5. kitchen
6. living/dining

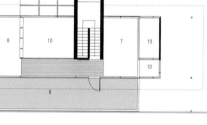

LEVEL TWO
7. sleeping loft
8. library
9. deck
10. open to below

TOP
Fashioned after nineteenth-century conservatories, a steel and glass enclosure protrudes from the rear facade, stepping out from the living/dining area and offering views of the nearby creek. Steel columns delicately lift the Jackson Family Retreat nearly 3 ft (1 m) off the ground, to reduce its impact on the land and protect it from flooding or damp soil.

ABOVE
A small gangplank leads to the entrance of the home, where a buttery yellow screen of Alaskan cedar slats extends horizontally across the south wall to shield the kitchen from the sun's glare. Glass of varying translucency allows the lofty open-plan interior to be filled with light – even when it's raining.

"...wild natural beauty and strict environmental regulations to protect it; extreme variations of canyon light, weather, and topography; and living spaces for both family reunion and retreat – for three generations... Resolving these opposing tensions in a compact house that would respect the land, reach for the sky, and communicate the relaxed intimacy of a Big Sur cabin was my inspiration and challenge."

Anne Fougeron

BIG SUR RETREAT

Located in the Big Sur area of Northern California, this 2,500-sq-ft (232-sq-m) two-bedroom house was built for a family to enjoy together on the weekends and holidays.

Jackson Family Retreat is a Modernist structure that sits lightly on the land acknowledging the ecologically fragile nature of the site. It took working with ten different consultants for three-and-a-half years to satisfy all the requirements of the local governing agencies that would have preferred to leave the site as it was – overgrown and uninhabited.

The house is composed of four volumes, all made of different materials that are interwoven and interconnected to create visually and spatially complex exterior and interior spaces.

USING THE CANYON

The steep walls of the canyon dominate the wooded site next to a creek. The house holds its own in this tall and cavernous place – neither dominating nor being dwarfed by it. The main volume of the house runs parallel to the canyon, with a butterfly roof and glass corners that reach out to the sky and the light at the open ends. The thin roof sits delicately above a band of extruded glass, connecting to the roof structure with thin rods that are invisible on the exterior.

At the corners of the house, two-story clear windows frame the views of the majestic redwoods and the sky at the ridge of the canyon. This volume is clad in standing seam copper.

FUNCTIONAL BEAUTY

On the front, the second volume is a one-story structure that includes all the service functions for the house and acts as a buffer from the dirt road, which leads to the other houses in this old subdivision. It is clad in yellow Alaskan cedar that is turned in three directions acting as a rain screen, a fence, and a railing. The material is left untreated, and as it ages naturally will become silvery gray in color.

The back of the house is open to the views of the creek with a custom steel and glass volume. Finally, the fourth volume of the staircase is both the seismic structural brace for the house and a visual foil to the shimmering and transparent volumes around it. It is clad with gray integral color stucco that wraps inside and out.

ABOVE
This glassy haven grabs every sliver of canyon light, looking out and up to grand views of Big Sur redwoods, ridges, and sky. Night exposes the transparency of the house, the glazed living/dining area acting as a welcoming beacon in the surrounding nature preserve.

RIGHT
The 52-ft- (16-m-) long roof deck stretches the length of the kitchen and bathrooms below, and is accessed via the steel bridge that bounds the living area. The private deck faces a grove of redwood trees.

On the ground floor, two bedrooms at opposing ends of the house sit either side of a two-story communal living space, fireplace room, and loft library above the living area. The 15-ft- (4.5-m-) high windows in the bedrooms dissolve the corners of the spaces, bringing light and views into the bedroom and living spaces of the house.

THE EFFECT OF GLASS

On the second floor, the space is open. The library and communal sleeping loft are separated from the upper level of the two-story bedrooms by glass walls.

A combination of transparent glass and extruded channel glass reflects and dapples the light on the inside, creating an ever-changing interior with a warm play of light and shadow throughout the day.

ABOVE
The compression and release of space evoke the architecture of Frank Lloyd Wright. Two-story corner windows in the first-floor bedrooms that bracket the central communal space not only create a soaring quality, as in Wright's designs, they also make the house look less large in relation to the site.

TOP RIGHT
The double-height living area is bounded by a steel bridge that connects a multipurpose room and loft library on the upper level.

OPPOSITE
The main living/dining area provides different kinds of spaces in which to be separate, yet connected. The focal point of this "retreat within a retreat" is an aingre-paneled fireplace inglenook with built-in seating, an area that exudes warmth and intimacy within the lofty room.

Kangaroo Valley House

KANGAROO VALLEY, AUSTRALIA

Glenn Murcutt

Construction	1996–1998
House type	Country house, single dwelling
Structure	Single level, reverse brick veneer on concrete slab, and steel frame roof

"The site is in a beautiful valley falling to the south. The house is sited as near as I could locate it along the contours, which provide a wonderful outlook to the escarpment. My clients wanted a very simple house, with living, dining, and kitchen together... It was very important to capitalize on the northern light to the rear of the house. The excavated earth was reworked to create a flatter terrace in front of the living space."

Glenn Murcutt

PROSPECT AND REFUGE

Located 120 miles (190 km) south of Sydney in New South Wales, between Nowra and Moss Vale, Kangaroo Valley House sits on a site of nearly 5 acres (2 ha). The site, which slopes to the south and faces and borders a national park, was formerly part of a large farm and includes grassland and "bush," the Australian term for untouched indigenous forest and shrublands. Pritzker Prize-winning architect Glenn Murcutt chose to locate the house relatively close to the road, and on part of the site that had previously been cultivated, so that the home's aspect would always include that of an untouched wilderness. As a weekender, this was to be an escape where one's view from the home would be a constant embrace of landscape – a classic description of one of Murcutt's favorite design themes: prospect and refuge.

TOUCH THE SITE LIGHTLY

Murcutt's next design strategy was to minimize the impact of the house on its site. He located the slim linear box with its single monopitch roof between two contour lines. The driveway came in from the east, also negotiating contours gently, so that on approach by car, the expanse and length of the valley was emphasized, and the presence of the car was made as unobtrusive as possible. Indeed the owner's car slips into and is hidden in one end of this linear block.

LINEAR PLAN

The plan of the house is a sequence of rooms laid along the contour. In line with, and following the garage are a studio, study/guestroom, bathroom, hallway (which splits the house in two), and then the true heart of the house – the refuge – a traditional farmhouse kitchen, which incorporates dining/living and a firebox, before the main bedroom, ensuite, and west-facing veranda/terrace. Murcutt is the master of the linear-planned house, and this plan form has been developed by him for more than thirty years. The single-room width plan (never more than 14 ft [4.3 m]) is also excellent for cross ventilation, and enables the capturing of sunlight and view, whatever the orientation.

TILTED ROOF, TILTED WINDOWS

The roof is tilted at 11° to parallel the slope of the land, and a continuous band of clerestory windows enables northern winter sunlight to penetrate the narrow plan. To the south, where the views are, large glazed sliding doors open up the kitchen/living/dining space entirely to the landscape. Elsewhere, there are tilted bay windows that serve a number of functions: shedding rainwater; incorporating ventilation flaps as sill panels; on the north side, external retractable venetian blinds for shade; while on the south, they have sliding timber screens to provide shade, privacy, and security. As Murcutt says, "It is one of my objectives to design openings to function in multiple ways."

SIMPLICITY IN MATERIALS

The materials palette for the house is understated, in contrast to the rich green of the surrounding pasture and soft gray-green of the distant landscape. Corrugated galvanized iron is used for roofing and for the four tanks that collect the home's drinking water. As winters can be cold in Kangaroo Valley, Murcutt chose to build the home in reverse brick veneer, with the internal brickwork walls clad in western red cedar. The double concrete floor has insulation between the slabs as well as cable heating. As a floor surface it was trowelled and given a latex finish. Elsewhere, joinery is painted white and benches are stainless steel.

ABOVE LEFT
The tilted bay window of the living/dining/kitchen space sheds water as well as acting as a shading device. External retractable aluminum venetian blinds can be closed to block out the summer sun. To the left is the front door. Above is the continuous band of clerestory windows and the repetitive series of tapering timber rafters.

ABOVE
In contrast to the openness of the living/dining/kitchen space is the enclosed refuge space of the main bedroom. A corner window frames a view of the escarpment landscape beyond.

TOP
A habitable veranda that can be completely closed or open is the theme of the home's major living space. Part traditional farmhouse kitchen, part elegant holiday pavilion, this is the sort of space that gives Murcutt's houses their universal appeal.

As a weekender, Kangaroo Valley House was to be an escape where one's view from the home would be a constant embrace of landscape – a classic description of one of Murcutt's favorite design themes: prospect and refuge.

RIGHT
The living/dining/kitchen space is the heart of the house. The proprietary firebox is built into a continuous stainless steel bench/joinery unit. The tilted bay window has as its sill, a series of ventilation flaps and insect screens, which can be opened and closed at will. Above, the tilted plane of the roof flies uninterrupted through the space.

Maison Goulet QUEBEC, CANADA

Saia Barbarese Topouzanov Architectes

Constructed	2003
Home type	Private residence
Structure	Steel-reinforced wood-frame construction, wooden frames, open wood metal trusses, and exposed plywood

"Maison Goulet is inextricably bound with its environment, designed in response to the site's topography, climate, and ecology. In planning and constructing in a dramatic landscape, isolated on a natural plateau, we noted the broader impact of design decisions on the local environment. Principles of sustainability formed an integral part of the design, informing every decision."

Mario Saia

ABOVE
At night the rooms throw a warm glow because of the reflected tones of the interior fir plywood paneling. The overall effect, from the outside looking in, is that of a sanctuary, secluded and safe from the extreme landscape outside.

TOP
Entry to the house is from the north, with stairs forming a buffer zone to the living areas situated to the south. On the north side, the facade remains closed to the harsh weather. The openings are few, and their dimensions reduced.

TOP RIGHT
The interconnected living spaces on the ground floor are extended into screened loggias at either end of the home. Seen here, the east loggia, which acts as a breakfast area. During the summer, the leaves of the trees filter the harsh southern sunlight.

RIGHT
A stone chimney terminates the western extension and signals the home's anchor point. The archetypal form of Maison Goulet refers to the traditional Quebecois rural residence, with its simple shape, practical roof form, and imposing chimneys.

A RETREAT FOR WORK AND LEISURE

A harsh landscape in the Quebec Laurentians and a steeply sloping site posed a challenge for the design of Maison Goulet. The slope runs from north to south toward a lake below. A sheer rock face forms part of the descent, acting as a retaining wall for the plateau upon which the house is situated. It is a long house, the shape being ordained by the projecting ledge that runs from east to west. Two chimneys, one located at the center, the other at the end of the house, anchor the steel-reinforced wood-frame construction. The zinc cladding provides an even finish.

THE WARMTH OF STONE

The house sits on a stone base. Prevailing winds are deflected by both trees and the walls of the house. The first level of the house, which lies on top of a 5-ft- (1.5-m-) deep stone core, covered by an irregular sawn-stone paving, serves to store the sun's heat. In the summer months, the foliage from the trees filters the sun's glare and heat. A ventilation system catches the warm air that has collected in the roof and then circulates it underneath the slab of the floor, keeping the house cool in summer and warm in winter.

The interior is lined with fir plywood, and the panels are placed horizontally, presenting a uniform continuous effect. There are no moldings or framing – there are simply openings, producing a dramatic outcome.

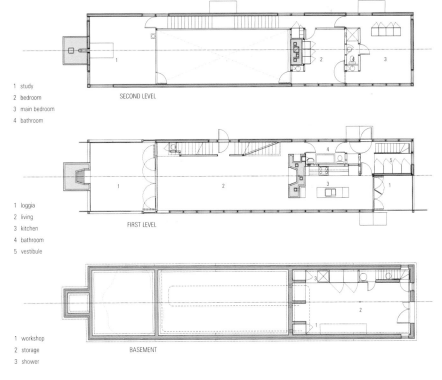

1 study
2 bedroom
3 main bedroom
4 bathroom

SECOND LEVEL

1 loggia
2 living
3 kitchen
4 bathroom
5 vestibule

FIRST LEVEL

1 workshop
2 storage
3 shower

BASEMENT

THE SYMMETRY OF STAIRS

The central space extends to the full height of
the house. Two independent staircases positioned
symmetrically, face to face allow access to the
second-floor bedrooms and the study. Although they
are on the same level, the study is quite separate from
the private area of the bedrooms.

The staircases are braced in parallel between the thick
northern wall and the second wall, which extends to
the level of the top plate, where the base folds at an
angle. This gives the effect of a sculpted-out space for
the living area below.

KEEPING THINGS IN PERSPECTIVE

In warmer weather, the large doors of the screened
loggias open out. Because the walls appear to disappear, the outside area gives the impression of making
the inside area much longer. On the second floor, a
series of "enfilade"(aligned openings) create the
perspective of length and continuity beyond the
east and west gable walls. This reinforces the initial
architectural concept and also orients the user toward
the landscape.

Because the architect kept the topography of the
site at the forefront of his mind, and also took into
account the climate and the position of the sun in
different seasons, the house is inextricably linked
to its surroundings.

Although the house at first glance may seem to have
many traditional characteristics, the simple lines and
volume of the home remove any superfluous details.
There is no ambiguity in the design and yet flexibility
is evident – there are a number of areas that offer
privacy and seclusion.

ABOVE
The private study and the bedrooms are located at opposite ends of the house on the upper floor, physically disconnected from one another with separate stair access.

TOP LEFT
In the winter, the sun is reflected in the snow, bouncing in through the windows and up to the ceiling. The intensity of the light makes the living area and the kitchen bright, as the windows are floor to ceiling. On a sunny day, changing patterns of light dance on the limestone floor.

Möbius House 'T GOOI, THE NETHERLANDS
UNStudio

Construction	1993–1998
Home type	Residential house
Structure	Glass and concrete on a concrete slab

"Möbius House represents a radical departure from long-held approaches to architecture that rely on traditionally aligned 'Platonic solids' in their design and construction."

UNStudio

GEOMETRIC GYRATIONS

This home was built using a principle of geometry known as the "Möbius Band" as the basis for its design. Imagine a strip of paper, turned once through 180° into a twisted figure eight, then attaching its two ends to produce one endlessly repetitive, non-orientable surface. Though not literally transferred to the building, the Möbius mathematical model can be found in architectural innovations throughout the house, including staircases, furniture, lighting, and in the way its occupants move through its interior. This endless repetition of the twisted figure eight is used in Möbius House purely as a design concept. It illustrates how two people can dwell together, yet be separate, while still sharing a common space. This premise lifts this residence out of the realm of architecture and into that of a provocative social experiment.

In an age where computers and computer modeling have become modern-day sketchbooks, experiments in constructing surfaces and solids based on pure mathematical formulas such as the Möbius Band are becoming increasingly common.

ABOVE
This view along the axis of the first-floor bedroom illustrates the profound relationship between the house and its surroundings. The project stretches over a 5-acre (2-ha) plot. The Möbius House is designed to provide an overwhelming sense of inter-connection with the environment.

ABOVE LEFT
The clients' wishes for their two working environments to be sited at opposite ends of the house can be seen to great effect here in Studio 1, a bold, cantilevered mass triumphantly forming the western end of the elevated ground floor.

TOP
Glazed exteriors are in the ascendancy on the southern elevation. Internal concrete partitions are clearly visible through the glass, highlighting the Möbius concept. The elongated design begins at left with Studio 1, which leads via an interior ramp to the meeting room (center) and through to the living room at right. The upper-level windows frame a guest bedroom and bathroom.

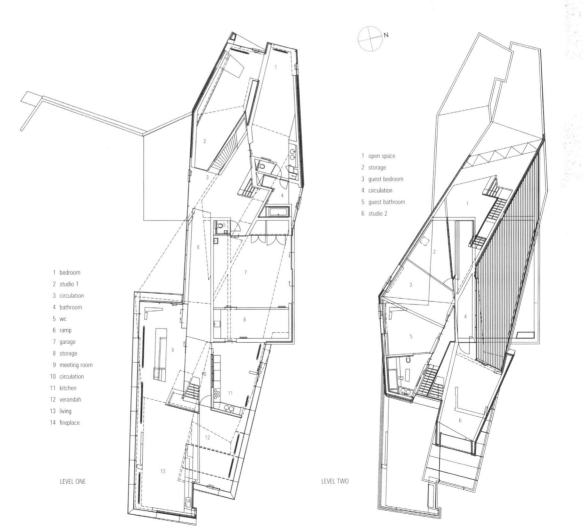

1 open space
2 storage
3 guest bedroom
4 circulation
5 guest bathroom
6 studio 2

1 bedroom
2 studio 1
3 circulation
4 bathroom
5 wc
6 ramp
7 garage
8 storage
9 meeting room
10 circulation
11 kitchen
12 verandah
13 living
14 fireplace

LEVEL ONE

LEVEL TWO

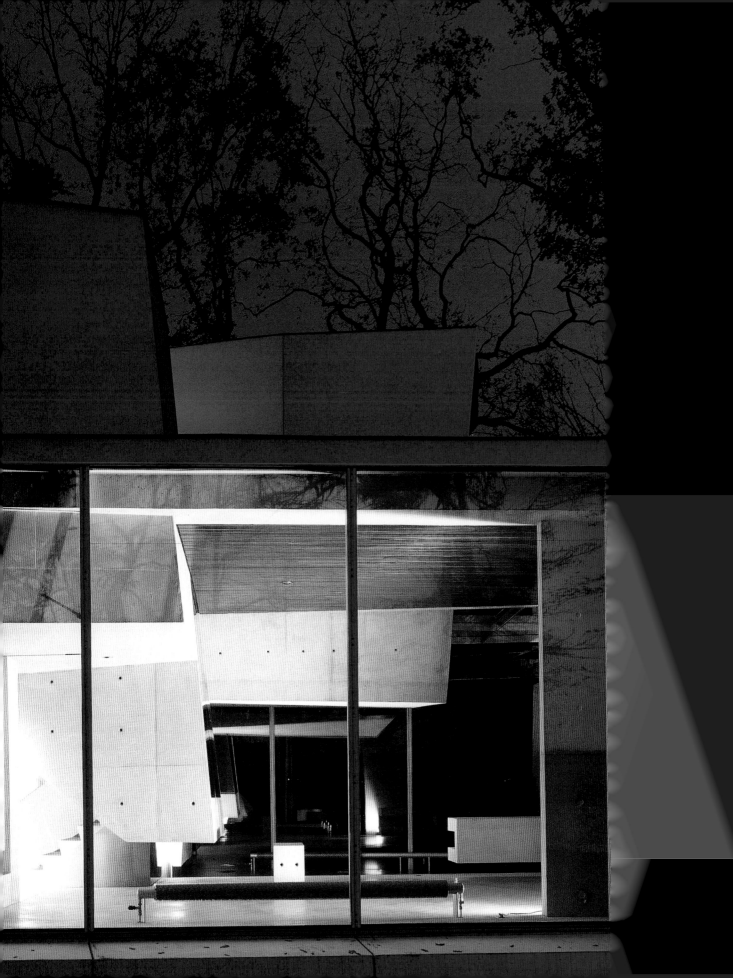

PREVIOUS PAGES
Even the structure's concrete slab has a part to play in the Möbius concept of intertwining elements. Extending beyond the building's perimeter, its role is transformed from the purely structural into the decorative and abstract, appearing to lift Möbius House serenely above its environment.

TRANSFORMING BOUNDARIES

Containing several interesting elements that can easily be applied to architecture, the Möbius Band's twist and continuity mean that, at least theoretically, floors can become walls, and walls can become ceilings. A design can be transformed so that the boundaries defining what is internal and external are so blurred that one can transmute into the other. This means it is possible to walk into an enclosed space and experience a spatial twist without having to walk upside down.

The exterior surfaces of Möbius House are so far removed from tradition that the glass is likened to a skin draped over concrete from one perspective, and a glass house framed in concrete from another.

The home's internal spaces represent a circular pattern of working, living, and sleeping, with the inherent deformation of the Möbius Band resulting in alternating forms and functions. The roles of glass and concrete structural elements have been reversed. Dividing walls are glass whereas tables are concrete. Furniture becomes a facade, a facade becomes a partition, a partition becomes furniture, and all simultaneously define and reveal spaces, culminating in an exciting sense of dislocation.

Unlike a traditional home with its clearly defined functional and social distinctions, the interior of Möbius House is akin to a continuous ribbon, where living areas, work spaces, and utilities all have their allotted place within the home's endlessly repetitious loop.

ABOVE
The concrete floor of Studio 2 on the upper level extends through the glass wall into the living area. Concrete forms such as this provide the necessary Möbius Band "intrusiveness" as well as adding dynamic points of reference.

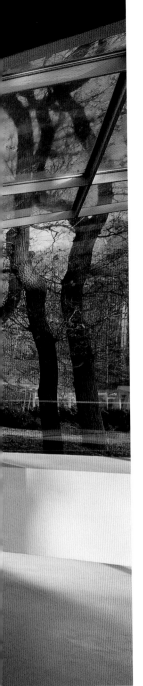

RIGHT
Form and function stand as shoulder-to-shoulder equals in Möbius House's meeting room. Multi-layered planes are interwoven into structural columns to add a Modernist style of ornamentation. The cantilevered concrete surface provides bench space.

ABOVE
Carefully placed internal glass walls divide the central corridor on level one from the meeting room. A first floor window floods the innermost recesses of the house with sunlight, bringing warmth to the cold, neutral concrete surfaces.

TOP
Much thought was given to the orientation and siting of Möbius House prior to its construction. Nestling it among a grove of trees succeeds in applying texture and human scale to the project, and helps counter the impersonal scale of the concrete.

Rose House KIAMA, AUSTRALIA

Ian Moore Architects

Constructed	2000
Home type	One-story family home
Structure	Reinforced concrete, steel, and glass

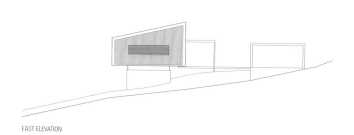

EAST ELEVATION

"The home is like a hovering viewing platform high on a mountain; its simple form and materiality inspired by the nearby utilitarian farm sheds – the external cladding forms an open-sided box, framing the view of the coast below. A simple subdivision of the plan, with parents at one end, children at the other, and the communal family space at the center create a comfortable living space."

Ian Moore

ABOVE
The north elevation of Rose House, showing the concrete entry bridge and the transparency of the living area, with a view of Seven Mile Beach to the south. A louvered roof over the entry bridge forms a shaded outdoor room.

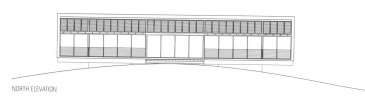

NORTH ELEVATION

ALL-ENCOMPASSING VIEWS

Saddleback Mountain is about a two-hour drive from Sydney, and the site for Rose House is the southern side of the mountain, some 165 ft (50 m) below the summit. There are spectacular views to Pigeon House Mountain in the south, the wooded hillside to the north, the coastal escarpment to the west, and the Pacific Ocean in the east.

To take full advantage of the views, the house has been built close to the road and centered on a north–south ridge, which also allows excellent views to the east and west. The site presented a challenge – the architect wanted to retain views to the south, yet still allow winter sunshine to permeate the house from the north, so he decided to design the roof to follow the natural slope of the site. This allowed for a clerestory with adjustable glass louvers to be placed in the northern part of the house. On the southern side, facing the prevailing winter winds, the glazing is lower in height.

THREE ZONES, THREE USES

The house is divided into three zones – the eastern zone is for the parents, the western zone is for the children, and the center of the home contains the kitchen, living, and dining areas. This not only allows private space for all the occupants, it also permits dazzling views from the central living space, with its floor to ceiling glazing.

TOP
View from the east, showing the house cantilevered above the concrete pods, which form the only contact with the ground. The profiled steel cladding and simple form recall the nearby farm sheds.

ABOVE
Night view from northwest, showing the single internal space subdivided into three zones by the bathroom pods, which pass through the floor slab to form the two concrete feet on which the house sits.

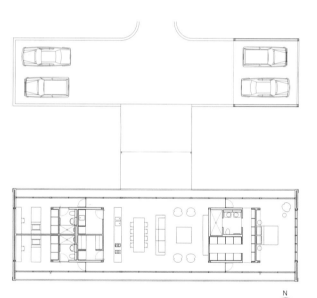

The eastern aspect is particularly inviting, looking, as it does, to the horizon – to maximize the vistas, a horizontal window was inserted in the main bedroom, so that the views can be enjoyed even while lying in bed. External aluminum louvers protect the room from the hottest sun.

To the north of the living areas, there is an open platform with an aluminum louvered roof. It functions both as the entry to the home, and as a shaded veranda. When the home is entered, the first sight is the view down the mountain to the south.

Narrow decks run down the length of the house on the north and south sides. They offer protection from the sun and wind. When the large sliding glass doors are open the entire living area becomes an open veranda space, permitting excellent cross-ventilation.

LOW IMPACT MATERIALS

Being attuned to environmental concerns, the materials for the site were carefully chosen. A light-weight steel structure was used, consisting of two trusses running along the length of the house. This was placed on reinforced concrete block storerooms underneath the house. This is the sole contact with the ground. The trusses allow the house to cantilever 12 ft (3.5 m) beyond the storerooms at the east and west extremities. Two service cores passing through the floor to ground level brace the entire structure. They also contain the plumbing.

The end walls and the roof are clad in gray-profiled steel sheeting, to harmonize with the farm sheds that are a common sight on adjacent properties. Windows and doors are sliding aluminum-framed glass.

TOP LEFT
The living area showing the
polished concrete floor slab
and the patterns cast by external
aluminum sun-control louvers.
The artwork on the wall is by
Australian artist John Coburn.

ABOVE
Living area and kitchen. The
elevated position of the house
affords dramatic views down the
mountain and over farmland. The
artwork behind the kitchen is by
Australian artist Sydney Ball. The
kit-set dining and coffee tables
were designed by the architect.

Tea Plantation House NILGIRI HILLS, INDIA
Rahul Mehrotra Associates

Constructed	2001
Home type	One-level family home
Structure	Load-bearing masonry, steel, and glass

"The intention was to make the houses touch the landscape as lightly as possible and yet root them in the site. The combination of a local stone base with a lighter superstructure in steel was used to achieve both objectives simultaneously ... the buildings seem to want to dive into the spectacular surrounding views."

Rahul Mehrotra

ABOVE
The home's front facade is fashioned in steel, accentuating the lightness with which the structure sits in the landscape. The tea bushes form a pleasant green border, framing each of the six individual homes in this rural hillside development.

TOP RIGHT
The corner windows in the main bedroom look outward to the viridescent "ocean" of tea bushes and the hills beyond. While the corner is made in fixed glass, the adjoining panels are movable, allowing for ventilation when required.

ALWAYS TIME FOR TEA

Overlooking an extensive tea plantation in the heart of the Nilgiri Hills in southern India, six identical contemporary houses sit on a hillside, marketed by the developer as "a few hours to a salubrious climate, clean air, amazing views, and a restful state." Set amid an emerald carpet of tea bushes, the Gurensey Estate homes lunge forward to embrace the spectacular vista. The house design combines metal, wood, and glass in a way that respects the land, while also achieving visual transparency to the views of the plantation. A cantilevered deck extends the usable space beyond the house and into the dramatic natural setting.

BORDERING ON COMMUNITY

Without the usual boundary fences, the arrangement of the houses on the site allows each owner a private yard, but also grants the residents the opportunity to become part of the community. Common infrastructure such as roads, electricity, and water are shared by community members, while a dense covering of tea bush helps unify the separate properties.

In this project, the architect attempts to address a contemporary issue facing tea plantations such as this, where adjacent existing towns are expanding rapidly and acquiring the cheap plantation land for development. It attempts to demonstrate how development can be accommodated in a fresh and innovative way, while still safeguarding the verdant ambience of the plantation. Achieving this kind of balance is a crucial issue for the burgeoning towns and settlements in the Nilgiris, where many South Indian tea plantations are located.

A HYBRID CONSTRUCTION

The method of construction employs both load-bearing masonry structure as well as lighter prefabricated steel frames. The choice of a hybrid construction stems from the difficulty involved in transporting materials to the site, coupled with the limitations of skills available in these presently remote locations.

Local stone was quarried partly from the site and partly from locales in close proximity. The stone was used to create a large plinth for each house, and also created

an architectural platform on which the lighter structure could be situated. The clear advantage of this strategy was that the elevation of the form protected the living spaces, lifting them above the plantation so that the areas could embrace the stunning views that surrounded them.

USING UNDERSTATEMENT

The houses were conceived as cool-climate retreats, far from the hot, crowded, and overwhelming cities. Architecturally, they were designed to be understated on approach, opening up dramatically to the wonderful vistas that are presented once the houses are entered.

The interiors received only minimal design treatment, allowing the views to take center stage. This also gives the occupants the choice to colonize the house according to their own tastes, and in keeping with standard development practices.

1 bedroom 2	6 bathroom 3
2 bathroom 2	7 kitchen
3 main bedroom	8 living/dining
4 main bathroom	9 veranda
5 bedroom 3	

ABOVE
A stone base solidly grounds each house in the high-altitude site, while the upper steel portion lunges toward the landscape. The louver panels help ameliorate the effects of sun and rain, and protect the veranda space, which juts into the surroundings.

Tree House DELAWARE, USA

Sander Architects

Construction	2004–2006
Home type	Three-level family home
Structure	Timber, concrete, and glass

"The house is on a magnificent small site with tremendous trees. The 100-year-old flood plain carved a small buildable area into the site, and thus we decided to go 'vertical' with the house. The site really constrained us in this way – it really decided the form of the house. This led to the magnificent additional benefit of being 'in the trees' on the third level."

Whitney Sander

ABOVE
The house sits on a mature wooded site. The living area on the second level features 20-ft (6-m) windows with an open corner, allowing views into the protected woods to the northeast.

RIGHT
A bar grating staircase rises away from the facade, then turns and stops abruptly at the landing, which functions as a viewing platform.

OPPOSITE
The front stairs move away to the left, while the open deck canopy twists to the right. A spiral staircase leads from the ground level to the roof deck, which doubles as an outdoor living space.

A HOME IN THE TREE TOPS

The design and building of the Tree House was a labor of love. The architect, Whitney Sander, designed it for his sister. When their father died, he left sufficient funds for her to build her dream house. It is also her first house.

The Tree House sits on a cul-de-sac at the end of a mature subdivision in Wilmington, Delaware. It is filled with 100-year-old deciduous trees, which form a magnificent canopy 150 ft (45 m) high. A gentle stream runs around the house, and due to certain restrictions imposed by the Army Corps of Engineers and also because of the potential for flooding, the buildable area is quite small. The architect solved the problem by designing a vertical house. The main living area is on the second level, while the main bedroom and ensuite occupy the entire third level. These spaces give one the feeling of being in the trees, of being part of the canopy itself.

There is one other bedroom on the ground or first level, and one overflow bedroom, which doubles as a study, on the second level.

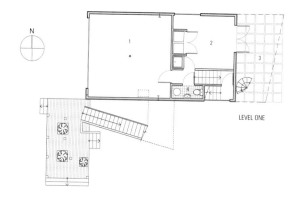

LEVEL ONE

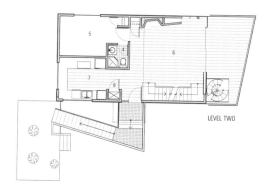

LEVEL TWO

1 garage
2 bedroom
3 patio
4 bathroom
5 study
6 living
7 kitchen
8 pantry
9 hallway
10 main bedroom

LEVEL THREE

STRIKING STAIRS

From the grade outside, one ascends to the main level on a grand stairway. This wood structure has galvanized metal bar-grate treads that allow you to see the ground below as you walk up. A landing projects over the site and provides a viewing point of the stream, which carved out the building site. The stairs inside the house were made at the owner's place of work. With two treads in each unit, the stairs are made of ½ in (13 mm) aluminum plate.

Various shades of purple set the color scheme for the house – a gray-purple slate encloses the fireplace wall and the media storage area, and the walls are complemented by full length drapes in a darker shade.

WINDOWS TO THE WORLD

Horizontal windows encircle the house, and provide select views of the surrounding landscape. In contrast to these small views, a great wrapping window in the double-height living room provides a dominant diagonal focus for the house, and allows views into the deep woods to the north and east.

A 35-ft (10.6-m) roof deck provides a sweeping view in all directions, and also a space for outdoor entertaining among the tree tops.

ABOVE LEFT
The stairs are made of ½ in (13 mm) plate aluminum. Each pair of treads is one unit, twisted together like the stair and canopy elements outside.

OPPOSITE
With its suspended lighting and slate feature wall like a scenery flat, the double-height living room is reminiscent of a theater. The floor to ceiling drapes draw back to reveal the view into the woods.

Villa Kaleidoscope NAGANO PREFECTURE, JAPAN
Cell Space Architects

Constructed	2005
Home type	Two-story cottage
Structure	Reinforced concrete with timber frame

"With this building, we strived to achieve a sense of connectedness with the environment, amplifying the number of surrounding trees by reflecting them in mirrors in the home's interior. Its occupants are immersed in nature regardless of where they are and in what direction they are looking."

Mutsue Hayakusa

ABOVE RIGHT
Villa K's upper level juts out on all sides beyond its reinforced concrete base. The home's timber exterior perfectly complements its rural setting.

TOP RIGHT
This view of Villa K's galley-style kitchen extends through to the entrance hall where the central tatami room lies to the left. A mirror is used to reflect the landscape, providing a sense of depth to the narrow space. Behind the mirror there is a generously sized storage area.

ABOVE FAR RIGHT
The assemblage of rooms on the upper level, including a living/dining room, kitchen, and west-facing balcony, revolve around a traditional raised tatami room. A floor to ceiling mirror to the left of the picture creates a "virtual reality" – where a forest panorama is visible. The predominantly cream-toned interior complements the changing seasonal colors outside.

Villa Kaleidoscope, also known as Villa K, is a family residence built as an occasional weekend retreat for a couple in their fifties and their daughter.

The aim of the project was to create a home that immersed its occupants in the natural environment through choice of site, extensive glazing, and a clever arrangement of internally placed mirrors.

A honeycomb-like arrangement of living spaces characterizes the upper level, which is cantilevered over the first-floor bedroom and its exterior of reinforced concrete and glass.

MOUNTAIN LOCATION

Located on a sloping, forested block in the popular mountain resort town of Karuizawa in Nagano Prefecture, the villa commands an enviable view looking toward Mt Asama.

Designed to appear as though it is transcending its surrounding stand of trees, the upper level contains all of Villa K's compact, functional living spaces – a living/dining room, generous west-facing balcony, kitchen, and bathroom, all constructed around the traditional raised tatami room. Carefully placed full-length mirrors serve to reflect the surrounding natural landscape, creating virtual perspectives of its forested environment and conveying them into every corner of the home.

Cooling breezes and dappled light from the surrounding trees bring relief from summer temperatures, with a fireplace in the living room a remedy for winter chills. An elongated external chimney echoes the verticality of the surrounding trees.

SMALL BUT SPACIOUS

The upper level's timber-clad exterior integrates the structure into its tranquil setting. Japanese cypress is extensively used throughout the interior and the pale, creamy color of its internal walls is a perfect accompaniment to the striking seasonal colors outside.

Although individually the rooms are small, Villa K's open design combines with its extensive glazed areas to give the impression of spaciousness. The mirrored walls add to the sense of openness and provide constantly changing perspectives of the house and its serene setting.

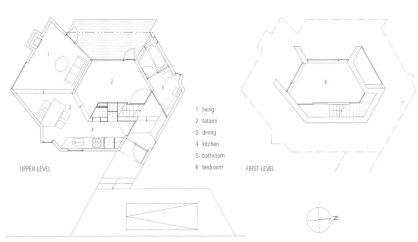

UPPER LEVEL

1 living
2 tatami
3 dining
4 kitchen
5 bathroom
6 bedroom

FIRST LEVEL

Chapter 13
By the
Water

Water is a dynamic life force that evokes feelings of serenity and vitality. A home by the water should capture the views and create a sense of place.

The primary design objective of a home by the water — whether it is a cottage on a sandy beach or a house perched on a cliff overlooking the ocean — is to capture and enhance the view of the water.

A home oriented toward the water has a view to an enormous amount of space. No buildings encroach on the water-side of the property, which creates a sense of tranquillity and seclusion, even if there are neighbors in close proximity.

Working with the client, the architect may strive to "diminish" the structure, making it simple and compact taking nothing away from drama of the site. Alternatively, the architect may experiment with shape, form, and color so the building makes a contrasting statement against the natural backdrop.

WORKING WITH NATURE

There are several challenges involved in designing a home to capture views: the site may be difficult to access and build on; while seeking out the view, the ideal aspect may be compromised; or the home may be exposed to the elements, such as salt-laden winds or tropical storms, defining the structure and many of the finishes in the architect's repertoire. Often too, an orientation to the water can ignore the potential for ancillary views from the sides and back of the house.

TELLING THE STORY

While maximizing the home's connection to the vista, the metaphorical challenge for the architect is to create variation for the occupants so they are not "saturated" by the views, rather like telling a story: the tale might begin with a strategically located window that captures a glimpse rather than a sweeping panorama; the story continues to unfold in the bathroom which admits an intriguing sliver of the outdoor scene; larger windows in the bedrooms and study further develop the plot, before the denouement in the living and dining areas, where panoramic views are revealed by a wall of glass.

CREATIVE SOLUTIONS

With so much on offer from the water-side, primarily solid walls may be the answer to other unattractive outlooks, where neighboring properties encroach, for example. On a rocky or steeply sloping site, a sensitive solution to the uneven building surface, may be a terraced footprint, rather than a cantilevered structure.

The terraced building fits the site like a waterfall collecting in pools as it spills down the slope. Connected by a series of stairs, each level of the home contains pavilions or a different set of rooms according to function — bedrooms on one level, living and dining on another, entertainment on the next.

OUTSIDE IS INSIDE

A home by the water should invite the outside in. Architectural ingenuity is put to the test to realize the clients dream: floor to ceiling "frameless" glass; a wrap of glass, angled and transparent at its edge; or walls of doors that vanish into a cavity, to create a truly indoor/outdoor space.

Balconies and exterior courtyards along the foreshore function as outdoor living spaces, bringing the occupant one step closer to the water beyond.

ABOVE
Peg Yorkin House,
Moore Ruble Yudell Architects
& Planners

TOP RIGHT
Sea Farm House,
Stefan Antoni Olmesdahl
Truen Architects

OPPOSITE
Rochman Residence,
Callas Shortridge Architects

Cape Schanck Residence VICTORIA, AUSTRALIA
Denton Corker Marshall

Construction	1997–1999; studio extension 2001–2004
Home type	Two-story holiday residence and separate studio
Structure	Steel frame, concrete floors, cement cladding

RECESSED LOWER LEVEL

MAIN LIVING LEVEL

STUDIO

"Although we don't design many single houses, it was great fun to work with the owner – an old friend – because as a graphic designer who had worked with us on many projects, there was a close understanding of what might be possible on this difficult site. We worked to achieve the expression of a simple and clear idea of a southern Australian house."

Denton Corker Marshall

A RUGGED RETREAT

The Cape Schanck Residence is located south of Melbourne on the Bass Strait coast. Intended as a holiday home and work retreat for a city-based professional and his family, the site contains a two-story house and a separate studio pavilion. Set on a rather steep site, and encircled by a golf course, the main house is positioned to maximize the stunning panoramic views to the ocean. The form of the house is simple and elegant, but it has a unique and irregular shape. The tubular form is twisted, with the chimney materializing from the wall at a jaunty slant. The cladding is raked and the lower windows are cranked. The overall effect is of something other-worldly, of something that has been carefully placed on the land as a unique and complete entity. It is unquestionably a dramatic form.

The studio is located as an extension to the rear of the main house. This self-contained work space is long, with clear lines defining its shape. A paved courtyard, complete with a long concrete bench, sits between the two structures. To accentuate the unusual shape, the bench has been placed at an angle.

TOUGH MATERIALS FOR TOUGH CONDITIONS

The shores of Bass Strait – the body of water separating mainland Australia from Tasmania – experience intense weather conditions, and the architects kept this in mind when designing the home. The windows facing the sea are kept to a minimum and both buildings are constructed using a steel frame.

The principal house sits atop the recessed lower level so that the second story rises above the local native trees. The exterior of the main house and studio is clad with gray cement sheets, while the lower level is colored a dull brown to merge with the coastal ti-tree vegetation. Entrance to this part of the dwelling is via a concrete staircase behind a glass screen.

FREEDOM IN LIVING

On the main level, the central living area looks west, out to dazzling views across the treetops, into the surrounding bushland, and out to the ocean. A fire-place sits in the eastern wall, set behind a stainless steel plate. Freestanding American maple-veneer cubes function as room dividers; these punctuate the length of the house, differentiating the living and dining areas, and the bedrooms.

The main bedroom and ensuite bathroom are hidden from the rest of the house by a concealed sliding door. There are two more bedrooms on the lower level, along with the laundry and a second bathroom.

The studio, which was constructed after the main house was completed, can be entered through sliding glass doors from the courtyard. It contains a comfortable sitting area, a kitchenette, and a bathroom. If necessary, the living space can double as guest accommodation.

ABOVE
The north-facing courtyard is cocooned from blustery winds by the dense and enveloping coastal vegetation. The living area and kitchen are separated from the main bedroom and ensuite by free-standing, timber-veneered boxes.

TOP FAR LEFT
The house sits atop a large sand dune like a twisted gray stick jutting out of the native ti-tree scrub. A slim slot window looks out to the sometimes tempestuous Bass Strait, its narrowness also buffering the occupants from the cold southwesterly winds.

FAR LEFT
The main house and studio are two buildings from the same extruded form, separated into two parts. As well as a spacious workspace area, the studio contains a sitting area, a kitchenette, and a bathroom.

ABOVE
Brightly colored contemporary furniture adds a quirky graphic focal point when placed against the gray, white, and silver backdrop of the living space and courtyard. The stainless steel fireplace on the right provides warmth during the colder months.

CENTER LEFT
The living, dining, and kitchen areas share the central streamlined volume of the house, with expansive views to the west across the treetops to the ocean. Beyond the kitchen is the ensuite box, which separates this area from the main bedroom. A further two bedrooms are incorporated into the lower level of the house.

LEFT
The bright white minimalist studio space includes a metal-clad bathroom box on the right. A sleek studio bench runs along the far wall, with a narrow slot window set above the bench providing glimpses to outside. The sitting area is used as a meeting place for clients, or it can be transformed into a guest bedroom when required.

ABOVE
The buckled form of the studio, and beyond it the main house, is accentuated by the raked cement cladding that forms the tough gray carapace of the buildings' exteriors. The sunny courtyard separates the two structures and is reached through the large sliding glass doors of both buildings.

Casa Fontana LUGANO, SWITZERLAND

Stanton Williams LONDON

Constructed	2000
Home type	Seven-level villa
Structure	Reinforced concrete

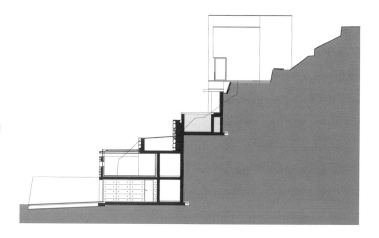

"Casa Fontana rises above the lake of Lugano in a series of terraces, each one boasting a different view. The house was carefully built around the views — exposing, protecting, or framing them, depending on the use of space."

Stanton Williams

TERRACED LAYOUT

Casa Fontana sits on a very steep, terraced slope above the city of Lugano in the Swiss-Italian county of Ticino. The biggest challenge for Stanton Williams was the panoramic view — of the lake, the mountains, and Lugano itself. He wanted his client to be able to escape the view from time to time so that he didn't become desensitized to it; and, at the same time, the architect didn't want the house to be overpowered by the landscape. The end result is a home that interacts with the landscape and the views so that the views are either concealed or revealed, depending on your location.

SEVEN LEVELS

The house is equivalent to a seven-story building and can be accessed from above and below. There are two distinct parts of the house. One part is intimate — set against the side of the mountain, shaded and cool in the summer, with a small fountain contributing to the calm and refreshing atmosphere. The other part is much more extrovert, looking out to the view.

The entry sits on a bridge, with light metal and glass stairs leading to the main bedroom and ensuite on the seventh level. Travertine stairs lead to the first level bedrooms, dining room, and kitchen. Across the bridge is the living room, a double-height space designed to maximize the impact of the 180° views. The room is overlooked by a minstrel gallery, and a slot in the ceiling allows light into the top part of the room.

The living room furniture is positioned on a patch of American oak treated with white oil. It is surrounded by travertine, a traditional local material, which extends beyond the glazing, making the observer feel as if they are sitting on a ledge overlooking the lake. There are no balustrades or barriers to obscure the view. The large fireplace reflects traditional rural houses and provides cosy winter warmth.

Downstairs, tucked against the mountain, are the domestic rooms, such as the open-plan dining room and the kitchen, where the challenge was to hide the cooking area while entertaining without blocking the view. This problem was solved by a sliding wall.

The way the house "plays" with the view is apparent in the quiet meditation space at the top of the house. The view is revealed at one end only, surprising the observer with the architect's game of hide and seek.

COOL SHADE

Spaces are characterized by light and shade, and also by temperature. The granite slope is exposed to the full effect of sunlight and heat during the afternoon. The "compressed" space between the house and the rock is shaded during the day and acts as a cooling element overnight. Light is drawn down through this space into the living areas.

The open terraces are cooled with water – a cascade and pool are carved into the rock midway up the site. The mirrored surface of the pool stretches out to the surface of Lake Lugano in the distance.

ABOVE
Drawn along the hillside, the main terrace was carved out to form an infinity lap pool with its own cascade – a cooling sound on a hot day. The pool is lined in locally sourced stone, giving the water a tone reminiscent of Lake Lugano far below.

TOP RIGHT
The concealed glazing and the continuity of travertine dissolves the interior and exterior spaces, allowing uninterrupted panoramic views. One can enjoy the vista in Jasper Morrison's The Thinking Man's Chair, which complements the dramatic views of the lake and mountains.

ABOVE
The concrete structure allows glass to fold around corners without an obviously visible means of support. The main public areas of the house have no thresholds or doors, allowing one space to flow into another.

RIGHT
The dramatic nature of the living room is highlighted by its double height and the blonde wooden floor. A wall to wall ribbon window frames the view of the lake, while a carved light slot animates the envelope of the room. The cantilevered open fireplace is faced in unfinished travertine – a local material that is historically and culturally significant in the area.

OPPOSITE
By "folding" travertine up from the first-level wall to the next level, the architect has high-lighted the fact that the house is carved into the mountainside. Key design elements and different spaces are connected by interlocking yet contrasting surfaces of unfinished and polished travertine.

1 entry
2 office
3 living room

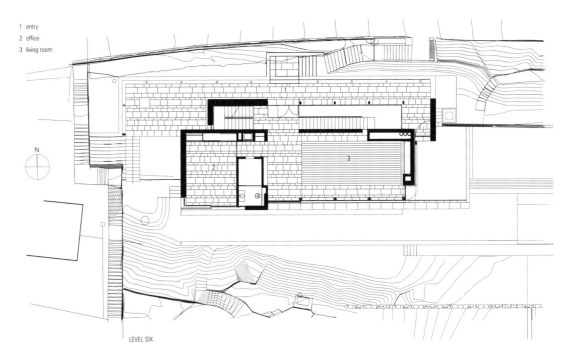

LEVEL SIX

Glass House KYUSHU, JAPAN
Shoei Yoh

Constructed	1991
Home type	Single-story family residence
Structure	Glass curtain walls and steel-frame reinforced concrete, cantilevered from concrete slab

> "I call this house 'Another Glass House Between Sea and Sky' as it unites the built environment with the natural elements. I wanted it to almost disappear into the landscape."
>
> Shoei Yoh

THE PERFECT SITE

After an exhaustive ten-year search for the site of his own dream home, Shoei Yoh purchased the land for his Glass House on a high ocean bluff in the town of Shimomachi, 20 miles (32 km) from Fukuoka on the island of Kyushu in 1983. Yoh, his wife, and two children were to spend the next eight years visiting the site every month, visualizing a dwelling that would one day capture the full splendor of the northern vistas provided by its 450-ft (137-m) vantage point above the Sea of Japan.

CANTILEVERED GLASS BOX

Echoing Farnsworth House, Ludwig Mies van der Rohe's seminal glass box built in 1951, Yoh's straight-forward single-story elevated glass and concrete creation is firmly anchored to its precipitous site by two vertical concrete slabs that extend dramatically southwards. Its living area faces north in a cantilevered space enclosed entirely in ¾-in (19-mm) glass curtain walls and railings. These are connected with silicone rubber and held in place by suspension rods that run down to the concrete base below in a complex network of tensioning. This results in a statuesque structure that seems to challenge the laws of gravity.

The glass provides an ideal barrier against the elements, integrating the home into its environment and connecting it to the outside world. The use of glass proved an ideal solution to Yoh's philosophy that architecture and nature should always strive to be integrated, never separate from one another.

AT ONE WITH NATURE

The region's heavy mists, harsh rains, and fierce winter winds, which once turned back the armies of Genghis Khan, combine to form wind pressures consistent with that of skyscrapers in typhoon-prone areas. Here, nature is confronted and absorbed by a house that was never intended to provide a sense of safety or security.

RIGHT
Silhouetted in Kyushu's early morning light, the Glass House boldly shows its majestic canti-levered north-facing elevation. The steel tensioning ropes almost seem a decorative afterthought, angling back to the two vertical concrete slabs that anchor the house to the site.

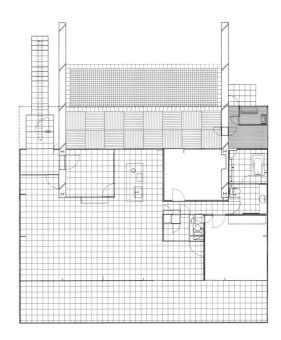

Yoh is very much at ease living in awe of nature and its destructive potential. The aim was to create a structure that would be as close to invisible as possible; one that blended into the landscape and became part of its fabric. Despite incorporating an array of Modernist materials in its construction, the home eventually came to reflect the age-old Japanese principles of transparency and flexibility. Like a traditional tatami room, its central living area has spaces that can be screened off. Inside the house, occupants are encouraged to go barefoot with the installation of heated white marble pavers that extend under the glass to the exterior deck. This also provides a striking sense of visual continuity.

From its inception, the sole determinant in Glass House's design was the extent to which the unfolding drama of nature could be witnessed. Its celebration of the struggle between humankind and nature led the architect to a refreshingly unorthodox use of transparent materials, resulting in a vulnerability that would not exist if he had designed the house for a client rather than for himself.

ABOVE LEFT
The glass curtain wall wraps itself around the house, providing 270° views of the Sea of Japan along with vast swathes of coastline. The wall is the architect's expression of the ancient Japanese notion that architecture and nature must always be in harmony with one another.

ABOVE
From inside, the ocean appears to be an extension of the house itself. The home's unadorned, minimalist interior offers few distractions, encouraging its occupants to focus beyond the humdrum of everyday life.

FOLLOWING PAGES
The architect's initial concept for the site was for a "watchtower," but this was impractical for a family of four. For all its outward sophistication, Glass House seems to embody the sense of isolation and singular purpose one expects from a lighthouse. Despite the setting, the bright lights of Kyushu's largest city, Fukuoka, are just 20 minutes away.

Gloucester House MASSACHUSETTS, USA
Charles Rose Architects

Constructed	2004
Home type	Three-level residence
Structure	Steel frame over concrete slab

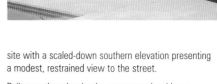

"My clients expressed a desire for a home with expansive water views and abundant natural light. At the same time they wanted a house that would offer a protected landscape on the unexposed side of the home. As well as a place to get away to, the owners wanted the home to be appropriate for entertaining. The views, the pool, and the soaring, open plan living spaces all contribute to this."

Charles Rose

ABOVE
In a house that possesses two very distinct focal points, this view of the southern facade gives no hint of the grandeur of the views. Windows and internal partitions have been carefully placed to allow views through the house to the ocean beyond.

TOP RIGHT
The overpowering presence of the lead-coated copper roof is quite dramatic as it extends out over the south-facing elevation, providing early morning and late afternoon shade to upper level spaces. The formality and structure of the pool surround is in stark contrast to the granite foreshore beyond.

The architects' approach to unified concepts that create innovative environments with a focus on open spaces and natural light finds full expression in their design of Gloucester House in Massachusetts.

HISTORIC SETTING

On the outskirts of the historic whaling port of Gloucester, the house is situated above a granite ledge next to the Atlantic Ocean. Its L-shaped floorplan provides expansive ocean views through a wall of windows in the living area. This is made possible by the sail-like quality of its roofline, which responds in scale to the ocean and the craggy rock formations of the coast.

Two environments have been created by the home's distinctive shape. While the ocean's crenellated, granite foreshore graces its northern and western boundaries, softened by a selective planting of indigenous shrubs, this is juxtaposed on the property's southern boundary to a rather traditional expanse of lawn facing the street. The lawn is ringed by a planting of mature shrubs and small trees, which find shelter from salt spray and damaging ocean breezes in the embrace of a home that is in perfect union with its surroundings.

NEW FOOTPRINT OVER OLD FOOTPRINT

Technically a renovation, the 5,000-sq-ft- (464.5-sq-m-) dwelling was constructed over the footprint of an old, dilapidated bungalow, and burrowed into its sloping

site with a scaled-down southern elevation presenting a modest, restrained view to the street.

Built over three levels, the uppermost level has a number of rooms that flow into one another creating a continuous space that opens onto the north- and west-facing balconies.

While the kitchen is an integral part of the surrounding space, it can be contained by closing off four sliding steel and glass doors.

NAUTICAL TOUCH

In catering to the client's desire for extensive water views, the sweeping roofline allows for the massive expanse of glass, which gives the ocean a palpable immediacy akin to being on the deck of a large boat. Lead-coated copper roofing and siding provide protection from the corrosive effects of the sea, while stainless steel railing and balustrade add to the home's nautical feel, as well as providing a low maintenance alternative to timber for the decking surrounds.

The home's patios, terraces, and walkways are made from a green-toned granite streaked with quartz, which ties in esthetically with the granite foundation upon which the home is built.

The architects' commitment to houses that have a sculptural quality is shown to full effect as Gloucester House rises from its surroundings beneath its spectacularly jagged, pitched roof. The home won the 2005 Boston Society of Architects Design Honor Award.

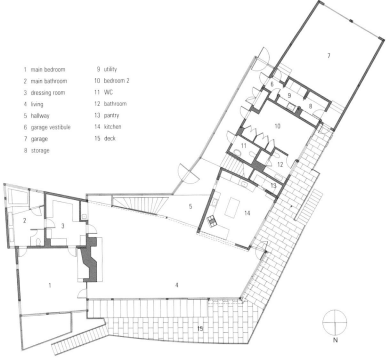

1	main bedroom	9	utility
2	main bathroom	10	bedroom 2
3	dressing room	11	WC
4	living	12	bathroom
5	hallway	13	pantry
6	garage vestibule	14	kitchen
7	garage	15	deck
8	storage		

ABOVE
The panorama of the surrounding seascape is pulled in and fully exploited beneath this soaring wall of glass. Triple-glazed to minimize heat loss, the panes are set within an almost abstract framework of mahogany, bringing a much-needed sense of warmth and texture.

TOP
Gloucester House seems to raise a defiant wall of glass, where the proximity and relationship of the house to the ocean is obvious. Granite boulders fall away to an eroded shoreline below, presenting an intriguing mix of strength and fragility.

MAIN LIVING LEVEL

N

Island House ONTARIO, CANADA
Shim-Sutcliffe Architects

Constructed	2001
Home type	Single family summer house
Structure	Wood frame, steel columns and beams with concrete retaining walls

"Our agricultural landscapes are a diminishing resource. This new building project is inserted into a clover meadow and asserts a unified and integrated relationship between building and its pastoral agrarian landscape. Simultaneously, the metaphor of island and water is created and extended though one's physical experience from the site to water's edge."

Brigitte Shim and Howard Sutcliffe

ROOFTOP MEADOWS

Built on a pleasant pastoral island in the majestic St Lawrence River, this summer home both engages the existing landscape and creates its very own distinctive perspective. The house is approached from a quiet rural road and presents itself as a long low concrete wall set into the gentle slope that leads down to the river. Both of the low roofs have been planted with wildflowers and essentially become their own abstract meadows. Above these flat roofs, the lantern-like living room is clearly visible.

From the road the entry to the house is arrived at by walking along a path set between two gentle berms. These clover-covered berms serve two important functions – they obscure the road from the house, and they establish a seamless continuity with the meadow and the adjacent farmland.

SIMPLICITY THE KEY

The simple plan of this house spatially interlocks two linear flat-roofed bars around a cubic living room pavilion. Located six steps down from the entry and to the west side of the living room are the dining room and kitchen. The kitchen leads on to a west-facing wooden deck, which has been set into the gravel dry garden.

On the east side of the entry is the rectangular bar containing the study, the main bedroom, and the main bathroom. The block that contains the bathroom and dressing area forms a freestanding island, sitting adjacent to an exterior deck that overlooks the river.

For visual continuity, the floor of the bathroom, dressing area, and external deck are constructed from the same timber. The thick north wall contains storage areas, stairs down to the basement level, and a water closet.

MAINTAINING THE PASTORAL

Ever mindful of the decreasing areas of natural vegetation, the architects ensured that the whole home maintained an air of unity and integration with the surrounding environment.

From the entry, one can look down through the living room pavilion – sitting like an island in a large tranquil reflection pool – across a meadow to the river beyond. The small rectangular island within the reflection pool has been planted with bulrushes. A freestanding fireplace acts as a pivot point between the living, dining, and entry areas.

The landscape and planting plan has attempted to reinforce both the meadow and the pastoral quality of the island in a more geometric form. Ornamental grasses have been set against natural field grasses, while large swathes of colorful wildflowers and clover form the bucolic palette, with water lilies and bulrushes acting as the detail elements. An attractive crushed limestone dry garden contains slabs of limestone that were removed during the excavation.

ABOVE
The lantern-like living room is visible above the wildflower-studded roof of Island House. The concrete walls and natural textures of this summer house complement the clover meadow that shrouds it from the road.

RIGHT
Both the living room on the left and the study beyond look out to the limpid reflection pool. Plantings of bulrushes, grasses, and water lilies add detail to the sweeping canvas of meadow.

LEFT
A custom-built vanity and medicine cabinet add rustic charm to the home. The bathroom enjoys views across the verdant pastureland.

ABOVE
The view from the light-filled living room across the meadow is punctuated by the calming reflection pool and a Robert Murray sculpture beyond.

1   entrance
2   living
3   dining
4   kitchen
5   outdoor deck
6   dry garden
7   winter garden
8   study
9   bedroom
10 outdoor deck

James-Robertson House SYDNEY, AUSTRALIA
Casey Brown Architecture

Constructed	2003
House type	Two-pavilion family home
Structure	Glass, steel, copper, timber, and stone

"The more you look at nature, the more intriguing is the relationship with the man-made. I prefer to look at shells, at rock overhangs, and the more that I see, the more I am attracted to an organic vision of form and to creating in harmony with the natural world."

Robert Brown

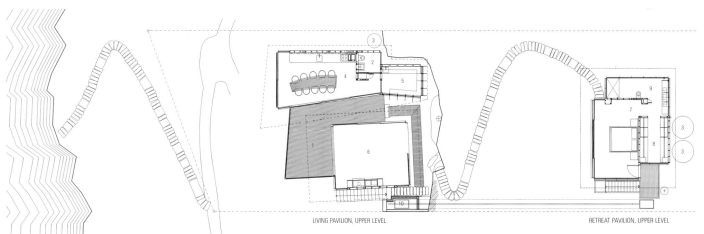

LIVING PAVILION, UPPER LEVEL

RETREAT PAVILION, UPPER LEVEL

1	deck	6	living
2	bathroom	7	main bedroom
3	water tanks	8	walk-in wardrobe
4	kitchen/dining	9	ensuite
5	pantry	10	inclinator

ABOVE
The glass doors between the dining room and the deck can be folded back in warm weather, so that the indoor and outdoor spaces become one. Trees hug the building, but the house is high enough to overlook the treetops to the views of Pittwater beyond.

RIGHT
A view to the northeast, toward Palm Beach lighthouse at the end of the isthmus. The double-height living room has louvered windows that control the air flow through the house. An inclinator connects the main part of the house with the owners' retreat pavilion up the hill.

IDYLLIC LOCATION

This house is situated on a steep 45° slope on the western side of Pittwater, less than one hour's drive from the Sydney CBD. National park surrounds the site, and the views are unparalleled – sweeping from Pittwater and Palm Beach to the mouth of the Hawkesbury River where it enters the Pacific.

Mackerel Beach is a small community linked to the mainland by the ferry that travels to and from Palm Beach. After the boat trip, reaching the house involves a walk across the beach and a climb up the hill. Apart from dealing with the challenges of the site itself, the architect was briefed to design a home that kept guest accommodation separate from the living areas. In addition, a separate pavilion was designed to be the main bedroom hideaway.

IN HARMONY WITH THE LANDSCAPE

Because the natural environment is so spectacular, the architect designed the house to merge with the landscape. Glass, steel, and copper pavilions constitute the makeup of the dwelling. A large sandstone retaining wall was excavated from the site and used to anchor the lower structure. Not only is the natural sandstone a beautiful local material, it also stabilizes the slope.

Dark colors were chosen to help the house harmonize with its bushland surroundings. The form of the house, and colors complementing the native vegetation, have the effect of reducing the visual impact of the building; you can hardly see the house from the water.

ABOVE
The sandstone base, hewn from the site, anchors the house to the boulder-strewn slope. The main bedroom sits further up the hill in a separate pavilion, above the living areas.

ABOVE RIGHT
Essentially, the frame of the house was designed to be taut and lightweight. The roofs seem to float over each other like the sails of a yacht or the wings of a bi-plane.

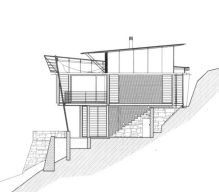

EXPERIENCING THE HOUSE

The lower level of the living pavilion contains a study, guest bedroom, and wine cellar. Above this is the double-height main pavilion, which contains the living areas. The floor-to-ceiling glass allows uninterrupted views of the natural surroundings. Directly outside the living area, the cliff face features a large Port Jackson fig tree, its distorted roots like a natural artwork. A timber boardwalk leads past this feature to the sandstone steps and the inclinator.

Copper's innate shine and the beautiful changes it undergoes over time made it the logical choice for the exterior walls and the roof. Its rich color also helps the home to be at one with its surroundings.

ADAPTING TO THE CLIMATE

The main exterior deck links the kitchen and dining area with the living area. When the glass doors are opened out, the inside extends to the outside. As the house is located in a mild sub-tropical climate, it was essential that the owners be able to use the outdoor space all year round. Interlocking layers of copper and steel hoods form the cover for this part of the house.

ABOVE
The house enjoys an intimate view of Mackerel Beach as well as grander ones such as those of Palm Beach to the northeast, and the Central Coast in the distance.

LEFT
The living room's stone and stainless steel mesh unit houses the entertainment system, as well as the floating fireplace. The floor is blackbutt.

ABOVE
View from the guest bedroom to the bathroom and study. The full-height, opaque, sliding glass walls and louvered exterior admit plenty of natural light but also provide these areas with privacy.

PERFECTLY PRIVATE

An inclinator connects the living pavilion with the retreat pavilion. Otherwise it's a steep climb, as this part of the house sits some 165 ft (50 m) up the incline. This separate building affords the owners the ultimate in private space.

Although the windows and glazed walls are large, generous overhangs and unusually shaped roof planes provide privacy from prying eyes and protection from the elements, while at the same time allowing light and warmth to enter.

SUSTAINABLE LIVING

A waste-treatment system and water-storage tanks that collect rainwater for drinking are featured. The design also allows the free flow of breezes through the pavilions, helping them to stay cool in hot weather. Steel hoods, which offer protection from heavy rain, conceal the mechanical blinds and outdoor lights. Minimal energy is used for heating – there is an open fireplace, and also radiant heating foils in the ceiling.

As well as being esthetically pleasing, the materials used in the construction – steel, glass, copper, timber, and stone – help keep the maintenance to a minimum. This is a must in an area that is subject to strong summer sun and salt-laden wind.

MATERIAL MATTERS

A major consideration in building this house was getting materials to the site, as there is no road access. Most materials had to be brought to the site by boat; some items even had to be brought in by helicopter.

Because of its resistance to bushfires and termites, steel was chosen as the major construction material. Durable corrugated copper sheets were used for the roof and walls. The copper will weather to a rich red-brown color, reminiscent of the iron colors in the Hawkesbury sandstone. The decks are teak, and the internal floors are laid with recycled blackbutt, another homage to the Australian bush.

The building fuses state-of-the-art
computer design with tried-and-true
traditional building techniques.

INVITING INTERIORS

To enhance the feeling of openness, the interior spaces
were customized, just like the fittings on a boat.
Because access to shops is difficult, adequate food
storage facilities were necessary and a modern
adaptation of the outback meat safe was custom-
made for the home. Complete with louvered screens,
the pantry adds charm as well as functionality.

THE LONG WEEKEND

The James-Robertson House is the owners' home,
not just a holiday house. The flexibility provided by
modern communications makes it possible to live
almost anywhere. For some, the weekender, in a
desirable seaside location, has become the permanent experience.

LEFT
A timber boardwalk links the
living area with sandstone steps
and the inclinator. The floodlit
aerial roots of the Port Jackson
fig tree form a natural artwork
against the rock face.

ABOVE
The landscape, with its stunning
views of Pittwater and Broken
Bay, was the defining factor
for this house. Even the table,
designed by Caroline Casey,
reflects the crescent curve
of Mackerel Beach.

Killcare House KILLCARE, AUSTRALIA
buzacottwebber

Constructed	2003
Home type	Three-level home with flat below
Structure	Traditional timber frame, masonry clad, steel-frame roof, floor, and deck; timber, steel, aluminum

"What makes this house special is the large, dramatic, cool, light-filled living areas which allow views out in all directions. This space feels different from the typical suburban house and its openness gives this house its contemporary beach house feel."

Stephen Buzacott

TOP
From the beach the house is seen in its bush context, perched high on the ridge between the ocean and Brisbane Water. The original dark brick has been bagged with a colored render which sets off the bush tones; the off-white roof dissolves the roof line in the sky.

TOP RIGHT
The large, calm volume of the living area, featuring its raked ceiling, provides a sense of spaciousness, and the glazed eastern wall allows full contact with the ocean view. A double-sided steel fireplace sitting on a stone tiled plinth mediates the space and delineates the dining area. This calming space is large enough to hold a crowd yet intimate enough for smaller groups to sit and converse.

RIGHT
This beautiful view due east to the sheltered northern end of Putty Beach, Bouddi National Park, and the Pacific Ocean sweeps south along to Killcare Beach and to the headlands of northern Sydney as far as Manly.

OUT WITH THE OLD, IN WITH THE NEW

This house was designed for a professional couple (lawyer and production designer) with no children, who have a wide circle of friends and love entertaining. The house was also designed for holiday letting.

Situated on a high, steep ridge overlooking the Pacific Ocean, the house was an existing three-level masonry veneer 1970s project house with dark klinker brick and timberwork painted mission brown. The original house had fantastic views of the beach and down the coast to Sydney's Palm Beach and Manly, but was in a very dilapidated condition due to poor construction and maintenance, and required extensive repairs. The house was poorly laid out with small pokey rooms, giving little access to the exterior or the views beyond.

MAXIMIZING THE OUTLOOK

A large building that could not be replicated under prevailing design rules, the house was largely rebuilt within the existing envelope with strategic changes to allow the full potential of the view to be revealed. A major element of the redesign is a dramatic raking steel-framed structure that supports the three new deck levels and the redesigned glazed eastern facade. The structure is supported on cantilevered beams with the rake allowing for three decks, widening out to the main upper deck. The whole house has been oxide color-rendered and re-roofed. The pool area has also been completely redesigned with a smaller pool built within an existing pool and surrounded by new timber decks accessed from a veranda off the kitchen.

CONTEMPORARY LIVING

The house is entered from the existing drive court directly off the street via a new timber pergola. Inside the gate a smaller external vestibule space opens to the tall entry space at the half level between the two upper floors. This leads to an open steel and timber staircase that goes up to the living floor and down to the bedroom floor. The living area has been totally opened up as one large double-height space, overlooking the dramatic eastern view and, via the open kitchen, the pool terrace to the west. The kitchen windows look south to Pittwater and the Barrenjoey headland. A new loft/study space above the existing garage overlooks the living areas. A bathroom and laundry complete this level.

The middle floor was completely redesigned to provide four large bedrooms, three opening to the view. The main bedroom has a bathroom and walk-in wardrobe, and a new WC and bathroom complete this floor. The lower floor, previously unusable, has been designed as a self-contained flat with separate access.

BRINGING IN THE TWENTY-FIRST CENTURY

This project is an example of how to sympathetically renovate a mid-twentieth-century project home which had reasonably good bones but lacked the imagination for contemporary living. The innovative revision of internal spaces to minimize circulation and wasted space, while linking the new spaces with the exterior in a more direct manner, allows the outside to become part of the decoration.

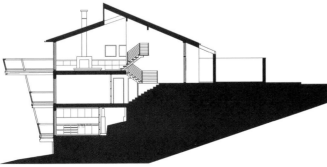

Lo House SINGAPORE

SCDA Architects

Constructed	2006
Home type	Three-level family home including basement
Structure	Timber, aluminum, granite, glass, and plaster

> "'Sentosa' means 'tranquility' in the Malay language, and this house was designed and built with this in mind. Set in an exclusive residential part of Singapore, the house is a sanctuary against the hustle and bustle of the real world."
>
> Chan Soo Khian

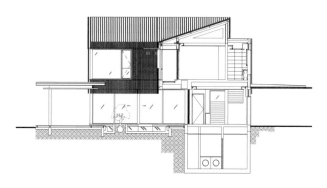

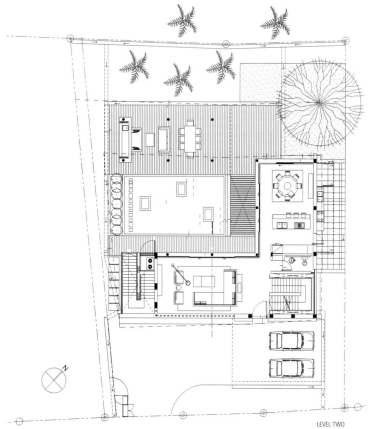

LEVEL TWO

SEASIDE LIVING

Singapore is a small island nation where space has always been at a premium. Many people live in apartments in the city, but there are also areas with lush gardens and glorious ocean views. This particular plot is part of a large tract of reclaimed land marketed as Sentosa Cove, only five minutes from the central business district. Sentosa is an elite resort island, most of which is covered with rainforest and teeming with wildlife. It has a villa community with marinas, golf courses, and a clubhouse.

Set in this beautiful location, the Lo House was designed using an L-shaped plan as the grid. The plan encompasses a carefully landscaped garden, which incorporates a peaceful reflection pool and an outdoor pavilion with views of the ocean.

ABOVE
This simple cantilevered carport, which doubles as a canopy over the entry area, has been carefully detailed using quality timber.

SEPARATING SPACES

The built form emphasizes the timber floor on the second level. It appears to float over the solid enclosure of the basement, and the whole effect provides a rather dramatic backdrop for the interior spaces that open out to the stunning ocean view.

A rough stone wall leads from the basement to the second level, and also separates the living areas from the road. On this side of the room the wall is topped by a long horizontal glass slit. The second story is lighter, wrapped in a "veil" of vertical timber battens.

The second level was conceived as an open plan, with strategically placed freestanding walls that screen the interior of the home from the road. The courtyard is a focal point, and the eye is automatically drawn there before moving on to the ocean beyond.

The third level of the home has a mono-pitched roof. This level has been interpreted as a kind of box that shelters the private areas of the house while keeping the views accessible, so the windows are openings cut into the facade. On this level there are four bedrooms, one guest room, and six bathrooms.

SMOOTH TRANSITIONS

The entry and carport, both in the shelter of a huge cantilevered canopy, lead to the living and dining rooms, which are enhanced by the delightful view of the courtyard and pavilion.

ABOVE
In the living room a floor-to-ceiling glass wall allows plenty of natural ventilation and access to the wonderful view.

LEFT
The main staircase features a bright red load-bearing wall that contrasts with the color of the timber steps, the stone, and the pale walls elsewhere.

ABOVE
The main material used in the construction of the house is timber. When coupled with the reflection pool and the tropical plants, this natural material creates a resort-like atmosphere that suits the house's location.

RIGHT
Cooled by sea breezes, the house has been designed as an L-shape so that the courtyard and reflection pool face the ocean. At different times of the day, the pool mirrors sections of both the house and the landscape.

The living room looks out at the view across a tranquil reflection pool surrounded by a timber deck, then through a pavilion toward the sea. There is also a void that overlooks the basement. Adjacent to the kitchen is the dining room, which enjoys the same views.

The staircase is set against a striking bright red wall. This contrasts with the palette of gray and brown that leads to the more private spaces of the bedrooms, the bathrooms, and the basement.

CHOOSING THE RIGHT MATERIALS

The architects chose materials for the Lo House that would bring a genuine unity to the entire structure, and gave a great deal of attention to connecting spaces. The house expresses modern sensibilities but also captures the essence of relaxed seaside living in the tropics.

"The brief was to clad the house in timber. During the day, the house is solid yet elegant, but in the evening its interior is expressed behind the timber screens both at the front and rear ends. This creates an openness and a lightness of expression."

Malibu House CALIFORNIA, USA
Kanner Architects

Constructed	2004
Home type	One-story family home
Structure	Concrete, plaster, glass, and wood (teak, mahogany, and vertical-grain Douglas fir)

"The project was supremely rewarding because it was a second chance of sorts. Kanner Architects had designed the house in the 1990s after the original home was destroyed by fire. A new owner with more money and bigger plans bought the project in 2002 and invited Kanner to come back and completely make it over. Square footage remained constant, but walls came down and every surface was updated and upgraded. The resulting house was closer to what the original might have been if not for budget constraints."

Kanner Architects

TOP
A courtyard is created by the U-shaped plan, which utilizes simple geometric forms. The white plaster shapes are strategically aligned in order to use the changing light of day and the resulting shadows to creative effect.

ABOVE
A look at the entry illustrates the varying heights of the home's different forms. Ceiling heights rise and drop throughout the house, creating a natural rhythm. The taller form at right includes the dining room, kitchen, and living room.

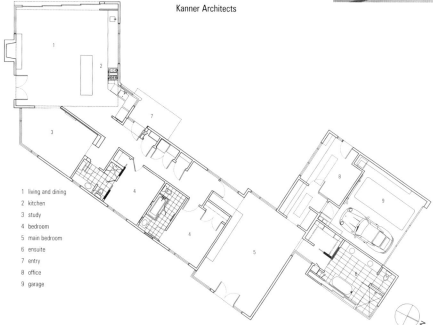

1 living and dining
2 kitchen
3 study
4 bedroom
5 main bedroom
6 ensuite
7 entry
8 office
9 garage

INSPIRED CHOICES

This house is inspired by the work of Luis Barragán, the Mexican architect, whose courtyard designs show a skilful use of light and space. Other influences are the houses of the Greek islands and the cubist work of Irving Gill, another specialist in internal courtyards.

FEEDING THE SENSES

The house is designed to take full advantage of its dazzling views of the Pacific. The stark white plaster exterior contrasts dramatically with the colors of ocean and sky. Inside, mahogany doors and cabinetry provide a warm complement to the austere exterior.

Varying ceiling heights create a ladder of space and volume, with vertical space being at its greatest in the living room, dining room, and main bedroom. The overall effect is one of compression and expansion, creating a bond between the rise and fall of room heights and the rolling Pacific Ocean.

OPENING TO THE WORLD

An interior courtyard doubles as the entry. When the glass walls are opened, the house extends out to the exterior spaces, and permits unencumbered views of the ocean and the mountains.

There are three bedrooms, three bathrooms, and a study. To increase the feeling of spaciousness without increasing the real space, the wall between the kitchen and the living and dining areas was removed, opening up views from all perspectives.

The main bathroom, which opens up to outside, is the gem of the house. It has stacked sliding glass doors and a butt-glazed corner in the shower. Black granite floor tiles are accented by a vertical-grain Douglas fir vanity and wall panels.

Another special feature of the 3,200-sq-ft (300-sq-m) house is the wall separating the pool area from the driveway and garage. A series of back-lit etched-glass panels stand on concrete bases in a reference to the simple geometric structures that compose the house. These panels create a glowing opaque barrier and light source for evening lounging or swimming.

JAPANESE TOUCHES

The owners are interested in Japanese art, so the architects chose a number of items that provide a distinct Japanese flavor to the home. Some of the most noticeable are the wooden shower fixtures in the bathrooms. The landscaping too, has an under-stated Japanese feel to it.

ABOVE
Retracting exterior glass walls fuse the inside and outside. Alder floors in the living area give way to a carpet of green grass outside. White walls trimmed in mahogany supply warmth for the open floor plan, which comprises the dining room, kitchen, and living room.

FOLLOWING PAGES
Malibu House's minimalist esthetic allows the natural beauty of the site and its views to dominate. With its retracting walls, the main bathroom opens to the pool deck. At right, a fence of translucent panels, which are 5 ft by 7 ft (1.5 m by 2.1 m), lines the driveway, hiding it from the pool area as well as creating an artistic sculptural element.

ABOVE
This view of the kitchen, dining, and living areas from the deck shows the spacious open floor plan. The home office at the rear of the garage can be seen through the dining room window.

TOP FAR RIGHT
Sliding mahogany-framed doors open the main bathroom to the pool deck, providing a stunning backdrop for bathing among ocean breezes. Both the floors and the tub platform are granite.

FAR RIGHT
The living room – with Mies van der Rohe's leather Barcelona chairs – opens to the deck and garden. The floors are alder and the wall panels are mahogany divided by stainless steel splines.

RIGHT
The island in the kitchen is mahogany – as are all the cabinets – and capped with granite. The vertical orientation of the stainless steel appliances interacts with the otherwise horizontal lines of the island, counters, and shelves. The ceiling height changes in the hallway to the right, and this change indicates the transition to another part of the house.

Martha's Vineyard House MASSACHUSETTS, USA

Architecture Research Office

Constructed	2005
Home type	Country house
Structure	Timber, steel, and concrete

"This house embodies qualities unique to the Chilmark shore. Its orientation and composition frame the passage from land to sea. The various shadows cast by the cedar siding allude to what occurs naturally on the site, where the scrub oak shadows change throughout the day."

Adam Yarinsky

TOP
The series of planes defining the entry court draw the visitor toward the entrance of Martha's Vineyard House, creating a sense of anticipation. Upon rounding the corner, an unexpectedly grand view of the ocean beyond is revealed.

ABOVE
A large fireplace of basaltina separates the living room from the dining room, while maintaining the openness of communal living spaces. The fireplace is complemented by oak floorboards, which have been laid in a staggered pattern in the living areas, as well as in the bedrooms.

AN ISLAND SANCTUARY

A peaceful hillside at the southern edge of a clearing in the woods is the site of this house in Martha's Vineyard, an island 7 miles (11 km) from the Massachusetts coastline. The home's elevation allows for expansive views across the water, and permits a blending of the home with the scrub oak trees that surround the site.

COMPACT FORM

To conform to stringent local code requirements and to stay within budget, the design of the home is compact and simple. Each of the three blocks composing the home have been arranged to define the world outside, making full use of the varying traits of the site. Entry to the house is through a protected, quietly landscaped entry court, which is formed by two of these blocks. From the entry, which looks through the living area, there is a view of the ocean and outlying islands in the distance. The main living block contains the entry foyer, living, and dining rooms. It offers views of a field and the water beyond. The main bedroom wing faces a densely vegetated gorge. The kitchen and guest wing faces out to the lawn and garden.

COMPLEMENTARY MATERIALS

Building materials were chosen to harmonize with the site. They also serve to delineate the interior and exterior areas. Two L-shaped cedar-clad walls, placed at a 90° angle, are the defining elements of the blocks. Cedar shingles are widely used in the Cape Cod region, and the architect varied the theme by alternating the widths of the siding, effectively creating something new and different. There is a genuine connection with the landscape here, emphasized by the parallel detailing on the walls. The architect chose zinc panels and wood windows, which achieve a bold contrast with the cedar. Zinc walls also feature in the living area.

SENSITIVE FINISHES

The cedar siding and cedar walls blend with the low stone landscape walls, all striking a chord of unity with the surrounding landscape.

White-washed ash has been used in the cabinetry; glass and marble tiles are the prominent elements in the bathrooms. Basaltina tiles run from the drive all the way into the foyer and stone is the defining feature of the kitchen and the outdoor dining terrace.

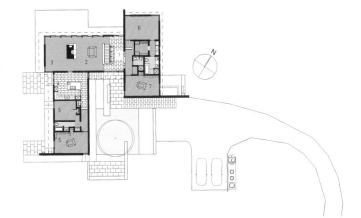

1 entry foyer
2 living
3 dining
4 kitchen
5 guest bedroom
6 main bedroom
7 study

TOP
The south wing of the house interlocks with the main living block at the kitchen. It houses the guest bedrooms. Tucked back into the site's gentle slope, this living block intimately relates to the site in contrast to the main living block.

ABOVE
The main living block of the house is stretched across the shoreline with a panorama of the waterfront and distant horizon.

Orleans House MASSACHUSETTS, USA
Charles Rose Architects

Constructed	2004
Home type	Two-level family home with studio
Structure	Steel, timber, concrete, and glass

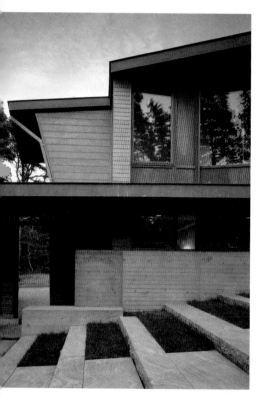

"The house is sited on a bluff overlooking a bay and the Atlantic Ocean to the east. The footprint traces a naturally occurring bowl in the landscape. The varying floor levels reflect the original rise and fall of the grade while providing spatial definition to the functional areas of the interior. The forms reflect the natural landforms and every effort was made to preserve the existing flora of the site."

Charles Rose

ABOVE
Granite stairs in the landscape provide an imposing access from the parking court to the main entrance of Orleans House.

TOP RIGHT
The two-level cabana sits on the western edge of the main house (in view, at left). The office on the upper level enjoys spectacular views of the bay and Atlantic Ocean.

ABOVE RIGHT
Floor to ceiling windows allow natural light to stream into the house, giving it a translucent quality. Generously sized overhangs and sunscreen trellises give the home plenty of shade and shelter from weather extremes.

COLOR, LIGHT, AND MOVEMENT

Orleans House is situated on a high bluff overlooking Pleasant Bay, Nanset Beach, and the Atlantic Ocean, and sits in a natural recess in the topography. The architects were briefed to design a house that would take advantage of the glorious water views, while still permitting comfortable living in all seasons. Winters get very cold in Massachusetts, so it was important that the design include adequate shelter and protection from the elements.

To take advantage of the views, large amounts of glass face the sea. This allows plenty of natural light and ventilation into the house. On the side away from the ocean, the house is covered with a low copper roof, which adds warmth and texture. The design encompasses the main house, an art studio, a self-contained guest apartment, and a separate cabana with an office above.

MASSACHUSETTS LIVING

The main house consists of a roomy single-story space. It contains the entry foyer, living room, dining room, kitchen, and gallery area. Although these spaces open into one another, they are separated by stepped floor levels and strategically placed walls.

Stepped exterior terraces emanate from the southern and western ends of the house. These are protected from the sun by roof overhangs and sunscreen trellises, bringing the outside into the inside and allowing more outdoor living.

The brief was to design a house that would take advantage of the glorious water views, while still permitting comfortable living in all seasons.

ABOVE
The entry to the house occurs along a natural rise in the landscape, and is framed by the architecture and the plantings.

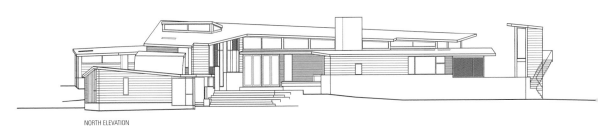

NORTH ELEVATION

The eastern side of Orleans House contains the library/media room. The south-facing, L-shaped master bedroom is also on this side. The intersection of the L is the spine of the house, and permits access to the guest bedroom level, the wine cellar, and an upper sitting room positioned underneath a roof window.

On the northern side of the house, the family room is linked to the main house by a covered walkway. Designed for a range of recreational activities, the family room was purposely set apart from the rest of the house. It has a charming aspect over the garden and surrounding landscape and also hides the parking court of the main house.

SEPARATE SPACES

On the western edge of the main house sits a towered cabana with a second-level private office. The room commands dazzling views to the bay and ocean beyond. It also contains a spa, shower, and toilet.

The separate guesthouse sits on the northern edge of the site. The first level of this space has large roller doors and contains an art studio. The upper level consists of the bedroom, a south-facing terrace, a small eating area, and a bathroom.

MATERIAL RESILIENCE

The materials used were chosen for their durability and practicality. The house has a conventional wood-frame structure, reinforced with steel columns and beams. On the exterior, exposed board-formed concrete foundation walls were used, as well as lead-coated copper walls and roofs, and cedar siding. The windows are framed in mahogany, and exterior stainless steel has been acid-finished to give it a brown color, making it blend with the outside.

Plaster walls and ceilings have been used inside. The doors are made of the exotic African wood anagre, while the floors are either jatoba wood or golden juperana granite.

ABOVE RIGHT
A view of the living area looking west. The client's artwork was considered in the development of each interior space.

LEFT
The stairs link the wine cellar on the lower level to a sitting area on the mezzanine level. The staircase is constructed from mahogany, acid-washed stainless steel, and glass.

1 cabana	16 library/media room
2 jacuzzi	17 WC
3 west terrace	18 main bedroom
4 dining terrace	19 main wardrobe
5 screen porch	20 main bathroom
6 dining	21 utility
7 sitting area	22 lower hallway
8 kitchen	23 bathroom
9 pantry	24 bedroom
10 gallery	25 utility entry
11 living	26 breezeway
12 pantry entry	27 motor court
13 south terrace	28 family/bunk room
14 north entry	29 bathroom
15 foyer	

LEVEL ONE

Peg Yorkin House MALIBU, USA
Moore Ruble Yudell Architects & Planners

Constructed	1997
Home type	Two-story family home
Structure	Concrete foundation, pre-cast concrete, timber frame construction, and sliding glass and aluminum panels

"The house evolved from understanding and embracing the complexities of the site and the social needs of the family. It is buffered and urban on the highway, transparent and transformable toward the water, and permeable and vertically connected to the animations of light and sky. It provides an urban refuge for three generations and can be shaped and tuned by them according to the season, or the needs of their varied social occasions."

Moore Ruble Yudell Architects & Planners

ABOVE
Toward the highway, the Peg Yorkin House is expressed as a collage of relatively solid forms of roofs and light-scoops that reach up to bring skylight and views into the house. Entry to the home is through a sequestered courtyard to the left of the palm tree.

LEFT
Facing toward the beach, the house is highly transparent giving it a "lightness" on the landscape. On the upper level, most bedrooms have a private, shaded balcony. At the lower level, sliding doors allow all major living spaces to open up to outdoor terraces and entertainment areas.

RIGHT
Toward the beach, the house is articulated to optimize views from individual spaces. Terraces and living spaces have varying degrees of shade, depending upon their requirements.

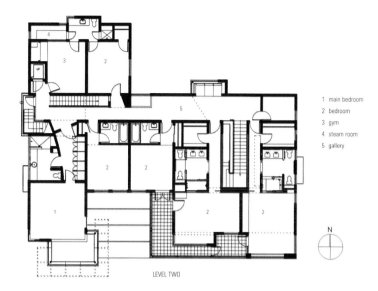

1 main bedroom
2 bedroom
3 gym
4 steam room
5 gallery

LEVEL TWO

N

RESPONDING TO THE SITE

The Peg Yorkin House evolved in response to the tensions of its site. It is on the edge of the busy city of Los Angeles, where the Santa Monica Mountains and the Pacific Coast Highway meet the ocean, with its dazzling and infinitely changing panoramas. Sitting snugly between the highway and the sandy beach is the Yorkin site, which provides an urban-edge refuge for three generations of a family with creative and social commitments.

The house is a social and familial retreat for the owner, her two adult children, and their families. All of them were intimately involved in the design process. It was critical that the house be comfortable for the individual as well as the group, and that the range of activities – both formal and informal – of each family member could be accommodated.

OPENING TO THE ENVIRONMENT

The urban courtyard is used as the basic building form and typology. A system of sliding exterior and interior panels allows the occupants to transform the home, creating varying degrees of openness to the environment. As well, these panels provide privacy when required. This transformability is reminiscent of the shoji screen systems found in traditional Japanese houses.

LAYERS OF MEANING

The house unfolds as a series of layers. Entry to the interior is through a courtyard of native beach grasses and over a wooden boardwalk. Inside there are dedicated family living areas, most of which retain a correlation to the exterior through sliding glass walls that lead to an outside courtyard, terrace, and beyond that, to the beach. The glass walls also permit the entry of plenty of natural light.

FAR LEFT
The primary staircase to the bedrooms is illuminated by clerestory light. Sliding color glass panels provide visual privacy, as well as "borrowed" light, to dressing areas of bedrooms. These panels can be moved to create an infinite number of abstract murals of colored light.

LEFT
A guest bathroom is animated by the simultaneous intensity and subtlety of integrally colored Italian plaster. Indirect light adds further richness to the spatial experience of this small room.

ABOVE
Highlighted by indirect lighting, the curve of the articulated ceiling in the main bedroom is reminiscent of the waves outside. To the left, a low bay provides a place for contemplation and viewing the everchanging panorama.

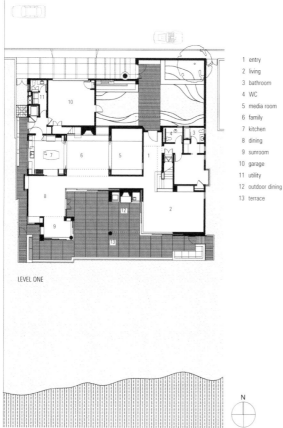

1 entry
2 living
3 bathroom
4 WC
5 media room
6 family
7 kitchen
8 dining
9 sunroom
10 garage
11 utility
12 outdoor dining
13 terrace

LEVEL ONE

N

ABOVE
The dining room space is more than doubled when the sliding glass walls are opened to the exterior terrace. These sliding glass walls are used extensively throughout the home to invite light in, and to unite internal and external spaces.

RIGHT
The home's centrally located family room opens out to an expansive terrace, which is the focal point around which all the major living spaces revolve.

A central courtyard is the focus of the house – it serves as the pivot around which the major living spaces of kitchen, family room, dining, and media room revolve. The courtyard, which is partially covered, includes an outside dining area and fireplace, and can be used year round.

Most of the bedrooms, all of which are located on the second level, have an individual ocean-facing terrace, allowing plenty of light and air to penetrate the house. In spite of this, each bedroom is completely private from the outside. There are six bedrooms and six bathrooms upstairs.

COASTAL COLORS

The colors and the materials were carefully selected to maintain a strong connection with the coastal setting of the house. It was important that materials be strong and durable enough to withstand the force of salt, sun, and seawater.

The outside walls are integral cement plaster, with concrete and pre-cast concrete details. The windows and doors are powder-coated aluminum. The exterior wood is teak, and the sun shades are stainless steel woven fabric or aluminum lattice. The roof is zinc with a matt finish.

ABOVE
The doors of the living room disappear into a wall cavity, creating a room completely open to the surrounding terrace and sea. The continuous deck creates the sense of a promenade on a large ship's deck.

Pond House ARIZONA, USA

Will Bruder Architects

Construction	2003–2005
Home type	One-bedroom home
Structure	Concrete block, structural steel, and wooden frame

> "Pond House runs along a creek bed outside the town of Cave Creek, north of Phoenix, Arizona, at the end of an isolated, unpaved road. As suggested by its solitary bedroom and isolated location, it was conceived as a place of reflection and contemplation for its owners."
>
> Will Bruder

DRAMATIC ENTRY

Thirty miles (50 km) north of Phoenix, Arizona, is architect Will Bruder's carefully crafted and modestly scaled retreat, Pond House, embedded in a rock outcrop in the midst of the Sonoran Desert.

The house, nestled into the rock banks of Cave Creek and overlooking a natural, year-round swimming hole, is approached by a natural gravel road. A vast 7-ft (2.1-m) steel plate emerges from the ground and gradually arcs away from the natural stone of the home's anchoring wall. An opening in the steel reveals the funnel-like approach to the house, and draws the visitor inexorably toward the heavy, raw steel entry door.

A natural spring, collected in a concrete cistern, overflows and trickles down the natural flagstone stairs toward the entry under the house, before reaching the creek below.

THE ORIGINAL INHABITANTS

The arc of the natural stones in Pond House's northern wall echo the crumbling remains of nearby irrigation ditches and the foundations of small abodes left by the Hohokan Indians, who inhabited this area from 800 to 1400 CE. They used the waters of Cave Creek to irrigate their land.

MAXIMIZING THE VIEW

Once inside, a small set of stairs descends into the central living/dining area and kitchen, featuring exposed concrete floors and maple veneer millwork, accented with a complex mix of plywood, steel, and natural stone. A panoramic view of the lush vegetation along Cave Creek floods in through Pond House's articulated custom windows of raw plated steel, set in weathered steel cladding beneath thin, broad eaves of re-sawn plywood.

ABOVE LEFT
The warm glow of the entry door resonates with the soft trickle of water from a natural spring between embracing walls of stone and steel to create an invitation into the home. A small window is set into the eastern wall under a heavy stone lintel, introducing to the living space views of the lush vegetation along the creek below.

LEFT
The low roofline and natural materials of Pond House allow it to easily meld with its desert surroundings. It seems to sit naturally within the rocky outcroppings above the swimming hole, bridging the transition between the creek vegetation and the Sonoran Desert beyond.

TOP RIGHT
The view looking back up the flight of natural flagstone steps leading from the entry, past a concrete cistern to the garage beyond, typifies the integration of Pond House into the landscape. The design of the house, and its form, location, and materials attempt to resonate with, rather than impose upon, the serene surrounding oasis.

ABOVE RIGHT
The rocky banks of the swimming hole seem to be part of the home's foundations. Reflective glass further softens the impact of the home by mirroring the surrounding landscape, while the cantilevered deck creates a dialogue between Bruder's idyllic hideaway and the harshness of the Sonoran Desert.

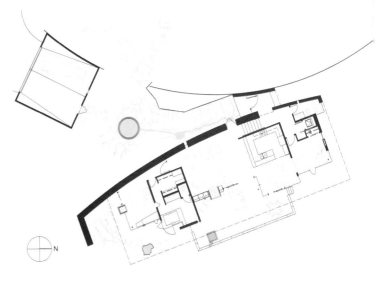

A cantilevered concrete deck, with minimal stainless steel guardrail, hovers effortlessly above its rocky escarpment, combining with large sliding glass doors to create a seamless transition between the interior and exterior spaces.

ATTENTION TO DETAIL

Native stone, rough-sawn plywood, and Venetian plaster characterize the home's interior, providing it with its warmth and scale. The eastern elevation is a fully glazed, intimate expanse of carefully selected textures and materials. This glazing offers views of the creek to each room, including the main living spaces, a large main bedroom, bathroom, and a home office, which can be converted to a guest room if required.

Pond House's natural stone western exterior doubles as an internal feature wall. This extends along the living/dining area and into the main bedroom, where a semi-frameless glass door permits the eye to follow the gentle arc of the wall. Beyond the bedroom, the stone wall turns east to define an intimate sunken garden. The bedroom faces southeast to enjoy this garden through large expanses of glass, complete with vent panels to allow natural ventilation.

PEACEFUL RETREAT

Pond House is replete with windows of glass and colored translucent resin that present a kaleidoscope of surprising, unexpected perspectives in a serene and peaceful setting.

ABOVE
The carefully chosen fabrics of the furnishings in the living/dining area combine with the natural stonework and woods to absorb, rather than reflect, the large volumes of diffuse light entering the east-facing windows. The small set of stairs from the entry on the left recede from the space, enhancing the peace of this desert oasis.

LEFT
Looking north along the generously scaled deck, one of the home's two slow-combustion wood fireplaces can be seen in the foreground. The wide overhangs of the roof help to shelter the deck, and filter early morning and afternoon light.

OPPOSITE
Echoing the building techniques of ancient communities across the southwest, from the abandoned Anasazi settlement of Mesa Verde in Colorado to the extensive ruins of Chaco Canyon in New Mexico, Pond House is both southwestern vernacular and desert modern.

Rochman Residence CALIFORNIA, USA
Callas Shortridge Architects

Construction	1998–2000
House type	Two-story family home
Structure	Wood frame construction with deepened foundation, stucco, steel

"The task at hand was to illuminate the inherent drama of the site and reflect that seamlessly in a natural architecture: as though the result of millions of years of geology and a human enterprise were logically intertwined."

Barbara Callas

IN CONSORT WITH NATURE

Precipitously perched above the curve of Pacific Coast Highway between the Palisades and Malibu, California, the Rochman Residence rises like an outcropping of angular granite, sculpted by the architects in consort with nature. The clients first approached Frank Israel to discuss the site; shortly afterward, the project was taken over by associates Steven Shortridge, David Spinelli, and Barbara Callas, who was the design principal.

Viewed from the roadway below, the home stands as a singular artefact and unique habitation. Large, thrusting parallel planes of eucalyptus-toned stucco jut from the upper reaches of the steep cliffs. The lines of the top level frame a wrap of glass, angled and transparent at its edge. This modern, mythic bird of prey stares silently out from its perch, sentient and all seeing.

The base of this expansive glassed room is the floor of the main bedroom below. Its face frames the ocean side of the structure as it bends crisply into a sharp, narrowing, structural support. The effect created by the acute angle of the column animates this essential function. The column seems to be a massive, mechanical knee, folded to brace itself into the substratum.

SHAPE AND FORM

A vertical wall of upthrust steel-trowelled plaster stands at the entry of the residence – both a practical and metaphorical subterranean anchor of Euclidian variation.

Adjacent to it, thin, elongated, and irregular concrete steps lead to the zinc-metal front door, which swings open to reveal a kinetic contrast between the muted exterior and a vibrant interior of color that is spontaneously enlivened by the transition. The geometry within becomes a subtle form of theater, where shifting shapes of angular walls and ceilings create visual intrigue against the endless panoramas.

LEFT
Indigenous vegetation was preserved, privacy heightened, and the naturally shallow-stepped site focused to give the structure a sense of lightness. Simultaneously, this achieved a solid anchoring into a perch that affords uninterrupted views of the coast from Santa Monica eastward to Malibu in the west.

ABOVE
Two non-native elements inhabit this western view – a eucalyptus tree included as a feature in the Spanish cedar deck, and the residence, which stands here like the prow of a ship heading out to sea. The deck is protected by steel and glass railings that provide increased solidity where previously there was only air. The mitered glass window leans in two directions to reduce the effect of enclosing the living area above.

ABOVE RIGHT
In contrast to the severe slope of the main residence, the entry is reached by climbing broad, slightly elevated, concrete steps that traverse the site, shifting axis while slipping through a displaced wall plane.

RIGHT
The drawings depict both a sectional elevation, through the axis of circulation, as well as a transectional axis, through the fireplace. In addition, reference is made, in the second vertical sketch, to the dining trellis that connects with the outdoor terrace.

ABOVE
The structure's transparencies are choreographed to produce energy while thrusting vertically, wrapping horizontally, or tilting at various angles. Southern California climatology and the proximity of the ocean allow fenestration, both fixed and movable, to substitute for forced air-cooling.

A SPECTRUM OF HUES AND VIEWS

In part, this design evolved as an internal logic in response to code demands that restricted the height and flexibility of roof permeations. The varied shapes of the interior walls are saturated with color. The hues, ranging from eucalyptus to deep orange, create a three-dimensional effect.

The upper level encompasses an office, living, and dining space, where a cedar trellis cantilevers over the deck to carry it outside to sense-saturating views of the Pacific. The lower peripheries of the view include the beach and the ocean.

BEAUTIFUL BEECH

Natural light dances upon the upper level's beech wood floor, which sets off the black and chrome chairs of the mahogany-stained dining table and dramatizes other space that is introduced by pronounced, straight-edged materials in radically contrasting tones.

The entry level is divided by a central, internal stair that descends as the base of an angled wall. Its treads continue the beech wood motif until they change to walnut-stained concrete at a platform two steps above the lower floor. This poured, richly burnished element is the surface on all lower level living space, including the main bedroom, its ensuite, and the adjacent gym.

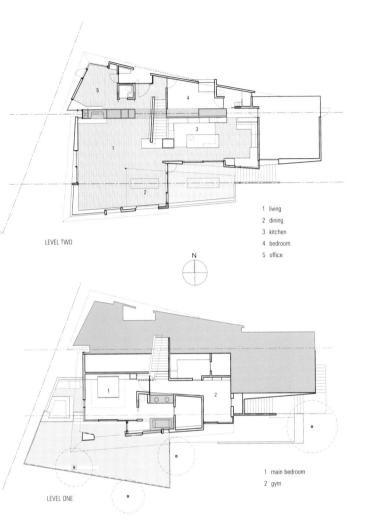

LEVEL TWO

1 living
2 dining
3 kitchen
4 bedroom
5 office

N

LEVEL ONE

1 main bedroom
2 gym

ABOVE

The thrust of a tilting plaster wall along the left flank of the entry procession carries the visitor into either the living room to the right, the dining room featured here, or beyond the dining room to the spaces that view limitless horizon. The ceiling is dramatized by ribs of Spanish cedar that pass by overhead to connect with the trellis, heightening the interior/exterior dialectic, ever present in the architect's design and implicit in California living.

LEFT

The base of the entry plaster wall functionally inverts in the lower spaces, providing privacy and separation between them and the main bedroom, seen beyond. The honeyed beech wood of the floor above continues as steps until they end at a stepped plinth of burnished concrete. The large section of Douglas fir pivots closed as a door, then comes to rest as a seamless wall.

LEFT

A 40-ft (12-m) continuous band of glass mitered at the corner of the living room contains a window seat that floats above the sea and mist. The ever-present eucalyptus softens the view and emphasizes the natural grounding of an otherwise incongruous site.

Sea Farm House HANGKLIP, SOUTH AFRICA

Stefan Antoni Olmesdahl Truen Architects

Constructed	2002
Home type	One-story family holiday home
Structure	Timber, stone, travertine, plaster

"The earliest inhabitants, the Khoisan, known as strandlopers ('beach walkers'), lived in caves or simple stone structures scattered along the coastline, living mainly on fish. Inspired by these simple dwellings, and the stone and lime-washed fishermen's cottages built later, the house has been designed to be very basic, virtually primal, and yet very sophisticated at the same time."

Stefan Antoni

RUGGED SETTING, STURDY STRUCTURE

This home is located on a rocky peninsula in a nature reserve, and is perched above a dramatic seascape with spectacular views of Hangklip Mountain. The area is home to indigenous fynbos and a vast array of sea life.

The walls are simple and heavy. The roof is thin and floats over voids created between the solid mass of stone and plastered wall, extending to form covered and open terraces tailored to the specific orientation of the space. The materials and finishes were chosen for their inherent qualities and relationship to the site.

LAYERING THE HOUSE

The linear homestead is layered horizontally, from the central living zones through the intermediate pause zone to the bedrooms and on to the bathroom areas that open out into the natural landscape.

To take advantage of the sea and surrounding views and to provide protection from the extreme coastal climate, the living spaces were designed with north–south orientations, resulting in an open, flowing space with sea and mountain terraces. The main living spaces form the link between inside and outside. The living area is on the sea side, and the dining room and kitchen, slightly raised and on the north, open out onto a deep-covered outdoor living terrace. This transparent center allows living to occur on either side of the house depending entirely on the prevailing weather conditions – in poor weather, the mountain-facing dining terrace is preferred; in fine conditions, living and entertaining takes place in the sea-facing area.

Natural colors and materials were used, including warm sandstone, ash-gray balau woodwork and a charcoal metal roof. There are large glazed areas with views from every room. Each aspect of the house has a private terrace or a deck.

ABOVE RIGHT
The holiday house, a linear single-story structure, is situated on the headland of a private nature reserve, surrounded by the Indian Ocean, indigenous fynbos, and Hangklip Mountain.

RIGHT
The doors to the bathroom slide back completely and open onto a private deck. A traditional timber "latte" screen adds privacy to the space. The bath is sunken, set on floor level to minimise its dominance in the space.

ABOVE
The lounge room opens up onto the front terrace, blurring the boundaries between inside and out. This space makes for easy living and stunning entertaining during fine, summery conditions. A Balau timber pergola frames the view and filters the natural sunlight, adding to the picture-perfect setting.

WITHOUT WALLS

The house appears to be "without walls." Nothing seems to contain the house, and its dual identity in terms of internal and external spaces is an integral part of the design: All the rooms, including the bedrooms and bathrooms, open up, extending beyond sliding glass doors onto decks with sweeping views to the horizon on all sides. Even the internal spaces trifle with the finality of walls — some do not meet the ceilings, yet they still fulfil their purpose of partitioning rooms.

Other spaces are subtly divided by contrasting surfaces, and elsewhere, heavy wooden beams are stopped abruptly by the sensual lines of a gentle arch which denotes a different zone.

The intermediate pause zones are enclosed in the stone walls and sculpted to create arched, cave-like, intimate, and cosy spaces. Each space contains a fireplace alcove on one side and the working part of the kitchen on the other. In contrast, the living spaces have high ceilings of thick timber beams and "latte," a material traditionally used in the construction of the thatched roofed houses of the Cape.

The result is a house with a strong yet understated character that is both elegant and timeless.

ABOVE

The dramatic view of the ocean, kelp, and rocks, which evokes a sense of seeing forever, is enhanced by the horizontal lines and expansive living room doors. The contrasting natural tones in the indoor space pick up on the coastal hues outdoors.

1 ensuite
2 dressing
3 WC
4 bathroom
5 bedroom
6 main bedroom
7 living
8 dining
9 kitchen
10 terrace
11 garage
12 parking
13 deck

N

ABOVE LEFT
The bathrooms, situated at each end of the house, afford sweeping water views. The bathroom areas open out into the natural landscape.

ABOVE
An arched ceiling cove flanked by stone-cladded walls provides a private zone in the main bedroom. The texture of the stone work adds a warmth to the space. The ensuite bathroom and dressing area are situated behind the alcove.

LEFT
The ceiling is constructed of deep, exposed timber beams with "latte" infill panels (timber slats) between. Clerestory windows provide additional natural light and cross ventilation. The differing ceilings and split-level floors help to define the individual spaces.

Shaw House VANCOUVER, CANADA
Patkau Architects

Constructed	2000
Home type	Private residence
Structure	Reinforced concrete

"The Shaw House is an essay in light, water, and concrete in which the material character of each, both ephemeral and enduring, is revealed by the presence of the others. Time enters in through changing light conditions and the movement of water – seen against the unchanging backdrop of concrete – to create a dynamic environment within which the daily events of domestic life unfold."

John Patkau

SMALL SITE, BIG IDEAS

The site for this house is a small waterfront property that enjoys wonderful views across English Bay to the North Shore Mountains that tower above Vancouver's city skyline. The site is 33 ft (10 m) wide and 155 ft (47 m) deep. Side yard setbacks required by the local government meant that the building – a private residence for one person – was limited to a width of 26.4 ft (8 m). The client requested the usual living spaces, as well as a single bedroom, a study, a music room, and a lap pool.

ORGANIZED LIVING

The arrangement of Shaw House is very simple. Living spaces are on grade (ground level), the music room is beneath grade, while the bedroom, study, and the lap pool are above it all. The pool was placed above ground level because putting it elsewhere would have compromised the size of the living spaces. It sits along the west side of the house and is connected at either end to terraces that merge with the study and bedroom, providing a seamless sense of continuity.

The narrowness of the house means that spatial expansion is only achievable upward through the volume of the house and outward over the water. The ceilings are quite high, having the effect of making small spaces appear bigger. The dining room, for example, rises from ground level to the upper level to a clerestory. Because the lap pool is on the west side of the house, it allows daylight – as well as reflected light from the pool – into the central area of the home.

ABOVE
From the street, the view of the Shaw House reveals wood-louvered skylights combined with cast concrete, creating a compositional calm, while also establishing a sculptural quality through the interplay between complementary textures and planes.

RIGHT
This perspective of the home demonstrates how the architects surpassed the constraints of a tight site. Long, parallel concrete walls and a narrow lap pool are positioned to navigate lines of sight toward the impressive views of the bay, the North Shore Mountains, and the city beyond.

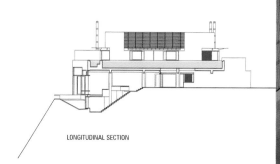

LONGITUDINAL SECTION

The entrance to the home is situated directly under the pool about halfway along the side of the house. The whole of this area is illuminated by the patterns of light that pass through the pool's glass bottom.

READY FOR ANYTHING

Vancouver, like many of the cities on the west coast of North America, is situated in an area of high seismic risk, so it was important to ensure that a strong structure was in place in the event that an earthquake should occur, particularly as the lap pool is located aboveground. The architect chose to construct the house almost entirely of reinforced concrete to provide resistance to any earthquake activity and its aftermath. White cement incorporated into the mix resulted in the house maintaining a bright external appearance even in wet weather, which is frequent in this part of Canada.

Inside the concrete exterior, the inside of the house is insulated and then clad with painted gypsum board. There are areas in the house that do not require insulation, and for these, the architect decided to leave the concrete structure exposed. The colors chosen for the interior are soft and muted, which allows natural light to make a real impact in the home.

TOP RIGHT
View from the living room toward the dining room and entrance to the home. Although the rooms are fairly narrow, a sense of space is achieved with high ceilings. This can be seen here where part of the dining/ living room ceiling rises from ground level to the upper level.

RIGHT
Sunlight is refracted through the lens of the pool's water and filters into the entry space below. This not only provides a natural light source, but also causes the concrete-clad space to come alive with the ever-changing patterns of rippling pool water.

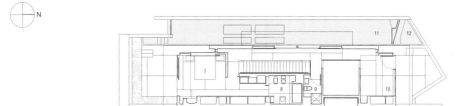

LEVEL ONE

N

LEVEL TWO

1 entry
2 dining
3 living
4 kitchen
5 WC
6 garage
7 bedroom
8 bathroom
9 guest bathroom
10 study
11 lap pool
12 hot pool

LEFT
Shaw House's well-situated terrace takes advantage of spectacular views of English Bay and the North Shore Mountains, as well as the beautiful city of Vancouver.

ABOVE
At night the white-tile-clad pool seems surprisingly shallow, and becomes almost like a light-box beaming against the darkened silhouette of the house.

Slat House CALIFORNIA, USA

David Hertz Architects

Constructed	2005
Home type	Three-level single family home
Structure	Concrete, typical wood framing, and some steel framing

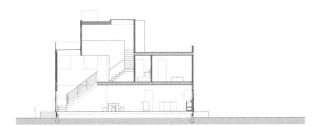

"The intent was to create a constantly changing facade on an existing elevation. Thin slats of Ipe wood provide a dynamic elevation defined by light and shadow...I've employed many environmental features — natural ventilation strategies, solar systems, solar hydronic radiant heating, and recycled content."

David Hertz

ABOVE
A clear view of the open kitchen/ dining room area and the cantilevered Ipe wood stair is offered from the entry and living room. The double height volume and open plan provide a passage for natural ventilation and allow for an abundance of natural light.

SENSITIVE REVAMP

Built for an architectural lighting distributor and his young family, Slat House is an extensive remodel to an existing single-family residence. The client desired the new residence, located three buildings from the sand in Marina del Rey, to have the look and feel of a contemporary beach house while maintaining environmental consciousness.

The previous residence was an unsightly shingle-siding and mansard-roof structure; however, its position and proximity to the street, not allowed by today's code, made it essential to do a renovation rather than a rebuild.

A DYNAMIC EXTERIOR

Keeping the existing setback preserved the view of the ocean and allowed for more space within the dwelling. The proximity to the street did not allow for any extension of the facade. Within this limitation and in order to reinvent the exterior, the architect chose to integrate slats of Ipe wood, thus creating a front elevation that is both consistent with the building requirements, but also dynamic through its constant play of natural light and shadows.

The facade is designed to display an open or closed form through sliding panels at the corners and front door of the residence. By opening the corners, the ocean view can be enjoyed from inside, and at night, with the panels closed, the structure glows through veiled openings. The Ipe slats extend upward past the roofline, serving as an open railing for the roof deck.

During the renovation, the interior was stripped down to the studs and an extensive mold remediation completed. The remodeled interior consists of typical wood framing, steel framing, and solar hydronic radiant-heated concrete flooring.

TOP LEFT
Building codes restricted a street-side extension, so the architect revitalized the facade with Ipe slats. The adjustable slats not only provide a more dynamic facade, they effectively modulate the passage of light and air into the interior.

TOP RIGHT
A home office, removed from the other areas of the residence, perches on the roof deck. The corner opens completely to the exterior, allowing fresh air to circulate through the space.

ABOVE
The structure within glows through the veiled openings, private without the need for draperies. The Ipe slats extend past the roofline, to become the railing for the roof deck.

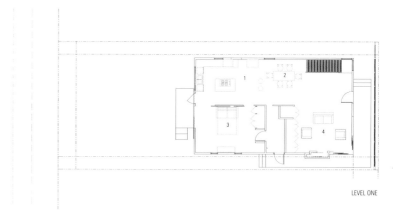

LEVEL ONE

1   kitchen
2   dining
3   family
4   lounge
5   bedroom
6   bathroom
7   WC
8   ensuite
9   main bedroom
10   hallway
11   utility
12   office
13   roof terrace

LEVEL TWO

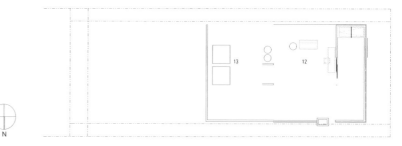

LEVEL THREE

N

ABOVE
The Ipe slats of the facade create an interesting display of interrupted light bands that track the sun's movement.

RIGHT
This *Ofuro*, or Japanese soaking tub, is tucked away to provide a space both private and tranquil.

BEACHSIDE LIVING

On entry, there is a double-height living room space that seamlessly blends into the dining and kitchen areas toward the back of the house. The open space, clean finishes, and light-filled aspect of the first level is typical of beachside living. Notably, the kitchen counters are made of a recycled lightweight concrete developed by the architect.

The vertical circulation, a three-story sky-lit volume, hugs the south wall of the house. The stair treads from the first to second level are made of Ipe slats supported by cantilevered steel beams, and rest on a lightweight concrete plinth. The staircase from the second to third level has bamboo treads. The second level hosts the main bedroom and ensuite, two more bedrooms, a shared bathroom, and a utility room.

SEPARATING WORK AND LEISURE

An open-air office was added to the roof deck in order to separate the work area from the living areas. The roof deck is a gathering space with views of the beach and exposure to cooling ocean breezes.

LEFT
The cantilevered Ipe slat staircase, naturally lit by the skylights above, leads to the second-story living spaces. The second set of stairs, made from bamboo, leads to the roof deck and third-story office. Both staircases were made with sustainably harvested materials.

Chapter 14
In Your
Dreams

The home of your dreams should be a unique form of self-expression. Its design and location are expressions of your lifestyle and personality.

Your dream home might be a luxurious penthouse in a vibrant city center, a cosy cabin in the woods, or an exhilarating place by the sea. Whatever your taste and lifestyle, the design of your dream home is a reflection of your preferred lifestyle. It is also informed by the location in which you build.

CAPTURING THE DREAM

The style of your dream home may be bold and vivacious or subtle and subdued. It may be organic in form, or have simple rectilinear shapes and clean lines. The interior could be a gallery that showcases a lifetime collection of treasures, or a stark and empty space, allowing the architecture itself to decorate your home.

It is the combination of the esthetic of your home and its surrounding context that truly reflects your personality — and the home of your dreams is the ultimate form of self-expression.

REFLECTS YOUR VALUES

The functions of the internal spaces will reveal your ideals and dreams. Perhaps the bathroom is a simple basin and shower, a purely practical space. Or maybe it is a room where you can bathe in a deluxe spa tub while gazing out at a breathtaking view. The function of such a space is to soothe your body and re-energize your spirit.

Your belief system is further revealed by the spatial sequence and hierarchy of rooms. Is the parent's bedroom separate or adjacent to the children's bedrooms? Is the focal point of the living room an entertainment system or a fireplace? Is the kitchen spacious enough to accommodate a large dining table, or is it a compact area used for food preparation only?

The building process also illustrates your values. If you are committed to the ethos of sustainability, you will choose materials and construction methods that are environmentally sensitive, minimizing the impact of your home on the environment and the drain on natural resources.

REFLECTS YOUR LIFESTYLE

Your dream home should be situated in a place that is ideal for the lifestyle you wish to live, and this setting ultimately determines the appropriate architectural style. A tropical seaside villa might be open on all sides, inviting the environment inside, whereas the urban retreat may be a haven of calm within high security walls.

Unlike a project home that can be built almost anywhere to meet most people's needs, the dream home is tailored to suit the precise requirements of the owner, from concept to detail, be it an infinity pool that meets the horizon, creating luxurious quarters for guests, or using hand-crafted materials.

Although the location of the home will in some way inform the architecture, many of the defining elements will be custom built rather than bought off the shelf.

In extraordinary landscapes, architects have worked with their clients to explore new ideas about what "home" might mean with new materials and alternative construction techniques. Many of today's dream homes are limited only by the imagination.

ABOVE
House Westcliff,
Silvio Rech & Lesley Carstens,
Architecture & Interiors

TOP RIGHT
Visiting Artists House,
Jim Jennings Architecture

OPPOSITE
St Leon House,
Stefan Antoni Olmesdahl
Truen Architects

Casa Cusenza PUERTO VALLARTA, MEXICO

Van Tilburg, Banvard & Soderbergh SANTA MONICA, USA

Construction	2003–2005
Home type	Two-story, single-family dwelling
Structure	Cast-in-place concrete frame, with slab on grade and partially raised first floor structural slabs, masonry walls

EAST ELEVATION – MAIN HOUSE AND GUESTHOUSE

"Nature was the catalyst for design, form, and function. From the moment I set foot on the site, three monumental higuera trees, towering well over 50 ft (15 m) above the jungle floor, became my focal point. Articulating design elements of glass, stone, and concrete beneath their protective canopy evolved into what is now Casa Cusenza."

Peter J Petraglia

ABOVE
An evening view of the guesthouse. The sloped concrete "butterfly" roofs add a sculptural element to the home. Strategically placed scuppers catch rainfall and create a series of waterfalls that cascade from roof to roof, and then drain into the natural stream below. The solid teak wood entry door was fabricated in Bali by Jerome Abel Seguin.

A TASTE OF PARADISE

The clients, successful business owners with an insatiable appetite for design and creativity, envisioned a contemporary oasis along the southern shores of picturesque Puerto Vallarta. They wished to create a Zen-inspired oasis embracing Vallarta's natural beauty, while at the same time pushing the envelope and redefining traditional construction techniques.

A lush tropical rainforest with mature specimen trees, natural waterfalls and streams, a private sandy beach, and breathtaking cobalt blue ocean vistas are just a few of the natural amenities to be found on the site.

WEAVING THE HOUSE INTO THE LANDSCAPE

After clearing the undergrowth, the main challenge was preserving the integrity of the land while at the same time creating the clients' dream home: This was to be contemporary with a minimum number of interior walls and a maximization of views – a home that seamlessly moved between interior and exterior spaces.

The next challenge was to incorporate the main house and guesthouse into lush hillside jungle, while preserving the natural beauty of the higuera trees, rambling streams, and a sandy beach. Landscaping the site and creating outdoor rooms became the primary design focus. Both architect and clients were acutely attuned to respecting nature and the gifts it had given them.

The main house was positioned beneath the large higuera trees, taking advantage of the shade from their canopy. Raising the foundation 10 ft (3 m) above the forest floor minimized the impact on the root structure and allowed the natural stream cutting through the site to run its course.

Smooth white plaster and concrete were the primary building materials, while limestone and natural rock veneers were used as accent finishes.

CONNECTING INSIDE AND OUTSIDE

Public rooms, including the main "gathering space," kitchen, and dining room are positioned on the first level to maximize a connection between inside and outside. Bedrooms are on the second floor to capture views and take advantage of natural ocean breezes. The guesthouse is across the natural stream facing the main house. A wooden bridge connects the guesthouse to the main entry, while a cascading terrace and lawn make the transition down to the edge of the pool.

Despite its soaring two-story volume, the main living space is the intimate heart of the house. Pocketing glass walls allow nature to flow through the space. Sheer fabric scrims and sliding glass panels create layers between interior and exterior — a design element echoed throughout the home. Sloped concrete "butterfly" roofs are a sculptural feature of the house. Rain scuppers are strategically placed to create a series of waterfalls that cascade from roof to roof, and then drain into the natural stream below.

ABOVE
Here the interplay between interior and exterior creates a "dreamy" ambience. The creamy white terrazzo slab floors seamlessly flow from the interior to the outdoor dining terrace, while the frameless corner glass panels, with floating concrete serving counter, redefine the lines between the spaces. A teak wood deck, punctured by the natural vegetation, extends out to the ocean's edge.

RIGHT
The two-story "gathering space" is the heart of the main house. All of the living spaces radiate from this central area. A living tree next to the floating wood slab staircase provides texture and contrasts with the contemporary lines of the space.

Creating seamless transitions
between interior and exterior space,
and blending the natural beauty of
the oceanfront site with the clients'
vision of their "dream home" presented
challenges that ultimately became
the genesis for the project.

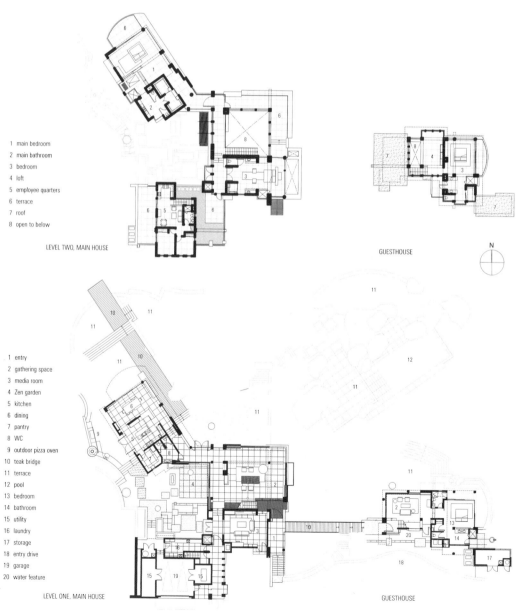

1 main bedroom
2 main bathroom
3 bedroom
4 loft
5 employee quarters
6 terrace
7 roof
8 open to below

LEVEL TWO, MAIN HOUSE

GUESTHOUSE

N

1 entry
2 gathering space
3 media room
4 Zen garden
5 kitchen
6 dining
7 pantry
8 WC
9 outdoor pizza oven
10 teak bridge
11 terrace
12 pool
13 bedroom
14 bathroom
15 utility
16 laundry
17 storage
18 entry drive
19 garage
20 water feature

LEVEL ONE, MAIN HOUSE

GUESTHOUSE

ABOVE
The cantilevered floor slabs and frameless corner glazing of the main home's "gathering space" reach out and embrace the natural beauty of the site. The sheltering canopies of higuera trees provide a natural enclosure for the surrounding terraces.

FAR TOP LEFT
A natural clearing on the site provided the perfect location for the guesthouse. Cascading concrete terrace steps flow gracefully onto the wooded lawn, which meets the travertine-lined pool at the ocean's edge.

RIGHT
Natural stone finishes – the travertine slabs in the pool, granite boulder chairs, and limestone buddha – ground the Zen garden, which is located just off the gathering space of the main house. Ocean breezes naturally cool the space as they pass through the terrace doors.

Casa Marrom SÃO PAULO, BRAZIL
Isay Weinfeld

Construction	2003–2004
Home type	Four-level family home
Structure	Poured concrete and steel

"Our clients are very informal people who wanted a house that expressed their relaxed way of living. Bright, wide living areas open onto the garden, patio, and pool allowing for full integration of interior and exterior spaces."

Isay Weinfeld

ABOVE
The three main elements of Casa Marrom can be seen in this view of the front facade – concrete, steel, and prefabricated plates made of cement and brown pebbles. These provide absolute privacy and a pleasing textural motif.

RIGHT
Timber was a logical choice for the external cladding on an upstairs bedroom because of its inherent ability to minimize heat. The living room below is oblivious to the vagaries of nature due to the presence of a large concrete overhang, which protects it from torrential tropical rains as well as providing much-needed shade.

NATURE-BASED RETREAT

In the teeming midst of the Brazilian city of São Paulo, with its 18 million inhabitants, a warm, comfortable residence has been conceived by architect Isay Weinfeld for his brother and his family.

Tropical trees stand in contrast to the muted grays of the property's high perimeter walls. The walls provide the home with an introverted focus and transform Casa Marrom into a retreat that helps reconnect its occupants with nature, and cocoons them from the city's tumultuous rhythms.

BEAUTY IN A BLIGHTED METROPOLIS

Weinfeld's engaging residences can be found spread across the city's wealthier neighborhoods, providing occasional glimpses of beauty and form in a metropolis the architect freely admits has no equal when it comes to ugliness.

His interest in design was first prompted by the city's high crime rate and population density, which, in turn, is forcing people to live in increasingly smaller spaces. São Paulian interest in design is a relatively recent phenomenon, with considerations of safety and economic well-being understandably taking precedence over mere visual esthetics.

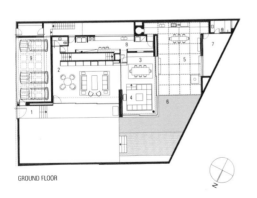

GROUND FLOOR

FIRST FLOOR

1 main entrance
2 living
3 dining
4 media
5 barbecue/dining
6 swimming pool
7 gym
8 kitchen
9 garage
10 bedroom
11 family

TOP
This view of the outdoor living area highlights its central role in the relaxed approach to life inherent in Casa Marrom. A kiln, a stove, and a grill are all to be found beneath the broad expanse of the glass-covered, wooden pergola. The swimming pool and living area combine to form a haven in the midst of the tumult of the city.

ABOVE
The entrance lawn on the building's northern facade, bordered by massed plantings of vibrant tropical foliage, abuts the main living room and its heavy concrete overhang. Glass doors slide into deep recesses in the walls to provide an exhilarating connection to this simple, elegant garden.

MATERIALS AND SCALE

Weinfeld's love affair with Brazilian raw materials yields an inviting tropical Modernism in Casa Marrom. Stone and timber have been used side by side to provide textual contrasts. A specially constructed design element involved prefabricated panels of cement and brown pebbles, used both as a facing on the street wall and facades, and as paving on the roof terrace. Steel and concrete also figure prominently. Experiments of scale are played out throughout the home where large sliding doors, when not recessed into the wall cavities, turn soaring, wide-open spaces into cozy, intimate nooks.

The 6,867-sq-ft (638-sq-m) house is constructed over four levels and begins with a step-up to the entry from street level. Wide living areas, designed in succession, open up to the garden, pool, and patio area creating a seamless integration of internal and external spaces. A large concrete overhang protects the living room from sun and rain.

Wooden siding and glass louvers characterize the upper level, while a rooftop terrace overlooks Casa Marrom's elegant L-shaped courtyard.

An outdoor swimming pool is connected to a deck via a stone pathway, before wrapping itself around the living room in its approach to the outdoor dining/barbecue area. This dining space is equipped with a kiln, grill, and a stove, all set beneath a large glass-covered wooden pergola, reflecting the clients' relaxed and informal approach to life.

The home also contains a basement level, complete with bedrooms and bathrooms for employees, a laundry, storage area, and a utilities room.

RIGHT
The exaggerated depth of the concrete overhang affords the living area a sense of separateness from the home's exterior even when its sliding doors are open. A pathway of stones creates an informal trail to the swimming pool deck.

Chesa Futura ST MORITZ, SWITZERLAND

Foster and Partners LONDON, ENGLAND
Küchel Architects ST MORITZ

Construction	2001–2004
Home type	Six apartments (with potential for 12) on three stories
Structure	Double-curved timber frame with wooden shingle cladding

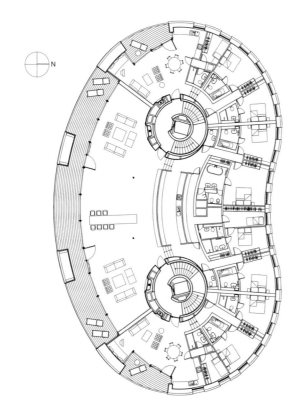

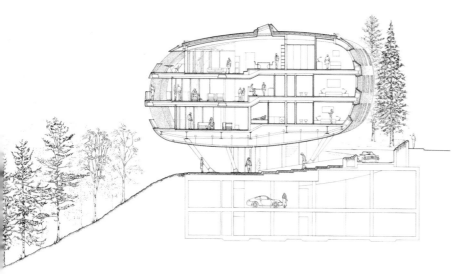

"Taken overall, Chesa Futura (literally, 'house of the future') might be regarded as a mini manifesto for architecture, not just here but in other parts of the world. Contrary to the pattern of sprawl that disfigures the edges of so many expanding communities, it shows how new buildings can be inserted into the existing grain at increased densities, while sustaining indigenous building techniques and preserving the natural environment."

Foster and Partners

ABOVE
The building's facades curve in two directions and are reminiscent of a boat's hull. The bedrooms sit along the highly insulated northern facade, whereas the living areas with terraces, pictured above, are to the south and make the most of the sunlight and the views. There is no storage against the external walls, only on the internal partitions, which radiate from the cores.

ABOVE LEFT
Visible to the right of the church spire, Chesa Futura, with its unique fusion of modern design ideas and centuries-old construction techniques, is noticeably different from surrounding buildings, but at the same time sympathetic to the alpine landscape. The building does not appear bulky because of its rounded form.

Chesa Futura apartment building lies in the densely built town center of St Moritz – the popular skiing resort in Switzerland, 6,000 ft (1,800 m) above sea level in the Engadin valley. Although small, the site is spectacularly located on the edge of a slope looking out across the village toward the lake. The building fuses state-of-the-art computer design with "tried and true" traditional building techniques. Considered novel in form, it uses age-old timber construction – one of the most sustainable methods of building.

A CHALLENGING SITE

The kidney-shaped, three-story structure contains six apartments sitting above the ground on eight "legs" – the architect's creative response to the multiple demands of the site, the local weather conditions, and the planning regulations. (In Switzerland, where snow lies on the ground for many months of the year, there is a long tradition of elevating buildings to avoid wood rot due to prolonged exposure to moisture.)

The site has a height restriction of 51 ft (15.5 m) above its sloping contours. A conventional rectilinear building would have protruded over the specified height, whereas the raised, sculptured form complies with planning regulations without compromising the overall floor area.

LETTING IN THE LIGHT

Large south-facing windows and balconies literally wrap around the convexly curved facade of the building. This allows generous amounts of sunlight into the apartments and makes the most of the spectacular view. The north-facing concave aspect gives protection from the coldest mountain weather. The building also provides insulation through its own thermal mass – the structural frame creates a 16-in- (40-cm-) wide cavity filled with insulating material. Small windows are punched into the northern facade, echoing traditional Engadin windows with their chamfered surrounds, to allow maximum light penetration.

PREFABRICATION IS THE KEY

The structure was developed in close collaboration with two engineering firms: Arups in England and Toscano in Switzerland. Construction was restricted to less than eight months of the year because of the winter holiday seasons, so a high degree of prefabrication was important. The tight site, which could only be approached via narrow winding roads, coupled with the length and width of the construction equipment, meant that considerable time went into the sizing of individual components.

STRUCTURE AND FUNCTION

The foundations consist of a sunken concrete box, which houses the plant rooms, car parking, and storage spaces. Above ground, the building is supported on a lightweight steel "table" approximately 65 by 130 ft (20 by 40 m) with eight steel legs. Two concrete cores, $6\frac{1}{2}$ ft (2 m) in diameter, housing the elevator shafts and stairwells, provide further stability. The remaining structure is timber.

The total weight of the structure (steel columns and table, the concrete cores, and the timber frame) is 2,750 tons (2,500 tonnes). The timber load-bearing frame reduces the dead load of the building by as much as 40 per cent.

The timber frame is made up of a series of prefabricated elements. Each element is composed of glue-laminated beams (thin pinewood planks, 1 in by 10 in by 40 ft/25 mm by 250 mm by 12 m, glued together to obtain the various geometric shapes), a skin of plywood, and OSB timber (oriented strand board). By using computer-driven cutting machines in the factory it was possible to obtain precisely sized elements with up to $\frac{1}{8}$ inch (3 mm) tolerance.

SHINGLES – SIMPLE AND SUBLIME

The larch shingles that make up the building's skin not only reflect local architectural traditions, but also combine harmoniously with the building's shape. Because local timber was used, little energy was expended in its transportation. The trees were cut during winter when the wood was dry and without sap, which helps prevent timber shrinkage.

By cutting the timber both laterally and radially, the wood was used in the most efficient way – 80 trees provided the required 8,500 cubic ft (240 cubic m) of shingles. The two different cuts combine beneficial water-draining characteristics with structural strength. They also provide an appealing variegated appearance.

The copper roof, chosen because copper is sufficiently malleable to be formed on site when temperatures drop below 12°F (-11°C), has long been used by locals and is sympathetic to surrounding buildings.

ABOVE
By raising the building on legs, each of the apartments enjoys a wood-framed alpine panorama. The small, densely populated skiing village of St Moritz, Switzerland, accommodates a resident population of 5,000 – a number that swells to 50,000 during the peak seasons.

The building fuses state-of-the-art
computer design with "tried and true"
traditional building techniques.

ABOVE LEFT
Eighty larch trees, taken from the surrounding landscape, provided the required 8,500 cubic ft (240 cubic m) of shingles for the building. To eliminate shrinkage, the trees were felled during winter when the wood was dry and without sap.

LEFT
The shingles were cut by a local family firm (that has practised the craft for generations) and applied to the roof by hand using nails. Over time, and in response to the weather, the shingles will change to silver-gray. They will last without maintenance for about 80 years.

ABOVE
By sculpting the building into a rounded form, the architects were able to maintain the desired overall floor area, while at the same time complying with building regulations – a conventional rectilinear building would have protruded over the specified height. The curved form allows windows to wrap around the facade, providing panoramic views of the town and the lake.

TRADITIONAL MATERIALS MEET COMPUTER DESIGN

The building's curved form was refined using a specially written computer program which converted flat plans into a three-dimensional form. The computer model acted like a conventional spreadsheet, enabling any part of the building to be altered and instantly generating a new overall form. Also, this allowed numerous design studies to be tested in a fraction of the time required for conventional modeling techniques. The computer model could be cut through any section to produce drawings of any part of the building.

The digital information was directly exported to cutting tools to build physical models and then ultimately to the machines that made the timber building components.

Chicken Point Cabin IDAHO, USA

Olson Sundberg Kundig Allen Architects

Constructed	2003
Home type	Two-level family holiday home
Structure	Concrete block, steel, and wood

ABOVE
This spectacular glass and steel door pivots up, opening the living room area of the cabin to the lake and surrounding countryside. The pivoting door is operated by an innovative hand-cranked mechanism that might be regarded as quaint in this age of remote controls.

"The idea here was to create a little house with a big window, so that the interior became the threshold, or link, between the lake and the forest — literally opening the cabin to the natural landscape of northern Idaho."

Tom Kundig

NOT YOUR AVERAGE LAKESIDE CABIN

The shore of a lake in northern Idaho is the setting for this unique vacation home. While the concept is of a lakeside shelter nestled in the woods, Chicken Point Cabin is far more than simply a holiday house. At first glance, it may resemble a little box with an outsized window, but it is a forest retreat and an artistic expression all in one.

WINDOW TO THE WORLD

The front entry to the house is an unusually tall and wondrous steel door, 19 ft (5.8 m) high. It opens to a narrow hallway, which in turn leads to the spacious living room, designed as a seamless extension to the exterior environment.

The living room measures some 22 ft (6.6 m) high and contains the home's most dramatic and defining feature: An enormous glass and steel window-wall measuring 30 ft by 20 ft (9 m by 6 m), which opens out the entire living space to the lake and forest. Operated by a specially designed hand-crank mechanism, named "the gizmo" by the architect Tom Kundig, the window-wall opens out rather like a garage door. Outside, on the concrete terrace, the family — a couple and their two children — can enjoy the tranquil views of the lake from the hot tub.

STAIRWAY TO HEAVEN

Just inside the entry door, there is a huge wooden staircase that leads up to the main bedroom, which is essentially a simple plywood box that seems to hover over much of the ground floor of the house, and which looks out over the lake. The children's bedrooms are

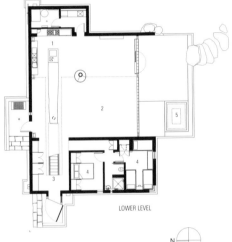

LOWER LEVEL

N

1 kitchen
2 living
3 staircase/entry
4 bedroom
5 sunken tub
6 main bathroom
7 sitting area
8 main bedroom
9 staircase/bridge
10 open to below

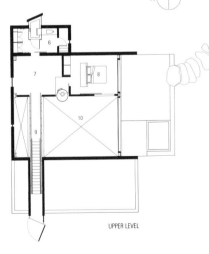

UPPER LEVEL

more of a bunk style and the house can sleep ten people at any time. There are two bathrooms. The roof of the cabin tilts upward to optimize the amount of light coming into the interior.

MATCHING MATERIALS WITH THE SETTING

The design of the cabin is in three main parts – a concrete block box with a plywood insert and a 4-ft (1.2-m) diameter steel fireplace. The fireplace is a feature in itself. It is constructed from a large steel pipe, which has structural as well as esthetic importance. Directly in front of the fireplace is a rock that is similar to rocks found on the lake's edge. It adds a natural texture to the floor, which is concrete.

The materials selected for the house are all low- or no-maintenance, and were chosen because of the way they age. The concrete and steel were left unfinished, so that as they age they acquire the natural patina that merges well with the forest landscape – the steel oxidizes a reddish brown and the concrete gathers moss.

The internal finishes also maintain this theme, being stainless steel, timber, and concrete. The whole effect is one of warmth and welcome.

ABOVE
The main bedroom area, a simple wood construction, is seen here hovering above the ultra-modern kitchen. Another feature of the living room is the fireplace (on the right), which is housed in an impressive steel pipe that reaches 22 ft (6.6 m) to the ceiling.

TOP RIGHT
The roof's wide overhang tilts upward, allowing plenty of light to reach the interior, while at the same time protecting the living spaces from the hot sun.

Coromandel Bach COROMANDEL, NEW ZEALAND
Crosson Clarke Carnachan Architects

Constructed	2002
Home type	Single dwelling
Structure	Timber-frame floor, walls, and roof with membrane roofing over plywoods

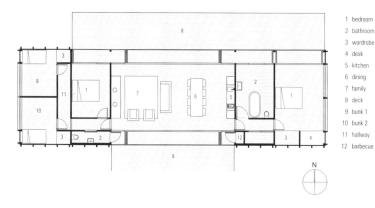

1	bedroom
2	bathroom
3	wardrobe
4	desk
5	kitchen
6	dining
7	family
8	deck
9	bunk 1
10	bunk 2
11	hallway
12	barbecue

N

"I was interested in designing a building that contrasted with living in the city, a building with a naturalness and openness to the outside — the sun, sea breezes, and view. By dissolving the walls the experience of common rituals is reinforced — showering in the sun, bathing under the stars, cooking outside, and gathering around the fire."

Ken Crosson

ABOVE LEFT
The open fire burns while the living room remains open to the outdoors — giving the home a "camp-like" quality.

ABOVE CENTER
The perfect weekend cottage is a shut up "box" while the owners are away. On arrival, the decks are opened down on either side, providing a stage for living.

TOP
The architects conceived the structure as a "container" sitting lightly on the land. The rich yellow joinery and interior plywood contrast with the naturally weathered cladding on the exterior. The silver gray exterior merges with the gray trunks of the Manuka tree-covered ridge.

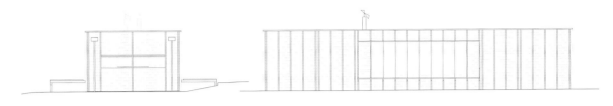

A PACIFIC HAVEN

The Coromandel Peninsula is just east of the North Island's biggest city, Auckland. It enjoys beautiful views over the Hauraki Gulf, and with its pristine beaches and stunning coastal scenery, is a favorite tourist and holiday destination for locals and international visitors alike.

REINTERPRETING TRADITION

The site is 26 acres (10.5 ha) and the house itself measures 1,378 sq ft (128 sq m). This house was conceived as a container sitting lightly on the land either for habitation or simply the dream of habitation. The intention was to reinterpret the New Zealand building tradition of the crafting of wood — the expression of structure, cladding, lining, and joinery in a raw and unique way. The construction is reminiscent of the "trip" or "rafter" dams that were common in the Coromandel region at the turn of the twentieth century. — heavy vertical structural members supporting horizontal boarding.

SUSTAINABLE MATERIALS, WARM RESULT

The structural posts of the house are Saligna, as are the exterior studs and joists. The cladding, decking, flooring, and rafters, as well as the bathroom gratings, are Lawson cyprus. This particular timber was chosen because of its durability and sustainability. The internal walls and ceilings are hoop pine plywood, as is the interior cabinetry.

The unadorned natural timber provides a connection to the natural environment. A simple mechanism to the deck allows the "box" to open on arrival, providing a stage for living, and to close on departure, for protection while the inhabitants are away.

SIMPLICITY AND STYLE

The house has a rectangular plan that sits across the contour in a patch of cleared bush, much like a rural shed, facing north and toward the view. The living room is open to the outside and the sun, acting as a metaphorical tent or campsite.

There are two main bedrooms with bifold doors that open the rooms to the outside. Additionally, two bunk rooms provide a shady haven from the hot summer sun with their small west-facing slot windows.

Further reinforcing the "camping out" experience, the bathroom opens to the outside. The bath itself is on wheels, thus providing the opportunity to bathe as one prefers — sheltered indoors, under the stars, or in front of the fire.

CAPTURING THE ESSENCE OF NEW ZEALAND

In New Zealand, "bach" describes a weekend cottage or house, usually located at the beach. With this bach, the architects have attempted to provide an environment that captures the essence of the New Zealand holiday spirit within its beautiful local landscape.

ABOVE
The dining table, designed by Ken Crosson, is an extension of the small kitchen. The kitchen is simple and open, unadorned and practical, with all crockery and utensils within easy reach. The plywood cabinetry has the same finish as the interior wall lining.

Crescent House CALIFORNIA, USA

Wallace E Cunningham

Construction	2000–2004
Home type	Multi-level family residence
Structure	Steel frame on concrete slab with cast-in-place concrete walls

"The clients required a residence that would provide a retreat from their active business lives as well as accommodate recurrent and extended family stays. An attempt has also been made to create a sense of isolation from the surrounding built environment."

Wallace E Cunningham

RAMP IT UP

Crescent House is a multi-story, concrete and glass residence situated on a clifftop in the southern Californian city of Encinitas. The area is known for its beautiful beaches, flat-topped cliffs, and steep mesa bluffs, and so the bedrooms, living areas, and terraces all boast expansive views of the Pacific Ocean.

From the street, a circular concrete ramp connects all three levels, wrapping around an overflowing crescent-shaped swimming pool that is surrounded by soaring walls of concrete and dominated by an expressive, triangular-shaped roof. This filters light into the interior spaces below.

GEOMETRIC FORMS

Because the home is perched on a clifftop, an extensive bluff retention system, which incorporated concrete tiebacks, was required to anchor it into the site. The building's opaque northern and southern elevations, closely bordered by neighboring properties, are punctuated by small, strategically placed openings designed to admit light into carefully selected spaces. A garage on the basement level has both a stairway and private elevator that serves the terrace and upper levels. The roof's complex geometric forms provide an exciting visual connection to the ocean while obscuring any views of neighboring buildings.

SURFACES AND FINISHES

The exterior surfaces of the home are a combination of cast-in-place concrete (which serves as both walls and facade), Portland cement plaster, clear frameless laminated glass with mirror-insulated glazing, and metal panels finished with a protective fluoropolymer coating that is stable in UV light.

The house's external decks are fashioned from metal, while the roof is constructed from a series of steel tube trusses that unfold across the house. In order to protect the exterior from the highly corrosive effects of the coastal surroundings, these elements (including integrated gutters) are also sheathed in flat-seamed fluoropolymer-finished metal panels for longevity.

TOP LEFT
Deeply recessed balconies provide shade from the afternoon sun on the western side of the house. From inside, the ocean views are dramatized through rectangular frameworks of cast-in-place concrete, the vertical slabs doubling as both internal walls and external facades.

ABOVE
Bold and complex geometric forms adorn the roof, angled to allow filtered light into various internal spaces in the home's upper level. These forms also act as a visual path to the horizon.

LEFT
A series of recesses – perhaps a Modernist version of Doric columns – provides an almost ornamental touch to the curved concrete wall. The sense of timelessness and classic strength is intensified by the water's reflection.

FOLLOWING PAGES
Surrounded by soaring walls of concrete, the three-level structure wraps around the overflowing crescent-shaped swimming pool that is the heart of this impressive house.

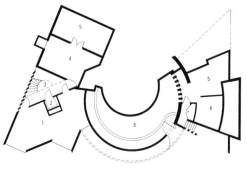

BASEMENT

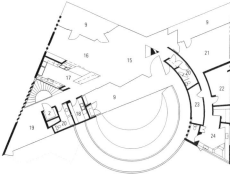

UPPER LEVEL (LEVEL THREE)

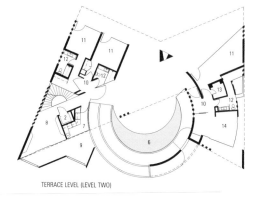

TERRACE LEVEL (LEVEL TWO)

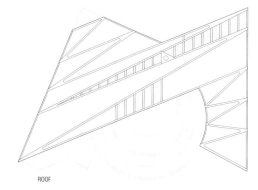

ROOF

1	garage	13	closet
2	elevator	14	gym
3	entry foyer	15	living
4	storage	16	dining
5	utility	17	kitchen
6	pool	18	pantry
7	laundry	19	media room
8	office	20	powder room
9	terrace	21	main bedroom
10	hall	22	walk-in robe 1
11	bedroom	23	walk-in robe 2
12	bathroom	24	ensuite bathroom

N

The interior walls are largely veneer plaster, architectural concrete, and fluoropolymer-finished metal panels; the internal stairs are stainless steel and glass. Throughout the 6,329-sq-ft (588-sq-m) home, the limestone flooring has an underlying hydronic heating system – hot water is pumped through a thermal mass floor, which absorbs the heat and radiates it to the living space.

SEA FOR MILES

Frameless glass panels in the capacious bedrooms on the terrace level afford expansive views of the ocean. On the upper level, the kitchen leads directly into the living room, where a spectacular triangular-shaped fireplace echoes the geometric forms found throughout the home.

LIGHT THE WAY

The innovative lighting design in Crescent House plays an important role in amplifying the home's geometric flow, particularly as sunlight fades. Recessed up- and downlights softly illuminate the generous interiors, producing dramatic wall shadows. Lights embedded in the concrete ramps and walkways direct and propel occupants through the different areas of the house.

The complex geometric form and scale of the house is tempered by its visually pleasing marriage of resolute Modernity and regal serenity. Crescent House's appeal goes beyond its architectural significance to encompass its pure and simple livability.

ABOVE
The main bedroom is a massive open space set amid a sea of glass and concrete. A minimalist approach to furnishing emphasizes the room's clean lines and functionality.

LEFT
The down-lit bar area is the perfect retreat for the owners from their busy city lives – a place to sit, relax, and relate the events of the day.

TOP
Lights embedded in the concrete ramp are an innovative alternative to ceiling lights. Slightly recessed, they provide an interesting wave effect – a nod of recognition to the home's waterfront location.

ABOVE
In the late afternoon light, the massed concrete forms of the interior generate bold and ever-changing shadows. The fireplace, perfectly positioned near the glass walls, is reminiscent of a Californian beachside bonfire.

House Westcliff JOHANNESBURG, SOUTH AFRICA

Silvio Rech & Lesley Carstens, Architecture & Interiors

Construction	1999–2001
Home type	Single dwelling for a family
Structure	African mud, thatch, and stone

> "We strive to make each project unique, handcrafting it down to the finer details so that the experience is a constant adventure in a cohesive whole."
>
> Silvio Rech, Lesley Carstens

House Westcliff is situated in suburban Johannesburg and built on what was considered a difficult and challenging site. Storm water ran through it and the land was overgrown. Yet its spectacular view over Johannesburg motivated Silvio Rech and Lesley Carstens to create something unique and striking underneath the forest canopy.

AT ONE WITH THE ENVIRONMENT

The architects had been building exotic bush camps for clients over the previous five years and wanted to use the same concept for their own home. One idea they favored was a mud African dwelling, as Rech and Carstens had great resources and connections to craftsmen and builders from all over Africa – Malawi, Tanzania, Zimbabwe, and South Africa – and their builder, Patrick Jonk, did not build conventional homes. So the African route was taken.

Basing the design on an African village was an inspired idea. The home is comprised of a series of rooms that form a compound – much as a series of huts do in the village context – ordered and connected along various axes. Rech and Carstens favor this "natural" form of architecture, fitting, as it does, with the surroundings.

There was an existing circular thatched building (rondavel) on the site, and this was retained as the heart of the building. The thatched roof was raised using a truss work of gum poles (round eucalyptus poles stripped of bark), the floor was re-screeded with brown pigment, and the walls were plastered with brown mud from the site. Large windows were placed into the front of the rondavel, their shape inspired by

ABOVE
The outdoor dining deck is built over the existing storm water run. The old pool pump house has been transformed into a conveniently positioned wine cellar. Its wooden doors with beaten metal spears were fashioned on site. Perched like sentinels above the doorway are temple birds from Java.

OPPOSITE
Reminiscent of a forest rockpool, the round-rim swimming pool features its own specially commissioned mosaic. Tumbled quarry tiles decorate the pool's perimeter; the retaining walls are constructed from local Magaliesburg rocks. A handhewn bed, purchased on a trip to Bali, sits on the deck outside the thatch-roofed dining room.

The spaces between rooms are circles, rectangles, or semicircles. These have niches carved into them in the classic African tradition, called "poche."

the windows of the Ngorongoro Crater Lodge in Tanzania, also designed by Rech and Carstens. Tanzanian artisans carved the entire 10-ft- (3-m-) high frame, which is flanked by two sculpted chimneys.

USING WHAT WAS THERE

The original rondavel contained a small altar and Rech and Carstens retained the suggestion of the altar and built a plastered bed 20 ft (2 m) above the floor in the center of the room. It is reached by a carved ladder. The architects' two young children sleep beneath their parents in a cosy little cube.

Because the room looks over the forest, a deck was added in front of the room to maximize use of the area. This steps down into the garden by means of a rock amphitheater, which gives a magical sense of drama to the garden.

One side of the room opens into a dressing room, which has a vaulted roof with handhewn wooden trusses. To the left lies a semicircular bathroom with sunken bath. The front of the bathroom is a large sliding window (with carved frames) that overlooks the vegetation, giving a sense of bathing in nature.

The spaces between rooms are circles, rectangles, or semicircles. These have niches carved into them in the classic African tradition, called "poche." The bathroom vanity is set into one of these niches — two white basins sit on top, much like an upturned lily pad.

The toilet room is conical shaped with a corbeled brick roof. A large steel screen with a metal cut-out motif sits behind the toilet. The basin, sitting on a mud pedestal, is a simple and elegant bowl hewn out of rock from Zimbabwe.

EVERYDAY LIVING

In the area between the bedroom and dining room a tree grows though the floor and roof. The dining room sits under a rough-thatched roof and the walls are built from local rock, packed tightly so the mortar joints cannot be seen. The room overlooks a stunning round pool, protected from street noise and prying eyes by dense vegetation and decorated with a mosaic of a man swimming — a calm and timeless image created by South African artist Clive van der Berg.

The separate kitchen has a vaulted roof made out of rough bricks and features a large curved glass window. The kitchen formwork was constructed from wires spanning the length of the room; rows of bricks were laid and then rubbed down with wire brushes to create a unified surface. The slight imperfections in the roof add to the home's handcrafted nature.

All the doors and window frames were custom made and designed for the house.

ABOVE LEFT
A temple bird sculpture from the island of Java is framed in a hand-packed rock wall niche, adding to the textural and handcrafted feel of this property.

ABOVE FAR LEFT
A network of stone paths and steps, as well as an extensive use of decking, help to link the individual huts in the complex. Glimpses across the shrub-filled garden, such as this one from the bedroom deck, reinforce the communal "village" ambience.

ABOVE
Light filters into the dressing room through a vaulted, sculptural roof. In front is the outdoor rooftop "sala", which affords a spectacular view across the garden. Constructed from gum poles, mass mud columns and a canvas roof, the sala is used as a sleeping retreat during the hot summer months.

1 kitchen
2 deck
3 dining
4 bedroom
5 dressing
6 bathroom
7 toilet room
8 pool deck
9 pool

ABOVE
The rock steps lead up the side of the amphitheater toward the main bedroom. The sculptural chimney stacks are flanked by Javanese water vessels. Large, intricately carved merbau doors were crafted by Tanzanians who had worked with Rech and Carstens on their exotic bush camp projects. All doors and windows for the complex were made on site.

Most of the furniture, screens, and light fittings in the house were designed by Rech and Carstens. (These were often prototypes for items later used in the various lodges the team designed.) The house contains an eclectic mix of furniture, with materials chosen for their tactile qualities, and shapes derived from natural forms and inspired by the African landscape.

A NATURAL GARDEN PARADISE

The garden has been left wild. Exotic plants were removed and native trees and shrubs were planted, so bird life is prolific – resident hadedas, paradise fly-catchers, as well as owls and eagles. The property is in the city, yet the jungle-like atmosphere sets it apart.

The storm water that ran through the property was stemmed and a small stream now links the various outdoor areas. An old swimming pool has been turned into a pond and the pool's pump house converted into a wine cellar at the bottom of the garden near the outdoor dining deck. It is decorated with a baroque gilt-framed mirror handcarved by Rech's father.

Reminiscent of the rooftop living quarters seen in hot and arid areas, such as Zanzibar and Egypt, small outdoor rooms (salas) were built on the flat roofs to capture some of the Johannesburg views. These are accessed by a series of wooden ladders. In summer, it is mild enough to sleep in these "nests" in the sky.

A HARD ROAD TO COMPLETION

Building the house was not a smooth process, as the architects were simultaneously involved with other projects in the Okavango Delta and in the Seychelles.

Because their buildings are unique handcrafted lodges in extreme places, the team were required to live on site for the duration of the building process. Meanwhile, their own house, House Westcliff, remained in a semi-finished state for some two years. However, it was well worth the wait.

ABOVE LEFT
The huge altar-like bed with its carved steps dominates the main bedroom. Underneath is a safe sleeping haven for the children. This structure is surrounded by seating topped with simple white cushions; animal skulls found on various sites around Africa are displayed on the walls. The back of the bed is framed by a suspended rock "curtain."

TOP
The toilet room houses a handcarved stone basin from Zimbabwe, set atop a mud plinth. The metal frame on the mud walls is made from strands of metal rod studded with white quartz stones, and is used for holding soap and candles.

ABOVE
The dressing room niche, one of many purpose-built niches throughout the complex of huts, provides a comfortable place for repose while dressing and preparing for the day ahead. The large standing sculpture, made from giraffe vertebrae, was crafted by Rech, as was the sensuously curved table.

OPPOSITE
Packed rock walls in the dining room support counters and display shelves for practical items as well as artefacts. The walnut table and chairs were skilfully crafted by Rech's father. Suspended above the table is a woven copper chandelier – a prototype made for the Ngorongoro Crater Lodge, one of the architects' award-winning bush camp designs.

John Lee House PETALING JAYA, MALAYSIA
Jimmy Lim

Construction	1999–2002
Home type	Multi-level family home
Structure	Concrete frame with brick infill, timber, and rendered plaster

SOUTH ELEVATION

"The main consideration in tropical architecture is to minimize heat build-up and maximize the cross-ventilation. My aim is always to create an environment where the client can enjoy their home and live life to the full."

Jimmy Lim

ABOVE
Columns provide a imposing aspect to the house facade, while the prominence of the pool and its proximity to the living spaces demonstrate the architect's careful response to his clients' specific needs and lifestyle.

RIGHT
A traditionally pitched roof combines with spreading, decorative eaves to provide protection from torrential tropical rains and the heat of the sun. White rendered plaster walls also reflect the sun, while narrow and vertical box-like windows permit the strategic entry of light.

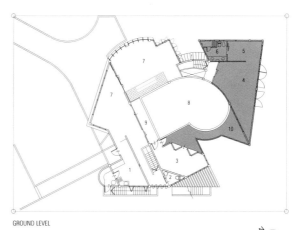

GROUND LEVEL

1	kitchen	5	dressing room	9	pool deck
2	toilet	6	main bathroom	10	main bedroom deck
3	dining	7	living		
4	main bedroom	8	pool		

TROPICAL RESORT

In the Petaling Jaya district, north of the Malaysian capital of Kuala Lumpur, architect Jimmy Lim has added to his already impressive residential portfolio with the vast 7,000-sq-ft (650-sq-m) John Lee House. Lim's fusing of traditional Malay architecture with the modern principles of design has resulted in a home that was conceived as a private resort, then planned around the needs and personal interests of his clients.

RECYCLED TIMBERS

The concrete-framed structure is raised on stilts, eliminating the need for expensive retaining walls and also allowing natural drainage during the heavy tropical rains. The pitched terracotta-tiled roof combines with both traditional and abstract stepped eaves to protect the interior from monsoonal rains and summer heat.

Recycled timbers have been used throughout the home. The exaggerated mortise and tenon joinery matches the workmanship of traditional craftsmen, resulting in a rough-hewn architectonic that expresses Lim's fondness for bold forms.

DIVE POOL

The heart of the home is a massive, 26-ft- (8-m-) deep kidney-shaped saltwater swimming pool, populated with tropical fish. It was purpose built for the clients, who wanted the luxury of being able to scuba dive without leaving home. The dining room's north-facing wall is a series of vertical slats that gently arc from east to west. They connect the external plate of the roof to the floor below. The slats draw in air, which then rises through the house and out through vents high in the walls, naturally ventilating the living spaces.

SEMICIRCULAR STAIRCASE

Forming a semicircle on the pool's northern side, the main staircase is a significant feature of the house. There is a study, and also a guest room on the ground floor. A further half-flight descends to two children's bedrooms and an audiovisual room, while another stairway leads beneath the lobby to an art gallery. The western end of the main stairway leads to an unusual, triangular-shaped main bedroom.

ABOVE LEFT
High ceilings are a natural defense against the build up of heat in the interior. Windows beneath the eaves permit the exit of warm air, while ceiling fans aid air circulation. Exposed beams provide both strength and an intricate web of ornamentation. Bi-fold doors lead from the generous living area to the kidney-shaped pool beyond.

ABOVE
This abstract collection of individual awnings rises in line with the arc of the main staircase leading to the main bedroom. Local chengal hardwood, known through-out Malaysia as the "king of woods," was chosen for its durability and water resistance, and is employed on both the supports and the awnings.

Mataja Residence CALIFORNIA, USA
Belzberg/Wittman Collaborative

Construction	1997–2000
House Type	Four-bedroom family home
Structure	Concrete with steel frame

> "When you watch the
> systematic construction of a
> building taking place,
> what you learn is freeing
> instead of controlling."
>
> Hagy Belzberg

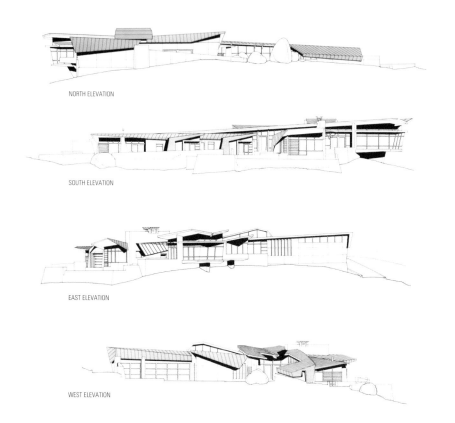

NORTH ELEVATION

SOUTH ELEVATION

EAST ELEVATION

WEST ELEVATION

SENSITIVE SURROUNDINGS

Situated about 2 miles (3.2 km) from the Pacific coast, in an environmentally sensitive area covered with native vegetation (mainly chaparral and coastal sage scrub), is the site of the Mataja Residence. Local planning authorities, including representatives from national parks, only approve those building sites that have a low impact on the natural surroundings. As a result, there are few new buildings in the area. Projects that do gain approval have been through a rigorous proposal process.

National parks border the north and east of the site, which sits at the western end of the Santa Monica Mountains. There are sweeping and spectacular views to the mountains, as well as some rugged rocky outcrops in the northwest corner. The area also holds significant historical importance – Chumash Indians lived here for hundreds of years, and their rock art and burial grounds can be found throughout the mountains.

SENSITIVE APPROACH

The architects had two major issues to address. First, there was the challenge of designing an efficient family home on an environmentally delicate site. Second, they had to adhere to the client's wish that the architects themselves actually do the construction. This meant being involved at every stage, and with every single aspect of the construction, a process that took three years.

LEFT
One of the requirements of developing the site was the protection of sensitive coastal vegetation. The area also has important historical significance, with burial grounds and rock art of the Chumash Indians located nearby.

FAR LEFT
The stately arrangement of volumes and roof planes demonstrates the interplay between the canyon's distinctive topography and the home's wraparound form. Rather than remove an imposing granite outcrop, the architects melded it into the design as a buffer against prevailing winds.

ABOVE
The National Park Service requested "an articulated roof line." The architects addressed this by breaking down the building into smaller volumes and fragmenting the roof lines, resulting in a composition that both reflects and complements the terrain.

ABOVE
Spectacular vistas are on
offer from every part of Mataja
Residence. The paved entry
courtyard boasts a view
through the family room to
the Pacific Ocean.

PREVIOUS PAGES
Perched high in its montane
surrounds, the cantilevered
dining room overlooks the
magnificent, misty panorama
of Mulholland Canyon below.

ENVIRONMENTAL WRAP

An existing granite outcrop on the site proved to
be a source of inspiration – rather than remove it,
the architects decided to wrap the house some
270º around it. This dramatic natural feature was
thus incorporated into the architecture itself, providing
protection to the courtyard and the house's interior
from northerly winds and inclement weather. There
was an added bonus – it helped to merge the house
into its surroundings, effectively concealing it from
visitors to the nearby national park.

MAKING MATERIALS MATTER

The architects believe composing and freely articulating the pattern and form of a building can be achieved
without having to use gauged, manufactured products.
They also developed novel ways to use standard
materials and were able to achieve impressive results
on site. Key segments of the roof face south and sit
at a 32º angle. This orientation maximizes the house's

solar heating system. The anglulation also permits
rainwater collection, thus reducing reliance on external
water sources. The framework is rigid steel, and the
windows have been double glazed, helping to keep
the house warm in winter and cool in summer.

The architects selected pre-formed concrete "trombe"
walls for the exterior, and installed honeycomb concrete slabs on the floor, both of which are insulated,
allowing for maximum heat retention.

INTIMATE INTERIORS

The house measures approximately 6,500 sq ft
(604 sq m) in area. It contains four comfortable
bedrooms and a spacious gallery. A three-car garage
is located on ground level, as are the lap pool and spa.

The hub of the house is the dining room and kitchen
area. The two rooms are intertwined, creating a
warm and welcoming ambience.

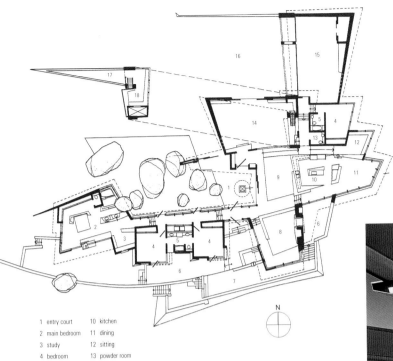

An existing granite outcrop proved to be a source of inspiration – rather than remove it, the architects decided to wrap the house around it.

1 entry court
2 main bedroom
3 study
4 bedroom
5 bathroom
6 terrace
7 lap pool
8 family
9 living
10 kitchen
11 dining
12 sitting
13 powder room
14 car gallery
15 garage
16 auto court
17 deck
18 loft

N

ABOVE
With breathtaking views over the canyon, the dining room's glass walls and vaulted ceiling bathe the space in day-long sunlight.

ABOVE LEFT
The family room intersects the integrated lap pool. The room's butterfly-shaped roof plays an important role in rainwater collection and solar heating.

LEFT
The dining room and kitchen interlink to create a continuous and harmonious flow of space.

Orchard House AHMEDABAD, INDIA
Rahul Mehrotra Associates

Constructed   2004
Home type   Single family weekender
Structure   Load-bearing walls clad in Porbunder stone, sand-faced cement plaster, and concrete

GROUND LEVEL

1 main bedroom
2 child's bedroom
3 bathroom
4 living
5 closet
6 maid
7 kitchen
8 dining
9 entry courtyard
10 terrace
11 lap pool
12 guest bedroom
13 central courtyard

"The house is designed like an oasis that one arrives at after driving through the orchard. On entering the house, the 'liquid' landscape of the water in the courtyard ... is a welcome contrast to the hot dry landscape the orchard is set in. The water also helps humidify and cool the breezes that blow through the house and work as effective air-conditioning in the semi-desert climate of Ahmedabad."

Rahul Mehrotra

HOT CLIMATE, COOL HOUSE

Orchard House is situated at the center of a mango orchard, just north of Ahmedabad in western India. Designed as a weekend retreat, the house is organized around a central courtyard, which contains a lap pool filled with fresh water. The water in the pool is used to recharge the wells on the property when the house is closed up during the week. The pool also harvests water during the monsoon months. Water management is critical in the hot dry climate of Ahmedabad, which is plagued by perpetual water shortages.

To further mediate the extreme climate, the house is sited in the center of the orchard rather than at the edge of the property. Besides being a naturally insulated location, the green canopy cover also provides visual relief in the summer months when the glare is uncomfortably intense. The terrace level, situated slightly above the treetops, gives wonderful views of the orchard. The use of terraces for recreation in the evenings or even for sleeping at night is a traditional practice in this region of the country.

AN OASIS IN SIGHT

Summer in this region is characterized by dust storms and extremely hot daytime temperatures. The house is designed as an oasis – a place to effectively escape the oppressive heat. The outer skin is local Porbunder sandstone, emphasizing the textures of a semi-desert

landscape. Entering the house brings an instant relief. The sight of lapping water in the courtyard and the vibrantly colored plastered surfaces give solace from the searing temperatures outside. The pool itself enters the living room space, as does one of its blue walls, enhancing the connection between inside and outside.

COLONIZING WITH CONSCIENCE

The broader issue addressed in this design is appropriate building practice on the periphery of India's cities. Weekend houses such as this symbolize the colonization of rural landscapes by urban people. If not appropriately positioned and situated, architecture can create a polarization between urban and rural communities. Siting the house in the orchard's center was an important move – not only climatically and visually, but also socially and politically. Being in the center, the house becomes integral to the landscape.

Furthermore, the orchard can be accessed through a courtyard door and produce grown can be cleaned in the courtyard facilities. As the central courtyard is the heart of the house, the use of this space by farmhands symbolically helps to break down the implicit polarities between country and city. In creating a softer threshold between the orchard and the central courtyard, perhaps the tenuous relationship between the weekend house and the rural landscape on the city's edge can be dissipated by spatial planning and design.

FAR LEFT
The floor of the living area is a mirror-polished gray limestone from the Kotah area in the state of Rajasthan. The furniture is designed as a series of platforms, leaving the space clutter-free, tranquil, and inviting.

TOP LEFT
The staircase leading up to the terrace has a screen wall made from cast-in-form reinforced cement concrete in lieu of the standard handrail. Integrated into the wall is small pantry counter to serve the pool area. The imprints of the wooden planks on the wall impart a handmade feel.

TOP RIGHT
The walls of the front facade are clad in sandstone from the Porbunder area of Gujarat. They form a distinctive and impressive base for the house, as well as a visual connection to the textures of the semi-desert setting. The entry porch and terrace pavilion are made from concrete.

ABOVE
The pool penetrates the envelope of the house, the water creating delicate reflective patterns on the ceiling and walls. The door on the right leads into the orchard. This gives farm workers direct access to the center of the house and courtyard to wash and dry the harvested produce.

Quito House MIRAVALLE, ECUADOR

Carlos Zapata NEW YORK, USA

Construction	1998–2002
Home type	Three-level family residence
Structure	Steel, concrete, and glass

"The main intention with this house was to maximize its cliff-top location to take advantage of its views across the Cumbaya Valley to Cotopaxi and the Andes Mountains to the south. Privacy is provided by the largely concrete, street-facing northern facade, which provides a secure, tranquil living environment."

Carlos Zapata

SPECTACULAR LOCATION

On a wooded hillside 30 minutes east of Quito, overlooking the Cumbaya Valley, stands the wing-shaped, glass and concrete Quito House.

The challenges the site presented to its designer, New York-based architect Carlos Zapata, were threefold — to maintain the privacy and security of the client; to integrate the residence into the surrounding landscape; and to maximize its unparalleled views over the Cumbaya Valley south to the Andes Mountains and Ecuador's Mt Cotopaxi, which, at 19,388 ft (5,909 m) high, is the country's highest active volcano.

A DRAMATIC RESPONSE

Dramatic vistas often demand a dramatic response in design. Quito House is wholly oriented toward the mountains, its southern facade faced with green-tinted glass, which not only provides views but also reflects the landscape, making the home all but invisible when it is seen from across the valley.

By contrast, a heavy band of reinforced concrete has been used on its street-facing northern elevation, which extends in a dramatic arc to form the external west-facing wall of the main bedroom and living room, providing a sense of privacy and insulating the home from noise.

The home hugs its clifftop location, the two main wings of the house opening in a wide angle, embracing the view and reaching toward it.

ABOVE
Despite its size, Quito House sits comfortably in its environment. Surrounding trees were not sacrificed in the pursuit of expansive views; the design contents itself with the vagaries of its hilltop setting.

RIGHT
The soaring glass facade of the living room and main bedroom are drawn forward in sensual communion with the panoramic mountain views. A cantilevered concrete terrace extends from the dining room, terminating in a small reflecting pool.

ABOVE
Massed volumes of reinforced concrete separate the living areas, their larger-than-life scale dwarfing the human figure but in keeping with the drama of the site and the scale of the living spaces,

TOP RIGHT
View of the home's entry and the underside cladding of the main staircase. Next to the stairs, the tilted wood wall continues up through the second level and pierces through the third level's glass facade.

SWIMMING IN SPACE

A cantilevered concrete terrace extends from the dining room at the extreme end of the main western wing; a deck and lap pool extend from the eastern wing providing balance and proportion.

Beginning inside the house and continuing outside, the pool runs along the home's eastern facade, then cantilevers over the cliff face. For the swimmer, this creates a sense of swimming in space.

GENEROUS LIVING

Within Quito House's sprawling 8,000 sq ft (745 sq m) of living space, there are four bedrooms, a kitchen with separate store, multiple dining areas, living room, playroom, family room, and an artist's studio, which is adjacent to the main bedroom.

Slabs of circular reinforced concrete in various sizes have been randomly placed within a manicured lawn between the home and the street, providing an unorthodox, visually stimulating alternative to a traditional driveway.

A SENSE OF PLACE

In Quito House, Carlos Zapata has simultaneously deferred to the drama of the site, as well as confronted it with the home's dramatic form. In making nature an intrinsic part of the home's environment, he has achieved a unique interaction between the landscape and the built elements of concrete and glass.

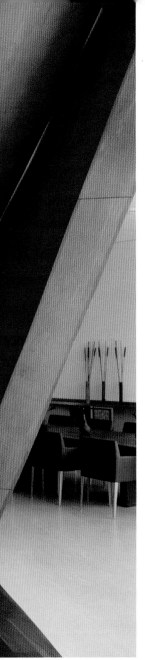

FIRST FLOOR

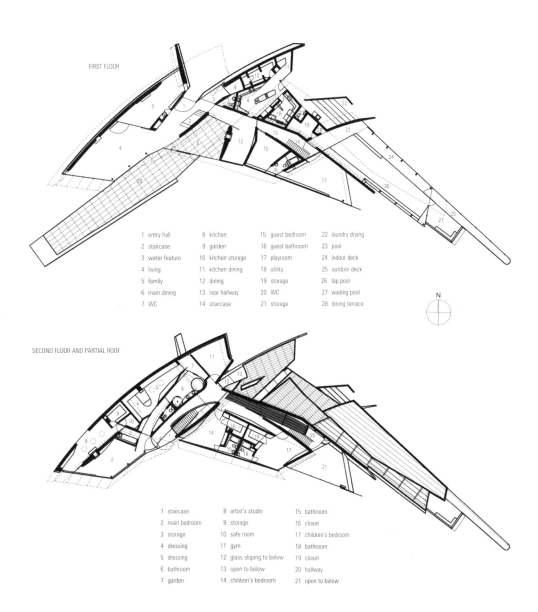

1	entry hall	8	kitchen	15	guest bedroom	22	laundry drying
2	staircase	9	garden	16	guest bathroom	23	pool
3	water feature	10	kitchen storage	17	playroom	24	indoor deck
4	living	11	kitchen dining	18	utility	25	outdoor deck
5	family	12	dining	19	storage	26	lap pool
6	main dining	13	rear hallway	20	WC	27	wading pool
7	WC	14	staircase	21	storage	28	dining terrace

N

SECOND FLOOR AND PARTIAL ROOF

1	staircase	8	artist's studio	15	bathroom
2	main bedroom	9	storage	16	closet
3	storage	10	safe room	17	children's bedroom
4	dressing	11	gym	18	bathroom
5	dressing	12	glass sloping to below	19	closet
6	bathroom	13	open to below	20	hallway
7	garden	14	children's bedroom	21	open to below

LEFT
The main living room is a functional, open space with ribbons of glass inset in the concrete facade, as well as large expanses of glass facing south and east to capture mountain vistas and early morning sun. The room also features several of the family's pieces of African and pre-Columbian sculpture.

TOP LEFT

The main bedroom has a curved, pivoting, solid timber door that closes away from the glass, extending the line of vision from the bed. The floor-to-ceiling angled glass reaches toward the mountain views.

LEFT

The lap pool begins within the confines of the house, continues to the outside, and is cantilevered over the cliff – for the swimmer creating a feeling of swimming in space. A deck following the pool extends further still.

ABOVE

This detail of the landing of the main staircase presents a kaleidoscope of overlapping geometric shapes. The handrail is recessed into the wall and lined with leather.

RIGHT

The base of the main staircase forms a powerful sculptural image, the curved wooden staircase anchored by its smooth concrete plinth.

Residence for a Sculptor CALIFORNIA, USA

Sander Architects

Construction	2001–2003
Home type	Single residence and studio/gallery
Structure	Steel and wood on prefabricated rolled-steel frame

"With this residence I had the chance to work with a billion-dollar view. I chose steel because it possesses strength in all directions. The clients admired the construction method, and understood truth in simplicity and in simple structures."

Whitney Sander

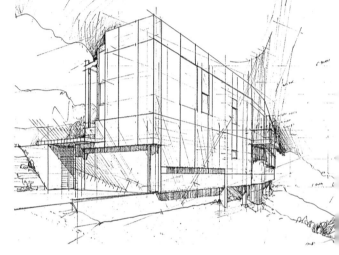

ABOVE
Built on the crest of a 4-acre (1.6-ha) allotment, the home from this rear perspective resembles a transport container, the steel girders like crane arms setting it in place.

HOME AND GALLERY

Whitney Sander's metal-clad Residence for a Sculptor is located 55 miles (88 km) north of San Francisco, perched on a wooded 4-acre (1.6-ha) hillside.

Situated in the midst of Sonoma County's 200 wineries with views extending over Jack London's Valley of the Moon, the house is an exciting mix of geometric shapes and curves. With its inherent qualities of adaptability and flexibility, metal lends itself well to the demands of the structure, which included a 22-ft (6.7-m) curved steel wall, and raised platforms for displays of the owner's pottery.

INDUSTRIAL APPEAL

The facade of Residence for a Sculptor is a mix of exposed structural framing and ribbed zincalume sheeting, the latter chosen for its durability, low cost, and quality of lightness, which seems to lift the home above its natural terrain.

The use of zincalume roofing as cladding for the home's external walls is a bold esthetic statement, complemented by a low-maintenance, uncomplicated exterior design. The sheet's recurrent, vertical ribbing, combined with the exposed steel girders that provide the home's structural framework, give the house an industrial appearance.

Galvanized high-tensile steel and, for lateral stability, a circular bolt pattern that does not require cross bracing, provide the home's stability, and meet all the state's seismic requirements.

HORIZONTAL OR VERTICAL?

The first impression of the house emphasizes its horizontal arrangement, suggesting an outward-focused experience might await. Paradoxically, the entry hall is stongly vertical and inward-focused, with a molded staircase along one side of a curving wall and a high curving, torqued steel wall on the other.

This entrance hall or "entry vessel" is an atmospheric space designed to capture some of the qualities of the sculptor's large clay pots. More than one third of the residence is dedicated to sculptural displays and the artist's studio.

The first level of the house contains the garage, a guest bedroom, a large, high-fire kiln, and two working studios totaling 1,500 sq ft (140 sq m). There is also an elevator for groceries and heavier loads.

STEPPING UP

The entry hall's curved steel staircase is anchored to the curved wall on one side but is free floating on the other. These stairs lead to the second level, containing the main bedroom with ensuite and dressing room. A bridge across the upper level of the entry hall leads to the home's expansive living/dining area with its exposed steel beams. The kitchen, family room, and study make up the remainder of the floor. It is here that the Valley of the Moon, bounded by the Maya-camas Mountains to the north and the Sonoma Mountains to the south, comes into full view through the home's large, metal-framed storefront windows.

LEFT
Zincalume's distinctive vertical ribbing defines the home's skin. The structural steel girders extend into the second level living areas. Both combine to form a durable, low-maintenance living space characterized by lightness and strength.

ABOVE
The unashamedly industrial facade is suggestive of the working space within. Modestly sized windows adorn the private living spaces to the left, whereas the kitchen, family room, and study at right of the balcony invite light and views within.

TOP
Large, metal-framed windows protrude from the facade and provide expansive views of the Valley of the Moon and the Sonoma Mountains. The balcony is accessed from the living room.

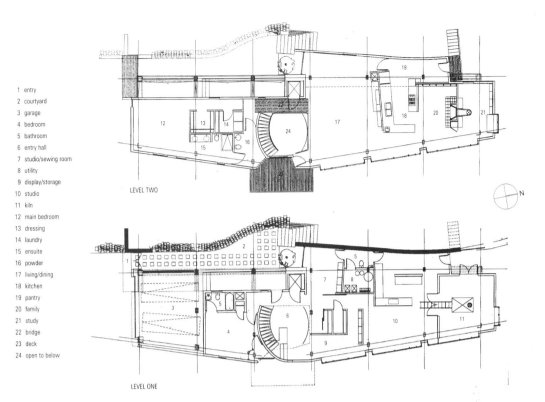

1 entry
2 courtyard
3 garage
4 bedroom
5 bathroom
6 entry hall
7 studio/sewing room
8 utility
9 display/storage
10 studio
11 kiln
12 main bedroom
13 dressing
14 laundry
15 ensuite
16 powder
17 living/dining
18 kitchen
19 pantry
20 family
21 study
22 bridge
23 deck
24 open to below

LEVEL TWO

LEVEL ONE

LEFT
The sculptor's pottery is superbly offset by the light and shade of the entry hall. The staircase, fabricated by Stockland Iron of Santa Rosa, is anchored to the wall on one side and free-floating on the other. It ascends from the entry level to the home's upper level, where a bridge connects the two sides of the home.

ABOVE
A profusion of geometric shapes and curves come together on the second-level of the entry hall. The penetrating light gives the shapes light and dark, creating its own work of art.

ABOVE
Softened by the dove-gray wall cabinet, furnishings, and sculpted forms, the hard-edged structural steel girders become an integral part of the gallery decor.

Sekeping Serendah SELANGOR, MALAYSIA
Seksan Design

Constructed	2000
Home type	Multi-level rainforest holiday retreat
Structure	Steel frame and concrete post foundations

> "Buildings can be erected without resorting to the 'slash and burn' approach so common in Malaysia today. The 'sheds' of Sekeping Serendah have been sensitively integrated into the landscape and are a kind of glorified tent. Staying here is all about enjoying the great outdoors."
>
> Seksan

One hour north of the Malaysian capital Kuala Lumpur, along winding dirt roads in the foothills of the Malayan Main Range, stands Sekeping Serendah, two contemporary structures designed by landscape architects Seksan and his partner Caroline Lau.

RAINFOREST RETREAT

Responding to the "slash and burn," "cut and fill" approach to construction normally associated with developments throughout Southeast Asia, these two multi-level, 700-sq-ft (65-sq-m) retreats rise above a sloping terrain of dense, pristine rainforest. Slender steel posts leave mountain streams to run their natural course, while effortlessly supporting the designers' light composition of glass, aluminum, and iron.

A COMMUNION WITH NATURE

Designed to represent a traditional *kampong*, the "sheds" contain no Balinese teak or travertine marble. There is no hint of pretentiousness here. The designers believe that materials transported over long distances tend to lose their "spirit" along the way. Instead, Sekeping Serendah reveals a communion with nature through the use of simple elemental materials that were carried to this 5-acre (2-ha) hideaway by hand, in order to minimize any environmental impact.

Materials used include construction chippings, corrugated iron, brick powder, asphalt, laterite mud, chicken wire, and old roof tiles — these buildings are as honest and uncomplicated as the landscape that surrounds them.

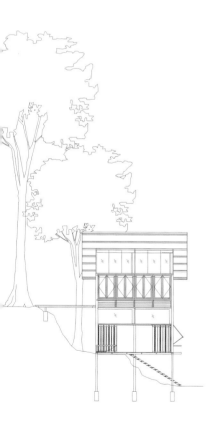

TOP
Strategically placed canvas awnings provide shade to the outdoor living area and day bed, where gaps in the rainforest canopy allow through the harsh rays of the tropical sun. They typify the approach used here – provide only what is necessary for the comfort of the users, unencumbered by unnecessary embellishments.

ABOVE
An elevated walkway protects a natural creek bed on the approach to Sekeping Serendah. From a distance the building is barely distinguishable from its dense tropical surrounds, achieving a sense of place rarely found in modern architecture.

LEFT
An absence of solid walls allows for 360° views of the rainforest, which itself is reflected in the building's glazed front elevation, further minimizing its visual footprint. Slender steel supports and an elevated floor plan are testimony to the environmentally sensitive approach to its construction.

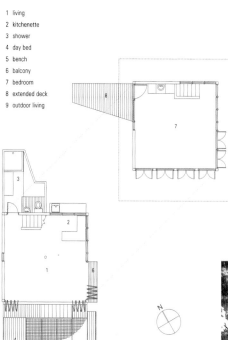

1 living
2 kitchenette
3 shower
4 day bed
5 bench
6 balcony
7 bedroom
8 extended deck
9 outdoor living

PRIMITIVE APPEAL

Sekeping Serendah is approached along a sinewy rainforest walking track, ending at a iron gate. The gate is flanked by gabion walls of local stones set in a framework of welded mesh. Past high mud walls thick with green moss, the track becomes a plinth that follows the terrain across a creek bed to where the glass and steel house rises up from the surroundings.

Mats and hammocks provide seating on the lower floors. A kitchenette with an unpainted zinc wall accentuates its primitive appeal. An outdoor living area, complete with a floor of industrial metal grating, a day bed, and seats that resemble a traditional *anjung*, flows out from the inside living area beneath the structure's cantilevered, corrugated iron roof.

Aluminum-framed bi-folding windows wrap around the internal spaces. Natural ventilation is provided by an extensive network of metal and glass louvers that eliminate the need for air-conditioning.

NATURE IS EVERYWHERE

Staircases lead to upper-level sleeping areas with mattresses laid on wire mesh bases, all set under a protective canopy that drenches Sekeping Serendah in day-long dappled light. There are no curtains. Transparency is everywhere, allowing the senses to experience the joy of nature in all its glory. A short walk along the valley is the spring-fed, cement-rendered swimming pool, set amid the rainforest

A cost-effective design respects the natural habitat and the traditions of surrounding communities, and triumphantly captures the intentions of its creators.

TOP LEFT
With its mix of louvers, casement windows, and wide timber floorboards, the bedroom strikes a contemporary pose. Glass and metal louvers are present throughout the retreat, allowing the regulation of natural breezes. With the absence of fly-wire screening on its windows, mosquito netting is essential.

LEFT
Aluminum, corrugated iron, and glass work together harmoniously to create a structure highly resistant to the corrosive effects of the harsh, tropical environment. The dominance of the surrounding rainforest and its penetration of the retreat help to soften the impact of the iron roof and metal walkways.

ABOVE
Rattan matting in the living area combines with the metal-meshed floor of the patio. A slender border of river pebbles and use of timber decking present a rich tapestry of textures. Bi-folding doors open the retreat to the forest, with Sekeping Serendah's splendid isolation ensuring privacy is not compromised.

Sky Arc Residence SAN FRANCISCO, USA
Will Bruder Architects

Construction	2003–2004
Home type	Two-level family home and separate music studio
Structure	Steel frame with concrete pier foundation

"The greatest charge at Sky Arc was to create a sensitive environment, an architecture rooted in this place. The house had to negotiate a challenging site – to engage the earth, recede into the trees. The simple volumes choreograph a pattern for living in an amazing landscape. The architecture amplifies the play of light and melts into the fog – a magical effect."

William Bruder

LEFT
The music room and studio is an 1,100-sq-ft (102-sq-m) haven, which is detached from the main residence. Constructed of board-formed cast-in-place concrete, it is set into the ground to minimize the intrusion of external noise. A suspended ceiling of origami-like fabric combines with walls of wood and fabric to enhance the room's acoustic properties.

ABOVE
The glassed living room glows at dusk, the suspended fireplace making a dramatic statement. The home is oriented to capture views that extend south from the Golden Gate National Recreation Area and eastward to San Francisco Bay.

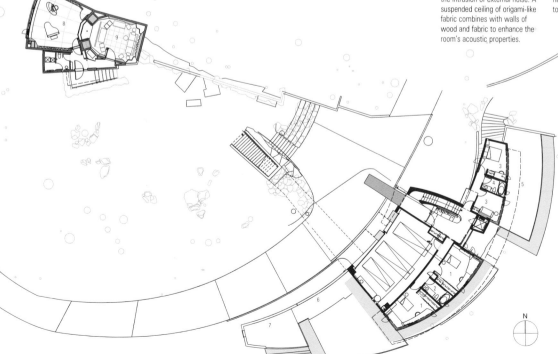

1 children's bedroom
2 bathroom
3 guest bedroom
4 guest bathroom
5 main bedroom below
6 gallery below
7 studio below
8 music room/ recording studio
9 studio control

UPPER LEVEL

N

PART OF THE LANDSCAPE

In Kentfield, just north of the Golden Gate Bridge in San Francisco's Marin County, is William Bruder's crescent-shaped Sky Arc Residence, set on 1.5 acres (0.6 ha) of forested hillside. It has dramatic views east over San Francisco Bay and south to the redwood and oak slopes of Mt Tamalpais.

The house is a collection of simple volumes. Sheathed in an external skin of pre-weathered, pewter-gray zinc and "solex green" glass, it easily recedes into the texture of the surrounding hills. This merging with the landscape is aided by the zinc's vertical, random ribbing, which harmonizes with nearby redwood trees.

CRESCENT SHAPE

The home's crescent shape embraces the natural contours of a rugged site, with the main residence located on the steeper eastern portion, and the garden and children's play area to the west, safely removed from dangerous precipices.

PANORAMIC VIEWS

Translucent fiberglass awnings encasing gossamer-thin filters replace more traditional overhangs and provide shade for the home's extensively glazed exteriors.

The upper level contains the children's bedrooms and a guest suite with bay views. A staircase descends to the "great room," with its sweeping 180° views from the bay to the mountains. Floors of Norwegian slate and mahogany are combined with birch and madrone casework and Venetian plaster, and there is a spectacular perforated metal fireplace suspended from the ceiling. This room is filled with a complex interplay of radiant, reflective textures.

The living room opens out to a wooden cantilevered deck and lawn terrace that uses perforated metal balustrades to blur any boundaries between the structure and the vistas beyond.

MUSIC STUDIO

Across the garden and detached from the house is a music room and recording studio. It is constructed of cast-in-place concrete, and features a reverberant concrete floor, all set several feet into the ground to minimize the penetration of external noise. Origami-like fans made of fabric form a false ceiling and, together with walls of wood, fabric, and plaster, diffuse, absorb, and reflect sound.

ABOVE
Fiberglass awnings containing blue filters replace traditional overhangs and glow luminously on gray, overcast days typical of the San Francisco Bay area. The crescent shape of the cantilevered wooden deck derives its form from the gentle, curvaceous topography of the surrounding northern California hills.

RIGHT
An external skin of pre-weathered zinc, with its vertical, randomly placed ribs, is designed to help the house recede into the texture of the landscape. Inspired by its site and exposed to the whims of nature, Sky Arc Residence promises to continually challenge and dazzle the senses.

St Leon House CAPE TOWN, SOUTH AFRICA

Stefan Antoni Olmesdahl Truen Architects

Construction	2003–2004
Home type	Single-family dwelling
Structure	Reinforced concrete, glass, marble, timber

"While being totally luxurious, the house also has a raw and robust quality to it. Materials and textures have been carefully selected to enhance the layered and magical experience. It is a house that needs to be given time to reveal itself."

Stefan Antoni

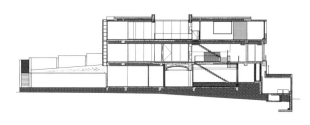

VIEWS TO DIE FOR

The magnificent site of St Leon House, nestled in a steep spur that separates Bantry Bay from Clifton, was the primary inspiration for architect Stefan Antoni's design. The property boasts breathtaking views toward the southwest, to the Twelve Apostle Mountains, across the beautiful Clifton beaches, and to the northeast over Robben Island toward the heart of Cape Town. Views from the back of the house frame Lion's Head.

The building is cut into the slope with approximately 50 percent of its rear face below the natural ground level. The engineers faced numerous challenges, the most critical being the large retaining walls that were required for the steep site, and the dramatic cantilevers, which were achieved by post-tensioning the beams. The third level of this imposing home floats over the extensively glazed southwest-facing second level, exaggerating the height of the building in relation to the adjacent first level.

CONTEMPORARY DESIGN, NATURAL FINISH

Although the design is uncompromisingly modern, the architects worked hard to soften the visual appearance by relying on the extensive use of natural finishes and textural elements.

Designed for a couple and their two children, the house also includes generous guest accommodation. The client, whose job requires him to travel between major cities, wanted a home that could cater for casual, intimate family occasions as well as large get-togethers with friends.

ABOVE
A dramatic view of the south-western elevation at sunset highlights the home's elegant angular lines and cantilevered slabs and roof.

RIGHT
Seemingly adrift in the black quartz-fringed infinity pool, the spa, with its balau timber deck, epitomizes the luxury and meticulous attention to detail incorporated into the house design. The unparalleled views of the Twelve Apostles Mountains can be fully appreciated while languishing in the warm water.

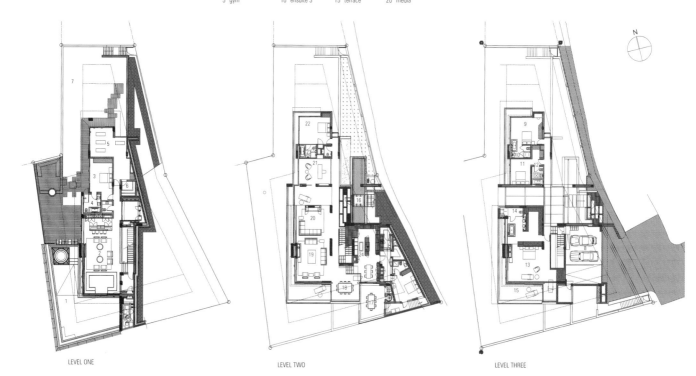

LEVEL ONE   LEVEL TWO   LEVEL THREE

ABOVE
Balau timber screens and a quartzite feature wall create a crisp contrast in colors and textures on the home's northeastern elevation.

RIGHT
Travertine stepping stones lead to the entry. Light floods into the living room beyond, with its magnificent ocean panorama. A timber screen provides privacy for the bedroom level above.

FAR RIGHT
The double-volume entry atrium "punches" through the quartzite feature wall. Glass balustrades reinforce the external/internal flow of the design.

COMPLEMENTARY INTERIORS

The architects' selection of exterior and interior finishes are complemented by the interior decorating skills of Antoni Associates. The third level main bedroom and ensuite have a lime-washed, solid oak ceiling that extends through and over the external terrace.

The building relates to the site by creating outdoor terraces at the first and second levels as the house steps down the slope. The kitchen opens up onto an intimate dining area, which includes a barbecue and pizza oven. This terrace has expansive views over the greenbelt alongside the house and down to the Twelve Apostle Mountains.

The large entertainment room, guest room, and gym on the first level open onto timber decks, a tranquil sculpture garden, and the large infinity pool.

LEVELS FOR LIVING

There are two levels devoted to living space and one full third level containing bedrooms. The first level entertainment room and cocktail bar open onto a timber deck, and are surrounded on two sides by the expansive infinity pool, and. The second level accommodates the entry and dramatic double-volume hall, and also the majority of living areas, including the kitchen, dining, two lounges, a study, and a guest room. Staff accommodation and the garden are at the back of the property on this level, below the garage. The third level has three generous ensuite bedrooms as well as a triple garage.

LINEAR LAYOUT

The house is organized in a linear manner, so that all the rooms face the magnificent sea view. Volumes and circulation penetrate the spaces vertically. The rear of the house offers a great deal of privacy – there are no openings other than the glazed double-volume entry space, which is shielded from the rear neighbors by a steel-framed timber screen.

To access the house from the street, one passes between heavy timber gates, past off-shutter, concrete-finished garden walls, over stepping stones and a water feature and, finally, through a minimalist Zen garden.

The design plays with transparency and translucency...The first impression is powerful and magical at the same time.

The main entry, at the rear of the second level, opens into a double-volume hall space framed by two stone walls. These cut perpendicularly through the main body of the building and frame a view of the sea and a sculptural palm tree. This space leads onto the main living wing of the house, which includes two lounges, a dining room, and a kitchen.

DRAMATIC LUMINOSITY

The design plays with transparency and translucency, with glimpsed views through timber screens into the entry, patterned voil curtains into the study, surprise glimpses into the kitchen, and views up to the bedroom bridge. The first impression is powerful and magical at the same time.

A sculptural stair leads up a triple-volume space from the entry to the third level. The west wing houses the main bedroom, which opens onto a terrace facing one of the most spectacular views of Cape Town. A bridge over the double-volume entry leads to the other two family bedrooms. Surprise glimpses of the distant views are revealed through the thin, tall end slots of the hallway, and between the timber screen and the face of the rear of the house. The bedrooms open up to provide sea views.

Accessed via the same stairwell, the first level includes a generous infinity pool, entertainment room, bar, and wine cellar. A gym and second guest room are also on this lowest level.

MAKING A STATEMENT WITH MATERIALS

The home is a reinforced concrete structure, and almost all the walls are full-height glass walls of either fixed frameless panels, or large sliding doors that slide into cavities. The wall and floor finishes are of natural textured plasters, silver-gray quartz cladding and natural timbers, and/or travertine tiling. The overall effect is warm and inviting.

TOP LEFT
Surrounded by panoramic views, the living room features textured plaster walls, lime-wash oak flooring, and a staircase clad in travertine.

ABOVE
The entertainment area boasts a bar clad in Marron Emperador marble as well as a tropical fish tank. To the left is an infinity pool flanked by palm trees.

OPPOSITE
Effective lighting creates a magical effect on the weathered balau timber deck, which leads to the infinity pool.

The Tree House CAPE TOWN, SOUTH AFRICA

Van der Merwe Miszewski Architects

Construction	1997–2000
Home type	Three-level family home
Structure	Steel, glass, and brick

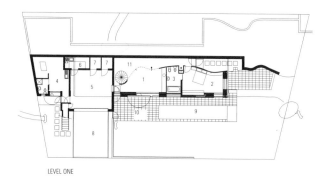

LEVEL ONE

1	study
2	bedroom
3	bathroom
4	bedroom
5	garage
6	laundry
7	store
8	driveway
9	pool
10	terrace
11	void over

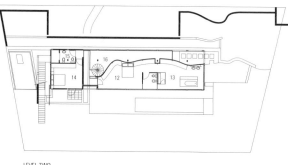

LEVEL TWO

12	main bedroom
13	main bathroom
14	bedroom
15	bathroom
16	void

LEVEL THREE

17	lounge/dining
18	kitchen
19	terrace
20	main entrance bridge
21	service stair
22	void
23	access bridge

"Trees are precious in Africa. They provide shelter for the elders at meeting time, for children from the midday heat, for all to shield against the elements. The building is an 'African folly' – immersed in, and inextricably linked with, the African landscape – a simultaneous dialogue between inside and outside, and outside and inside, neither taking precedence over the other."

Van der Merwe Miszewski Architects

A NATURAL INSPIRATION

The majesty of the African landscape and the defining canopy of the surrounding umbrella pine trees form the setting and inspiration for the Tree House. Five tree-like structures root the house to the earth. Over this framework is an enclosure of transparent glass and steel, which opens the house to the trees outside.

SEPARATE ROOF, UNIFIED HOUSE

The structure supporting the roof – made of steel and timber – is completely separate from the actual enclosure, which consists of a base, a middle section, and a top section. The brick base is clad in black slate. The doors can be pulled back into the walls, and the security screens perform their utilitarian function while at the same time accentuating the weight of the base.

The middle part of the house is covered by the steel "shaft" of the structure. On the northern side, glass infill panels merge the boundaries between interior and exterior. On the southern side, timber infill panels create the kitchen and services spaces of the house. There is a timber theme here, the motif extending to the fireplace, which appears to hover above the floor.

A LAYERED EXPERIENCE

Layering is a theme that continues throughout the structure of the Tree House. A steel bridge connects the outside with the inside. A screen wall provides protection from the sun, and privacy from prying eyes.

ABOVE
The north facade of the Tree House showing the heavy ground-level base with steel-and-glass structure above. Enclosed within the steel framework, the tree-like columns support the roof.

The front entry door opens to the interior bridges. One bridge leads to the working spaces of the home, such as the kitchen. Another leads to the welcoming center of the home, where side panels of transparent grating create a sensation of being suspended above what lies beneath. The bridges have an inner lining of maple, which provides warmth and texture.

A cylindrical staircase wrapped in a metal perforated screen covering takes the visitor down to the lower levels. The maple motif continues with the triple volume curved wall that winds its way through the house.

The main bedroom, bathroom, and a self-contained staff flat are located on the middle level. The walls of the main bedroom are glass, with opaque spots for privacy. The guest bedroom and study are on the ground level and open onto the garden, the swimming pool, and the nearby river.

Natural shade is provided by the surrounding trees, and the internal temperature is kept reasonably constant because of the triple volume of the space.

THE BRANCHES OF THE TREE

The tree-like structure was carefully thought through. The "trunk" is constructed of two folded mild steel plates welded together and bolted to the base.

The top of the roof is accessible, providing a deck that hovers above the surrounding trees with magnificent views of the sea and mountains.

ABOVE
The upper level living room with triple volume void to the left of the tree-like columns. The undulating timber-clad wall separates the rooms below from the void space, while the spiral staircase in the foreground links the three levels vertically.

RIGHT
A circular skylight above the spiral staircase accentuates the cylindrical form of the expanded metal sheath that encloses the structure.

Visiting Artists House CALIFORNIA, USA
Jim Jennings Architecture

Constructed	2003
Home type	Two joined, self-contained suites
Structure	Concrete, steel, glass, and wood

"By the act of cutting through the hill, the long walls integrate into the curve of the land, in essence creating their own site. It is an architecture of containment and an architecture of connection. At its most subterranean, the building is most open."

Jim Jennings

ABOVE
The main gravel courtyard lies below ground level and joins the two units of the dual residence. At the north end, the transparency of the enclosed living area allows unobstructed views through to a small lake beyond. Glass curtain walls, steel crossbeams and metal roof decking contrast with the thick concrete walls.

CONTAINMENT AND CONNECTION

On the crest of a hillside that was once home to a northern California sheep ranch, this starkly minimalist building – consisting of two joined, self-contained suites for artists while on site – now boasts sculptures by Richard Serra, Bruce Nauman, Martin Puryear and others. Two seemingly parallel poured-in-place concrete walls cut through the hill, diverging at the north and converging at the south. Throughout the length of the structure, the stepped floor constantly reconfigures the horizontal and vertical planes, accentuating the perspective of elongation and foreshortening of space.

THE ART OF TRANSPARENCY

Jim Jennings conceived the building as an intervention in the landscape rather than as an object on top of it. His response to the program was the simple act of cutting through the hill and occupying a void in the landscape. He opened both ends, connecting the inside and outside, making the building a visual link between a small lake on one side and a major sculpture in the landscape on the other.

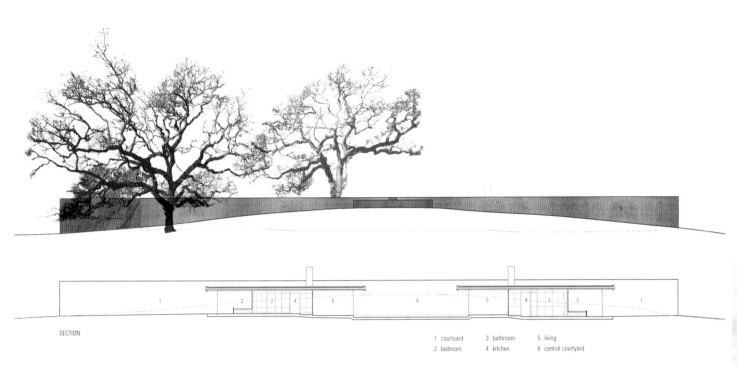

SECTION

| 1 courtyard | 3 bathroom | 5 living |
| 2 bedroom | 4 kitchen | 6 central courtyard |

LEFT
The concrete walls cutting through the hill are unadorned on their exterior surfaces and are carved into a sculpture by David Rabinowitch on the inward-facing sides. The walls at the northern end diverge slightly outward, just as their counterparts at the southern end converge.

ABOVE
A gravel pad edged with steel forms an entry platform for the paired stairs leading to the courtyard below. The recessed entrance is situated at the top of a knoll on the vast property.

FOLLOWING PAGES
The transparency of the house at night is striking. A band of fiber optic light is buried in the ground at the base of the walls, leaving visible a 4-in (10-cm) strip on each side that illuminates the interior edges of the building from below. A light source hidden in the ceiling closely replicates the patterns of daytime light. Mechanical shades provide privacy when desired.

1 courtyard
2 bedroom
3 bathroom
4 kitchen
5 living
6 central courtyard

SEEING DOUBLE

The house is 1,700 sq ft (158 sq m) in area and is composed of two nearly identical suites that contain basic living functions. In each, the central core element – bathroom, kitchenette, and fireplace – is the same. The suites differ slightly in size, each offering a richness of spatial experiences throughout as the walls converge and the floors step down.

CARVING A DIALOGUE

A site-specific work by the New York artist David Rabinowitch is carved directly into the inward-facing surfaces of the concrete walls, in concert and in dialogue with the architecture. The sculptor's intent was not to ornament or define the spaces but to involve the architecture in a relationship of rhythm and shape. For his part, Jennings used a fine aggregate in the concrete and added a non-reinforced area of 4-in (10-cm) thickness to the 10-in- (25-cm-) deep structural walls as a "canvas" for Rabinowitch's work.

ART REFLECTS LIGHT

The house was designed for two artists to share at any one time, and the emphasis is as much on privacy as it is on communal living. Each pavilion opens from the living area to the central common courtyard as well as from the bedroom to a private graveled terrace whose outlook varies from its counterpart. Mechanical shades can be utilized to enclose and set off the pavilions; pocket doors pulled from the core structures out to the walls also allow a degree of demarcation if needed.

Narrow skylights fitted inside the walls wash the surfaces with light during the daytime; at night, lighting designed by Dan Dodt approximates the daylight effect. A band of fiber optic lighting runs the length of each side of the building – a unifying element that, even in the day (when it is far less dramatic than at night) adds a hint of pale blue color to the decidedly neutral palette.

ABOVE LEFT
Each of the two bedrooms, which are oriented to views of the bucolic landscape, has a maple and aluminum unit containing a built-in headboard and bed that abuts a private bath on the other side. The maple floor steps down toward the main living space.

ABOVE
A freestanding aluminum kitchenette is contained within the living area's fireplace wall. Steel and glass doors open to the central courtyard, designed as a meeting place for the artists in residence.

LEFT
Artist David Rabinowitch carved 4 in (10 cm) deep into the concrete walls' interior sides, which were then honed and sealed; 10 in (25 cm) of wall remains structural. It took four stone carvers eight months to execute the sculpture. The gravel continuing outside from the maple floor adds to the continuity of space and the indoor–outdoor character.

ABOVE
Furnishings were kept to a minimum throughout. Natural light washes the concrete walls to accentuate the carvings. Monopoint light fixtures project from the slatted-wood ceiling to provide multidirectional sources of illumination.

Yudell-Beebe House CALIFORNIA, USA

Moore Ruble Yudell Architects & Planners

Constructed	2001
Home type	Two-story, family holiday home
Structure	Concrete foundation, timber frame, and aluminum-frame glazing

1 living
2 dining
3 main bedroom
4 ensuite
5 porch
6 guest bedroom
7 bathroom
8 kitchen
9 garden courtyard
10 garage

N

ABOVE LEFT
The exterior of the house, with its natural timbers and sympathetic color scheme, merges with the native landscape. From this perspective, the visual impact of the stepped roof line makes a bold statement, contrasting beautifully with the blue hues of ocean and sky.

LEFT
A courtyard of native plants, including mosses and grasses, catches the morning sun while offering protection from prevailing winds. The rocks mimic the formations of the local area and help the ground to drain well.

"In harmony with its environment, the house celebrates craft and materials and shapes a retreat for quiet contemplation or spirited social interaction. The house developed in close response to the rhythms and materials of the rugged coast of northern California."

Moore Ruble Yudell Architects & Planners

BONDING WITH THE SITE

This house at Sea Ranch was designed by and for its inhabitants, architect Buzz Yudell and colorist and painter Tina Beebe, who fell in love with a site near a dramatic cove on the rugged coast of northern California. They wanted to create an intimate house for work and play, where they could entertain friends and family.

Local planning authorities have imposed strict architectural guidelines in the area, and these were embraced by the owners, as they have a strong bond with nature and the environment. At the same time, they wanted their home to have an individual character.

RESPONDING TO THE SITE

Each part of the house responds to its specific site conditions. The north elevation presents a rugged entry, while the west elevation opens to the ocean with full or partial shading. The east screens the interior from houses across the meadow. The north is shaped as an intimate court with mountain views. The garden's native grasses and rocks reinforce the bond between ocean and mountain.

The interior design is elegant and simple with different feelings created by different internal shapes. The varying layers and levels offer a variety of views from various parts of the house.

FRAMING VIEWS

The windows frame the landscape and allow ample light into the house in this northern climate. The north-facing courtyard catches the morning sun and screens prevailing winds. The studio towers also collect light and serve as markers in the landscape. The house is arranged as a one-room deep array and all spaces have multiple exposures, optimizing both daylight and ventilation.

The main living space of the house can be seen either as one great room framed between the ocean and the courtyard, or as a sequence of spaces from kitchen to dining, living, and library. This provides intimacy for a small group or, conversely, accommodation of a larger gathering.

The main bedroom runs at an angle to this. Aligned on a north-south axis framed by the meadow and the courtyard, it has ocean views. A guest bedroom and bathroom are detached for privacy but linked by a south-facing protected porch.

Stairs in the courtyard lead to two small studios, which provide ideal work spaces. The studios are positioned as "tower" rooms, and have views to the ocean, meadow, mountains, and the home's courtyard.

NATIVE LANDSCAPING

The courtyard garden is populated with rocks, moss, and native grasses. In fact, the landscaping for the entire site contains predominantly native plants, mostly grasses and shrubs. The garden's rock pattern reflects the nearby natural rock formations, and also provides effective drainage for the outside.

COMPLEMENTARY MATERIALS

The materials used for the house are similarly inspired by the site and region. The external walls are redwood siding, from local sources. The windows are gray powder-coated aluminum, and the roof is a light matt gray powder-coated corrugated aluminum, which mirrors the varying conditions of the sky.

Inside, the walls are skim-coated, integral color plaster. The colors complement the native grasses and wildflowers. The exposed beams and window reveals are Douglas fir. The floors are end grain hemlock, and the built-in furniture and cabinets are beech.

TOP
The hearth provides an anchor for the major living spaces. The color scheme, reminiscent of native grass and wildflowers, counterpoints the natural timber and plaster. The cutout windows that sit flush on the main wall allow shafts of natural light to filter through, acting as organic spotlights on various surfaces in the space.

ABOVE
The aspect of this tower studio – one of two in the house – frames views of ocean, meadow, and sky. The essentials for a creative work space – natural light, clean surfaces, and an inspiring outlook – are well catered for.

Index

Picture Credits

Efforts have been made to contact the holder of copyright for each photograph. If any errors or omissions have occurred, Millennium House would be pleased to hear from copyright owners.

t = top; b = bottom; l = left; r = right;
c = center; tl = top left; tr = top right

2–3 Erhard Pfeiffer; 4 Fawn Art Photography; 6-7 Nigel Young/F&P; 8–9 Undine Prohl; 13 Paul McCredie; 14–15 Mark Callanan.

Introduction (US edition)
16 t, John Edward Linden; 16 b, © Hester + Hardaway Photographers; 17 t, Leonardo Finotti; 17 c, John Edward Linden; 17 b, TEN Arquitectos; 18 t, Bill Timmerman; 18 b, 19 l, Undine Prohl; 19 t, Howard Sutcliffe; 19 b, Eric Staudenmaier; 20 tl, Kim Zwarts; 20 tr, Richard Barnes Photography; 20 c, Cesar Rubio; 20–21 b, Tim Griffith; 21 tl, Benny Chan/fotoworks; 21 tr Marvin Rand.

Introduction (South African edition)
16, 17 t & bl, 18 l, 'Ora Joubert; 17 br, Peter Rich; 18–19 t, Dook Photography; 18–19 b, Mario; 19 tr, Hugh Fraser; 19 tc, Wieland Gleich of Archigraphy; 20 tl & tr, Van der Merwe Miszewski Architects; 20–21 b, 21, Stefan Antoni.

Introduction (Australian edition)
16 t Patrick Bingham-Hall; 16 bl, John Gollings; 16–17, Anthony Browell; 17 tl, Ross Honeysett; 17 tr, Adrian Boddy; 18 tl, John Gollings; 18 tr, Stephen Varady; 18 c, Adrian Boddy; 19, Eric Sierins; 20 t, Anthony Browell; 20 b, Willem Rethmeier; 21 tl, Rocket Mattler; 21 tr, Shannon McGrath; 21 c, Adrian Boddy.

Introduction (New Zealand edition)
16 t, Patrick Reynolds; 16 b, Ken Crosson; 17 t Mark Smith ©; 17 br & bl, Patrick Reynolds; 18 tl, Mark Smith ©; 18–19, Patrick Reynolds; 18 b, Paul McCredie; 19 Ken Crosson; 20 l, Paul McCredie; 20 tr, Megan Rule; 20 cr, 21 t, Patrick Reynolds; 21 b, Mark Smith ©.

Introduction (All other editions)
16 t, Stefan Müller-Naumann; 16 b, Manuel Herz; 17 t, Leonardo Finotti; 17 b, David Pisani / METROPOLIS; 18 t, Stanley Chou/©Millennium House; 18–9, 19 t, Christian Richters; 19 b, John Gollings; 20 l, John Edward Linden; 20–21, Benny Chan/fotoworks; 21 tr, Caramel; 21 br, Eugeni Pons